OCR

A2
Geography

Michael Raw

Philip Allan Updates, an imprint of Hodder Education, an Hachette UK company,
Market Place, Deddington, Oxfordshire OX15 0SE

Orders

Bookpoint Ltd, 130 Milton Park, Abingdon, Oxfordshire, OX14 4SB
tel: 01235 827720   fax: 01235 400454
e-mail: uk.orders@bookpoint.co.uk

Lines are open 9.00 a.m.–5.00 p.m., Monday to Saturday, with a 24-hour message
answering service. You can also order through the Philip Allan Updates website:
www.philipallan.co.uk

© Philip Allan Updates 2009

ISBN 978-0-340-94794-4

First printed 2009
Impression number 7 6 5 4 3
Year 2014 2013 2012 2011 2010

Ordnance Survey map extracts reproduced by permission of Ordnance Survey
© Crown copyright. Licence No 100027418

This textbook has been written specifically to support students studying OCR A2
Geography. The content has been neither approved nor endorsed by OCR and
remains the sole responsibility of the author.

Front cover photograph © Robert Harding Picture Library Ltd/Alamy

All efforts have been made to trace copyright on items used.

Printed in Italy

Hachette UK's policy is to use papers that are natural, renewable and recyclable
products and made from wood grown in sustainable forests. The logging and
manufacturing processes are expected to conform to the environmental
regulations of the country of origin.

Contents

Contents

Introduction

This textbook has been written specifically to meet the needs of students following the OCR A2 Geography course, though much of the content is also relevant to the other A-level specifications. The book provides comprehensive coverage of the OCR specification and makes extensive use of original case studies.

The book has several special features.

➤ Each of the six topics that comprise the *Global Issues* unit (F763) has a separate chapter and a structure that follows the same order as the specification.

➤ A chapter devoted to *Geographical Skills* (F764) provides an in-depth description and analysis of geographical methodology, which draws heavily on the author's own research and fieldwork experience over the past four decades.

➤ Within each chapter, sub-topics are introduced by a list of key ideas that use the same wording as the specification. These ideas provide both the framework for studying the text and the themes for external examination questions.

➤ Feature boxes, separated from the main text, develop important ideas and challenge students to think more deeply about a topic and research it in more detail.

➤ Numerous case studies drawn from MEDCs and LEDCs and contrasting environments at a variety of scales imbue general geographical patterns, processes and issues with a real sense of place.

➤ Examination questions consistent with the style of questions set by OCR are provided at the end of each chapter.

Online resource

While the main aim of the textbook is to deliver the content of the OCR specification, the crucial area of examination matters is dealt with by a supporting online resource (go to www.hodderplus.co.uk/philipallan). This resource includes advice to students on preparing for the A2 examination and on how to answer evaluative essay questions. There are also sections on how to satisfy the synoptic requirements and typical command words and phrases used at A2. Finally, the resource has further specimen questions and mark schemes for each part of the specification. The mark schemes contain a summary of indicative content and include examiners' comments on errors as well as the on the qualities that make a successful answer.

Taken together, the textbook and supporting online material provide a complete resource that covers all aspects of the course, from knowledge, understanding and skills, to assessment and examination preparation. For each sub-topic, students might use the resources by:

1 learning the key ideas that introduce each sub-topic
2 learning the themes, principles and processes that underpin each sub-topic
3 using the themes, principles and processes as organising frameworks for constructing relevant case studies

4 studying the mark schemes in the online resource for the exemplar examination questions and writing timed answers (or plans)

5 writing timed answers (or plans) to the examination questions in the textbook

Acknowledgements

I owe a debt of gratitude to a number of people who have assisted in the preparation and writing of this book: in particular to Patrick Fox and Katie Blainey at Philip Allan Updates for their editorial advice and superb organisational skills; to Charlie and Nicky Linfield for their kindness in inviting me to tour southern Africa and South America with them; to generations of sixth form geographers at Bradford Grammar School who have, unknowingly, fuelled and sustained my passion for geography; and especially to Diana for her loving support, despite the hectic demands of the family and her own professional life.

Michael Raw
Ilkley, West Yorkshire
March 2009

Unit F763

Global Issues

Section A Environmental Issues

Earth hazards

Natural hazards

Key ideas

➤ Natural hazards are naturally occurring events that impact adversely on people.

➤ Earthquakes and volcanic eruptions are primarily caused by plate tectonics.

➤ Earthquakes and volcanic eruptions have a range of social, economic and environmental impacts on the areas they affect.

➤ Earthquakes and volcanic eruptions give rise to a range of human responses, both short term and long term.

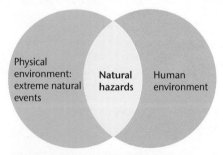

Physical environment: extreme natural events

Natural hazards

Human environment

Figure 1.1 The occurrence of natural hazards

Natural hazards are naturally occurring events, such as earthquakes, volcanic eruptions, floods and landslides (Photograph 1.1). What makes these natural events hazardous is the adverse effect they have on economy and society (Figure 1.1). They often cause death and injury, destroy property and infrastructure, and disrupt social and economic systems.

Natural hazards only occur when natural events interact with people. For instance, a volcanic eruption on an uninhabited island is by definition non-hazardous. When

Photograph 1.1 The physical impact of natural hazards: (a) earthquake (b) floods (c) landslide

natural hazards result in major loss of life, injury and economic damage, they are known as **natural disasters**.

Despite their name natural hazards can be caused or made worse by human activities. An example of this is deforestation, which, as we shall see later, can trigger mass movements and cause serious flooding. People have a more direct effect on the impact of natural hazards. The distribution and density of population, levels of economic development, and preparedness, are just some of the human factors that influence the impact of hazardous events.

Earthquakes

Earthquakes are major natural hazards. Caused by sudden movements of the Earth's crust, they result in violent shaking of the ground, surface faulting, **liquefaction**, landslides and tsunamis.

Seismic waves travel outward from the site or **focus** of the quake within the Earth's crust (Figure 1.2). The greater the magnitude of the quake the more powerful and destructive are the earthquake waves. Places closest to the **epicentre** experience the most powerful shocks. Earthquake depth also affects intensity. Other things being equal, shallow quakes are more destructive than deep quakes.

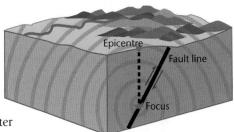

Figure 1.2
Earthquake focus, epicentre and fault line

About 130 million people are exposed to earthquake risk. Globally, earthquakes and related hazards caused 603 000 deaths between 1980 and 2005 (Table 1.1, p. 4). Indonesia, Pakistan and Iran had the highest death tolls.

Causes of earthquakes

Earthquakes result from stresses in the Earth's crust. Figure 1.3 shows that most earthquakes occur close to tectonic plate boundaries. This is not surprising. Plates

Figure 1.3 Global distribution of earthquakes

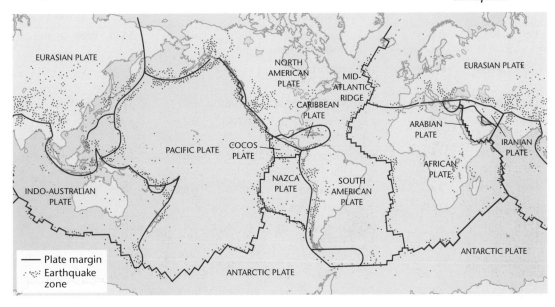

Table 1.1 *Largest and deadliest earthquakes by year, 1990–2005*

	Largest earthquakes				Deadliest earthquakes			
Year	Date	Magnitude (Mw)	Fatalities	Region	Date	Magnitude (Mw)	Fatalities	Region
2005	28/03	8.7	1313	Northern Sumatra, Indonesia	08/10	7.6	80361	Pakistan
2004	26/12	9.0	283106	Off west coast of northern Sumatra	26/12	9.0	283106	Off west coast of northern Sumatra
2003	25/09	8.3	0	Hokkaido, Japan region	26/12	6.6	31000	Southeastern Iran
2002	03/11	7.9	0	Central Alaska	25/03	6.1	1000	Hindu Kush region, Afghanistan
2001	23/06	8.4	138	Near coast of Peru	26/01	7.7	20023	India
2000	16/11	8.0	2	New Ireland region, Papua New Guinea	04/06	7.9	103	Southern Sumatra, Indonesia
1999	20/09	7.7	2297	Taiwan	17/08	7.6	17118	Turkey
1998	25/03	8.1	0	Balleny Islands region	30/05	6.6	4000	Afghanistan–Tajikistan border Region
1997	14/10	7.8	0	South of Fiji Islands	10/05	7.3	1572	Northern Iran
	05/12	7.8	0	Near east coast of Kamchatka				
1996	17/02	8.2	166	Irian Jaya region, Indonesia	03/02	6.6	322	Yunnan, China
1995	30/07	8.0	3	Near coast of northern Chile	16/01	6.9	5530	Kobe, Japan
	09/10	8.0	49	Near coast of Jalisco, Mexico				
1994	04/10	8.3	11	Kuril Islands	20/06	6.8	795	Colombia
1993	08/08	7.8	0	South of Mariana Islands	29/09	6.2	9748	India
1992	12/12	7.8	2519	Flores region, Indonesia	12/12	7.8	2519	Flores region, Indonesia
1991	22/04	7.6	75	Costa Rica	19/10	6.8	2000	Northern India
	22/12	7.6	0	Kuril Islands				
1990	16/07	7.7	1621	Luzon, Philippine Islands	20/06	7.4	50000	Iran

Source: USGS

move relative to one another along these boundaries and it is there that tectonic forces — compression, tension and shearing — are greatest.

Compression

Compression bends rocks until they fracture and move suddenly along fault lines. This process releases huge amounts of energy as seismic waves. Compressive forces are most obvious at destructive plate boundaries or **subduction zones** where they give rise to low-angled reverse faults known as **thrust faults** (Figure 1.4). Crustal movement along these faults can produce high-magnitude earthquakes such as the Sumatran quake in December 2004 (magnitude 9.0 Mw), and the Kashmir quake in October 2005 (magnitude 7.6 Mw).

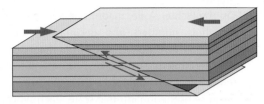

Figure 1.4
A low-angled thrust fault caused by compressive forces in the crust

Michael Raw

Photograph 1.2
Rifting on the western edge of the Thingvellir Valley in Iceland

Figure 1.5 Normal faults and rifting in the east Africa rift valley in Kenya

Tension

Tensional forces are associated with constructive plate boundaries or **mid-ocean ridges**. There tension stretches the crust and causes normal faulting and rifting (Photograph 1.2). Rifting is when blocks of crust slip downwards along a series of parallel faults — a movement that produces shallow earthquakes (Figure 1.5).

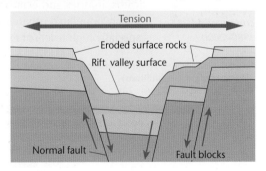

Figure 1.6 Strike-slip fault and shearing at a conservative plate boundary

Shearing

Earthquakes at conservative boundaries are due to horizontal or shearing movements. These boundaries are known as **strike-slip** or lateral faults. The San Andreas fault in California is a massive strike-slip fault (Figure 1.6). The Pacific and North American plates shear past each other along this fault line. Movement is erratic and sudden and produces violent quakes in the San Francisco and Los Angeles regions.

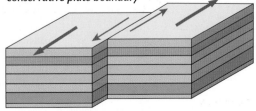

Box 1.1   Earthquake magnitude

- The Richter scale, developed in 1935, measures the magnitude of an earthquake.
- The scale is determined from the logarithm of the amplitude of waves recorded by seismographs.
- On the Richter scale, magnitude is expressed in whole numbers and decimal fractions. Recordable earthquakes range from magnitude 2.5 Mw (micro-earthquakes) to magnitude 9 Mw (great earthquakes).
- Because of the logarithmic scale, each whole number increase in magnitude represents a tenfold increase in measured amplitude.
- The amount of energy released by a magnitude 7 Mw earthquake is around 30 times more than

a magnitude 6 Mw quake, and 900 times greater than a magnitude 5 Mw quake.
- Great earthquakes have magnitudes of 8.0 Mw or higher. On the average, one earthquake of such size occurs somewhere in the world each year.
- The Richter scale has no upper limit, though the largest known quakes have had magnitudes in the 8.8–9.0 Mw range.
- The Richter scale is not used to express damage. The damage caused by an earthquake is determined not only by magnitude, but by many other factors such as population distribution and density, rural and urban populations and earthquake preparedness.

Exposure and vulnerability to earthquake hazards

We have seen that earthquakes result from powerful tectonic forces. Human activities play no part in earthquake causes but they have a huge influence on their impact.

Exposure to earthquake hazards depends on the frequency of earthquakes and the number of people living in the area around the quake's epicentre (Figure 1.7). In other words, the more people who live in an earthquake zone, the more deaths, injuries and economic damage you would expect. For this reason, large, densely populated urban areas such as southern California and Mexico City have especially high levels of exposure.

Figure 1.7 Physical exposure to earthquakes, 1980–2000

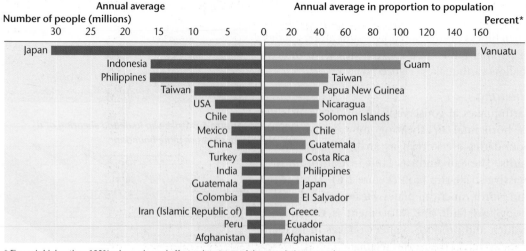

* Figure is higher than 100% where a hazard affects a large part of the population more than once a year

However, exposure is not the same as vulnerability (Figure 1.8). While southern California's urban dwellers have high exposure, they are less **vulnerable** than Mexico City's population. Why?

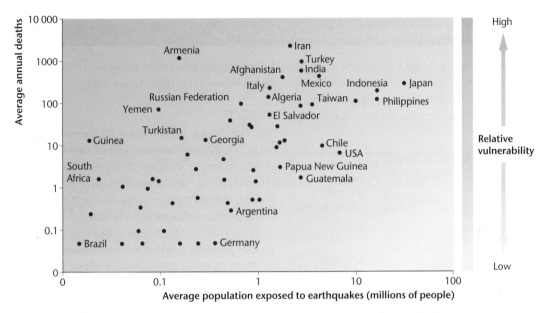

Poverty is the critical factor that affects people's vulnerability to earthquakes. Governments in rich countries can afford to mitigate the effects of earthquakes, and in this way reduce risk and vulnerability. Mitigating actions include seismic codes to prevent building collapse and fires; training and coordinating emergency services; educating the population on how to respond to earthquake disasters;

Figure 1.8 Relative vulnerability to earthquakes, 1980–2000

Photograph 1.3 Cross bracing on a high-rise tower in San Francisco; cross bracing allows the building to be more flexible and to twist during a large earthquake

7

mapping earthquake risks; and planning for the immediate and longer term aftermath of a major earthquake including the provision of emergency water, food, shelter, medical supplies and reconstruction.

Case study   The Northridge earthquake, California

On 17 January 1994 at 04.30 a magnitude 6.7 quake struck the town of Northridge in the Los Angeles basin (Figure 1.9). The quake originated on an unknown thrust fault and proved to be the costliest in US history.

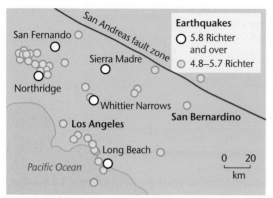

Figure 1.9 Location of Northridge, showing fault lines and earthquake occurrences

Exposure

Exposure to earthquake hazards is especially high in southern California. The Los Angeles metropolitan area, with a population of 16.5 million, and an average density of 2437 persons per km², is the second largest concentration of population in the USA.

Southern California is also one of the most seismically active regions the USA. Five large earthquakes measuring between 5.9 Mw and 6.8 Mw occurred in the Los Angeles basin between 1978 and 2004. Crustal instability results from the convergence between the Big Bend of the San Andreas fault and the north-west motion of the Pacific Plate (Figure 1.10). North–south compression forms the Transverse Ranges running parallel to the Pacific Ocean and the San Fernando Valley, filled with soft sediments. Scores of hidden thrust faults lie beneath the Los Angeles basin. The Northridge quake resulted

from a sudden movement along one of these faults, 16 km below the surface (Figure 1.10).

Impact

The Northridge quake killed 57 people, injured 9000, left 20 000 homeless, and caused more than US$20 billion of damage. If the human cost was relatively light, the economic costs were huge. Indeed, the Northridge quake was at the time, the costliest natural disaster in US history.

Given that the Northridge quake was not exceptionally powerful and that the urban environment of southern California is designed for seismic resistance, why was its economic impact so great?

Most significant was the depth of the quake. Its focus was shallow and as a result the seismic shocks were violent. Ten to twenty seconds of strong shaking collapsed buildings, brought down freeway interchanges, ruptured pipelines and damaged bridges. Add to this the fact that the earthquake struck a large densely populated urban environment and the scale of the economic impact begins to make sense.

But compared to the 2005 Kashmir quake, Northridge (and the San Fernando Valley) got off relatively lightly. Building codes, earthquake preparedness, accessibility and emergency procedures limited the impact on the built environment and saved many lives. Near the epicentre well-engineered buildings withstood violent shaking without structural damage.

However, some structural failures pointed to deficiencies in design or construction methods. Freeways, including the 1-5/SH-14 interchange, collapsed at seven sites and 170 bridges sustained varying degrees of damage (Photograph 1.4). Most residential buildings escaped undamaged, although several low-rise apartment buildings, built above open-air parking spaces, collapsed. In one such building 16 people died. Over 150 steel-framed

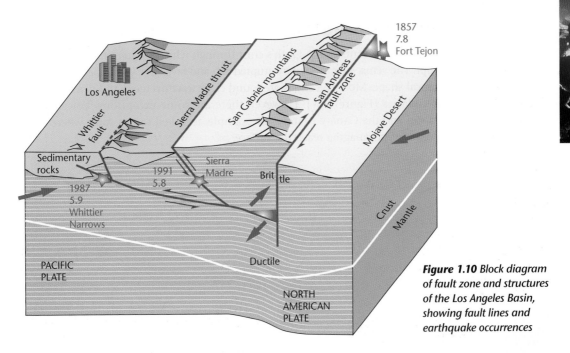

Figure 1.10 *Block diagram of fault zone and structures of the Los Angeles Basin, showing fault lines and earthquake occurrences*

buildings, including hospitals and schools, suffered damage. Cracking of steel beam and reinforced column connections was common, despite being built for seismic resistance.

Investigations after the earthquake showed a further need to improve building codes. For example, masonry walls could be prevented from collapsing by properly tying them to adjacent walls and roofs.

Photograph 1.4 *A collapsed freeway overpass after the Northridge earthquake*

Volcanic eruptions

Volcanoes are vents in the Earth's crust through which molten magma and gases erupt. The vents, surrounded by erupted ash and lava, give volcanoes a distinctive conical shape. Most volcanoes are found close to convergent and divergent plate boundaries (Figure 1.11). However, there are some exceptions. Volcanism in Hawaii and the Canary Islands, for example, is linked to hot spots where rising plumes of hot magma reach the surface.

Figure 1.11 Global distribution of active volcanoes

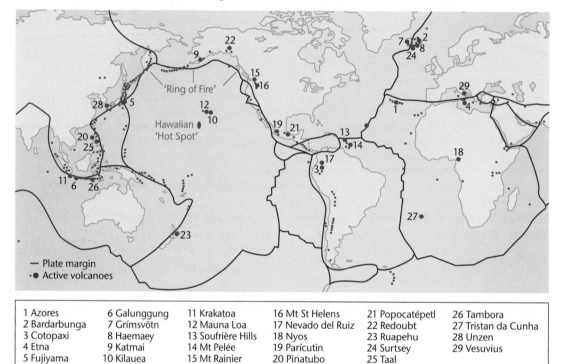

- Plate margin
- ● Active volcanoes

1 Azores	6 Galunggung	11 Krakatoa	16 Mt St Helens	21 Popocatépetl	26 Tambora
2 Bardarbunga	7 Grímsvötn	12 Mauna Loa	17 Nevado del Ruiz	22 Redoubt	27 Tristan da Cunha
3 Cotopaxi	8 Haemaey	13 Soufrière Hills	18 Nyos	23 Ruapehu	28 Unzen
4 Etna	9 Katmai	14 Mt Pelée	19 Parícutin	24 Surtsey	29 Vesuvius
5 Fujiyama	10 Kilauea	15 Mt Rainier	20 Pinatubo	25 Taal	

Volcanism at convergent plate boundaries

Tectonic plates converge at active margins (Figure 1.12). One plate underthrusts the other and slowly subducts into the mantle. The Pacific 'Ring of Fire' is the best-known example of a convergent margin. Stretching from New Zealand through North and South America, and across the Bering Straits to Kamchatka, Japan, the Philippines and Indonesia, the 'Ring of Fire' has three-quarters of the world's active and dormant volcanoes. All around the Pacific slabs of oceanic plate are subducted beneath the lighter continental plates of Eurasia and the Americas. At depth the subducted oceanic crust, mixed with water and sea floor sediments, melts. Then the magma migrates slowly towards the surface where it erupts through volcanoes and fissures as **andesite** lava and **tephra**.

Andesitic magma is highly viscous and forms steep-sided **stratovolcanoes**. Viscous magma traps gases, increasing pressure inside volcanoes, and causing explosive eruptions. Thus, stratovolcanoes like Vesuvius, Soufrière Hills and Mount St Helens are extremely hazardous.

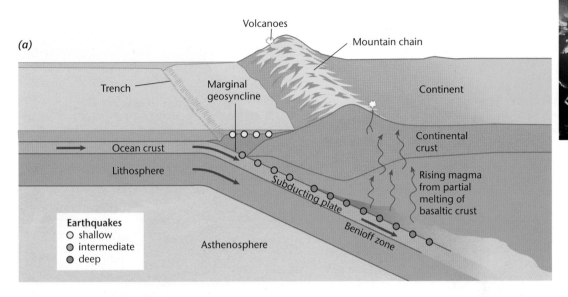

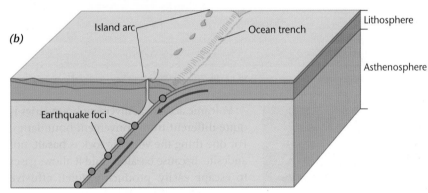

Figure 1.12
Convergent plate boundary zones and volcanic activity:
(a) ocean–continental boundary
(b) ocean–ocean boundary

Volcanism at divergent plate boundaries

Tension in the crust and lithosphere occurs where magma forces its way to the surface at divergent plate boundaries (Figure 1.13). As the hot rock approaches the surface and pressure falls, it starts to melt. Eventually lava, tephra and hot gases erupt through volcanoes and fissures.

Because divergent boundaries are found along spreading (mid-ocean) ridges, most eruptions occur unseen on the ocean floor. There is, however, one place where a divergent boundary can be observed on land — Iceland. Iceland sits astride the mid-Atlantic ridge (Figure 1.14). It is one of the most active volcanic regions in the world and is literally being torn apart along a huge rift valley (Thingvellir) which separates the North American and Eurasian plates (Photograph 1.5).

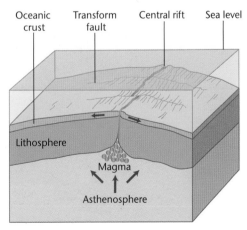

Figure 1.13 *A divergent plate boundary and spreading centre*

Michael Raw

***Photograph 1.5** Rifting along a spreading ridge: the western end of the Thingvellir rift valley, Iceland*

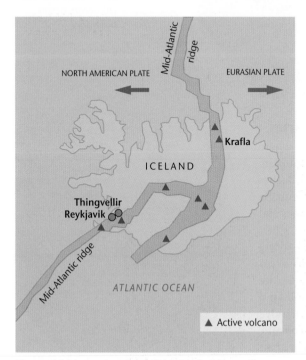

***Figure 1.14** Iceland and the mid-Atlantic ridge: a divergent plate boundary*

Volcanic activity at divergent boundaries is quite different from convergent boundaries. For one thing the volcanic rock is **basalt**, not andesite. Because basalt is fluid it allows gases to escape easily, producing quiet, **effusive** eruptions. Fluid basalt lava can flow tens of kilometres before it cools and solidifies. In the process it makes huge, low-angled **shield volcanoes** such as Iceland's Skjaldbreidur.

Hot spots

Not all volcanic activity occurs at plate boundaries. Hawaii, arguably the most volcanically active place in the world, lies at the centre of the Pacific plate — thousands of kilometres from the nearest plate boundary. Its volcanism is caused by a **hot spot**. Although hot spots are not fully understood, one theory suggests they are places where a plume of magma rises from the mantle, punches a hole through the lithosphere and crust, and erupts at the surface.

Michael Raw

Photograph 1.6
El Teide on Tenerife in the Canary Islands; despite its location on a hot spot, El Teide is a stratovolcano that is known to erupt explosively

Volcanism at hot spots and divergent plate boundaries is similar. The main eruptive material is basalt; eruptions are effusive rather than explosive, and volcanoes are massive shield-types such as Mauna Loa on Hawaii. However, there are exceptions. The Tenerife volcano — El Teide — in the eastern North Atlantic, is a stratovolcano (Photograph 1.6). Despite its location on a hot spot, it is known to have erupted explosively in the past, with evidence of pyroclastic flows and thick tephra deposits from ashfalls (Figure 1.15).

Figure 1.15 *Types of volcanic hazard*

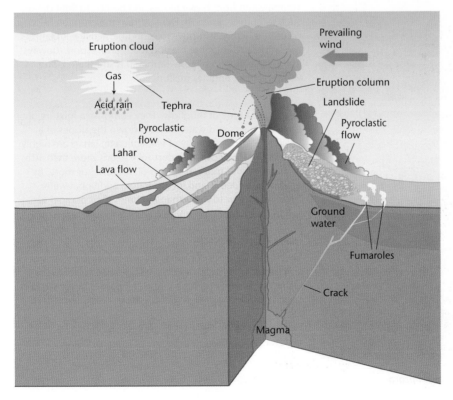

Hazard		Description
Lava flow		Lava flows are masses of molten rock that pour from volcanoes and fissures during an eruption. The characteristics of lava flows, such as speed and run-out distance, depend on the lava's viscosity. For example, basalt is runny and fast flowing; rhyolite is thick and pasty and flows more slowly. Everything in the path of a lava flow will be bulldozed, buried or burned. Though lava flows destroy property they are rarely life-threatening. Lava flows can bury settlements, crops and land under tens of metres of volcanic rock. For this reason, rebuilding and repair of devastated areas is not possible.
Pyroclastic flows		Pyroclastic flows are ground-hugging avalanches of hot ash, pumice, rock fragments and gas. They rush down the slopes of volcanoes at speeds of 100 km h^{-1}. Temperatures within pyroclastic flows may exceed 500 °C. Pyroclastic flows destroy everything in their path. Even on the margins of pyroclastic flows death and serious injury to people and animals are caused by burns and inhalation of hot ash and poisonous gases. The pyroclastic flow released when Mount Pele in Martinique erupted in 1902 killed 28 000 people.
Ashfalls and tephra		Tephra is a general term for fragments of volcanic rock that are blasted into the atmosphere by explosive eruptions. Tephra varies from heavy blocks and bombs to light debris, such as pumice, and ash. Fall-out from the eruption column is highly disruptive to economic activity. It blankets the landscape in tephra making roads and airport runways impassable. Roofs collapse, farmland is smothered, and vehicle and jet engines malfunction.
Lahars		Lahars are a type of mudflow. They comprise a mixture of rock fragments and water flowing down the slopes of a volcano. With the density of wet concrete, lahars are highly destructive. They can transport rock debris more than 10 m in diameter and move at speeds of 50 km h^{-1} or more. By eroding rock debris and incorporating additional water, lahars can grow to more than ten times their original size. Lahars cause serious economic and environmental damage. Buildings and land not destroyed may be buried under thick layers of rock debris. So long as loose, unconsolidated ash covers the slopes of volcanoes, lahar hazards continue for many years. In the vicinity of Mount Pinatubo in the Philippines heavy rainfall triggers fresh lahars even though the last eruption was in 1991. Lahars caused by the Nevado del Ruiz eruption in Colombia in 1984 swept through the town of Armero, killing 23 000 people.

Table 1.2 *Types of volcanic hazard*

Case study   The eruption of Nyiragongo in 2002

Nyiragongo is a stratovolcano in east Africa's rift valley in the Democratic Republic of Congo (DRC). The east African rift valley is a divergent plate boundary that extends for nearly 2000 km, from Malawi in the south to the Gulf of Aden in the north. Volcanism in this region results from tension and stretching of the continental crust and lithosphere. In the DRC and nearby Rwanda it gives rise to a chain of eight active volcanoes. One of these volcanoes is Nyiragongo (Figure 1.16). Nyiragongo is one of Africa's deadliest volcanoes, spewing lava and toxic gas. Its magma is low in silica and its fast-moving lava flows are major threats to life and property.

Nyiragongo has one other unusual feature: its enormous summit crater. Over 500 m deep, this crater contains an active lava lake. From time to time cracks develop in the flanks of the volcano, causing the lava lake to drain suddenly. This happened in 1977 and 2002, generating lava flows that engulfed surrounding villages and the nearby city of Goma (Figure 1.16).

Toxic gases — especially sulphur dioxide — are a further hazard. Vents on the slopes of Nyiragongo release up to 50 000 tonnes of sulphur dioxide a day: emissions that are highly dangerous and threaten human health, livestock, crops and forests.

2002 eruption

The most recent eruption of Nyiragongo began on 17 January 2002. Lava drained from the crater and poured down the volcano's steep eastern and southern slopes, into the nearby city of Goma and Lake Kivu (Figure 1.16). This was the first time a city had ever been devastated by lava flows.

Lava flows, 50 m across and 6 m high, flattened and burned everything in their path. Fourteen villages and one-fifth of Goma, including its commercial centre, were destroyed. One hundred and ten people died, 120 000 were made homeless, and the city's water treatment plant, cathedral and hospital were flattened. The lava flowed across the runway at Goma's airport, preventing access by large aircraft

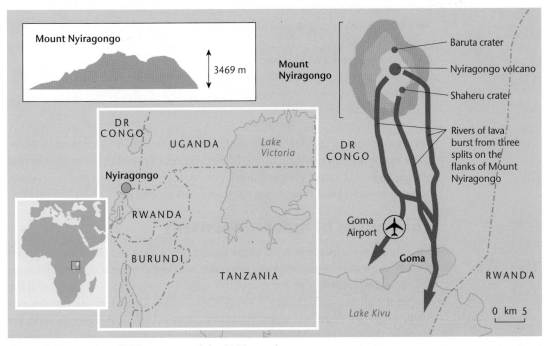

Figure 1.16 Location of Nyiragongo and the 2002 eruption

and hindering emergency relief supplies. In total, 400 000 people were evacuated with thousands fleeing to neighbouring Rwanda where they were housed in temporary shelters. Acid rain formed by sulphur dioxide emitted by the eruption damaged crops and forests, and polluted drinking water.

In the days immediately following the eruption there was a fear that infectious disease would spread through the population. Poor sanitation, people living in overcrowded refugee camps (many of whom were undernourished) and shortages of potable drinking water added to the risk. Fortunately, cholera and diarrhoea, which are endemic in this part of Africa, were contained.

Exposure and vulnerability

Exposure to volcanic eruptions on the DRC–Rwandan border is high for two reasons. First, Nyiragongo is one of Africa's most active and deadly volcanoes. Second, nearly 500 000 people live in the volcano's shadow.

Levels of vulnerability are equally high. The local population is poor, depends heavily on subsistence farming, and has few resources to buffer it against natural hazards. The 2002 eruption destroyed 80% of the local economy. Vulnerability was also increased by civil war in the DRC, which has made economic conditions even more dire than usual.

The Nyiragongo volcano will remain a major hazard to local people for the foreseeable future, hence the need for close monitoring and hazard mapping. Education is also a priority in reducing the vulnerability. Leaflets have been distributed to raise awareness of the risks and videos made that explain the hazards and the early warning and evacuation procedures.

Mass movement

Key ideas
➤ There are three types of mass movement: slides, flows and creep.
➤ Mass movements and slope failure are influenced by physical conditions and human activities.
➤ Mass movement is often caused by the interaction of physical and human factors.
➤ The impact of mass movement hazards can be economic, social and environmental.
➤ The human reaction to mass movement disasters is both short term (e.g. emergency rescue) and long term (e.g. planning and management).

Mass movement is the downhill transfer of slope materials as a coherent body. Some mass movements, such as landslides and mudflows that occur rapidly and unexpectedly, are extremely hazardous. Others, such as soil creep and frost heave, occur slowly and pose little threat to people and property.

The causes of mass movement

Rapid mass movements indicate slope failure. To understand why this occurs we need to know that slopes represent a balance between driving and resisting forces. Gravity is the major driving force. It pulls materials downslope and varies with the sine of the slope angle (Figure 1.17). Other driving forces include the mass of material on the slope and water. Resisting forces act upslope. They include, for example, the shear strength of the slope materials, the frictional resistance between slope materials and the binding effects of vegetation.

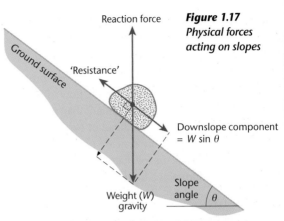

Mass movement occurs when the downslope forces exceed the upslope forces. In these circumstances mass movement lowers the slope angle and restores stability. A number of factors may tip the balance and trigger slope failure:

➤ Steepening and undercutting at the base of a slope increases the driving force. This can result from natural erosion (e.g. a valley-side slope undercut by a river) or human activity (e.g. a road cutting).

➤ Loading the slope increases the driving force. The most common cause of loading is heavy rain which adds to the mass of material on the slope. Loading may also result from rockfall and building on slopes.

➤ Heavy rain lubricates slope materials and decreases the resisting force.

➤ Heavy rain increases water pressure within the pores of mineral materials, reducing their coherence and decreasing the resisting force.

➤ Deforestation removes the binding effect of tree roots on slopes and increases the amount of water absorbed by slope materials. Its effect is twofold: to reduce the resisting force and increase the driving force.

➤ Earthquakes reduce the resistance of slope materials through violent shaking.

Figure 1.17
Physical forces acting on slopes

Force of gravity acting on a slope particle

Slides and flows

There are three types of mass movement: slides, flows and heaves. Only slides and flows give rise to major hazardous events (Figure 1.18).

Slides are masses of material that move across a clearly defined slide plane. This means that velocity is uniform throughout the sliding mass (Figure 1.19). Flows, in contrast, decrease in velocity with depth. Both slides and flows vary in their speed of movement, water content and particle size. Most hazardous slides and flows are fast moving and give people little time and warning to prepare for evacuation.

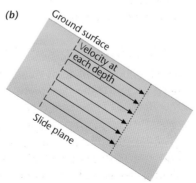

Figure 1.18
Types of mass movement

Figure 1.19 Types of mass movement (a) Flow (b) Slide

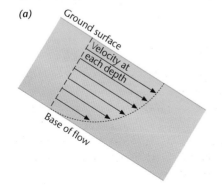

Box 1.2 Some types of mass movement hazard

Earthflows

Earthflows are the most common type. They consist of bodies of granular regolith which flow downhill. Earthflows have a lower water content than mudflows.

A steep scarp defines the head of earthflows. In a long profile earthflows are concave near the head and convex upward near the toe. Rates of movement range from a few centimetres a month to over 100 km h^{-1}.

Mudflows

These are more mobile, saturated flows comprising clay and silt-sized particles. Mudflows are more rapid than earthflows. They are most common in areas of sparse vegetation cover. In hot deserts mudflows often form large fans at the foot of mountain slopes. In areas of active volcanism, where loose ash is easily transported by runoff, mudflows are known as lahars.

Debris flows

This consists of coarse regolith (including boulders) and other debris (e.g. timber). Rates of flow can reach 50 km h^{-1}. Debris flows are associated with extremely heavy rainfall events. They produce coarse lobe-like deposits (alluvial fans) along mountain fronts.

Rotational slide

Deep landslides usually take place across a curved slide plane. The moving mass shows evidence of rotation with tilted back slopes. Rotational slides often occur on steep slopes where basal undercutting (by a river or waves) steepens the gradient. Classic slides are found where permeable caprocks overlie impermeable rocks such as shale or clay.

Debris slides and mudslides

Debris slides are mass movements of loose rock debris. The material slides or rolls downslope, forming an irregular hummocky deposit resembling a moraine.

A mudslide is a fast-moving landslide of mud. Mudslides resemble flows because of their high water content. But unlike mudflows, all movement occurs across a basal slide plane. They occur when torrential rain saturates steep hillslopes until they become unstable. Some mudslides can be massive.

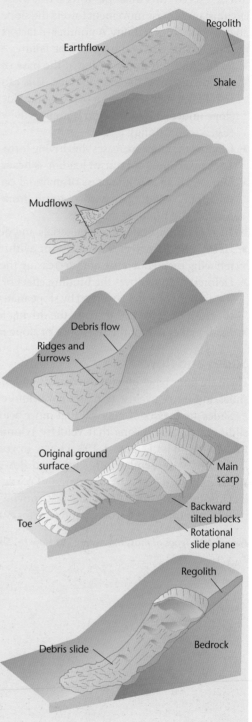

Case study **Debris flows in northern Venezuela**

In December 1999, Vargas province on the northern coast of Venezuela was devastated by massive debris flows. Debris flows are fast-moving masses of water together with sand, gravel, boulders, trees and other materials, with the consistency of wet concrete. Estimates of the final death toll in Vargas ranged from 15 000 to 30 000. In total the disaster affected 214 000 people of whom 44 000 became refugees. The economic impact was also severe: 20 000 houses destroyed and 40 000 damaged; low-rise houses buried to the roof; and the collapse of several high-rise buildings hit by giant boulders. Hundreds of houses in Carmen de Uria were swept away, and large areas of Caraballeda, Macuto and Carmende were buried by debris.

Causes of the disaster

A combination of climatological and geomorphological factors caused the Vargas disaster. Between 8 and 19 December a slow-moving cold front deposited 914 mm of rain in the coastal mountains. This extreme weather triggered landslides, flash floods and debris flows.

Three features of the region's geomorphology also contributed to the debris flows. First, in this part of northern Venezuela the Cordillera de la Costa runs parallel to the coast. The summit ridge, 2000–2700 m high, is just 10 km from the sea. As a result the seaward-facing slopes are very steep, runoff is rapid and streams have high energy. Second, the igneous rocks that form the mountains have been deeply weathered. The mountains are mantled in easily eroded clay (phyllite) which feeds large amounts of sediment to debris flows. Third, widespread deforestation has further increased runoff and erosion.

Exposure to debris flow hazards

Exposure depends on the size of the debris flows and the population at risk. There is no doubt that the debris flows were an exceptional event. Boulders up to 5 m in diameter were transported to the coast and 2 million m^3 of debris was added to coastal alluvial fans. In fact so much debris was transported from the mountains that in places the coastline was extended seawards by over 250 m.

The distribution of population along the coast also meant that thousands were exposed to risk. Because the mountains drop abruptly to the sea there is little flat land for settlement. Alluvial fans,

USGS

Photograph 1.7
Debris flow damage to Caraballeda, northern Venezuela, 1999

formed where rivers emerge from the mountains onto the narrow coastal plain, offer some of the few sites for settlement. In recent years rapid population growth (6.3% in Vargas state between 1990 and 2001) has concentrated urban development on the alluvial fans. Caraballeda, a plush resort, occupies such a location.

Not surprisingly the coastal towns sited on alluvial fans were hit hardest (Photograph 1.7). These locations are at high risk from flood and debris flow hazards. Indeed the alluvial fans themselves owe their formation to successive floods and debris flows over the centuries. Thus thousands of people were living unwittingly and without any protection in the path of massive debris flows. Sooner or later disaster was going to happen.

Hazard mitigation: the human reaction

Lack of preparedness and any strategy for disaster management increased the vulnerability of the coastal population of Vargas to debris flow and landslide hazards.

Early signs of imminent debris flow hazards are given by the accumulation of sediments in stream channels in the mountains. Only when sediment accumulations are large is the risk from debris flows significant.

A priority should have been the removal of slums built on steep slopes near the coast. The President of Venezuela announced shortly after the disaster that victims of the floods would be re-settled away from the coast. But given that many people live in the coastal slums to escape the hardship of life in the interior, the logic of this policy is questionable. After the disaster, 100 000 people whose homes had been destroyed were temporarily evacuated to neighbouring regions.

In future the canyon plains of the Uria and Cerro Grande rivers will not be suitable for settlement unless check dams are built in the mountains to hold back debris flows and floods. Flood channels could be constructed on some alluvial fans to allow the passage of large scale debris flows. Other responses designed to mitigate the impact of debris flows include monitoring and early warning of exceptional rainfall and runoff events in the mountains; land-use control in mountain catchments; and the alignment of new buildings and streets in the direction of debris flows.

Case study   Philippines mudslide 2006

A devastating mudslide hit the Philippine village of Guinsaugon in southern Leyte province on 17 February 2006 (Figure 1.20). The slide covered 9 km², was 3 km wide and in places 30 m thick.

Causes: torrential rain and deforestation

The main cause was exceptionally heavy rainfall associated with a La Niña event in the western Pacific. Two hundred centimetres of rain fell in 10 days, loading slopes and weakening slope materials. However, there were other contributory causes. Slopes in the region are steep and mudslides and other mass movements occur frequently. Widespread deforestation during the past 70 years has also increased slope instability. The ultimate event that triggered the slide was a small earthquake measuring 2.6 Mw.

Figure 1.20
Location of the Guinsaugon mudslide

A hazard becomes a disaster

The mudslide moved at speed as half a mountain collapsed behind the village of Guinsaugon. People had no time to escape. Survivors described how a 'wall of mud' descended on the village, killing over 1000 people, including 246 children at the elementary school. Virtually every one of the 300 houses in Guinsaugon was destroyed. The slide also killed thousands of livestock and buried surrounding farmland. Altogether around 16 000 people were affected.

Exposure

Exposure to mass movement hazards is high in this part of the Philippines. In 1991, 5000 people were killed when typhoons triggered several landslides. A similar event in 2003 killed 133 people. A deadly combination of physical conditions makes mudslides and landslides a constant threat:

- heavy and prolonged rainfall from typhoons
- steep hillslopes comprising deeply weathered volcanic rock
- extensive faulting and earthquake activity

Human factors also contribute to high exposure levels. Many villages, sited at the foot of steep slopes, occupy the run-out zone of mudslides and landslides. Rural population densities are high (208 persons per km^2), putting thousands at risk. Deforestation has also added to slope instability. This is partly the result of rapid population growth and the demand for fuelwood and new land for cultivation.

Vulnerability

The impact of natural hazards is only partly explained by exposure. The proportion of the exposed population killed by the 2006 mudslide is a measure of vulnerability. In this example, vulnerability is high. Prominent in the list of factors contributing to vulnerability are poverty and population growth. Southern Leyte is one of the poorest regions in the Philippines. Between 1995 and 2000 the population grew by 2.73%, placing even more pressure on environmental resources and forcing people to live in high-risk zones.

Deforestation results from commercial logging as well as population growth. Logging bans have not been enforced by the government. Policy failures have their roots in corruption among politicians and government officials. Even where sustainable logging has been practised, deep-rooted forest trees have often been replaced by shallow-rooted coconuts, increasing the risk of slope failure.

Inadequate hazard mitigation measures have added to vulnerability. Hazard maps exist for southern Leyte but are not detailed enough to pinpoint villages at risk from mass movements. Following heavy rains and the deaths of 20 people in a nearby village, hazard warnings were issued between 4 and 17 February and several hillside villages were evacuated. Even so, many people could not afford to abandon their livelihoods and chose to stay despite the risks.

Human responses to the disaster

In response to the disaster evacuation centres were set up around St Bernard, the capital of southern Leyte. Emergency aid in these centres provided safe drinking water, sanitation and health services. But southern Leyte is remote and its poor communications slowed disaster response times. Two hundred rescue workers were brought to the disaster site. However, unlike earthquakes, mass movement disasters have few survivors. International aid was provided by the Red Cross and Red Crescent and a disaster appeal raised US$1.6 million. The government, concerned to better identify the areas most at risk from mudslides, has commissioned a new US$1.5 million geohazards survey and mapping map of southern Leyte.

USFG

Photograph 1.8 *Guinsaugon mudslide*

Floods

Key ideas

➤ Floods are caused by a combination of physical and human factors that vary from place to place.
➤ Floods have a range of social, economic and environmental impacts.
➤ The human reaction to floods is both short term (e.g. emergency rescue) and long term (e.g. management and planning).

Flood hazards at a global scale

Floods are possibly the world's greatest natural hazard (Figures 1.21 and 1.22). Every year nearly 200 million people in more than 90 countries are exposed to severe floods: more than the number at risk from earthquakes and hurricanes. Between 1980 and 2000 floods caused an estimated 170 000 deaths.

India, Indonesia, Bangladesh and China have the largest populations exposed to flooding. The main reason is because millions of people in these countries live on floodplains and coastal deltas.

The number of deaths from flooding as a proportion of the size of the exposed population provides a measure of relative vulnerability. Figure 1.22 shows that the most vulnerable populations are in China, India, Bangladesh and Indonesia. However, based on lives lost, Venezuela had the highest vulnerability between 1980 and 2000. This was due to the disastrous floods and debris flows in northern Venezuela in 1999 which killed over 30 000 people.

Figure 1.21
Physical exposure to floods, 1980–2000

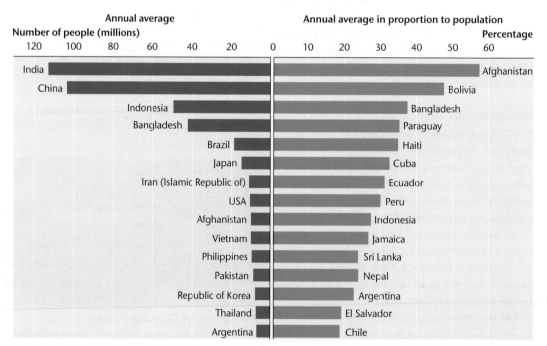

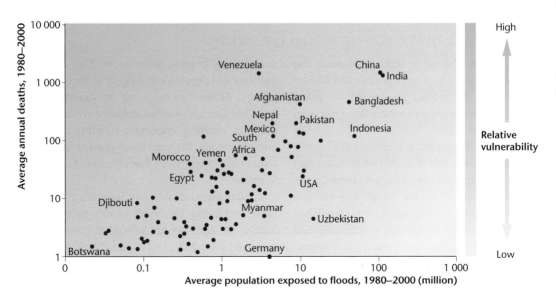

Figure 1.22
Relative vulnerability to floods, 1980–2000

What are river floods?

Floods are natural events and most rivers normally flood once or twice a year. But floods only become a hazard when floodwaters threaten property and put lives at risk.

Floods occur when rivers burst their banks. This may be due to an exceptional rainfall event or rapid snowmelt. It may also be due to land-use change such as deforestation and urbanisation, which speed the transfer of rainfall into rivers.

The severity of any flood hazard depends partly on its predictability. **Flash floods** caused by sudden, torrential downpours develop rapidly and are difficult to predict (Box 1.3). This makes them particularly hazardous. In contrast heavy and prolonged rainfall often produces **slow floods**. When rivers rise slowly people have time to protect their property and evacuate their homes. In large parts of tropical Asia, Africa and South America flooding is a predictable feature of climate. Indeed, millions of people in India and Bangladesh depend on the annual monsoon floods for their survival. In countries like these, human activities have adapted to the annual cycle of floods which are essential to farming.

Box 1.3 Flash floods

Flash floods are unpredictable and often violent. A combination of physical factors is associated with flash floods in the UK. These include:

- upland areas, where mechanical (orographic) uplift intensifies convectional storms
- small and steep catchments with high drainage density, which speed runoff and shorten lag times
- impermeable geology
- limited tree cover

These conditions were a common feature of the Ryedale floods in North Yorkshire in 2005, and the flash floods at Boscastle in Cornwall in 2004 and Lynmouth in Devon in 1953.

Box 1.4 Climate change and flooding

Future climate change is likely to increase the severity, frequency and costs of river and coastal flooding. For this reason governments in many MEDCs are developing sustainable flood management strategies.

Climate models predict that global warming will increase surface pressure in middle latitudes and reduce it in high latitudes. This will speed up the westerly circulation in the North Atlantic and increase the number of severe storms. Meanwhile in the tropics, rising sea surface temperatures will fuel more powerful hurricanes and tropical storms. These changes will increase flood risks in coastal regions. But the problem is made worse by another factor. Global warming will raise sea level by at least 25–30 cm by 2050 as polar ice and glaciers melt and the oceans expand thermally.

Protecting the entire coastline of the UK by strengthening sea defences is economically unsustainable. Faced with this problem the UK government has adopted a new strategy of managed realignment. Along some stretches of coast, sea defences will not be maintained, and in places they will be deliberately breached. A new line of flood defences will be established inland. On the seaward side of these defences mudflats and salt-marshes will develop naturally, and absorb wave energy. As well as requiring no maintenance, mudflats and saltmarshes deliver environmental benefits, creating important habitats for birds and marine life. Managed realignment is already happening in parts of Lincolnshire, Essex and Somerset.

Global warming will also intensify the water cycle and bring increased rainfall to northern Britain. By 2080 winter rainfall is predicted to increase by 10–25%. This is particularly worrying because runoff is greatest in winter when flood risks are at their highest. Although summer rainfall amounts will decrease, higher temperatures will increase convection, bringing a greater risk of flash floods. Sustainable river management will mean abandoning some flood protection structures. In places, flood embankments will be removed, allowing rivers to connect with their floodplains once more. Water stored temporarily on floodplains will reduce flood risks downstream. Meanwhile tighter planning controls will restrict the building of houses and businesses on floodplains where risks are high.

Case study   Flooding on the lower River Severn

The River Severn is the third largest British river, draining a catchment of nearly 11 500 km^2 (Figure 1.23). It rises in the mountains of central Wales above 800 m. On leaving the mountains, it initially flows east, before turning south to its estuary in the Bristol Channel. Two major reservoirs in the upper catchment — Lakes Vrynwy and Clywedog — provide floodwater storage. However, the lower catchment, especially between Worcester and Gloucester, fed by major tributaries such as the Avon and the Teme, is particularly vulnerable to flooding (Figure 1.24).

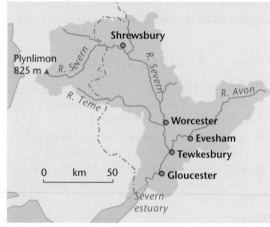

Figure 1.23 The Severn catchment

Physical factors affecting flooding

A number of physical factors influence flooding on the lower Severn, including rock type, relief, climate and vegetation. Large parts of the upper catchment in central Wales are above 300 m, where slopes are steep and the main rock types have low permeability. As a result runoff is rapid and small tributaries, which feed into the main river, are highly responsive to rainfall and therefore liable to flash floods.

The main relief feature in the lower catchment is an extensive floodplain, only a few metres above sea level (Figure 1.24). Much of the land adjacent to the River Severn floods regularly in winter. Flooding is also more likely to occur in the lower catchment because of the convergence of a number of major tributaries in this area. The Warwickshire Avon joins

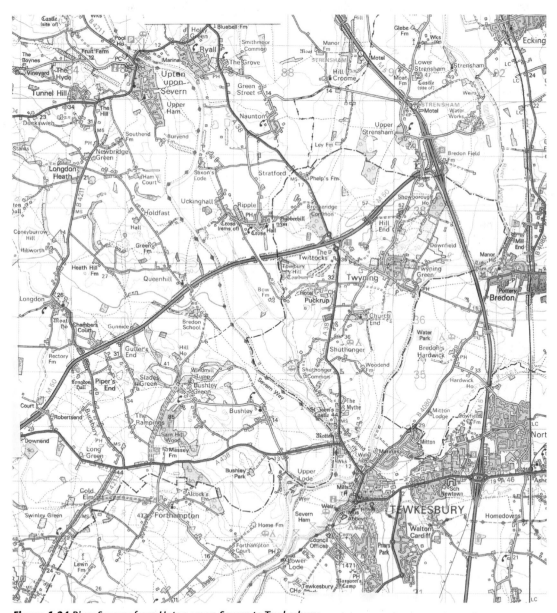

Figure 1.24 River Severn: from Upton-upon-Severn to Tewkesbury

Figure 1.25 Flood risk map of area around Tewkesbury

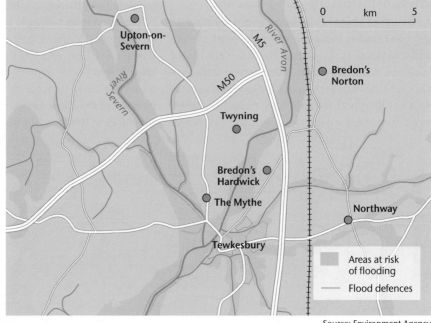

Source: Environment Agency

the River Severn at Tewkesbury, and the River Teme's confluence with the Severn is just south of Worcester.

Mean annual rainfall in the mountains in central Wales exceeds 2000 mm, and because of orographic uplift, rainfall is often intense and prolonged. Low rates of evaporation mean that most rainfall is converted to runoff and river flow.

Vegetation cover influences rates of interception, evapotranspiration and runoff. Nearly 45% of land use in upper catchment comprises rough pasture and moorland. This promotes rapid runoff and increases the flood risk.

Human factors affecting flooding

The main human factor contributing to the flood risk is building on the Severn floodplain. Figures 1.24 and 1.25 show that large parts of the settlements of Upton-upon-Severn and Tewkesbury occupy the floodplain. Without adequate flood defences, these areas are exposed to a high level of risk. Within the lower Severn and Avon catchments there is evidence that recent urbanisation has accelerated the loss of floodplain land, reducing natural water storage and placing more properties at risk.

Rural land-use change and land-use management may also have contributed to higher peak flows. Improved drainage of farmland speeds the movement of rainwater into rivers; so too does the conversion of pasture to arable and the clear felling of forestry plantations.

The lack of hard flood defences also exposes much of the lower Severn valley to flooding. There are few flood embankments, and other forms of river engineering such as flood relief channels, channel widening and straightening are absent.

The July 2007 floods

Large parts of England and Wales, including Humberside, South Yorkshire, the lower Severn valley and the Thames valley were affected by severe flooding in the summer of 2007. The floods in the Severn valley followed an extreme rainfall event on 20 July, when 135 mm of rain fell at Pershore in just 16 hours. This was exceptional rainfall with a recurrence probability of only 0.1% a year (Figure 1.26). Flash floods in several small catchments such as the Isbourne in Worcestershire then fed into the major rivers, raising the Severn at Worcester nearly 6 m above normal and the River Avon at Evesham to the highest level ever recorded. The severity of flooding was due only to exceptional rainfall (2007 was the wettest summer since 1766), but also to soils already saturated by heavy rains in June. Where flood defences were overwhelmed it was because the flow level exceeded their design.

By the 21 July flooding had occurred in towns and villages on the Avon's floodplain to a depth of 2 m. At Tewkesbury, flood waters entered the town's medieval abbey for the first time in 247 years, and there was widespread flooding all along the River Severn from Upton to Gloucester (see Table 1.3 below and Photograph 1.9 on p. 28). The flood wave peaked on 23 July, when Gloucester city centre narrowly avoided flooding.

Human reaction to the July 2007 floods

General management responses towards river flooding in the UK are shown in Table 1.4 on p. 29. In the specific example of the July 2007 floods, the reaction was both immediate and long term. Immediate responses included the erection of temporary flood barriers and flood warnings issued by television, radio, the Environment Agency's 'Floodline' and the internet.

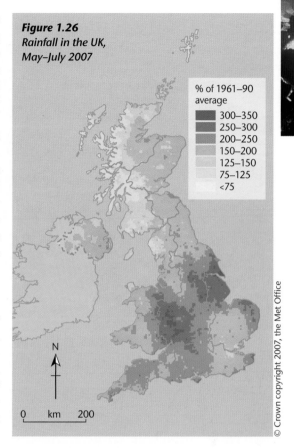

Figure 1.26
*Rainfall in the UK,
May–July 2007*

% of 1961–90 average

- 300–350
- 250–300
- 200–250
- 150–200
- 125–150
- 75–125
- <75

N

0   km   200

© Crown copyright 2007, the Met Office

Table 1.3 *The societal, economic and environmental impact of the July 2007 floods*

Societal	Considerable disruption to electricity and water supplies. Flooding of a sub-station near Gloucester left 50 000 households without power (some for up to 2 days). A water treatment plant in Tewkesbury was also flooded with the result that water supplies for 140 000 households were cut off and without water for at least 5 days. Safe drinking water was not restored until 7 August. Ten thousand motorists were left stranded on the M5 and surrounding roads and forced to abandon their cars.
Economic	The total insured loss estimated for the 20 July flood event was £1–1.5 billion. These losses include damage to property, motor vehicles, disruption to businesses and the expense of providing temporary accommodation for those forced to leave their homes. There was large-scale damage to property and disruption of businesses: 27 000 domestic insurance claims and 6800 business claims were made. Many motor vehicles were damaged completely, and abandoned vehicles blocked roads and traffic flows. The M5 was closed due to flooding and landslides on 20 July. Crops were submerged and maize, potatoes and hay crops lost. Where floodwater contained sewage, crops had to be destroyed.
Environmental	Thousands of small mammals drowned, ground nesting birds were badly affected and large numbers of mature fish were left stranded on the floodplain when water levels receded.

Environmental Agency

Photograph 1.9 *Flooding of the River Severn at Tewkesbury, July 2007*

The Severn Trent water authority's response to the disruption to water supplies was the immediate distribution of 5 million litres per day of bottled water and the deployment of 1500 water bowsers. The government provided £87 million of emergency aid for funding schools, transport and businesses hardest hit by the floods and the European Union contributed a further £31 million in compensation.

Overall spending on flood defences by the UK government doubled between 1997 and 2007 and the experience of the 2007 floods prompted the government to pledge an increase in spending on flood defences to £800 million by 2010–11 (an increase of £200 million since 2006). However, apart from the provision of temporary flood barriers for Upton-on-Severn, and raising some flood embankments around Gloucester, the Environment Agency (EA) has no plans for major new flood protection schemes in the lower Severn valley. People living in the flood-prone areas (in September 2008 Tewkesbury Abbey and the town centre once again became an island surrounded by floodwater) will have to learn to live with floods, and rely on the EA's flood warning system and on flood insurance. Huge investment in new river flood defences, like coastal defences, is seen in the long term as being unsustainable.

Table 1.4 *Approaches to river flood management in the UK*

Non-structural measures		
Approach	**Description**	**Advantages/disadvantages**
Catchment flood management plans (CFMP)	A holistic approach to environmental management of drainage basins. The primary concern is sustainable flood management. Other environmental issues include water abstraction, pollution, land-use change and wildlife conservation in drainage basins. The first pilot study (River Ribble) was completed in 2007. Eventually there will be around 80 CFMPs covering England and Wales.	Drainage basins are natural units. Until now they have been managed piecemeal by different agencies, e.g. water authorities, Environment Agency (EA), DEFRA. CFMPs provide an opportunity for coordinated planning of environmental resources within natural geographic units.
Afforestation and land-use change	Changing land use in headwaters can help to prevent flooding. Afforestation slows runoff, increases water loss through evapotranspiration, and reduces peak flows. Discouraging artificial drainage in upland catchments and conserving areas of wetland can also reduce peak flows.	There is difficulty in getting landowners to agree to land-use changes. Changes such as afforestation and wetland conservation often benefit wildlife and improve amenity.
Controlling development on floodplains	The government provides local authorities with guidelines aimed at controlling floodplain development. Climate change will increase flood risks so floodplain development must be sustainable. Currently 10% of England is exposed to significant flood risks. The annual cost of flood damage could rise to £20 billion a year by 2080.	There is a huge demand for new housing in the UK and limited space to accommodate it. The government wants to encourage redevelopment of brownfield sites. However, many of these are close to rivers and are vulnerable to flooding.
Flood insurance: exposure and vulnerability	The average claim for a house flooded to a depth of 1 m in winter is £35 000. Insurance premiums can be assessed more accurately thanks to detailed flood-risk maps being compiled by insurance companies. Vulnerability to flooding can be reduced by designing homes where the ground floors are garage spaces, and where materials are less easily damaged by floodwater.	Insurance premiums will rise as flood hazards increase with climate change. Many householders may be unable to afford premiums, or will be forced to buy insurance with large excesses (e.g. they pay the first £20 000 of damage).
Washlands or flood basins	Floodwaters are stored temporarily on floodplains reducing the flood peak and saving settlements downstream from potential flooding.	Washlands can be used for grazing for most of the year and when flooded provide valuable refuges for wildlife. Washlands work with nature because they occupy areas that flood naturally.
Flood warnings	The EA provides information on flood risks through telephone 'Floodlines' and websites. There are three levels of alert: flood watch; flood warning; and severe flood warning. A flood warning means that flooding is imminent and people at risk should take immediate action.	Flood alerts allow people to prepare for flooding and minimise the damage to property and the threat to life.
Flood risk maps	The EA publishes maps on its website which show areas at risk from river and coastal flooding.	The EA's flood maps at 1:50 000, give only a general view of areas at risk. More detailed maps, based on GPS data, will eventually become available end enable insurance companies to assess risk more accurately.

Structural measures		
Approach	Description	Advantages/disadvantages
Flood embankments or levées	Flood embankments are walls (often earthen) on either side of a river's channel. By increasing channel capacity they reduce the risk of floodwaters spilling onto the floodplain.	Flood embankments are often unsightly and may cause rivers to flow above the floodplain. If flood embankments fail the potential damage is much greater than a normal flood. Embankments can also raise flood levels, accelerate channel erosion, are expensive to build and maintain, and in the long term are unsustainable.
Dams and reservoirs	Damming of rivers and their tributaries allows floodwaters to be stored and released gradually.	Dam construction involves huge capital costs and reservoirs may flood valuable farmland and/or environmentally important valleys. Unusually large flood events can overtop dams (e.g. Prague floods, 2002). Apart from flood management, dams have other benefits, e.g. HEP production, water supply, water-based recreation and leisure such as Glen Canyon dam, Arizona and Lake Powell, Utah.
Channel straightening	Meanders are removed, increasing channel gradient, flow velocity and depth. To prevent meanders reforming, straightened channels may have to be lined with concrete.	Increasing gradient gives a river surplus energy which results in it scouring its bed, eroding laterally, and re-establishing its meandering channel. Straightening a river is only sustainable if the channel is hardened to prevent erosion. Channel straightening is also unattractive aesthetically.
Flood relief channels	Artificial channels are constructed, diverting some of the flow from a river to reduce the risk of flooding. The Jubilee River scheme created a relief channel on the River Thames to give flood protection to communities in Maidenhead, Windsor and Eton.	Flood relief channels are effective in preventing flooding in places they were designed to protect, but do nothing to stop flooding further downstream. They are used infrequently and when empty are unsightly concrete boxes.

Coastal flooding

Coastal flooding is much rarer than river flooding. However, in England and Wales exposure to coastal flooding is high. One third of the population lives within 10 km of the coast and without coastal defences 2500 km^2 would be at risk.

There are two types of coastal flooding. The first and less common, is when water levels exceed the height of coastal defences, overflowing or breaching them. This is most likely to happen when high spring tides coincide with storm surges, driven by low pressure and strong winds. This type of flooding can result in major disasters. In February 1953 a storm surge in the southern North Sea overtopped flood embankments in eastern England killing 307 people, damaging 24 000 homes and flooding 400 km² of farmland.

The last major flood of this type in the UK was at Towyn in North Wales in February 1990. A deep depression in the Irish Sea generated gale-force winds and a storm surge 1–2.5 m high. The sea wall, unprotected by beaches or saltmarshes, took the brunt of storm waves and was breached at high tide. Water poured through the breach and in minutes flooded 6.5 km² and damaged 3000 properties. In Towyn the floodwaters reached a height of 5.4 m.

Case study   Coastal flooding in Bangladesh

Bangladesh is situated astride the Tropic of Cancer, between 20° and 26°. It is bordered to the north, east, and west and by India, to the southeast by Myanmar. It is a low-income country and one of the most densely populated in the world. The coastal districts suffer high levels of exposure to flooding.

Physical factors affecting coastal flooding

Few places in the world are at greater risk from flooding than the coastal districts of Bangladesh (Figure 1.27). A number of physical factors contribute to the country's high exposure to coastal flooding. First, most of Bangladesh occupies the Ganges-Brahmaputra delta, a vast area of alluvial islands, shifting river channels and tidal inlets only a metre or two above sea level. Flooding occurs frequently when strong onshore winds and low pressure in the Bay of Bengal coincide with exceptional spring tides.

Figure 1.27 Bangladesh: coastal districts most exposed to flooding

But while tidal flooding is routine, there is a second physical factor that can result in disastrous floods. Storm surges up to 10 m high, generated by tropical cyclones that originate in the Indian Ocean and track northwards through the Bay of Bengal, slam into the delta every few years causing massive devastation and loss of life. These cyclones, powered by the ocean's warm surface waters, drive storm surges towards the delta coast.

The natural funnel shape of the Bay of Bengal steepens the storm surge which overwhelms the low-lying tidal floodplains of the delta. In 1970 a cyclone and its accompanying storm surge killed an estimated half a million people and caused utter devastation. A similar surge in 1991 resulted in 138 000 deaths. As a result of this disaster millions lost their homes, and farmland and infrastructure were destroyed.

Photograph 1.10 *Cyclone shelter in Bangladesh*

Human factors affecting coastal flooding

Bangladesh's densely populated delta lands add to the region's exposure to coastal flooding. In 2008 Bangladesh's total population was 154 million, with approximately 40 million living in the coastal zone. The average population density is nearly 1150 km², making Bangladesh arguably the most densely populated country in the world. Pressure of population on the land forces millions of people to risk their lives and live in places exposed to storm surges and tidal flooding. So too does poverty: Bangladesh is one of Asia's poorest countries, its GDP per capita being just US$423 in 2005. Roughly two in every five Bangladeshis cannot afford enough food to sustain a healthy life, making the population even more vulnerable to flooding and other natural disasters. Meanwhile, on the UN's human development index Bangladesh was ranked the 140th poorest country in the world (out of 177) in 2007.

In the past, a dearth of investment in coastal defensive structures such as levées, storm surge shelters and flood warning systems has also left the population highly vulnerable to flood disasters. The huge death toll in the 1970 and 1991 floods could have been much lower with better flood mitigation and adequate warning systems.

However, there has been no repeat of the 1991 disaster. This is due to progress in hazard mitigation which has reduced the vulnerability to storm surges. Many flood embankments have been strengthened and new ones built. Mangrove forests have been planted on the coast, trapping silt to build up mudflats, and absorb wave energy. Thanks to foreign aid, new cyclone shelters, strong enough to withstand 7 m storm surges, have been completed (Photograph 1.10).

The impact of Cyclone Sidr, 2007

Cyclone Sidr made landfall on the southwest coast of Bangladesh on 15 November 2007. A category 4 cyclone, Sidr was the most powerful storm to hit Bangladesh since 1991 (Figure 1.28). Its impact was

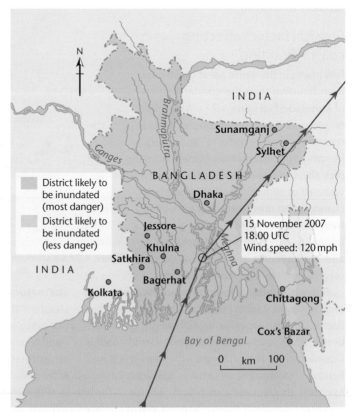

Figure 1.28 *Impact of Cyclone Sidr*

widespread and devastating. At its height winds reached speeds up to 240 kph and generated a 5m storm surge which swept inland. Large areas of the coast were flooded, and over 4000 people died. Over 1.5 million homes were damaged and 1 million ha of crops destroyed. The total economic cost was around US$450 million and nearly 9 million people were affected. There was also an ecological cost. It was estimated that one-quarter of coastal mangrove forests of the Sundarbans — a World Heritage Site with a unique ecosystem — was badly damaged by the storm surge and hurricane-force winds. Parts of the forest could take 40 years to recover.

The human response

Significant progress on hazard mitigation in Bangladesh occurred between 1991 and 2007. This is evident in the relatively low death toll caused by Cyclone Sidr compared to previous cyclones.

Following the 1991 disaster, the USA and the European Union (EU) supported a cyclone preparedness programme. Satellites monitored the progress of Sidr and the authorities were able to provide early warning and evacuate over 1 million people in the most hazardous areas. Many took refuge in the 1800 disaster shelters dotted around the coast (Photograph 1.10). Cyclone walls, planted with trees, also saved lives in some of the most exposed areas. All of these measures helped to reduce the vulnerability of the coastal population and saved thousands of lives.

Short-term aid in the form of disaster relief funds, emergency food, blankets and clothing came from the USA and the EU and from NGOs such as Oxfam and the Red Cross. The World Food Programme sent food rations for 400 000 people, and for longer term relief, the World Bank pledged US$250 million in aid.

Case study   Flood and storm damage in Cornwall, 2004

A more frequent type of coastal flooding occurs when storm waves overtop sea defences such as sea walls and flood embankments. The resulting floods usually last for 1 to 3 hours around high tide. Damage caused by this type of flooding is often fairly localised.

On 27 and 28 October 2004 a deep depression hit the coast of southern Cornwall (Figure 1.29). Winds gusting to 90 km h^{-1} whipped up huge waves. The storm coincided with the spring tide. Waves overtopped and damaged the sea wall at Penzance causing extensive flooding to properties along the promenade. Flooded homes had to be evacuated, roads were closed and rail services suspended. In Looe, 30 homes and businesses were flooded. Flooding was also reported in Porthleven and Flushing near Falmouth.

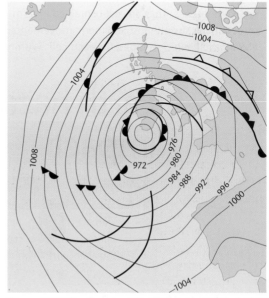

Figure 1.29 *Weather chart for 28 October 2004 at 12.00*

Box 1.5 Coastal flood management

Like river flood management, coastal flood management relies on two approaches: hard engineering and soft engineering.

Hard structures raise the level of the coastline and provide a barrier to the sea. On shallow low-energy coasts such as East Anglia and Lincolnshire, earth embankments are widely used. Where wave energy is greater and where important settlements need protection, sea walls are built. But sea walls are expensive (£3 million km^{-1}) and require constant maintenance. They are only justified where the value of property they protect exceeds their cost of construction.

Hard structures can also cause problems within the coastal system. For example, sea walls stop erosion and the input of sediment to the coastal system. Nearby stretches of coast, unprotected by sea walls, starved of beach sediment may suffer accelerated erosion.

Current policies of coastal flood management in England and Wales are based around Shoreline Management Plans (SMPs). The coastline of England and Wales is divided into 11 natural units or sediment cells. They are self-contained in terms of sediment supply and sediment movements. SMPs have been developed for each cell. Within each cell smaller lengths of coastline or sub-cells have been defined. Management policies for the sub-cells state whether existing sea defences are to be:

- Advanced — moving coastal defences into areas now covered by the sea.
- Maintained — keeping the shoreline in its present position.
- Abandoned — allowing the shoreline to be moved inland in a controlled manner, i.e. managed realignment or managed retreat.
- Ignored — literally doing nothing and allowing nature to take its course.

The new philosophy is to work with nature wherever possible, even if this means abandoning sea defences and allowing the sea to encroach on some areas. Working with nature means interrupting sediment movements as little as possible; allowing the sea to recreate the natural boundary between land and sea; getting rid of some hard structures which squeeze salt marshes and mudflats and result in their erosion; and recognising that rising sea levels will in future make the costs of maintaining and increasing existing defences unsustainable.

Earth hazards: the human impact

Key ideas

➤ The impact of earth hazards varies over time and location.
➤ The impact of earth hazards is influenced by economic and technological development, population distribution and population density.
➤ The impact of earth hazards varies from immediate to long term.
➤ Earth hazards can be managed in a number of ways to reduce their impact.

In this section we shall look at a number of case studies of earth hazards to show how their human impact is influenced by a range of factors such as levels of development, management, urbanisation and population distribution. All of these factors contribute to the vulnerability of a population or society to natural hazardous events.

Impact of earthquakes in MEDCs

 Case study **Earthquakes in Japan**

Japan occupies one of the most seismically active zones in the world, where four major tectonic plates converge (Figure 1.30). Ocean trenches such as the Japan Trench and the Sagami Trench mark plate boundaries where subduction occurs off Japan's Pacific coast.

Exposure to earthquake risk is not just a function of tectonic activity. It also results from the distribution and density of population in Japan. Population densities in Japan are highest on the Pacific coast of Honshu, the areas most at risk from earthquakes. Tokyo (33 million), Osaka (14.1 million) and Nagoya

(6.9 million) are situated only a few hundred kilometres from active subduction zones.

The vulnerability of Japanese cities to major earthquake disasters

The Kobe earthquake in January 1995 destroyed Japan's myth of safe cities. It showed that even the richest and best prepared MEDCs are not immune from major earthquake disasters. The Kobe quake (6.9 Mw) caused 6400 deaths and destroyed or partly destroyed 200 000 homes. It forced Japan to take a critical look at its disaster prevention strategies.

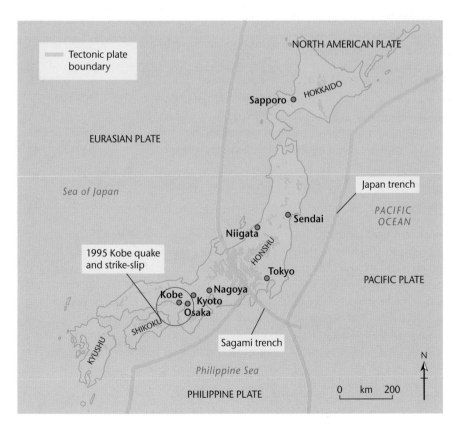

Figure 1.30
Tectonic plates, ocean trenches and seismic activity in Japan

The conclusion was stark: Kobe and other major Japanese cities, including the capital, Tokyo, were highly vulnerable to major earthquake hazards.

How great is the earthquake risk in Tokyo?

Thirteen earthquakes measuring between 5.3 and 7.9 Mw on the Richter scale were recorded in Tokyo in the twentieth century. The 1923 Great Kanto quake was by far the biggest and most damaging. It killed over 140 000 people and injured a further 104 000. It also destroyed or partly destroyed a quarter of a million homes in the city. Massive **interplate** earthquakes in Tokyo have a recurrence interval of 100–200 years.

Intraplate quakes, with their focus directly beneath Tokyo, have also occurred in the past. These quakes are generally smaller than interplate quakes, usually measuring less than 7 Mw. Despite their smaller magnitude, most intraplate quakes have a shallow focus which increases their intensity and can cause severe damage. Tokyo's Ansei Edo quake of 1855, which had its focus directly below the mouth of the Arakawa River, resulted in over 4000 deaths.

Making Tokyo an earthquake-resistant city

A huge amount of management and planning is currently taking place to mitigate the effects of a major earthquake in Tokyo. Current planning for disaster prevention is based on the assumption that a repeat of the Great Kanto quake would result in 150 000 deaths. In the past 60 years, rapid urbanisation and urban growth has actually increased exposure and the risk of a major earthquake disaster in Tokyo. Damage estimates for the central 23 wards of Tokyo based on a 7.2 Mw earthquake (similar to the Kobe quake) are shown in Table 1.5.

Disaster planning in Tokyo involves the Tokyo Metropolitan Government (TMG), the individual and the community. Following the Kobe earthquake in 1995 the TMG stepped up its earthquake disaster planning. A revised disaster plan, due for completion by 2017, aims to make Tokyo a disaster-resistant city. Priority is given to making as many buildings as possible earthquake resistant. The plan identifies 25 high-risk districts in the city most urgently in need of improvement. High-density wooden housing in these districts is a major fire risk. Fire-proofing will help to reduce these risks.

Table 1.5 *Estimated impact of 7.2 Mw earthquake in Tokyo*

Structures destroyed by fire	324 288 (18.9%)
Deaths	6717
Serious injuries	15 384
Residents forced to live in refuge sites	1 259 875
Houses totally destroyed	36 971 (2.2%)
Houses partly destroyed	83 743 (4.9%)

Box 1.6 Super structure construction method: Tokyo Metro Building 1

Tokyo's metropolitan government buildings are designed with a small base area relative to their height. The main building is 243 m high but only 44 m wide at the base. The usual method for skyscraper construction — the flexible structure or Rahmen type — was unsuitable. The degree of bending in an earthquake would be too great. Thus the Metropolitan Building is a rigid structure, designed to resist earthquakes by absorbing the force with gigantic pillars and beams. Its box-shaped reinforced concrete pillars were constructed using iron plates with a thickness of 1 m × 80 mm. Four of these pillars were erected at each corner and the ones in the core part of the building were connected to each other by K-type braces, forming a super pillar measuring 6.4 m². Strength and resilience is also provided by connecting these super pillars with super beams every ten floors. The super beams take up space equivalent to one floor each.

The TMG is also strengthening roads, express-ways, bridges, riverbanks, coastlines and essential infrastructure such electricity, gas and water pipelines. Important buildings such as government offices, police stations, fire service offices and hospitals, vital in the event of a major quake, are also being strengthened. For many years high-rise buildings have been designed to withstand high-magnitude quakes.

Tokyo's disaster plan also identifies hundreds of open spaces where people can assemble following a major earthquake. These refuge sites are provided with emergency supplies, including tents and other makeshift shelters. People will also be accommodated in 3000 public shelters (e.g. schools) with a planned capacity of 4.27 million.

Rapid recovery and long-term reconstruction will be vital after an earthquake. The disaster plan sets out priorities and targets for the first few months and years of the post-quake period. It also includes recon-struction plans, restrictions on building rights, and the formation of recovery organisations. In this way it is hoped that reconstruction can take place smoothly and as quickly as possible.

Earthquake preparedness and public safety are also the responsibility of each individual and the community. The TMG plans to build a 'strong society' against earthquakes by raising public awareness of earthquake hazards and getting across the message of working together to overcome disasters.

Conclusion

Japan's geography and geology place the country at high risk from earthquakes. There is no doubt that a major earthquake will strike Tokyo sooner or later. The TMG, through its earthquake disaster plan, aims to increase the city's preparedness and reduce its vulnerability. In this way it hopes to avoid the massive destruction and loss of life that occurred in Kobe in 1995.

Impact of earthquakes in LEDCs

Because LEDCs often lack the economic resources to reduce earthquake hazards, their populations are more vulnerable than those of MEDCs. A glance at Table 1.1 (p. 4) confirms this. The 6.9 Mw earthquake that struck the Japanese city of Kobe in 1995 killed 5530 people. Ten years later, the Kashmir quake of similar magnitude killed over 87 500 people in rural Pakistan and India. In Kashmir the people were particularly vulnerable because they could not afford to build safe housing. Their vulnerability was increased by rescue services hampered by a lack of equipment and their isolation. Cut off by landslides, tens of thousands were without emergency aid for days, and in some cases weeks.

 Case study **The Kashmir earthquake**

At 08.50 local time on 8 October 2005, a 7.6 Mw earthquake struck the province of Kashmir in northern Pakistan and northern India. The epicentre was 105 km north of Islamabad, close to the towns of Muzaffarabad and Balakot (Figure 1.31).

This region occupies the collision zone between the Indian subcontinent and Eurasia. Collision causes faulting and frequent earthquakes, and over the past 50 million years has created the world's highest fold mountain range — the Himalayas. In Kashmir thrust faults dip northwards beneath the mountain ranges. It was movement along one of these faults that caused the Kashmir earthquake (Photograph 1.11).

The earthquake also triggered secondary hazards, including landslides, which blocked rivers and led to flooding. Steep, unstable mountain slopes and

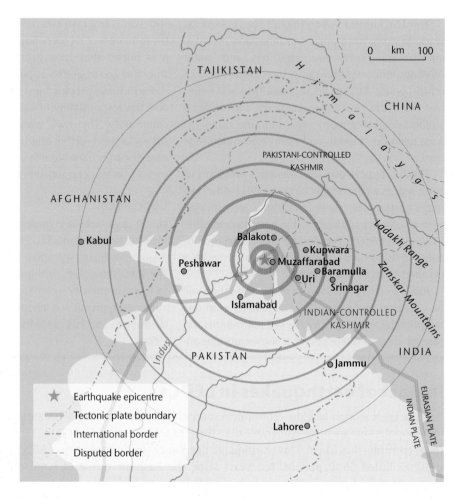

Figure 1.31
Location of the Kashmir earthquake

deeply incised river valleys make the whole region extremely susceptible to mass movement events.

Impact of the disaster

In terms of loss of life the Kashmir earthquake was the most costly in recent history. Over 87 000 people died and more than 3 million were affected. Eighty-four per cent of those affected lived in rural areas. Collapsed buildings caused most deaths. Further deaths resulted from landslides, exposure to severe winter conditions and disease. Four-hundred thousand people live above the winter snowline in Kashmir. Most of these people were made homeless and had to survive temperatures as low as −15°C.

The economic cost of the disaster was also high. In Muzaffarabad, the quake destroyed half of all buildings. There was extensive damage to roads, bridges, electricity supplies, schools and hospitals. Eighty per cent of all crops and 50% of arable land was destroyed, the maize crop was lost, grinding mills were broken, and 100 000 cattle were killed. Overall, the economic cost of the disaster was US$5 billion — a huge sum for such an impoverished region.

Exposure and vulnerability

Kashmir's large population — 15 million — has grown rapidly in the past 50 years and has increased the region's exposure to earthquake risk. Eighty-four per cent of the population lives in rural areas, many in isolated villages in the mountains.

Although rural–urban migration is taking place in

Kashmir, the region remains weakly urbanised. This rurality increases the population's vulnerability to earthquakes. So too does poverty. In Kashmir one in three people lives below the poverty line. Many of those hit by the 2005 quake were already living on the edge, with few resources to fall back on in the event of a major disaster.

Remoteness simply adds to vulnerability. It took several days to get emergency aid to survivors in some mountain villages. In the 200 km-long Neelum Valley, 160 000 people were cut off for 6 weeks by massive landslides with access impossible except by helicopter.

International appeals for emergency aid met with a slow response. Many survivors had no heating and by December 2005, 40% were not getting enough food. Two million people depended on food aid and 1.7 million were living in tents. Poor sanitation, contaminated drinking water and the reluctance of farmers in the mountains to abandon their land and livestock added to the death toll.

However, the main cause of death was poor building construction and engineering. Close to the epicentre nearly all buildings, whether made of stone, block masonry or reinforced concrete, collapsed. Twenty-five kilometres from the epicentre one-quarter of all buildings collapsed and half were severely damaged. Hundreds of deaths occurred in single-storey unreinforced stone buildings. Walls made of undressed, irregular or rounded stones laid in a weak sand or mud mortar (or even dry stone walls) simply disintegrated. In towns many reinforced concrete structures also collapsed due to poor quality concrete and mortar, and poor design. The lack of seismic building codes underlines the low state of earthquake preparedness in LEDCs such as Pakistan and India.

Conclusion

The people of Kashmir were particularly vulnerable to earthquake hazards because they could not afford to build safe housing. Their vulnerability was increased by rescue services hampered by a lack of equipment and the remoteness of the region. Cut off by landslides, tens of thousands were without emergency aid for days, and in some cases weeks.

Caro/Alamy

Photograph 1.11 *Damage caused by the Kashmir earthquake, 2005*

Box 1.7   Rural and urban populations and the Kashmir quake

Rural populations in the mountains and the deep valleys of Jhelum and Neelum were hit harder than urban populations. The impact of the quake was particularly severe in rural areas because:

- Few buildings in rural areas are earthquake-proof.
- Destruction of crops, livestock and arable land devastated the rural economy.

- The remoteness of mountain villages meant that aid was slow to reach many rural areas.
- Steep, unstable slopes in the mountains are susceptible to secondary hazards such as landslides and other mass movements triggered by earthquakes.
- The harsh winter climate in the mountains added to the problems of earthquake survivors.

Managing earth hazards

Case study   **Managing a volcanic eruption: Montserrat**

Montserrat is a small volcanic island in Caribbean. It belongs to the Lesser Antilles island arc: a curved chain of volcanic islands formed by subduction along the margin of two oceanic plates (Figure 1.32). In this instance the subduction of the North American plate explains the 19 active volcanoes in the island chain which have erupted 33 times in the past 200 years.

The island of Montserrat owes its existence to the Soufrière Hills stratovolcano. For over four centuries the volcano had been dormant. Then in July 1995 it suddenly burst back to life. Between 1995 and 2005 the volcano spewed out nearly $0.5\,km^3$ of magma. Recent eruptions have been violent and have followed the growth and collapse of lava domes inside the crater. The principal hazards are pyroclastic flows, tephra falls, debris avalanches and occasional lava flows.

Impact of eruptions

Eruptive activity peaked in 1997, when 19 people were killed and Plymouth, the island's capital, was destroyed by pyroclastic flows, fires and tephra deposits (Photograph 1.12). Managing the eruption involved designating the southern half of the island an exclusion zone and evacuating its population to safe areas in the north (Figure 1.33). However, over half the displaced population migrated overseas.

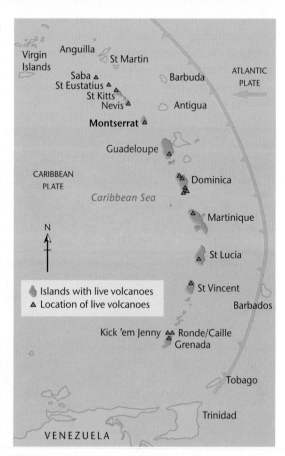

Figure 1.32 The Lesser Antilles subduction zone

Photograph 1.12
Plymouth: the clock tower and war memorial, before and after tephra deposits from the Soufrière Hills eruptions

Many islanders took up permanent residence in the UK and others left for the USA and nearby islands such as Antigua. Montserrat's population, which stood at 10 728 in 1990, plummeted to just 6409 by 2000. Out-migration was a social and economic disaster. It undermined the islanders' sense of community and a disproportionate number of better educated islanders (especially young women) left.

The physical impact of the eruptions devastated Montserrat's economy. Two-thirds of the island is now uninhabitable. Pyroclastic flows and ash falls destroyed most of the fertile agriculture land in the south. Before the eruptions tourism was the lifeblood of the economy, generating around 40 000 visitors a year. Today most of Montserrat's tourism infrastructure — its hotels, roads and airport — is in ruins.

Yet as the eruptions have subsided a new optimism has emerged. Slowly the island's infrastructure is being rebuilt. A new airport has been completed and the UK and EU have spent around £200 million on regeneration projects.

Conclusion

Overall levels of exposure on Montserrat to volcanic hazards have been moderate. Although the eruptions have been violent and prolonged, the total population at risk has been relatively small. Even so, 6000–7000 thousand people living closest to the volcano (including those in the capital, Plymouth)

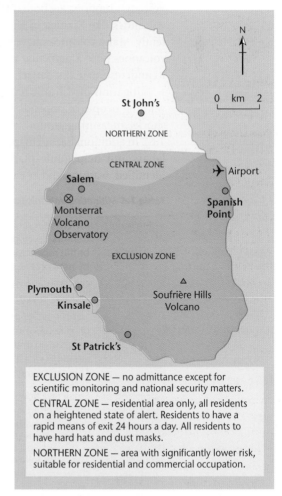

EXCLUSION ZONE — no admittance except for scientific monitoring and national security matters.

CENTRAL ZONE — residential area only, all residents on a heightened state of alert. Residents to have a rapid means of exit 24 hours a day. All residents to have hard hats and dust masks.

NORTHERN ZONE — area with significantly lower risk, suitable for residential and commercial occupation.

Figure 1.33 *Risk map of Montserrat, September 1997, showing the exclusion and safe zones*

lost everything. Nothing could be done to save either their homes or their farmland.

In contrast, vulnerability was high because the eruptions occurred on a small island. Many islanders had little option but to emigrate. Others, who evacuated to the north, lived for several years in overcrowded and squalid conditions. The Montserrat eruption shows how natural disasters can devastate small island communities. Not only did the eruptions destroy a large part of the island's resources, they

also had a huge knock-on effect on the economy and society.

On the positive side vulnerability has been reduced by hazard mitigation measures and the overall loss of life has been relatively small. Since 1995 scientists have closely monitored the Soufrière Hills volcano. Using data on seismic activity, volcanic gases and ground deformation, they have been able to give early warning of deadly pyroclastic flows and prepare the people for evacuation.

Mitigating volcanic and mass movement hazards

Volcanic eruptions are both difficult to predict and unpreventable. Although a few volcanoes like Kilauea in Hawaii are continuously active, most erupt intermittently. Many volcanoes have not erupted within living memory. These dormant volcanoes pose a particular risk, however, because people living near them tend to underestimate the danger.

Mitigation of volcanic hazards depends almost entirely on monitoring, and warning people of impending eruptions. Monitoring includes recording seismic shocks, measuring ground inflation, and collecting gas and lava samples (Table 1.6). In addition, hazard mapping can show areas most at risk from lava flows and lahars and help guide planning decisions. Once high-risk areas have been identified, warning and evacuation procedures follow.

Table 1.6 Mitigating volcanic hazards

Monitoring	Increases in seismic activity often precede an eruption. Earthquakes and tremors develop as magma forces its way to the surface and fractures brittle rocks inside volcanoes. The resulting seismic waves are recorded by networks of seismometers on the volcano's surface.
	Gravity is also measured. As magma fills the reservoir within the volcano, gravity increases.
	Gases emitted by fumaroles are sampled. Increasing levels of sulphur dioxide (SO_2) and hydrogen chloride (HCl) emitted by the magma are a sign of an impending eruption. So too is ground deformation (or inflation) which results from magma accumulating below the surface. This can be measured remotely by GPS to within an accuracy of 1 cm.
Diversion of lava flows	Small lava flows on the flanks of Mount Etna in Sicily have been successfully diverted away from centres of population. At Heimaey, in Iceland, the fishing harbour was saved from destruction by lava through spraying with sea water.
Hazard mapping	The paths followed by ancient lahars can be mapped from sediments to show areas which historically have been at most risk.
Warning and evacuation	Lahar detection warning systems have been installed in the vicinity of Mount Rainier in Washington state. Detection triggers an automatic alert and emergency managers initiate evacuation.

Table 1.7 *Mitigating mass movement hazards*

Drainage	Reduce the water content on slopes by installing drainage systems e.g. concrete interceptor drains at the top of the slope. Water adds to the mass of material on a slope and pore water pressure weakens the material, making it incoherent and less stable.
Reduce slope angles	Slopes can be regraded. Lower slope angles reduce the gravitational force acting downslope.
Retaining walls	Build walls (or gabions) at the base of a slope to provide support and reduce undercutting (by erosion and weathering) and the risk of slope failure.
Rock bolts	Less stable materials on a slope can be anchored to solid bedrock using a system of rock bolts.
Reafforestation	Trees reduce the amount of soil moisture in slope materials and tree roots resist downslope forces.
Hazard mapping	Using aerial photographs and fieldwork, identify slopes that are at risk of failure and map the hazards. Situations which might lead to mass movements include steep slopes, bedding planes inclined downslope, hummocky topography and slope scars indicating previous slope failures etc.

Examination-style questions

Section A
Resource 1

The Sichuan earthquake occurred along a thrust fault between the Longmen Shan mountains, which mark the eastern border of Tibet, and the Sichuan Basin at a depth of 10 km. Tectonic instability is caused by the collision between the Indian sub-continent and Eurasia. Heavy shaking in the area was amplified by the soft sediments of the Sichuan Basin. In the mountains, shaking triggered numerous landslides, which buried entire villages. Elsewhere, landslides blocked rivers and created over 30 temporary quake lakes. 200 000 people were at risk when a dam impounding a quake lake at Beichuan threatened to burst.
Source: USGS

1 Resource 1 focuses on an area of western China hit by a powerful earthquake in May 2008. Outline an issue indicated in Resource 1 and suggest appropriate management. (10 marks)

Section B

2 To what extent is poverty the real killer in earthquake disasters? (30 marks)
3 Discuss the view that the management of earth hazards is more successful in urban than in rural areas. (30 marks)

Ecosystems and environments under threat

Ecosystems

Key ideas
➤ Ecosystems comprise physical and biological components.
➤ The physical and biological components of ecosystems interact through energy flows and nutrient cycles.
➤ Ecosystems and environments are subject to constant change due to the interaction of physical, biological and human factors.

Ecosystems are communities of plants, animals and other organisms (the biotic component) and the physical environment (the abiotic component). Within ecosystems, living organisms interact with one another and with the physical environment through flows of energy and the cycling of nutrients. Four sub-systems can be identified in terrestrial ecosystems: the primary production system; the grazing-predation system; the detrital system; and the soil system (Figure 2.1).

Figure 2.1
Ecosystems and sub-systems

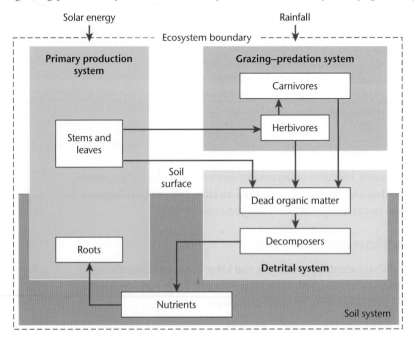

An ecosystem is a type of **open system**; 'open' in the sense that both energy and matter can cross its boundaries. For example, local ecosystems such as heather moorland or deciduous woodland receive inputs of energy in the form of solar radiation, and matter such as precipitation, carbon dioxide and mineral nutrients. Outputs comprise heat, water (through runoff and evapotranspiration) and mineral nutrients (through leaching). Closed systems on the other hand, are 'open' to energy, but not matter.

Table 2.1 The biotic and abiotic components of ecosystems

Biotic components	Abiotic components
Plants (primary producers or autotrophs)	Rocks
	Slopes
Animals (heterotrophs i.e. herbivores, carnivores, omnivores)	Atmosphere and climate
	Soil
Fungi, bacteria (detritivores)	Water
	Solar energy
People	Fire
	Gravity

Holisticity

Although ecosystems consist of many individual parts, they operate as functioning, interdependent wholes. The multiplicity of relationships within ecosystems binds their separate parts together. In this sense ecosystems often behave like a single organism: a quality known as holisticity. One consequence of this is that change in any one component invariably has knock-on effects that cascade throughout the entire system and cause widespread (and often unexpected) change elsewhere.

Feedback

Ecosystems are self-adjusting. Short-term changes are corrected through the process of negative feedback, which restores stability. Figure 2.2 shows an example of **negative feedback** in a tundra ecosystem. **Positive feedback**, on the other hand, occurs when change induces further change. As change spirals out of control it may lead to declining productivity, reduced biodiversity and environmental degradation. Positive feedback is rare in natural ecosystems and usually results from unsustainable human activity such as deforestation.

Figure 2.2 Negative feedback in a tundra ecosystem

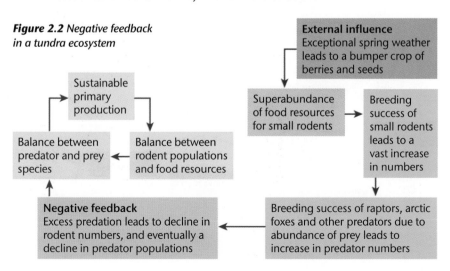

External influence
Exceptional spring weather leads to a bumper crop of berries and seeds

Sustainable primary production

Superabundance of food resources for small rodents

Breeding success of small rodents leads to a vast increase in numbers

Balance between predator and prey species

Balance between rodent populations and food resources

Negative feedback
Excess predation leads to decline in rodent numbers, and eventually a decline in predator populations

Breeding success of raptors, arctic foxes and other predators due to abundance of prey leads to increase in predator numbers

Box 2.1 Ecosystems and dynamic equilibrium

Most natural ecosystems, unaffected by human activity, exist in a state of dynamic equilibrium. They are dynamic (rather than static) because they have continuous inputs, throughputs and outputs of energy and materials. Although small variations occur naturally from year to year in plant productivity and animal populations, in the long term natural ecosystems remain stable and maintain their equilbrium.

Energy flows in ecosystems

The starting point of energy flows is the capture of sunlight by green plants, and its conversion into chemical energy. This fundamental process is known as photosynthesis.

$$6CO_2 \quad + \; 6H_2O \quad \rightarrow \quad C_6H_{12}O_6 \; + \quad 6O_2$$

carbon dioxide + water → glucose + oxygen

In photosynthesis, sunlight provides the energy for carbon dioxide and water to be transformed into glucose and oxygen by chloroplasts in the green leaves of plants. This energy is then transferred along **food webs** and **food chains** to consumer organisms (Figure 2.3). Energy flow within ecosystems takes place in a number of stages or **trophic** (feeding) **levels**.

➤ At the base of the food chain, photosynthesisers (mainly green plants but also some algae and bacteria) are the **primary producers** or **autotrophs** (self-feeders), transforming light energy into chemical energy.

➤ **Heterotrophs** or consumers either feed directly on plants (**herbivores**) or indirectly by eating other animals (**carnivores**). Non-specialist consumers, which eat both plants and animals, are called **omnivores**.

➤ The consumer at the end of a food web or food chain is known as the top or apex predator. Depending on the number of trophic levels, top predators may be secondary, tertiary or quaternary consumers.

***Figure 2.3**
Simplified food web in a North American montane forest*

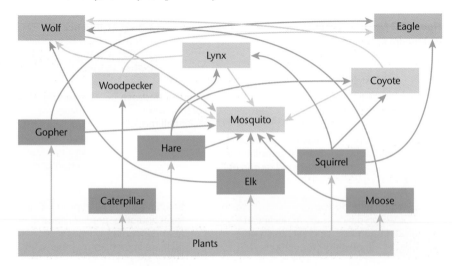

➤ At each trophic level, **detritivores** such as fungi and microbes decompose dead organic material and animal faeces. In this way they consume energy and release gases such as carbon dioxide to the atmosphere, and mineral nutrients to the soil.

Box 2.2 Measuring primary production

The rate of photosynthesis is called gross primary production (GPP). It is usually measured in $g\,m^2\,year^{-1}$. Net primary production (NPP) is the amount of energy fixed in photosynthesis minus the energy lost in respiration. NPP is the amount of chemical energy theoretically available to the primary consumers in an ecosystem. It is influenced by environmental factors such as light intensity, temperature, moisture and soil nutrients. The NPP of selected ecosystems is given in Table 2.2.

Table 2.2 Net primary production in selected ecosystems

Ecosystem	NPP ($g\,m^2\,year^{-2}$)
Tropical rainforest	2200
Temperate deciduous forest	1200
Savanna grassland	900
Boreal coniferous forest	800
Temperate grassland	600
Tundra and alpine	140
Desert and semi-desert	90

At each tropic level there is a loss of energy. On average only 10% of the energy received by one tropic level is passed on to the next. Energy loss occurs because living organisms convert only a small proportion of the energy they consume into living tissue. Ninety per cent is used to keep the organism alive and is lost in respiration. The equation for respiration is the reverse of that for photosynthesis:

$$C_6H_{12}O_6 \; + \; 6O_2 \; \rightarrow \; 6CO_2 \; + \; 6H_2O$$
$$\text{Glucose} \; + \; \text{oxygen} \; \rightarrow \; \text{carbon dioxide} \; + \; \text{water}$$

Pyramids of biomass and pyramids of numbers

In food chains, the gradual reduction of available energy with distance from the source of primary production explains:

➤ the pyramid of biomass, comprising the total mass of living material at each trophic level (Figure 2.4)
➤ the pyramid of animal numbers, with primary consumers outnumbering secondary consumers by roughly 10:1 and so on up to the top predator
➤ why animals towards the end of the food chain are particularly vulnerable to human pressure and habitat change

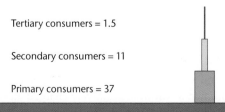

Tertiary consumers = 1.5

Secondary consumers = 11

Primary consumers = 37

Producers = 807

Figure 2.4 Pyramid of biomass

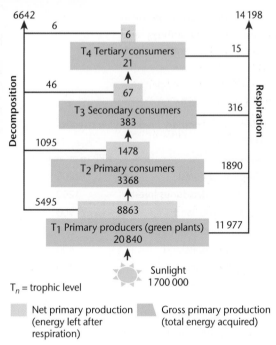

Figure 2.5 *Energy transfers in the food chain at the Silver Springs ecosystem, Florida*

The actual shape of the pyramid of biomass and pyramid of numbers depends not just on the 10% rule, but also on the efficiency with which different consumers assimilate what they eat.

Figure 2.5 shows energy flows through a river ecosystem in Silver Springs, Florida. Energy flows are measured in kcal m^2 year^{-1}. The energy transfers at Silver Springs show that at each trophic level:

➤ Net production is only a fraction of gross production because the organisms lose energy through respiration.
➤ Much of the energy stored in net production is lost to the system by decomposition.
➤ There are large losses in net production as energy is transferred from one trophic level to another.
➤ The ratio of net production at one level to net production at the next higher level — the **conversion efficiency** — is low, ranging from 17% from primary producers to primary consumers to 4.5% from primary to secondary consumers.

Nutrient cycling in ecosystems

Nutrients

Nutrients are the chemical elements and compounds needed by living organisms. Green plants need 16 essential nutrients. These are shown in Table 2.3. Those nutrients required in relatively large quantities, such as nitrogen, are known as macronutrients. Micronutrients, or trace elements, like copper are needed in much smaller amounts.

There are three sources of plant nutrients:

➤ Rocks are the ultimate source of most nutrients. Nutrients such as iron and calcium are released into the soil from rocks by chemical weathering.
➤ Carbon, oxygen and hydrogen are obtained in gaseous form from the atmosphere.
➤ Some mineral nutrients are present in rainwater. Tropical rainforest plants such as epiphytes have aerial roots and rely on the mineral nutrients in precipitation.

Table 2.3 *Plant nutrients*

Macronutrients	Micronutrients
Nitrogen	Iron
Phosphorus	Manganese
Potassium	Copper
Calcium	Zinc
Magnesium	Molybdenum
Sulphur	Boron
Hydrogen	Chlorine
Oxygen	
Carbon	

Soils are an important store of mineral nutrients where they exist as charged atoms. Positively charged atoms are known as **cations**: negatively charged atoms are **anions**. Plants absorb these nutrients through their roots. Nitrogen, phosphorus and potassium are the most important nutrients for plants.

Nutrient cycling

Unlike energy, the supply of nutrients is finite. For this reason plant nutrients have to be continuously recycled. New mineral nutrients enter the soil system through the weathering of rocks. These inputs are balanced by losses through **leaching** (the removal of nutrients in solution from the soil) and runoff (Figure 2.6). Mineral nutrients are stored for variable lengths of time in the soil, living plants and animals (biomass), and in dead organic matter (litter). Nutrients such as nitrogen, oxygen and carbon have a gaseous phase and are also stored in the atmosphere.

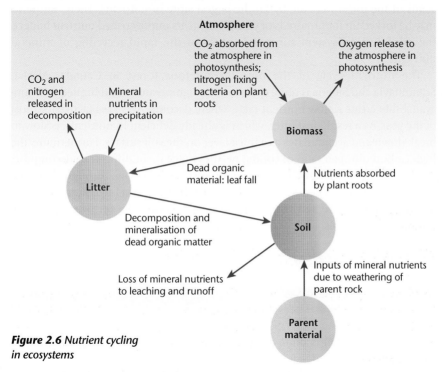

Figure 2.6 Nutrient cycling in ecosystems

The size of the soil, biomass and litter stores, and the speed and volume of nutrient flows between stores, vary between ecosystems (Figure 2.7). A number of factors influence the speed of nutrient cycling. They include temperature, rainfall, soil types, the chemical composition of leaf litter and the relative importance of trees, grasses and herbs.

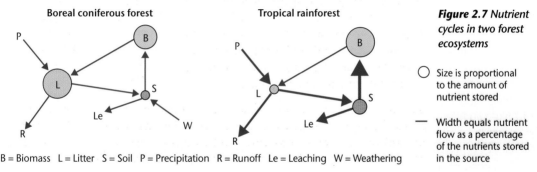

Figure 2.7 Nutrient cycles in two forest ecosystems

○ Size is proportional to the amount of nutrient stored

— Width equals nutrient flow as a percentage of the nutrients stored in the source

B = Biomass   L = Litter   S = Soil   P = Precipitation   R = Runoff   Le = Leaching   W = Weathering

Nutrient cycles in tropical rainforest and boreal coniferous forest ecosystems

Figure 2.7 shows simplified nutrient cycles for the tropical rainforest and boreal coniferous forest ecosystems. Mineral nutrients are recycled quickly in the rainforest. High all-year-round temperatures and abundant rainfall mean that decomposition of dead organic material is rapid. Thus the litter store is small. The soil is also a relatively small reservoir of nutrients. Once released from the litter, nutrients are quickly absorbed from the soil by the shallow-rooted forest trees. The stems of the forest trees are by far the largest store of nutrients. There, nutrients may be locked up for hundreds of years. Despite its impoverished nutrient budget, the rainforest ecosystem survives because of the rapid recycling of mineral nutrients.

The nutrient cycle of the boreal coniferous forest in Canada, Alaska, Scandinavia and Siberia is quite different. Low temperatures and limited moisture availability create a slow nutrient cycle, where decomposers are inactive for most of the year. As a result, leaf litter, which is already deficient in nutrients, is slow to break down and accumulates as a thick layer on the soil surface. Furthermore, the high carbon:nitrogen ratio of conifer needles make them difficult to decompose. So slow is the nutrient cycle that some forests only survive through lightning strikes which result in periodic ground fires that burn the leaf litter. Burning speeds up the nutrient cycle, releasing mineral nutrients into the soil where they are absorbed by the trees.

Change in ecosystems

 Case study   **The Greater Yellowstone Ecosystem**

The Greater Yellowstone Ecosystem (GYE) is one of the world's largest, relatively intact temperate zone ecosystems (Figure 2.8). It covers 7300 km² of wilderness in the Rocky Mountains of Wyoming, Montana and Idaho in the western USA. It includes Yellowstone and Grand Teton national parks, parts of seven surrounding national forests and three national wildlife refuges. This area is renowned for its wild beauty and for its spectacular mammals including grizzly bears, cougars, coyotes, elk, moose and bison (Figure 2.9).

Human impact

A century ago the gray wolf was the dominant large carnivore and the primary force shaping the GYE. However, a policy of predator eradication led to its relentless persecution by farmers and hunters.

As a result, by 1944 wolves had disappeared from Yellowstone.

Top predators like wolves are 'keystone' species in natural ecosystems. They play a crucial role maintaining the stability of food webs and food chains. Yellowstone's wolves were no exception. They had a 'top-down' influence. Through predation, they directly controlled the numbers of large herbivores and the intensity of grazing and browsing. This in turn had an impact on plant growth and populations of insects, birds and small mammals.

The return of the gray wolf

In 1995, 31 wolves were released into Yellowstone National Park, and 35 into central Idaho. This was part of a controversial programme to re-establish the species in the GYE. Ten years later the wolf population

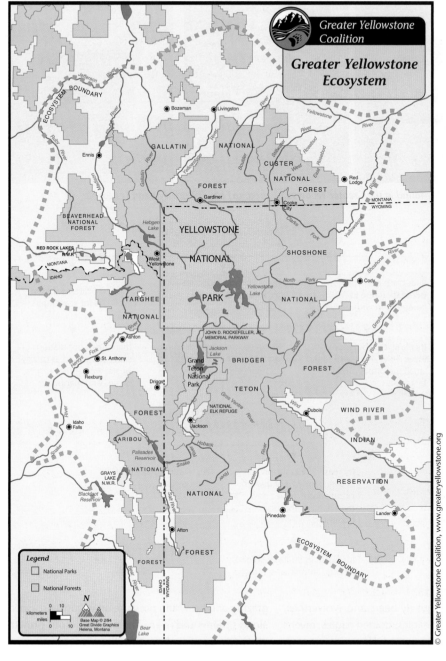

Figure 2.8 *Greater Yellowstone Ecosystem*

© Greater Yellowstone Coalition, www.greateryellowstone.org

had increased to 300, half of them in Yellowstone National Park.

The return of the wolf has had a dramatic effect on the ecosystem, triggering a 'trophic cascade' (Figure 2.9, p. 52). As predicted, the main impact has been on the elk population, the wolf's main prey species (Figure 2.10, p. 53). Ninety per cent of wolf-kills of large herbivores have been elk, causing elk numbers to halve in just 10 years. This in turn has benefited scavengers that feed on wolf-kills.

Photograph 2.1 *Wildlife found in the Greater Yellowstone area: (a) elk, (b) grizzly bear, (c) coyote*

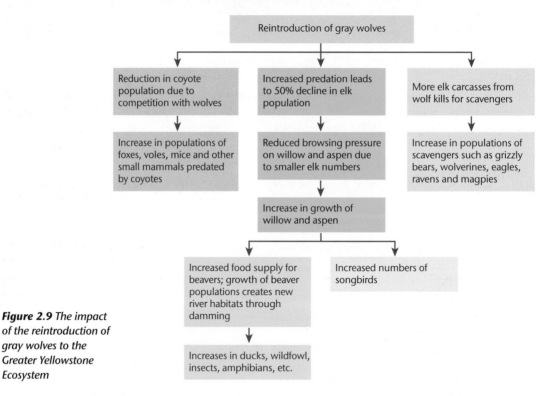

Figure 2.9 *The impact of the reintroduction of gray wolves to the Greater Yellowstone Ecosystem*

Thus populations of grizzly bears and wolverines, and birds such as bald eagles, golden eagles, ravens and magpies have all increased. However, coyotes, unable to compete with more powerful wolves, have declined significantly.

The indirect effect of wolves has also cascaded down to plants and other animal species. Drastic reductions in the elk population and changes in their distribution and behaviour have relieved grazing and browsing pressure on willow and aspen along streams and rivers. The more vigorous growth of these species has benefited songbirds and beavers. Streams dammed by beavers have also attracted more waterfowl, frogs, trout, voles, shrews and insects. Meanwhile, the decline in coyote numbers has triggered an increase in small mammals, which has boosted populations of red foxes and birds of prey.

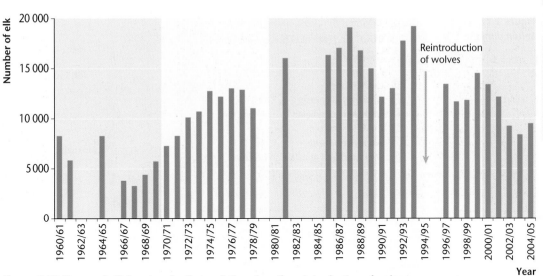

Figure 2.10 *Changes in Yellowstone's elk population since the reintroduction of wolves*

Because of the inter-dependent nature of ecosystems, reintroduction of wolves is having a profound impact in Greater Yellowstone. 'Like a stone thrown into a pond, rippling out in all directions' (*Yellowstone Science*, Vol.13, No.1) wolves are restructuring the entire ecosystem.

Case study

A local ecosystem: Sefton Dunes, Merseyside

Coastal dunes cover around 545 km² in the UK. They support highly distinctive and localised ecosystems.

The Sefton dunes in northwest England stretch for 17 km along the Irish Sea coast between the Mersey and Ribble estuaries and are the largest area of coastal dunes in England (Figure 2.11). A number of factors favour dune development along this coast:

- a plentiful supply of sand delivered to the coastal zone by the Mersey and Ribble rivers
- a shallow offshore gradient which at low tide exposes extensive areas of sand
- prevailing onshore winds which blow the sand inland
- a lowland coast where blown sand can accumulate

Environmental conditions

The dune environment consists of three principal features that run parallel to the coastline: mobile dunes, fixed dunes and dune slacks.

Mobile dunes

The youngest dunes, located within 100 m of the shoreline, are highly mobile. Their sparse vegetation cover reflects the harsh environmental conditions for plant growth (Photograph 2.2, p.54). The problems for plants include:

- exposure to strong winds and lack of shelter
- the absence of dense vegetation to anchor the dunes, exposing plants to the abrasive effects of blown sand
- shortage of fresh water due to the high porosity of sand
- saline conditions in the dunes closest to the beach
- lack of plant litter to allow soil development
- alkaline sands (due to the presence of shell fragments) which many plant species cannot tolerate

As a result, few plant species have colonised the mobile dunes and biodiversity is low. Net primary

Figure 2.11
Sefton dunes

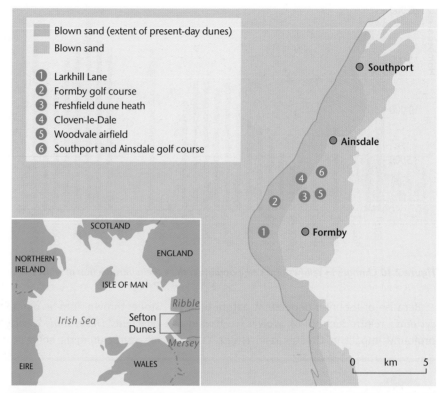

Blown sand (extent of present-day dunes)

Blown sand

① Larkhill Lane
② Formby golf course
③ Freshfield dune heath
④ Cloven-le-Dale
⑤ Woodvale airfield
⑥ Southport and Ainsdale golf course

Southport

Ainsdale

SCOTLAND

NORTHERN
IRELAND

ENGLAND

ISLE OF MAN

Ribble

Irish Sea

Sefton
Dunes

Mersey

EIRE

WALES

Formby

0   km   5

Photograph 2.2
Mobile dunes

Michael Raw

productivity, limited by environmental conditions, is also low and food webs are short.

Fixed dunes

The older dunes, 200 m or so from the shoreline, have complete vegetation cover and are fixed permanently in position (Photograph 2.3).

Environmental conditions are altogether more favourable for plant growth. The fixed dunes are more sheltered, and support thin but well developed soils that provide mineral nutrients and moisture for plants. As a consequence both net primary productivity and biodiversity are higher, and there is a richer nutrient cycle.

Michael Raw

Photograph 2.3
*Dune ridge and
slacks*

Slacks

The depressions or slacks between the dune ridges create a very different physical environment. In the slacks the water table is at or near the surface. Instead of drought, excess water is a problem. Specialised plants adapted to wet and aquatic conditions such as creeping willow, rushes and flag iris colonise the dune slacks creating a freshwater **hydrosere** (Photograph 2.3).

Ecological succession in sand dune environments

Primary ecological succession in sand dune environments is known as a **psammosere**. Because the dunes get older inland from high-water mark, we can view the process of succession on the ground as a series of vegetation zones running parallel to the shore (Figure 2.12).

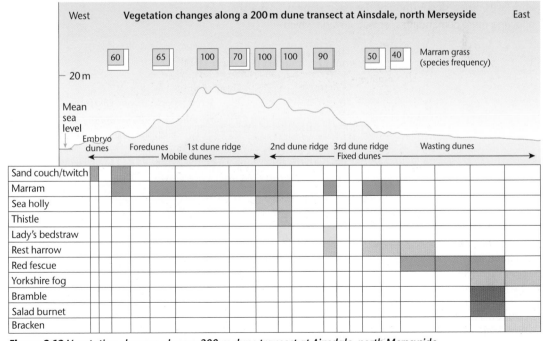

Figure 2.12 *Vegetation changes along a 200 m dune transect at Ainsdale, north Merseyside*

Box 2.3 Ecological succession

The sequence of vegetation changes that occur on a site through time is called **ecological succession**. There are two types of succession: primary and secondary. Primary succession describes the vegetation changes on previously unvegetated sites such as sand dunes, mudflats and lava flows. Secondary succession occurs on sites where the original vegetation cover has been destroyed. Examples of secondary succession include the destruction of forests by the blast from the Mount St Helens volcanic eruption in 1980 in Washington state and the massive fires in Yellowstone National Park in 1988.

In primary succession, ecological change occurs in a number of stages or **seres**. The progressive development of seral communities over time is accompanied by increases in biomass, biodiversity and net primary production.

Primary succession starts when the first plants colonise a new surface. These initial colonisers are **pioneer species**, adapted to extreme environments such as bare rock, sand dunes, mudflats and lakes. They slowly modify the environment, allowing more demanding species to invade which

eventually displace them. Over time one sere succeeds another, until stability is reached and **mesic** conditions prevail (Figure 2.13). In this final or **climax** stage the vegetation is in balance with prevailing environmental conditions. Providing the environment remains stable, the climax vegetation will persist indefinitely (Figure 2.14). A **sub-climax** occurs when an arresting factor such as a sandy soil determines the character of the final successional stage. A **plagio-climax** describes a final successional stage which is in balance with environmental factors and human activities such as burning and grazing, e.g. lowland heath.

We recognise two principal types of primary succession: **xeroseres** and **hydroseres**. In xeroseres, the limiting factor to plant growth is drought. Sand dunes (psammoseres) and solid rock surfaces (**lithoseres**) are types of xerosere. In hydroseres the initial limiting factor is excess water. Dune slacks and raised bogs are examples of freshwater hydroseres. Salt water hydroseres are known as **haloseres** and include tidal mudflats and salt-marshes.

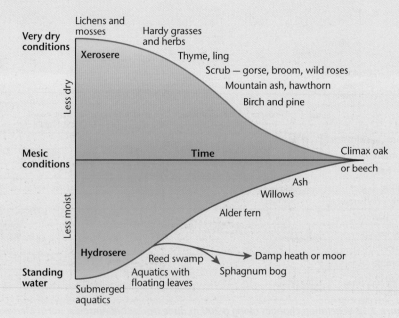

Figure 2.13
Summary of the relationships between primary successions and convergence to the climax of ecological succession

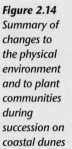

	Sere 1	Sere 2	Sere 3	Sere 4 (climax)
Biomass/productivity/ ground cover				
Biodiversity				
Energy flows				
Exposure				
Nutrient cycle				
Soil depth/moisture/ nutrients				
Soil alkalinity				

Figure 2.14 Summary of changes to the physical environment and to plant communities during succession on coastal dunes

Embryo dunes

The embryo dunes that form close to the high-water mark are just a few centimetres high. They have a sparse covering of sand couch grass (or sand twitch): just enough to trap sufficient sand to elevate the dunes above the mean high-water mark. In the transect in Figure 2.12, sand couch is the only species present on the embryo dunes and covers just 25% of the area. The rest is bare sand. Sand couch grass is a true pioneer species. It is highly specialised and has one great advantage over other species: it is able to extract freshwater from salt water.

Foredunes

A few metres inland from the embryo dunes, the foredune ridge rises to 2 m or so above the shoreline. The foredunes are less exposed than the embryo dunes, and salt water incursion is less of a problem. At Ainsdale, sand couch grass and marram grass dominate the foredunes, though around 40% of the dunes still comprise bare sand.

Michael Raw

Photograph 2.4 Marram on 1st dune ridge

Table 2.4 *Adaptations of marram grass to dune environment*

Extraction of water	Marram's exceptionally long roots enable it to tap freshwater deep below the dunes.
Reducing water loss	Marram's leaves curl up in dry weather to conserve moisture. Its leaves have hairs which trap moist air and reduce transpiration, and sunken stomata which also increase humidity close to the leaf and reduce moisture loss.
Blown sand	Marram can survive being buried by blown sand (in fact, swamping with sand stimulates growth).

1st dune ridge

This is the most impressive feature of the Ainsdale dunes, rising nearly 20 m above the beach. Its size shows the effectiveness of vegetation in trapping wind-blown sand (see Photograph 2.4). Marram is by far the dominant species on the 1st dune ridge; sand couch grass has disappeared, and the only other species are sea holly, thistles and lady's bedstraw. Marram grass is a true **xerophyte**, superbly adapted to the dry, exposed dune environment and able to out-compete all other species (Table 2.4).

Marram has a major impact on the sand dune environment. Its dense growth adds organic matter and mineral nutrients to the sand, forming a skeletal soil which retains some moisture. Dense stands of marram also stabilise the sand, and provide shelter for other species downwind.

The fixed and older dunes

Plant succession has greatly modified the environment of the fixed dunes. With a complete cover of vegetation there is less blown sand and, thanks to shelter afforded by the 1st dune ridge, winds are much lighter. Organic plant material mixes with the sand to form a shallow soil that is neutral or slightly acidic. The soil is both a store of mineral nutrients and moisture. Although specialised xerophytes like sea spurge are still found, a wide range of species (including localised plants such as bloody cranesbill and round wintergreen, and more common species

Photograph 2.5 *Succession in old dunes*

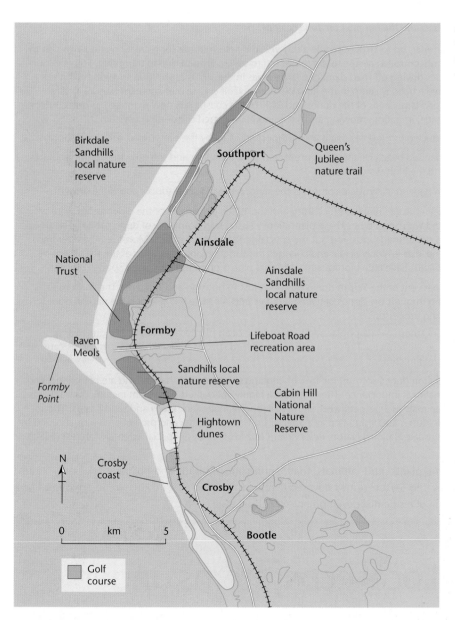

Figure 2.15
Conservation and recreation on the Sefton coast

like bird's foot trefoil, dandelion, daisies, hawkweed and pansies) thrive (Photograph 2.5). Further inland woody plants and shrubs such as heather, sea buckthorn and hawthorn start to make an appearance.

Under natural conditions, the final vegetation community on the oldest dunes would be a climax mixed oak-birch woodland. However, in the Sefton dunes this is replaced by plantations of Scots pine,

planted as shelter belts between the late nineteenth century and the 1930s.

Human influences on the Sefton dunes' ecosystem

For the past 100 years, human activity has been the dominant factor driving change in the Sefton dunes' ecosystem (Figure 2.15 and Table 2.5). For the most part these changes have damaged the fragile dune

Table 2.5 *Human activities and their impact on dune ecology*

Recreation	In summer, up to 10000 people a day visit the Sefton dunes for recreation and leisure. In the past, uncontrolled access to the dunes led to severe erosion due to trampling. Four-by-four vehicles driving off-road damaged large areas in the 1970s and 1980s. In 1968 Pontin's opened a holiday camp in the Ainsdale dunes. Golf course management has drastically changed large areas of the dunes and 25% of the coastline is now managed as golf courses. Drainage, irrigation, mowing and fertilising have altered the dune ecosystem.
Sea walls	By reducing erosion, sea walls at Southport and Crosby have interfered with sand supply.
Beach management	Mechanised beach cleaning has prevented sand accretion and the growth of embryo dunes around the high-water mark.
Car parking	Beach parking at Ainsdale compacts the sand, reducing sand supply and dune growth.
Forestry	Between the late nineteenth century and the 1930s large areas of the older dunes were planted with Scots pine. These plantations caused significant loss of dune habitat. The trees cast a dense shade, pushing out the specialised sand dune plants. Moreover, the litter from pine needles is highly acidic and changes the structure and chemistry of the soil. The pine woodlands have little biodiversity and Scots pine is often the only plant species present.
Development	Fifty per cent of the Sefton dunes has been lost to housing and building. The coast road cutting through the dunes between Birkdale and Ainsdale has stopped the natural dune building processes.
Introduced species	Sea buckthorn, white poplar and balsam have been planted to stabilise the dunes and provide shelter belts. These and other introduced species have colonised large areas causing nutrient enrichment.
Conservation	The Sefton dunes account for 15% of England's coastal dune habitat and are of national and international importance. They support a highly specialised ecosystem including rare plants and animals such as petalwort, dune helleborine, natterjack toads and sand lizards. The Sefton dunes are designated as a Special Conservation Area and protection is also afforded by the Ainsdale National Nature Reserve and dozens of Sites of Special Scientific Interest (SSSIs).

environment, and the plants and animals that it supports. Originally the Sefton dunes covered $30\,km^2$. Now, as a result of residential development, golf courses, roads and holiday parks, only $20\,km^2$ remain. Of this, just $10\,km^2$ are in anything like a natural state.

Local ecosystems under threat from human activity

Key ideas
➤ Human activity poses threats to physical environments in both planned and unintended ways.
➤ Human activities such as agriculture, forestry, settlement, transport, industry and mineral extraction threaten and impact on the physical environment and ecosystems.
➤ Conservation can reduce the threat to the physical environment.

Case study — Thorne and Hatfield Moors

Thorne and Hatfield Moors lie between Doncaster and the head of the Humber estuary in South Yorkshire and Lincolnshire (Figure 2.16). Covering 34 km², the Moors are the largest area of lowland raised bog in the UK.

Raised bog is a type of wetland environment that provides a unique habitat for many rare plants, insects and birds. It represents the later stages of succession in a freshwater hydrosere. Its main feature is a thick layer of peat, formed from the partly decayed remains of wetland plants, particularly sphagnum moss (Photograph 2.6). Normal decomposition of dead plant material is inhibited by the wet boggy conditions and the lack of oxygen. Raised bog gets its name because the accumulation of peat over thousands of years creates a gentle dome-like surface raising the bog surface several metres above the surrounding land (Figure 2.17).

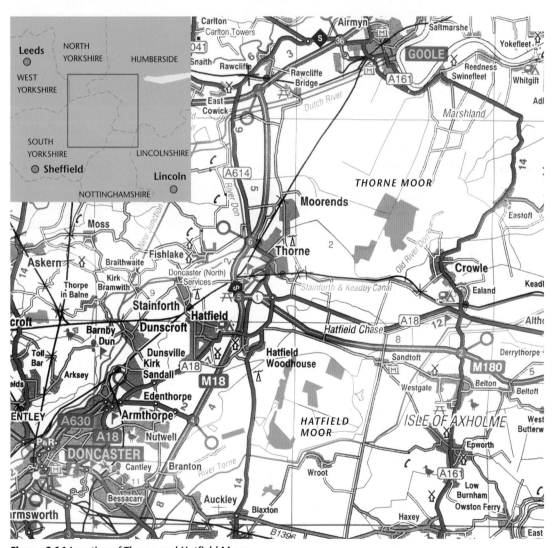

Figure 2.16 Location of Thorne and Hatfield Moors

Photograph 2.6 Hatfield Moor: a unique exosystem and the largest surviving area of lowland raised bog in the UK

Michael Raw

Figure 2.17 Raised bog, formed by the accumulation of dead plant material in open water

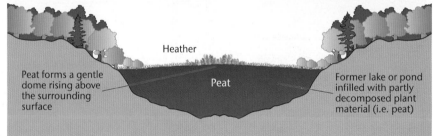

Heather

Peat forms a gentle dome rising above the surrounding surface

Peat

Former lake or pond infilled with partly decomposed plant material (i.e. peat)

Ecosystem

Raised bog is a rare and threatened environment. It supports a rich ecosystem, with a unique assemblage of wildlife. Over 5500 different species of plants and animals have been recorded on Thorne and Hatfield Moors. Typical wetland plants at the base of the food chain include cotton grass, sphagnum moss and cranberry. Over 200 bird species have been recorded on the Moors and there are breeding populations of rare species such as nightjars and nightingales. Further along the food chain there are raptors such as merlins, hobbies, marsh harriers and short-eared owls as well as healthy populations of grass snakes and adders. Yet in spite of its biodiversity, raised bog is acidic and deficient in plant nutrients. This explains the carnivorous plant species such as round-leaved sundew. The survival of the Thorne and Hatfield Moors ecosystem depends crucially on maintaining groundwater levels and ensuring that the bog does not dry out.

Human activities

In the past, peat was a valuable fuel and small-scale peat cutting has taken place on Hatfield and Thorne Moors since the fourteenth century. However, in the 1960s industrial-scale extraction began. Surface milling machines mined thousands of tonnes of peat not for fuel, but for use in gardening and horticulture. In addition, deep trenches were dug, lowering the water table and causing the peat to dry out. The result was an ecological disaster. By the turn of the century only 6% of the original area of raised bog on Hatfield and Thorne Moors remained.

Conservationists fought for many years to stop peat extraction and finally succeeded in 2002 when English Nature reached agreement with the peat extraction industry to halt production.

The ecological importance of Thorne and Hatfield Moors has given them protected status. There are several SSSIs, Special Protection Areas, and Special Areas of Conservation under European and international directives. Conservation is controlled by the government agency Natural England, which manages a large part of the area as a National Nature Reserve, and the Lincolnshire Wildlife Trust.

Already, abandoned peat cuttings are reverting to bog as natural succession takes hold. However, if left undisturbed the natural succession will ultimately result in a mixed woodland of alder, willow and birch. To prevent this, controlled grazing by sheep keeps out scrub and woody plants and encourages the formation of raised bog dominated by cotton grass and sphagnum. Management also includes maintaining the water table at a high level to conserve biodiversity.

While peat extraction is no longer a threat to the Moors, planning permission for wind farms in the area is being sought. In 2005 alone there were 21 proposals for development. Thus a new threat to environment and further challenges appear likely in future.

Case study: The Breckland: a lowland heath environment

The Breckland is a gently undulating plateau covering 950 km² in southwest Norfolk and northwest Suffolk (Figure 2.18). It is the largest area of lowland heath in England. Like raised bog, lowland heath is one of Europe's rarest and most threatened habitats.

Environment and ecosystem

The Breckland has a semi-continental climate, with warm summers and cool, frost-prone winters. It is the driest part of the UK with annual precipitation averaging just 550 mm. Its soils are also distinctive. Based on glacial sands, they are **podsolised**, and typically acidic, free-draining and nutrient-poor (Figure 2.19).

Breckland's dry climate and infertile soils provided few opportunities for farming before the eighteenth century. As a result much of the region was left uncultivated. These heathlands were common lands, providing grazing for sheep and cattle as well as fuel and building materials. A combination of grazing and burning maintained the open character of the heaths and prevented the invasion of trees and scrub. The heaths are dominated by evergreen shrubs such as heather, ling and gorse (Figure 2.20). Plants such as ling and heather are well adapted to dry heath-

Figure 2.18 Breckland Environmentally Sensitive Area

land, their tiny leaves and sunken stomata reducing transpiration loss.

Lowland heath vegetation has the status of plagioclimax. This means that it is in balance with climate, soil and human activities. For example, when grazing pressure is removed rapid changes occur with invasion by bracken, brambles, scrub and later woodland. Without controlled grazing the natural process of succession takes over and the specialised heath plants and habitats eventually disappear.

Figure 2.19 Profile of
an iron-humus podsol

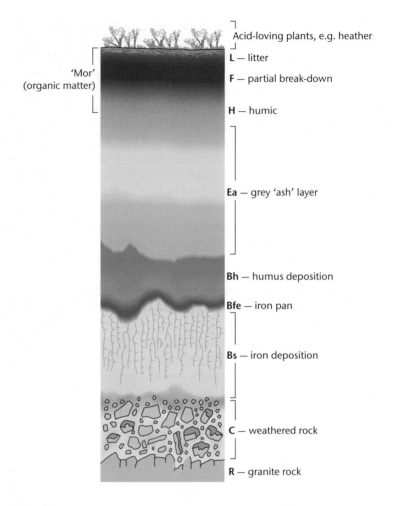

Acid-loving plants, e.g. heather

L — litter

'Mor'
(organic matter)

F — partial break-down

H — humic

Ea — grey 'ash' layer

Bh — humus deposition

Bfe — iron pan

Bs — iron deposition

C — weathered rock

R — granite rock

Figure 2.20 Heath
nutrient cycle

Heathland environment
A dry, open habitat that
allows low-growing woody
plants such as heather, ling
and gorse to survive. It also
favours rare bird species
such as stone curlews and
woodlarks. The open habitat
has been maintained by
human activity such as
grazing of sheep and
burning. Thus, heathland
has the status of plagio-
climax, not climatic climax.
Once traditional human
activities are removed,
without management,
heathland is invaded by
scrub and birch.

Drought
Free-draining sandy soils, underlain by sand and chalk mean that water is in short
supply. The Breckland is also the driest area of England with just 550 mm of rain a year.

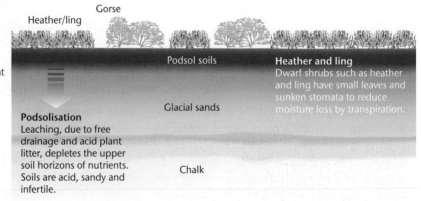

Gorse

Heather/ling

Podsol soils

Heather and ling
Dwarf shrubs such as heather
and ling have small leaves and
sunken stomata to reduce
moisture loss by transpiration.

Glacial sands

Podsolisation
Leaching, due to free
drainage and acid plant
litter, depletes the upper
soil horizons of nutrients.
Soils are acid, sandy and
infertile.

Chalk

Despite its poor soils, low net primary productivity and lack of biodiversity, heathland provides important habitats for many rare species (Photograph 2.7). They include plants such as Spanish catchfly and spiked speedwell; insects like the silver studded blue butterfly; and birds such as stone curlews, woodlarks and nightjars.

Threats to heathland

The area of heath in Breckland has decreased dramatically in the last century. In 1900, 29% of the region was covered by heath. One hundred years later this proportion was down to 11%. Large areas have been lost to farming, forestry and military training. Today only 45 km² remain (Figure 2.21).

Although the Breckland soils are naturally infertile, chemical fertilisers, liming and draining have allowed farmers to convert large areas of heath to productive arable land (Figure 2.21). In addition, spray irrigation has solved the problem of summer water shortage, though at the cost of lowering the water table over wide areas.

Photograph 2.7 *The heathland habitat:*
(a) spiked speedwell (b) silver studded blue butterfly
(c) stone curlew

Figure 2.21 *Pressure on Breckland's heaths*

Between 1934 and 1980, 86% of Breckland's heath was lost to afforestation, agriculture and military training. Only 45 km² of original heath survives today. Much of the original heath is fragmented.

Urban development
Although protected today, in the past heath was often regarded as wasteland. As a result it was the first land seized for new roads, factories and housing estates.

Military training
The large Stanford military training area is retained for military maneouvres. It is inaccessible to the public but retains some original heaths. The heaths are maintained by controlled grazing of sheep.

Thetford

Ely

Mildenhall

Bury St Edmunds

Agriculture
In the 1930s, large areas of heath were converted to productive arable farming thanks to mechanisation, irrigation and enrichment of soil fertility. After 1945, government policies further encouraged the expansion of arable at the expense of heath. Today 60% of Breckland is arable land.

Afforestation
A massive programme of reafforestation sponsored by the government occurred between 1922 and the late 1930s. Plantations were mainly Scots pine and exotic conifers such as larch and fir.

Following the First World War, huge conifer plantations were established in the Breckland to meet national shortages of timber (see Figure 2.21). Scots pine, other species of pine, larches and firs were planted by the Forestry Commission and private landowners on over 200 km². These plantations transformed the environment, modifying the soils, increasing humidity, reducing wind speeds and altering local energy exchanges.

Today the Breckland heaths are recognised as rare and valuable habitats and are protected against development and land-use change. Yet, while the expansion of farming and forestry is no longer a problem, there are threats from other sources:

■ Neglect and lack of management of the heaths — Without controlled grazing, scrub and trees invade changing habitats and push out the more delicate heathland species.

■ Runoff from arable land and free-range pig farming — This leads to nutrient enrichment of soils, causing vigorous vegetation growth which smothers indigenous heathland plants.

■ Acid deposition – This causes nutrient (especially nitrogen) enrichment of soils which also favours alien species.

■ Summer fires and trampling caused by informal recreation — Several bird species are vulnerable to the disturbance associated with recreation.

Conservation

The ecological importance of Breckland is recognised both nationally and internationally. Large areas of the heath have now been given statutory protection. There are, for example, four National Nature Reserves and 42 SSSIs in Breckland. However, the need to protect the landscapes and wildlife of the entire region, led to the whole of Breckland being designated an Environmentally Sensitive Area (ESA) in 1988. Farmers who belong to the ESA scheme farm the countryside in traditional and environmentally responsible ways in order to conserve its landscapes, wildlife and historic features. In return they receive financial compensation from the government for lost production. Breckland farmers belonging to the ESA scheme must:

■ maintain traditional management of the heathland, including controlled grazing by sheep

■ allow suitable cultivated land to revert to heathland

■ increase the benefits of arable land to wildlife by leaving uncropped wildlife strips around the margins of fields and conservation headlands

■ where appropriate convert arable to pasture

■ maintain a stubble cover on arable fields in the winter

■ allow public access to conservation areas

The impact of human activity on the physical environment

Key ideas

➤ The impact of human activities on the physical environment varies with economic and technological development.

➤ Human activity can have both positive and negative effects on the physical environment.

➤ The impact of human activity on the physical environment can both increase and decrease with economic, social and technological development.

Wolfgang Kaehler/Alamy

Photograph 2.8
Terraced rice fields in Java

The factors explaining the impact of humankind on the physical environment are summarised in the equation devised by Commoner, Ehrlich and Holdren in the 1970s:

I (impact) = P (population) × Affluence (per capita consumption) × Technology

Let us look at each of these factors in turn. First, population: the size and density of a population will influence the pressure on natural resources such as soil, water, forests and grasslands. For example, small bands of shifting cultivators, such as the Iban in the rainforests of Borneo in Indonesia, have minimal impact on the ecosystem. The contrast with the neighbouring Indonesian island of Java is stark. There rural populations live at average densities of $500 \, km^2$. Over the centuries the sheer pressure of population has transformed the natural rainforest ecosystem. Even the steepest hillslopes have been cleared and the trees replaced by small fields for intensive rice cultivation (Photograph 2.8).

But demands on natural resources are not just determined by population. The affluence or wealth of a population directly affects resource consumption. Ireland provides a clear example. In the mid-nineteenth century Ireland's population was around 4.5 million. Most people were poor subsistence farmers and relied on local resources for food, shelter and fuel. One hundred and fifty years later, Ireland's total population has actually fallen to 4.1 million. However, the country's per capita wealth has soared, giving Ireland the second highest GDP per capita in the EU and the seventh highest in the world. With rising wealth has come a massive increase in resource consumption. Whereas in the past resources were sourced locally, today they are procured worldwide. As a result Ireland's **ecological footprint** is now global.

The third (and arguably the most important) factor influencing the human impact is technology. Humankind's increasing impact on, and control of, the environment is linked with expansion of technology. Technological growth has accelerated so rapidly in the past 150 years that human activity is now the main driver of environmental change at the global scale. Yet despite advances in technology, in many countries in the less economically developed world, food production and energy supplies still depend on technologies that are thousands of years old. So while modern technology in MEDCs makes jet travel commonplace, generates electricity from nuclear power and allows a single farmer to cultivate 1000 ha of wheat, millions of people in the less economically developed world depend on simple technologies such as animal power, fuelwood and scratch ploughs.

Case study   The human impact in the Netherlands and Bangladesh

Geographically, the Netherlands and Bangladesh share a number of similar characteristics. Both are small countries: the Netherlands is roughly half the size of Scotland, and Bangladesh is about the same size as England. Both are densely populated: the Netherlands, with nearly 500 persons per km^2 has the highest density in the Europe; and Bangladesh, with 1150 persons per km^2, has arguably the highest density in the world. As a result land is scarce in both countries and there is considerable pressure on resources. The physical geography of the two countries is also similar. Most of Bangladesh and a large part of the Netherlands occupy estuarine deltas. Bangladesh is at the mouth of the Ganges, Brahmaputra and Meghna river systems, which drain northern India and the eastern Himalayas. The Netherlands is situated at the mouth of the Rhine, Maas and Schelde rivers, which drain much of western Europe. And because of their delta locations, large tracts of land in both countries are at risk from river floods and storm surges.

While there are many geographical similarities between the Netherlands and Bangladesh there are huge economic differences. The two countries are

at opposite ends of the development spectrum (Table 2.6). The Netherlands is a rich, post-industrial country with access to advanced technology. Bangladesh is a LEDC where 80% of the population lives on less than US$2 a day and where low technology is the norm. As we shall see, such economic and technological differences are the key to understanding the extent to which these two countries can control and modify the physical environment.

The Netherlands

There are few countries where people have had a greater impact on the environment than the Netherlands; hence the saying that 'God created the world, but the Dutch created the Netherlands'. Over the centuries human activity has transformed the geography of the Netherlands, and in particular the western regions of Holland and Zeeland.

Most of the western Netherlands comprises a huge estuarine delta, at the mouth of Rhine-Maas-Schelde river system. Like all deltas, it is barely a metre or two above sea level and criss-crossed by hundreds of waterways. One thousand years ago this region was a vast wetland, flooded by rivers,

Table 2.6
Economic comparison of the Netherlands and Bangladesh

	The Netherlands	Bangladesh
GNI per capita (US$)	37 580	2340
HDI (ranking among 177)	9th	140th
Internet users (per 1000 people)	439.5	0.8
Per capita energy consumption (oil equivalent kg^{-1} year^{-1})	4761.5	145.1
Per capita electricity consumption (Kwh year^{-1})	6559.4	103.6

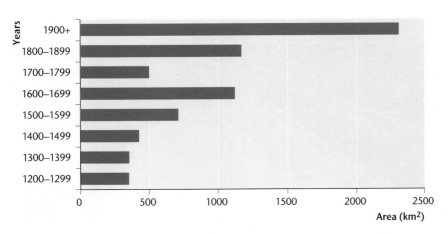

Figure 2.22 *Land reclamation in the Netherlands*

tides and storm surges. The first settlements were built on artificial mounds or 'terps' and by the thirteenth century, thanks to the development of the windmill for lifting water, the process of land reclamation had begun (Figure 2.22). The key to understanding the Netherlands' man-made landscape is water control.

Over the centuries the advance of technology allowed the Dutch to drain large areas of wetland and become expert at land reclamation. These newly reclaimed lands were known as polders. At the same time dykes were built to keep the sea out, rivers were embanked and the coastline was shortened. Even areas of shallow seafloor were reclaimed.

In the twentieth century land reclamation added nearly 7% to the Netherlands' land area, providing much needed space for housing, industry, commerce and farming. Meanwhile, the need to protect people and settlements from flooding in such a vulnerable environment was a spur to remodel the coastline and waterways. As we shall see, land reclamation continues today.

Explaining the human impact

We have already seen that the human impact on the environment depends on population, affluence and technology. All three have been instrumental in transforming the Dutch landscape, especially in the past 100 years.

Draining and land reclamation is expensive and complex. For example, the enclosing dam alone in the Zuider Zee project cost the equivalent of US$1 billion at today's prices (Photograph 2.9). For the Dutch people such schemes are not only technically feasible but also affordable.

As the engineering technology of land reclamation and flood control advanced, more ambitious schemes were attempted. One-quarter of the Netherlands' land area lies below sea level. Draining this land requires water to be raised and pumped into nearby rivers and canals. Until the nineteenth century this was done by wind power. The introduction of steam pumps allowed water tables to be maintained at lower levels and land several metres below sea level to be drained. The reclamation of the 180 km² Haarlemmermeer in the 1870s used steam power. By the 1930s diesel and electrically driven pumps had replaced steam. Technology had advanced sufficiently to construct the 30 km enclosing dam (Afsluitdijk) across the Zuider Zee and complete the long-anticipated reclamation of this area.

The Zuider Zee project

The Zuider Zee is a shallow inlet of the North Sea. The oldest plans for drainage and reclamation date to 1667. However, it was only in the early twentieth century that technology was sufficiently advanced to make reclamation feasible. The enclosing dam (Afsluitdijk) was completed in 1932. The Wieringermeer was drained in 1930, the North East Polder in 1942, East Flevoland in 1957 and South Flevoland in 1967. The project added about 6% to the Netherlands' land area, shortened the coastline

Photograph 2.9 *Zuider Zee dam*

and reduced the risk of flooding by the sea. Land reclamation was initially to increase the agricultural area, and over 90% of land in the oldest polders is used for intensive farming of cereals, sugar beet, market gardening crops and bulbs. The newer polders, such as South Flevoland, have a more varied land use: housing, commerce, industry, transport and recreation, as well as farming, are important. The two largest urban centres are the new towns of Almere (181 000) and Lelystad (73 000), and South Flevoland has become a commuter province for Amsterdam. The Zuider Zee project has provided other benefits, for example water-based recreational activities (sailing, fishing and swimming), a large freshwater reservoir, wetland habitats and nature reserves, and improved communications (across the Afsluitdijk) between Randstad and the northeast Netherlands.

The Delta Project

The southwest Netherlands (Zeeland) is occupied by the Rhine-Maas-Schelde delta. This region suffered badly in the disastrous floods and storm surge of 1953. Engineering work to seal off most of the delta, which began in 1950, was not completed until the mid-1980s. The total cost was US$5 billion.

The main purpose of the Delta project was flood control. It reduced the length of the coastline from 800 km to 80 km and greatly improved communications between Rotterdam and the southwest region. There were environmental costs. Many saltwater tidal inlets were replaced by freshwater lakes, destroying coastal habitats and wildlife. Important fisheries were destroyed and a number of harbours lost.

The environmental impact of the closure of the eastern Schelde was diminished by building a storm surge barrier with sluice gates, rather than a solid dam. This meant that the eastern Schelde remained saline and tidal. Valuable areas of mudflat and salt-marsh were preserved for wildlife and the local oyster fishery was saved. New freshwater lakes such as Grevelingenmeer provided opportunities for water-based recreational and leisure activities.

Maasvlakte2

A major land reclamation project started in 2008 at the mouth of the New Waterway, 15 km west of Rotterdam (see Figure 2.24). Known as Maasvlakte2, this scheme will create 20 km² of new land from the North Sea to allow further expansion of the port of Rotterdam (see Figure 2.23). Maasvlakte2, will

Art Kowalsky/Alamy

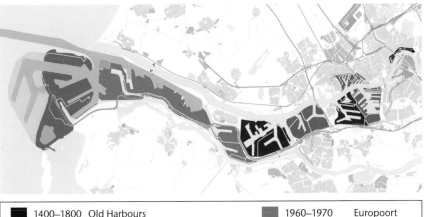

■ 1400–1800	Old Harbours	
■ 1800–1900	Former Trade areas	
■ 1920–1960	1st and 2nd Petroleumhaven, Merwehaven, Waalhaven	
■ 1946–1960	Botlek, Eemhaven	

■ 1960–1970	Europoort	
■ 1970–present	Maasvlakte1	
■ 2008+	Maasvlakte2	

Figure 2.23
Expansion of the port of Rotterdam

handle the largest container ships and provide sites for the chemical and distribution industries. The initial phase will be completed within 5 years and the first ships will begin using the new facilities in 2013. However, final completion will not be until 2033.

Maasvlakte2 is just the latest phase in the expansion of the port of Rotterdam (Europe's leading port) that began in the early twentieth century (Figure 2.23). Growth in trade led to the steady downstream expansion of the port, seeking deeper water to accommodate larger ships, and space to build new harbours. By mid-century the port had reached Botlek. Then in the 1960s and 1970s the huge Europoort complex with its specialist terminals for oil refineries and petrochemicals works was added. When trade outgrew even this facility, land was reclaimed from the North Sea. This was Maasvlakte1. Now, 25 years on, work is about to begin on Maasvlakte2 (Figure 2.24).

Environmental impact

The main impact of Maasvlakte2 is on marine ecosystems along the coast and immediately offshore. First, 20 km² of seabed will become dryland and second, this new land, up to 5m above sea level, will consist of sand dredged from offshore. Suction dredgers will mine 325 million m³ of sand from three locations on the seabed. Although these areas support no plant

Figure 2.24 *An artist's impression of the finished project*

life, there are important habitats for a variety of marine life, including molluscs, crustacea and fish. Small invertebrates on the seabed provide food for fish and, higher up the food chain, for fish-eating birds, seals and porpoises.

Closer inshore, engineering operations will release silt and other fine particles into the sea, making coastal waters cloudier. This will disrupt primary production which will cascade throughout the marine food web (Figure 2.25).

The engineering works at Maasvlakte2 are also likely to disrupt the movement of sand northwards along the Dutch coast, which could affect sand

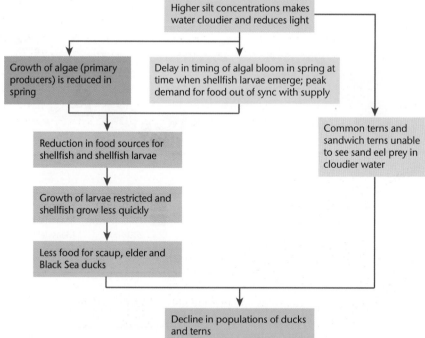

Figure 2.25 *Local impact of engineering operations on food chains in coastal waters*

supplies for dune building. There will also be some damage to dunes and their flora in the Voorne, just south of Maasvlakte.

Sustainable development

The Maasvlakte2 site is in the Voordelta bay — a protected nature reserve. The new development will lead to some loss of habitat for birds and marine life and a reduction of feeding grounds. However, under the terms of the EU's Natura 2000, the Dutch government is obliged to compensate for any habitat loss.

For this reason, a new 250 km² seabed protection area has been planned to the southeast of the Maasvlakte, compensating for the loss of seafloor in the construction of Maasvlakte2. Human activities such as fishing that disturb the seabed will be banned in the protection area. Moreover, the extent of the planned seabed protection area is ten times larger than that of the projected land recovery.

A new dune area north of Maasvlakte, between Hook of Holland and Ter Helje, will be created to compensate for the loss of some dunes and damage to flora in Voorne. In addition, three new recreational areas on the edge of Rotterdam, totalling 7.5 km² will

be established. These landscape parks will provide the public with opportunities for recreation such as walking, cycling and other outdoor activities.

Although the Maasvlakte development will result in the loss of the popular Slutterstrand beach, two new beaches, with access, parking and cycling routes, will be created on the edge of the new port area (Figure 2.26). Overall the Maasvlakte2 project has been planned to ensure that there is no net loss of environmental resources.

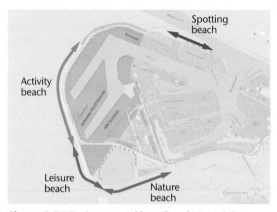

Figure 2.26 *Environmental benefits of Maasvlakte2*

Bangladesh

Bangladesh is a densely populated country with an acute shortage of land. Indeed it is one of the few countries in the world that could be described as overpopulated (Figure 2.27). Eighty per cent of Bangladesh's population are rural dwellers engaged mainly in agriculture and fishing. Pressure of population has reduced the average farm holding to less than 1 ha. Despite favourable farming conditions, most farms are too small to be self-sufficient. Meanwhile millions of rural dwellers are landless, and are forced to work as labourers.

If Bangladesh were a wealthy country with access to investment funds and the advanced technology, land reclamation would be a serious consideration. Faced with similar pressures, MEDCs such as the

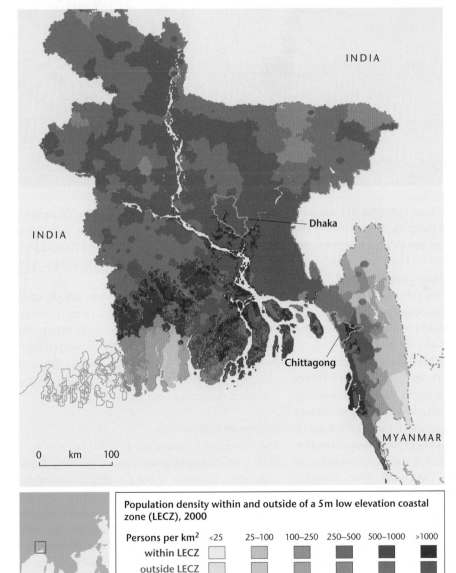

Population density within and outside of a 5 m low elevation coastal zone (LECZ), 2000

Persons per km²	<25	25–100	100–250	250–500	500–1000	>1000
within LECZ						
outside LECZ						

Largest urban areas

Figure 2.27 Population distribution and density in Bangladesh

Reproduced by permission of Centre for International Earth Science Information Network (CIESIN), Columbia University (2007)

Christopher Pillitz/Alamy

Photograph 2.10
A flooded village in
Bangladesh

Netherlands and Japan have opted for this solution. But poor countries like Bangladesh have neither the economic resources nor the technology to modify the natural environment on this scale. Farming, for example, relies on traditional methods: human labour and livestock are still the main sources of power; technology has changed little over the centuries and for millions of farmers simple wooden ploughs drawn by bullocks are the norm.

The lives of people in the delta and floodplains are shaped by the annual floods. Every year one-fifth of the country floods for up to 45 days due to the monsoon rains and meltwater from the Himalayan snowpack. High-magnitude floods, which occur once every 6 years on average, flood more than 35% of the land area. Moreover, these high-magnitude events that occurred in 1987, 1988, 1998, 2004 and 2007 are becoming more frequent.

While annual floods provide irrigation water and silt that are essential to the farm economy, they are destructive and a serious threat to lives. According to one estimate, the 1998 floods covered 84 000 km² and left 30 million people homeless (Photograph 2.10). Even more serious is the threat posed by tropical cyclones. In 1970 a storm surge caused by a cyclone in the Bay of Bengal killed 300 000 people. In a similar event in 1991 138 000 lost their lives. Most recently Cyclone Sidr, which hit Bangladesh in November 2007, killed over 3000 people and destroyed 250 000 homes.

Apart from human misery, the floods have massive economic consequences. They damage crops, livestock, housing, small business enterprises and infrastructure. In the 1998 floods, output from Bangladesh's export industries fell by one-fifth and hundreds of factories were forced to close. Typically the floods reduce the country's GDP by 2–5%.

Responses to flooding

The Netherlands' approach to flood hazards is to build hard structures which prevent flooding. Flood prevention, however, is not a practical solution for Bangladesh. The scale of Bangladesh's rivers and the violence of tropical cyclones make a technological fix much more difficult. But in addition, Bangladesh, even with the help of international donors, has neither the technology nor the resources to implement a comprehensive flood protection programme. Instead, the focus is on flood mitigation and measures such as flood warning systems, disaster management and cyclone shelters. For example, cyclone shelters provided refuge for 1.5 million people when cyclone Sidr struck in 2007.

In contrast to the Netherlands, flood prevention structures in Bangladesh are scarce. Flood embankments extend for just 5700 km, including 3400 km in coastal areas. In addition, there are 4300 km of drainage canals. However, without constant maintenance earthen embankments are easily damaged by river erosion and breaching is commonplace. The lack of flood protection structures in Bangladesh is very different to the situation in the Netherlands and demonstrates the country's limited ability to control and modify the environment.

In the 1970s and 1980s the World Bank and other international donors supported major flood prevention schemes. These have not been implemented, partly because they were impractical and partly because there were insufficient resources. Even smaller-scale schemes such as riverbank protection, the construction of coastal embankments and disaster shelters have stalled. Meanwhile, with rapid population growth, urbanisation and climate change, the risks of flooding in future can only increase. The Netherlands, on the other hand, can afford to be relaxed about future sea level rises and climate change. Wealth and technology have made the country secure against all but the most extreme flood events.

Managing physical environments sustainably

Key ideas
➤ When human activity impacts on physical environments, the environment may need to be managed sustainably.
➤ Sustainable environmental management includes conservation, planning controls and restricted use.

Case study | Jasper National Park

Jasper National Park, together with Banff, Yoho and Kootenay (Figure 2.28), is one of four national parks in Canada's southern Rockies that collectively have UN World Heritage status. Jasper covers nearly 11 000 km² and forms part of the Yellowhead ecosystem, a much larger area roughly the size of Scotland. Jasper is famous for its outstanding scenery, especially its mountains, glaciers, forests and alpine meadows. It is also home to spectacular wildlife including large carnivores such as wolves, grizzly bears, cougars and wolverines, and herds of elk, woodland caribou, moose and white-tailed deer.

Most of Jasper National Park is wilderness, though few areas have been unaffected by human activity. The park originated as the Jasper Forest Park in 1907 and was granted national park status in 1930.

The national park is managed by the government-run Parks Canada. Management has two main purposes. The first is to protect and maintain the natural environment in a way that leaves it unimpaired for present and future generations. The second is to further the education and enjoyment of visitors in a way that does not damage the park's ecological integrity (Box 2.4). Park management must, in other words, be sustainable.

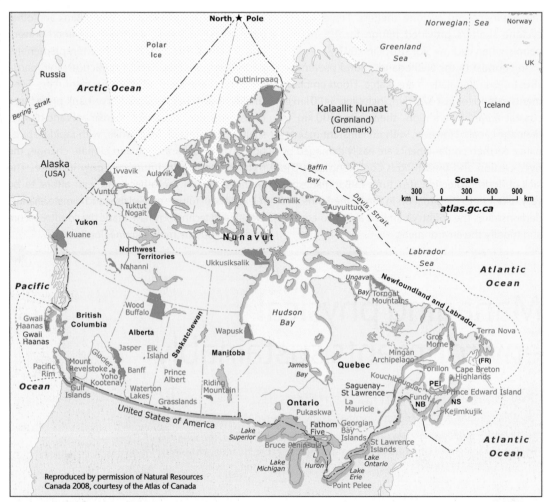

Figure 2.28 *Canada's national parks*

Managing visitor pressure in a fragile environment: Mount Edith Cavell

Mount Edith Cavell is a popular destination for visitors and a prominent landmark in the Athabasca Valley, southeast of the town of Jasper. Among its attractions are its easy accessibility, glaciers, moraines and breathtaking scenery (Photograph 2.11). As a result Mount Edith Cavell is one of the most popular day-trip areas in the Jasper National Park.

However, the pressure of visitor numbers poses a significant threat to the environment which requires careful management. Mount Edith Cavell is ecologically very sensitive. Its meadows are important rutting, calving and wintering grounds for woodland caribou, an endangered species numbering no more than 300 to 400 animals in the park. The area also supports rare plant communities.

While protection of the area's fragile ecosystem has priority, there is also a need allow public access and to improve the quality of visitors' experience. In Mount Edith Cavell the national park authorities aim to:

- Tackle the problem of traffic congestion caused by visitors at peak times.
- Provide high-quality interpretation of the ecosystem.
- Protect and maintain rare plant communities and old-growth sub-alpine forest.

Box 2.4 Ecological integrity

The concept of ecological integrity is central to national park management in Canada. Ecological integrity means that ecosystems have their natural components and supporting processes intact, and that human impact is minimal. This concept guides management in national parks, where the aim is to maintain ecosystems in, or restore them to, their natural state. It means, for example, retaining biodiversity (i.e. the composition and abundance of individual species and biological communities such as forests and tundra), not suppressing natural processes such as flooding and forest fires, and ensuring that predator-prey balances are preserved.

The basis of environmental management is the park's management plan. It sets out the objectives, goals and strategies for the maintenance and restoration of ecological integrity. The park authorities also work with the tourism industry to encourage appropriate recreational activities such as hiking, rock climbing and skiing.

A number of pressures threaten Jasper and other national parks in the Rockies. They include habitat loss, habitat fragmentation, losses of large carnivores such as grizzly bears which upset predator-prey relationships, air pollution, pesticides, the invasion of alien plant species and overuse by visitors.

Rollie Rodriguez/Alamy

Photograph 2.11 *Mount Edith Cavell, Jasper National Park*

- Protect the wood caribou's rutting, calving and wintering grounds.

It is planned to achieve these goals by taking the following actions:

- Reduce the demand for parking at peak periods, possibly by imposing traffic quotas or restriction on the use of private vehicles.
- Improve interpretation so that visitors can understand better the ecological and geological diversity, including glacial features.
- Ecourage visitors to take advantage of guided tours.

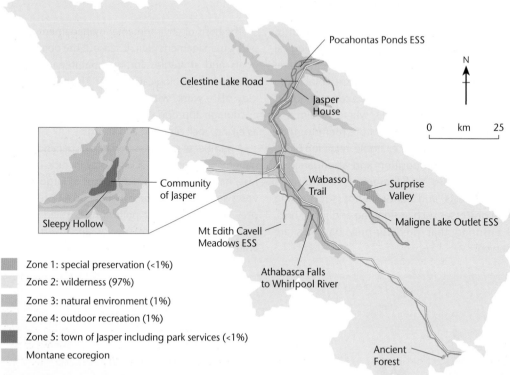

Zone 1: special preservation (<1%)

Zone 2: wilderness (97%)

Zone 3: natural environment (1%)

Zone 4: outdoor recreation (1%)

Zone 5: town of Jasper including park services (<1%)

Montane ecoregion

Figure 2.29 Jasper National Park zoning map

- Close the meadows to visitors in the autumn in order not to disturb the caribou during the rutting season, and again in early spring to reduce damage to vegetation caused by trampling.
- Build hardened trails in the Cavell Meadows to prevent damage to rare plants, and where necessary, re-route some trails.

Land-use zoning is a management device applied throughout Jasper National Park. Its main purpose is to resolve the conflict between ecological integrity and visitor pressure. The park is divided into geographical areas or zones according to the need for environmental protection and suitability for recreational activities (Figure 2.29).

- Zone 1 comprises special preservation areas. It covers less than 1% of the park and protects unique or endangered natural and cultural features. It includes ancient forests, karst scenery and archaeological sites.

- Zone 2 is wilderness and covers 97% of the park. Minimal human interference is allowed here and motorised access is not permitted. It includes steep mountain slopes, glaciers and lakes. Service provision is limited to trails, alpine huts and backcountry camp grounds.

- In Zone 3 (natural environment areas), visitors experience the park's natural and cultural heritage through outdoor recreational activities that require few services and facilities. However, facilities in Zone 3 exceed the acceptable standards for Zone 2. Again, motorised access is not permitted. Access routes and land associated with backcountry commercial lodges are in this zone.

- Zone 4 is reserved for outdoor recreational activities and popular tourism such as sight-seeing, appreciation and enjoyment of the park's heritage, and facilities such as information centres and parking lots. It accounts for less than 1% of the area of the park. Direct access by motorised

vehicles is permitted. Zone 4 includes rights of way along park roads (including the main Icefield Parkway route between Jasper and Banff) and popular locations such as the Columbia Icefield and the Sunwapta Falls.

■ Zone 5 comprises the town of Jasper, the principal centre for tourism and administration in the park.

In addition to the five zones, there are environmentally sensitive sites that require special protection such as Lake Maligne and Mount Edith Cavell Meadows, and the Montane ecoregion (Figure 2.29). The latter covers the lower slopes of large valleys, and being milder, drier and sheltered, provides important refuge areas for wildlife in winter and corridors for the movement of larger animals. In the past much of this area has proved attractive to economic activities and what little is left needs to be managed to prevent further losses.

Wildfire management

Park managers used to view wildfires as a destructive force: their policy was to suppress wildfires whenever and wherever they occurred. Today's policy is very different. Fire is recognised as an essential process in the park's forest ecosystem: one that has shaped landscapes and ecosystems of Jasper and the southern Rockies.

Forest ecosystems need fire to thrive. In the Canadian Rockies, where winters are cold and long, decomposition is slow. Conifer needles, branches and stems pile up on the forest floor. Fire mineralises this material, releasing nutrients for plant growth. Periodic wildfires also create openings in the forest which warm the soil and stimulate new growth. The result is a vegetation mosaic providing a variety of habitats which sustains biodiversity. Some plant species need fire to survive. For example, lodgepole pine and jack pine have resin-coated cones that only open and release their seeds when fire melts the resin. Without fire, regeneration is impossible.

Many animals also benefit from forest fires. For example:

■ Woodpecker populations soar after forest wildfires as they feed on the glut of insects that colonise newly burnt trees.

■ Moose and elk browse on new-growth aspen, raspberry and other species that sprout after fire.

■ The Canadian lynx benefits as snowshoe hare populations boom in newly burned areas.

In contrast we now know that preventing wildfire has harmful long-term effects on the forest ecosystem.

■ Forests become older and more closed-in.

■ Open habitats and the species they support become scarcer.

■ As the vegetation mosaic is lost, biodiversity is reduced.

■ Dead organic material builds up on the forest floor, depriving the trees of nutrients and increasing the hazard of highly destructive crown fires fuelled by large quantities of dead wood and litter.

Fire programme

The restoration of fire to the park's forest ecosystems is vital to their ecological integrity.

While Parks Canada accepts its responsibility to protect people and settlements against forest fires, it also has a policy of controlled burning.

Controlled burnings take place in the spring when temperatures rise and the snow melts. For example in 2007 the park undertook prescribed burns at Hawk Mountain (5.6 km²), 15 km north of Jasper close to the Athabasca River; Vine Creek (7.3 km²) 5 km north of Hawk Mountain; and Pyramid Bench. In the last location, burning was confined to the day and the fires completely extinguished at night.

Examination-style questions

Section A
Resource 1

Trump snubs experts over golf course threat to rare dunes

Donald Trump...the billionaire property developer will fly into the UK today to give evidence to a month-long public inquiry into his controversial plans to spend £1billion building a golf resort with 950 timeshare flats, a 450-bed hotel and 500 homes on the coastline north of Aberdeen.

His proposals...have met concerted opposition from residents and conservation agencies because the first of two 18-hole golf courses will be built over part of a large but very fragile stretch of dunes — the Foveran Links site of special scientific interest.

Backed by Scotland's first minister, Alex Salmond, local businesses and tourism agencies, Trump claims the 'great vistas and majestic dunes' have that 'magical quality' which would allow him to create the finest course on the planet. It 'appears to grow out of the land', he exclaims in his advance evidence to the inquiry.

However, two independent ecological surveys commissioned by Trump warn in great detail that his proposals will have a 'severe' and 'significant' effect on the ecology of the dunes.

The fate of the dunes — described by Scottish Natural Heritage as unparalleled in the UK — is central to the inquiry, at which protesters will also oppose Trump's plans to build 500 new homes and four eight-storey blocks of timeshare flats overlooking the dunes to finance the golf resort.

In advance testimony to the inquiry, Trump confirms he rejected his experts' pleas to move the course since it would affect only roughly a tenth of the dune system....If he is told to move off the dunes, he will abandon the entire project, he states.

Source: Severin Carrell. the *Guardian*, 9 June 2008

Resource 2

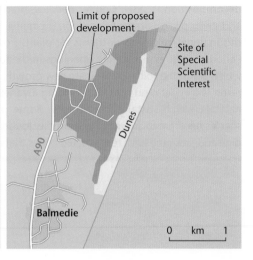

Foveran coastal dunes

1 Resources 1 and 2 focus on the Foveran coastal dunes in northeast Scotland, which are the site of a proposed links golf course. Outline an issue indicated and suggest appropriate management. (10 marks)

Section B

2 Discuss the view that the negative impact of human activity on ecosystems increases with levels of technological development. (30 marks)

3 *'As civilization creates cities, builds highways, and drains marshes, it takes away, little by little, the land that is suitable for wildlife. And as their space for living dwindles, the wildlife populations themselves decline.'* (Rachel Carson)
How valid is this viewpoint? (30 marks)

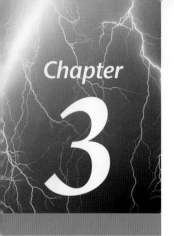

Climatic hazards

Hurricanes and tornadoes

Key ideas
➤ Tropical storms and tornadoes develop under particular atmospheric conditions to become major hazards.
➤ Hazards associated with tropical storms and tornadoes have serious environmental, social and economic impacts on the areas they affect.
➤ The degree of impact of tropical storms and tornadoes on an area depends on a variety of factors including economic and technological development and population density.
➤ Impacts can vary over time from immediate to long term.
➤ There are a variety of ways to manage or reduce the impacts of hurricanes and tornadoes.

Hurricanes

Violent tropical storms in the Atlantic region are known as hurricanes. In east Asia the same storms are called typhoons, and in south Asia they are known as tropical cyclones. Despite their different names, all these storms have a number of common features. They:
➤ sustain wind speeds of more than $119\,km\,h^{-1}$
➤ deposit massive amounts of rain in a short time
➤ give rise to deadly storm surges in coastal areas
➤ are highly destructive

Hurricane formation and decay

Hurricanes form over tropical oceans between latitudes $8°$ and $20°$. Three conditions favour hurricane formation:
➤ high humidity and therefore plenty of water vapour
➤ light winds which allow vertical cloud development (i.e. little or no wind shear)
➤ sea surface temperatures (SSTs) of at least $26-27\,°C$ and a deep layer of warm water down to $60-70\,m$. This warm layer prevents cold water rising to the surface and killing the system.

These conditions are found in the summer and early autumn in the tropical North Atlantic and North Pacific Oceans. As a result the hurricane 'season' in the northern hemisphere runs from June to late October. By November ocean waters are usually too cool to generate hurricanes.

The first signs of a hurricane are tropical disturbances: clusters of thunderstorms which develop over the ocean. In the tropical North Atlantic these disturbances often form as easterly waves. Indeed most Atlantic hurricanes can be traced to easterly waves that originate as far away as Africa.

Given favourable conditions, some tropical disturbances become better organised. Pressure falls in the area around the storm as condensation releases latent heat and warm air starts to rise. Soon a distinctive cyclonic circulation (counter-clockwise in the northern hemisphere) develops in response to the Earth's rotation. All the while rising air cools, condenses and releases more latent heat. This warming creates high pressure near the top of the storm. As a result the central area of a hurricane behaves like a giant chimney: high pressure aloft forcing air outwards; low pressure at the surface sucking air in (Figure 3.1). In this way the hurricane gets a constant supply of vapour — the energy that drives the storm.

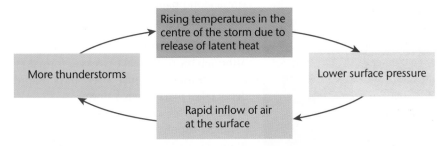

Figure 3.1 Positive feedback and hurricane growth

Once sustained wind speeds reach $37 \, \text{km h}^{-1}$, tropical disturbances are called tropical depressions. As winds increase to $63 \, \text{km h}^{-1}$, tropical depressions are upgraded to tropical storms. Eventually, when wind speeds reach $119 \, \text{km h}^{-1}$ tropical storms become hurricanes (Figure 3.2).

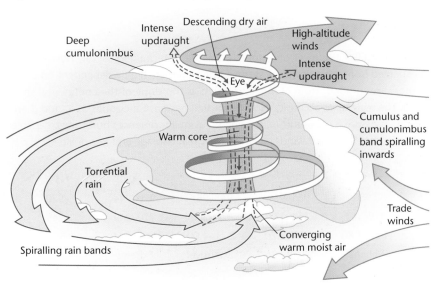

Figure 3.2
The anatomy of a hurricane

NASA

Photograph 3.1 *Satellite image of a hurricane*

Hurricane structure

Mature hurricanes have a number of distinctive features. First, at the centre of the hurricane there is a 10–65 km diameter cloud-free area of sinking air and light winds. This is the eye, a cylinder of relatively calm air (Photograph 3.1). As the air sinks, it is compressed, warming the atmosphere, which becomes cloud-free.

Bordering the eye of a mature hurricane is the eye wall: a ring of tall thunderstorms that produce heavy rains and very strong winds. This is the most destructive part of the storm. Curved bands of clouds surround the eye wall and trail away in a spiral fashion. These cloud bands produce heavy bursts of rain and strong winds.

Hurricane decay

Although hurricanes take weeks to form they often disappear in just a few days. Rapid decay takes place when a storm:
- moves over cooler water that can no longer supply warm, moist air
- moves over land, where it abruptly loses its power source — warm, moist air
- moves into an area where the large-scale flow aloft is either subsiding or where there is strong wind shear

Box 3.1 The Saffir–Simpson Scale

The Saffir–Simpson scale quantifies the level of damage and flooding expected from a hurricane. On this scale hurricanes are graded from 1 (weakest) to 5 (strongest). The scale takes account of a hurricane's central pressure, maximum sustained winds and storm surge. Sustained wind speeds are the determining factor, however, as storm surge values are highly dependent on other factors such as the slope of the continental shelf in the landfall region. Categories 3, 4, and 5 are considered as major (intense) hurricanes, capable of inflicting great damage and loss of life.

Scale number	1	2	3	4	5
Central pressure (mb)	>980	965–979	945–964	920–944	<920
Wind speed (km h^{-1})	119–153	154–177	178–209	210–249	>249
Storm surge (m)	1.20–1.80	1.81–2.70	2.71–4.00	4.01–5.50	>5.50
Damage	Minimal	Moderate	Extensive	Extreme	Catastrophic

Hurricane hazards

Hurricanes bring three types of natural hazard: damaging high winds, storm surges and heavy rain.

Winds

Wind speeds can reach 250 km h⁻¹ in the wall of the hurricane, with gusts of up to 360 km h⁻¹.

Destruction results from both direct impact and flying debris (Photograph 3.2). Wind speed is a primary cause of damage to trees and crops: entire forests can be flattened by hurricane-force winds. Tall buildings are also vulnerable to collapse. Sudden pressure changes may cause buildings to explode while suction can lift up roofs and entire buildings. However, most destruction, death and injury is due to flying debris. Poorly fastened roof sheets, tiles, telephone poles and other building parts are the most common projectiles.

FEMA

Photograph 3.2
Hurricane wind damage to a mobile home in Florida

Storm surges

A storm surge is water pushed toward the shore by the force of the winds. An advancing surge combined with high tides creates a hurricane storm tide, which can increase mean water level by 5 m or more. Meanwhile low atmospheric pressure pushes up the sea surface. The resulting rise in water level can cause severe flooding in coastal areas (Photograph 3.3). Much of the densely populated Atlantic and Gulf Coast coastlines of the USA, no more than 3 m above mean sea level, are at high risk from storm tides.

Storm surge heights are also determined by the slope of the continental shelf. A shallow offshore gradient allows a greater surge. Coastlines with steeper continental shelves experience less flooding. Storm tides, waves and currents in confined harbours severely damage ships, marinas and pleasure boats.

Photograph 3.3
*Floods caused by
storm surge in
New Orleans*

Rainfall

The rains that accompany hurricanes can be extremely heavy and may last several days. Local topography, humidity and the forward speed of a hurricane are important factors influencing rainfall amounts.

Intense rainfall causes three types of hazard:

➤ water seepage into buildings may result in their collapse from the weight of the absorbed water
➤ inland flooding by rivers
➤ mass movements such as landslides, mudslides, mudflows and debris flows (see Photograph 3.5 p. 93)

Managing hurricane hazards

Hurricanes are probably more closely monitored than any other natural hazard. Sophisticated measuring of temperatures, humidity and wind speed and tracking storm paths using satellites, aircraft, ships and buoys mean that accurate forecasts can be issued by agencies such as the National Weather Service. In the USA the National Hurricane Center is responsible for measuring and monitoring hurricanes in the Atlantic and eastern Pacific.

Storm surges are the most deadly hazard caused by hurricanes. On the Gulf Coast in the USA, major cities are protected by flood embankments or levées. In LEDCs such as Bangladesh and India, storm shelters, built on stilts, provide temporary refuge from storm surges (see case study: Coastal flooding in Bangladesh, page 31). Where storms are closely monitored, early warning may trigger mass evacuation of vulnerable populations away from the main storm track. Mass evacuation occurred in New Orleans in 2005 (Hurricane Katrina), Bangladesh in 2007 (Cyclone Sidr) and Houston in 2008 (Hurricane Ike).

Box 3.2 Measuring and monitoring hurricanes

Monitoring begins in the early stages of storm development in the ocean. At this stage only indirect measurements are possible, using satellites, ships and buoys moored at sea. Closer to land direct measurements are made by aircraft and radiosondes. Data are fed into computer models which forecast storm intensities and tracks.

- **Geostationary satellites:** provide information on the size, intensity and movement of storms.
- **Ships and buoys:** provide air temperature, sea surface temperature, wind speed, wind direction, pressure and humidity data.
- **Aircraft:** fly into the storms to measure wind speed, pressure, temperature and humidity.
- **Radiosondes:** small instrument packages and radio transmitters are attached to balloons and released into storms. They provide additional information on temperature, wind speed, pressure and humidity.
- **Radar:** radar images provide information on rainfall intensity.

The National Hurricane Center issues two categories of warning on approaching hurricanes:

- **Hurricane watch:** announcements are made for specific coastal areas that hurricane conditions are possible within the next 36 hours.
- **Hurricane warning:** announcements for specific coastal areas that sustained winds of 119 km h^{-1} and above are expected in the next 24 hours.

Case study Hurricane Katrina: the world's costliest natural disaster

Hurricane Katrina slammed into the Gulf Coast of Louisiana on 29 August 2005. Although by the time Katrina made landfall it had weakened slightly from a category 5 to category 4 hurricane, its effects were devastating. The storm killed 1422 people, of whom 1104 were in Louisiana. Three-hundred-and-fifty thousand people were evacuated and the damage — US$75 billion — made Katrina by far the costliest natural disaster in US history. A storm surge flooded 80% of New Orleans and was responsible for most of the deaths (Photograph 3.3).

Exposure

The Gulf of Mexico is no stranger to hurricanes. Every year three or four major storms batter this coast, leaving a wake of destruction in Florida, Alabama, Louisiana, Mississippi and Texas. Hurricane activity has been above average in the Atlantic region since 1995. Even so, the 2005 hurricane season broke all records. There were 14 hurricanes in the Atlantic region, including three — Wilma, Rita and Katrina — which were category 5. This was the first time that more than one category 5 storm had developed in the Atlantic region in a single season.

Although it is too early to be certain, there could be a link between the frequency and magnitude of hurricanes and global warming. Hurricanes get their energy from the oceans and rising sea surface temperatures (SSTs) should generate more frequent and more powerful storms. In recent years SSTs in the Gulf of Mexico have been the highest recorded, and in 2005 were 1 degree above normal.

Hurricane Katrina was the fourth most powerful hurricane to make landfall in the USA. At its peak sustained winds speeds reached 281 km h^{-1} with gusts exceeding 344 km h^{-1}. These high winds and a central pressure of just 902 mb created a storm surge of 8–9 m which breached the levées separating New Orleans from Lake Pontchartrain.

Adding to exposure are the 11–12 million people living in coastal counties along the Gulf of Mexico between Louisiana and Florida (Table 3.1). Several large metropolitan areas are also situated along the Gulf Coast where overall population densities are more than twice the US average. Moreover, there has been rapid population growth in these areas: a three-and-a-half-fold increase since 1950, and a 6.7% rise between 2000 and 2004 (Figure 3.3).

Figure 3.3 *Major metropolitan areas along the Gulf Coast*

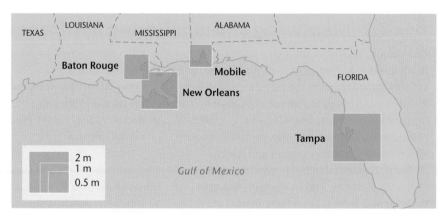

Table 3.1 *Population of coastal counties along the Gulf of Mexico, 2004*

	Population in coastal counties	% of total state population in coastal counties
Alabama	727 090	16
Florida	6 800 000	39
Louisiana	3 555 628	79
Mississippi	667 635	21

Vulnerability
Loss of wetlands

Hurricane Katrina was an exceptional natural event, but this alone does not explain its massive impact. As well as exposure, vulnerability on the Gulf Coast is high. Flooding caused by the storm surge was made worse by the loss of wetlands in the Mississippi delta. Over the years large areas of wetland and salt-marsh have become open water. In the past these wetlands acted as a buffer, absorbing water and giving protection against storm surges and flooding. The main cause of wetland losses is subsidence due to the extraction of natural gas. The levée system is also significant. While it allowed farms and industries to expand into the delta it prevented the Mississippi River from flooding, starving the delta of new sediment which would raise the level of the land surface.

Short-term mitigation

No country is better prepared to deal with hurricane hazards than the USA. Katrina's progress was closely monitored and tracked as it developed from a tropical depression to a tropical storm and finally to a category 5 hurricane (Figure 3.4). Before Katrina made landfall, the National Weather Service issued hurricane watches and warnings. Accurate predictions of the location and time of landfall were made, and evacuation of the areas most at risk was organised.

Although these measures did little to reduce the physical and economic damage caused by the storm, they probably saved thousands of lives. President Bush declared a state of emergency in Alabama and Mississippi 2 days before Katrina made landfall. The governor of Louisiana declared a state of emergency on 26 August, and the mayor of New Orleans ordered an evacuation of the city on 28 August. The city's superdome sports arena and conference centre were designated 'refuges of last resort' for the 150 000 people unable to flee the city.

Long-term mitigation

New Orleans is a city surrounded by water: Lake Pontchartrain lies to the north and the Mississippi River to the south. Adding to the flood risk is the city's site which on average is 2 m below sea level (Photograph 3.4). Without flood defences New Orleans simply could not exist. It relies on protection from a 560 km levée system, built to withstand a category 3 hurricane.

Sooner or later a major flood disaster was bound to happen. It occurred on 28 August 2005 when the levées between the city and Lake Pontchartrain failed. The levées were not designed for a hurricane of Katrina's power, but the situation was made worse by the Mississippi Gulf Outlet. This 200 m-wide canal

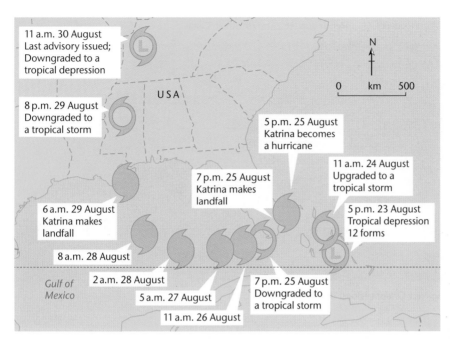

11 a.m. 30 August
Last advisory issued;
Downgraded to a
tropical depression

8 p.m. 29 August
Downgraded to
a tropical storm

USA

N

0   km   500

5 p.m. 25 August
Katrina becomes
a hurricane

11 a.m. 24 August
Upgraded to a
tropical storm

7 p.m. 25 August
Katrina makes
landfall

6 a.m. 29 August
Katrina makes
landfall

5 p.m. 23 August
Tropical depression
12 forms

8 a.m. 28 August

Gulf of
Mexico

2 a.m. 28 August

5 a.m. 27 August

7 p.m. 25 August
Downgraded to
a tropical storm

11 a.m. 26 August

Figure 3.4 *Storm track of Katrina*

acted as a funnel for the storm surge, increasing its height by 20% and doubling its speed.

Despite the known risks of flooding, the levée system had been poorly maintained and was in urgent need of strengthening. Aware of the problem, a year before the disaster the US Army Corps of Engineers asked the federal government for US$105 million to strengthen the New Orleans' flood defences. It got just US$40 million.

Following the Katrina disaster a multi-billion dollar scheme was launched to strengthen New Orleans' flood defences (Figure 3.5). The aim is to raise the levées and floodwalls around the city to a level capable of withstanding a category 5 hurricane by 2011. New water-pumping stations are being built to remove water from the city. However, some experts question whether protecting areas of the city up to 2 m below sea level is in the long term sustainable. Rising sea levels and the sinking delta may eventually mean that these areas have to be abandoned.

Photograph 3.4 *New Orleans: a city surrounded by water*

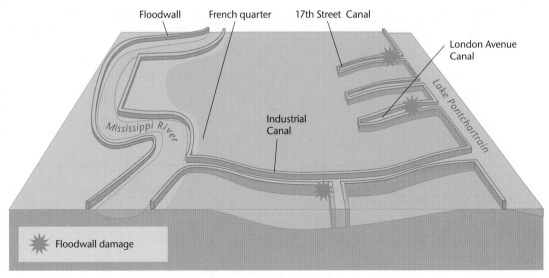

Floodwall   French quarter   17th Street Canal

London Avenue Canal

Mississippi River

Lake Pontchartrain

Industrial Canal

✳ Floodwall damage

Figure 3.5 *Strengthening New Orleans' flood defences*

Flooding and the geography of poverty

It is often said that poverty is the real killer in natural disasters and there is no doubt that Katrina hit the poor and most vulnerable hardest. One-hundred-and-fifty thousand citizens did not respond to the order to evacuate New Orleans. They were trapped by rising floodwaters either because they were too poor to own a car, or too old or physically disabled. Adding to their misery the poorer people were disproportionately concentrated in cheaper housing in the low-lying, most flood-prone areas of New Orleans. Most of them were black.

> Americans…discovered that it was mainly white folks who lived on the higher, safer ground, while poorer black families had to huddle in cheaper, low-lying housing — that race, in other words, determined who got hit. They….also learned that 35% of black households in the area do not have a car…Or that 28% of the people of New Orleans live in poverty and that 84% of those are black…Or that some people in the city were so poor, they did not have the money to catch a bus out of town — that race, in other words, determined who got left behind.

Conclusion

Hurricane Katrina shows that even the richest countries in the world are not immune from major natural disasters. This was the costliest natural disaster in history; despite advance warnings and the most sophisticated monitoring systems, more than 1400 people lost their lives. Why was this?

A combination of factors explains the disaster.

- New Orleans' site is hazardous, with the risk of flooding and storm surges exceptionally high.
- The city's flood defences were inadequate and were not built to withstand a category 5 hurricane.
- The loss of wetlands in the Mississippi delta and the construction of the Mississippi Gulf Outlet amplified the storm surge.
- Evacuation by the federal and city authorities before and planning after Katrina struck was slow, inadequately resourced and poorly organised.

However, it is hard not to conclude that, had a similar hurricane hazard hit a poor country such as Bangladesh, the death toll and the suffering would have been immeasurably greater (see Chapter 2, the impact of Cyclone Sidr, in case study: Coastal flooding in Bangladesh, page 32).

Case study **Hurricane Mitch: the deadliest Atlantic storm**

Figure 3.6 Track of Hurricane Mitch

In October 1998 Hurricane Mitch left a trail of destruction in Central America. It was the deadliest Atlantic hurricane for over 200 years. It swept through Honduras and Nicaragua killing over 10 000 people while thousands of others went missing, presumed dead. Three million people were made homeless and damage to infrastructure was estimated at US$5 billion. Hurricane Mitch was a massive setback to development for many poor countries in Central America.

Exposure

In just 2 days Mitch developed from a category 1 to a category 5 hurricane. It sustained winds of 290 km h^{-1} for over 15 hours and gusts of over 320 km h^{-1} were recorded. Slow moving, Mitch finally made landfall on the north coast of Honduras on 29 October (Figure 3.6). Then, after devastating the coastal region, it weakened and drifted westwards into the mountains. There the combined effects of orographic uplift and slow movement produced enormous amounts of rain. Between

1000–2000 mm fell in the mountains of Honduras.

The hazardous events caused by Hurricane Mitch were due to the magnitude and intensity of this deluge. Floods, debris flows, mudslides and other mass movements destroyed whole villages. Thousands of people were swept away by flood waters and buried by mudslides. In Honduras floods destroyed infrastructure and 70% of all crops. They also devastated parts of neighbouring Nicaragua, Guatemala, El Salvador and Costa Rica (Figure 3.7).

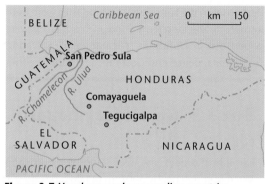

Figure 3.7 Honduras and surrounding countries

Table 3.2 *Honduras and Nicaragua: development indicators*

	Infant mortality (1000)	Life expectancy (years)	HDI	Literacy (%)	GDP per capita (US$)
Honduras	25.82	69.33	116th	80.0	2665
Nicaragua	28.1	70.63	112th	76.7	3262

Table 3.3 *Population growth (millions): Honduras and Nicaragua 1950–2006*

	1950	1960	1970	1980	1990	2000	2006	% change 1950–2006
Honduras	1.431	1.951	2.760	3.401	4.792	6.347	7.326	+512%
Nicaragua	1.097	1.492	2.052	2.805	3.683	4.932	5.570	+508%

Hurricane Mitch: an unnatural disaster?

Human activity in the mountainous interior greatly increased vulnerability, helping to turn Hurricane Mitch into a major disaster. Agricultural colonisation by subsistence farmers, commercial logging, mining and the collection of firewood by local people were responsible for deforestation, which triggered floods and mudslides. The situation was worst in Honduras. The country lost 31% of its forest cover between 1990 and 2005.

Deforestation is closely linked to population growth and poverty (Tables 3.2 and 3.3). Between 1950 and 2006 the populations of Honduras and Nicaragua increased five-fold. This growth placed extreme pressure on the environment. The outcome — a more fragile and hazardous environment, with people being forced to live in areas of high risk — increased the vulnerability of thousands of Hondurans to hurricane hazards.

Responses to the disaster

Responses to the Hurricane Mitch disaster were both immediate and long term. Food and cash crops were wiped out in Honduras, Nicaragua, El Salvador, Guatemala, Belize and Costa Rica. Flooding either washed crops away or buried them in silt. As a result, food availability was compromised, while thousands of rural dwellers were out of work and had no income. Inevitably the poorest families, with few assets and little access to credit, suffered most. An emergency disaster appeal raised US$22 million and the World Bank made US$200 million available to assist Honduras, Nicaragua, Guatemala and El Salvador. Relief operations concentrated on kick-starting local food production by providing farming communities with basic inputs such as seeds, fertilisers and hand tools.

The UN's Food and Agriculture Organization estimated that Hurricane Mitch had destroyed more than 20 years of economic progress in Central America. A long-term management strategy was needed to address the human factors such as deforestation and the cultivation of marginal land, which had contributed so much to the disaster. The UN and other agencies are working on long-term plans that include land conservation and rehabilitation, and drainage basin management. In addition, future food security will be improved by crop intensification, water control and crop diversification programmes.

Box 3.3 Secondary hazards triggered by Hurricane Mitch

Flood hazards

For almost 5 days, the near-stationary Hurricane Mitch dumped nearly 500 mm of rain a day on the uplands of Honduras and Nicaragua. In north-west Honduras, the rains turned the Ulua and Chamelecon Rivers into a vast lake, and ruined

most of the nation's banana crop.

Tarpaulin-tent refugee camps, set up on supposedly safe high ground were swept away. Meanwhile floods rose two storeys high in the capital, Tegucigalpa. The floods even swept away people who had climbed onto rooftops.

In Nicaragua the heaviest rain fell in the northern mountains. There, floodwaters cut deep ravines in hillsides and destroyed a third of the country's major cash crops. Before the rains began two-thirds of Nicaragua's children were already malnourished. Many who survived the floods died later from disease. Other survivors in the most isolated areas faced starvation.

Mass movement hazards

Torrential rain triggered several hundred mass-movement events within the cities of Tegucigalpa and Comayaguela and in the surrounding countryside (Figure 3.7). Most of these were debris flows, travelling at up to 50 km h^{-1}) and with run-out distances ranging from several metres to several hundred metres.

A major landslide occurred below the summit of Cerro El Berrinche in Tegucigalpa. It totally destroyed the shanty town (colonia) of Soto and parts of several neighbouring colonias. The slide dammed the Río Choluteca, creating a lagoon of stagnant, sewage-filled water.

Photograph 3.5
Landslide damage in Tegucigalpa after heavy rain caused by Hurricane Mitch

Tornadoes

A tornado is a violently rotating column of air extending from a thunderstorm to the ground. A distinctive funnel, made visible by the dust sucked up, and by condensation of water droplets, extends towards the ground from the cloud base. Within the funnel wind speeds may reach 500 km h^{-1} (Photograph 3.6). Tornadoes are localised and highly destructive because their energy is concentrated in a small area, often no more than 100 m wide. As a result areas of total devastation may be adjacent to areas completely unscathed.

The US mid-west, between the Rockies and the Appalachians, is popularly known as 'tornado alley' (Figure 3.8). No other

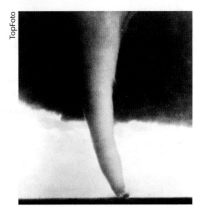

Photograph 3.6 *A tornado in Kansas*

Figure 3.8
Tornado alley

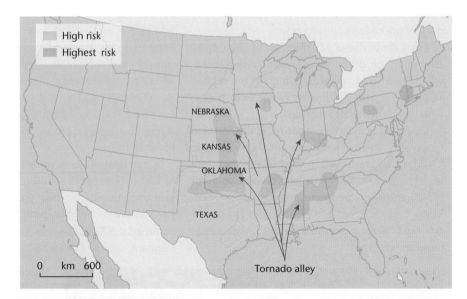

Figure 3.9 *Synoptic situation for tornado formation*

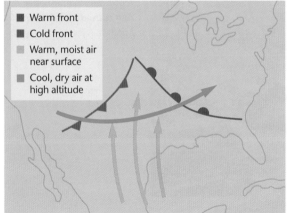

region suffers so many damaging tornadoes. There tornadoes occur most often in spring and early summer when cold dry air from the Rockies collides with warm humid air from the Gulf of Mexico (Figure 3.9). As these contrasting air masses meet, the warm humid air moves upwards generating enormous cumulonimbus clouds growing up to 18 km tall. Ascent may be assisted by uplift caused by the Rockies. Occasionally, thunderstorms group together to form supercells. The most dangerous tornadoes originate in these supercells, which also produce intense rainfall and damaging hail showers.

Box 3.4 Development of tornadoes

- Two airmasses, one cold and dry, the other warm and humid, meet.
- The boundary between the warm and cold air forms a cold front. Sharp contrasts in pressure exist on either side of this, causing the wind to veer abruptly and change direction with height.
- Cold dry air lies above the warm humid air.
- Powerful updraughts develop as warm air becomes unstable. Rapidly rising air inclines the initial spinning motion towards the vertical.
- Eventually, rapid rotation extends downwards towards the surface as a tornado.

The impact of tornadoes

In an average year, about 1000 tornadoes are reported across the USA. They cause around 80 deaths and over 1500 injuries. Damage from tornadoes is caused by violent winds and by flying debris. In the most powerful tornadoes wind speeds can reach $500\,km\,h^{-1}$. Winds of this strength can pick up cars, and rip houses to shreds. Damage paths can exceed 1.5 km wide and 80 km long.

Damage is measured on the Fujita scale (Table 3.4). Unlike hurricanes, tornadoes are assigned a damage scale after the event. This is because they develop too rapidly for monitoring to take place before they strike.

Level	Wind speed ($km\,h^{-1}$)	Degree of damage
F0	97–117	Light damage
F1	118–180	Moderate damage
F2	181–253	Considerable damage
F3	254–332	Severe damage
F4	333–418	Devastating damage
F5	419–512	Incredible damage

***Table 3.4** Fujita tornadic damage scale*

Case study — Tornado outbreak in the US mid-west

On 2 and 3 April 2006 an area of the US mid-west (Figure 3.10) straddling the Mississippi River in eastern Kansas, northwest Tennessee and Missouri was struck by powerful tornadoes.

A thunderstorm supercell spawned seven separate tornadoes. They touched down in the afternoon and early hours of the morning. The most powerful were rated 3 on the Fujita tornadic damage scale. Winds up to 300 km h^{-1} were recorded. The tornadoes left a trail of destruction throughout the region, destroying houses, flattening trees and bringing down power lines and grain silos. Some of the damage tracks were over 30 km long, and damage paths were up to 1 km in width. Much of the town of Marmaduke in Arkansas (population 1200) was destroyed. In total the tornado outbreak killed 25 people and injured 176.

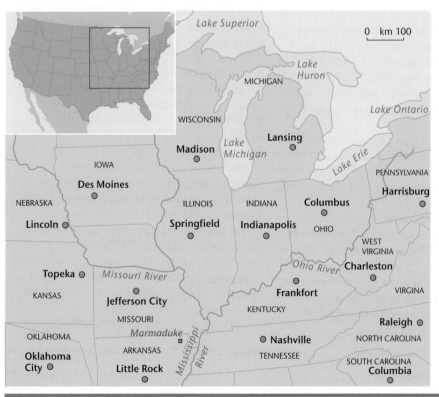

Figure 3.10
US mid-west

Tornado wreaks havoc in suburbs of Birmingham

Multi-million pound damage as roofs are ripped off and cars are wrecked

Roofs were ripped off houses, cars hurled across roads and trees uprooted after a tornado struck high street shops and suburban streets in Birmingham yesterday, injuring at least 12 people.

Rows of houses were left with gaping windows as the twister turned the sky a dull brown, tore Victorian turrets off a primary school, and littered the area with glass, bricks, furniture and everything from shoes to fruit, torn from shop displays.

Three of the victims were seriously injured by what one shopkeeper described as "bricks, slates and other debris whizzing down the road". At one stage paramedics set up an emergency field centre to cope with cuts and broken bones.

Damage is certain to run into millions of pounds, according to the city council and West Midlands fire service, which deployed emergency plans for a major incident.

The devastation centred on Ladypool Road in Sparkbrook and parts of King's Heath and Balsall Heath, where the tornado ploughed a narrow, zig-zag trail of damage across residential roads and a park.

Witnesses said the sudden onslaught at 2.30pm after torrential rain had been short-lived but terrifying, with initial attempts to run for cover blocked by falling trees or a hail of debris at every turn.

King's Heath high street was sealed off after a car park attendant's wooden hut was blown from one side to the other, splintering the front of an Iceland store.

Three men, thought to include the car park attendant, were taken to hospital, along with six children and three women, one with leg and arm cuts caused by a flying street sign.

None have life-threatening injuries but last night medical teams, police and firefighters were still searching damaged buildings for other possible victims.

Brian Cassidy, 30, a carpenter from Balsall Heath, said that the tornado had virtually "unscrewed" a roof from a house, lifting it with a twisting motion. "I could see grown men on a garage forecourt crying, holding their ears. It was like breaking matches. Ladypool Road is a write-off."

He had run to help a woman and two girls who were huddled, crying hysterically, in a house which no longer had a roof.

Kamran Ishtiaq, 22, who owns a supermarket in King's Heath, watched in horror as another woman just managed to free her baby from a buggy which was then tossed across the road.

His friend Zishan Parvez, 21, said: "The wind was so strong I had to grab hold of a lamp-post to stop myself being sucked into the air."

Graham Batty, 34, a delivery driver, just managed to dive out of his van before a tree collapsed on to the cab. He said: "I'm lucky to be alive, my instincts just took over. I'd pulled up behind another car when the sky went dark, and I looked up and could see the tree coming straight for the windscreen.

"Everything was going in slow motion. There was nowhere for me to move the van so I jumped out of my seat as the tree trunk came smashing into the windscreen."

The stricken area is less than half a mile from the scene of a storm in 1999 when high winds blew over a roadside tree on to several vehicles, killing three people. The King's Heath area was also struck by a similar tornado in 1931, when there was one fatality.

Source: Martin Wainwright, *Guardian*, 29 July 2005

***Figure 3.11** Tornado damage in the UK*

Box 3.5 Tornado warnings

Forecasting tornadoes is difficult. Many different weather patterns can lead to the formation of tornadoes. However, tornado development requires a combination of instability, moisture, lift and wind sheer.

Local communities in the USA are responsible for tornado warnings. There are two stages of alert: first a tornado watch and second a tornado warning. A tornado watch alerts people that tornado development is possible. A tornado warning occurs when a tornado is imminent, i.e. it has been sighted or indicated by radar. In Elk City, Oklahoma, a tornado warning is accompanied by a siren lasting for 3 minutes and television is interrupted to give exact details of the tornado's location and track. Following a tornado warning, people are advised to seek shelter, ideally in a storm cellar basement. If outdoors, people should lie flat in a ditch or culvert. They should never shelter in a mobile home.

Tornado disaster in West Bengal and Orissa

The impact of tornadoes is highly localised. Although they can devastate whole communities, their relatively small scale means that outside the USA and other MEDCs they get relatively little publicity. None the less, tornadoes are found worldwide.

In March 1998 an extremely powerful tornado struck 20 coastal villages near Dantan just west of Kolkata in India (Figure 3.12). Winds estimated at 500 km h^{-1} (5 on the Fujita scale) killed 160 people and injured 2000. Nine labourers died when they were lifted several metres into the air and slammed back to the ground. Thirty-five children who had taken refuge in a primary school died when the building collapsed. Fifteen thousand houses, mostly made from mud and roofed with thatch, became death traps when they collapsed on their occupants. Emergency medical teams, ambulances and the fire brigade were hampered in their rescue effort by fallen trees.

Figure 3.12 *Location of Dantan in West Bengal, India*

Even in the USA, tornadoes are notoriously difficult to predict. Perhaps unsurprisingly, in India and many other LEDCs, people are largely unprepared for tornado hazards. Rarely are there systems in place warning of tornado hazards. Tornadoes hit the Dantan area without warning; and the vulnerability of local people was increased by an absence of basement shelters, and flimsy houses that offered no protection.

Extreme weather conditions

Key ideas

➤ Anticyclones, air masses and depressions can produce extreme weather.

➤ Extreme weather can result in hazards for people.

➤ Extreme weather hazards have various social, economic and environmental impacts on the areas they affect.

Extreme weather conditions are exceptional events such as storms, droughts, heat waves, severe spells of cold weather, and heavy rainfall and snowfall. By their very nature these events occur infrequently and their scale and intensity is often hazardous to people and economic activities.

Anticyclones

Anticyclones bring settled weather conditions and occasionally extreme temperatures and rainfall. Once established, anticyclones often persist for days or even weeks, making conditions even more extreme.

Box 3.6 Anticyclones: processes and weather

Anticyclones are areas of high pressure. On average they control the weather in the British Isles on one day in four. Central pressures are typically in the range 1020 to 1050 mb. Anticyclones have a roughly circular pattern of isobars on weather charts. Pressure increases towards the centre. Light winds spiral outwards in a clockwise direction (in the northern hemisphere) (Table 3.5).

Figure 3.13 shows that, in anticyclones, air is subsiding throughout the lower atmosphere (troposphere). Subsiding air is the key to understanding anticyclones. Because air warms as it sinks towards the surface (due to adiabatic compression caused by increases in pressure), the troposphere remains cloud-free. As a result anticyclones nearly always bring dry weather. Clear skies also bring lots of sunshine, and night-time frost in winter. However, the sinking air may diverge before reaching the surface (as in Figure 3.13), creating a shallow temperature inversion. In these circumstances, stratus clouds often fill the inversion layer and create overcast conditions. In winter, radiation fog may form at night and, trapped in the inversion layer, it may persist all day.

In summary anticyclonic weather is likely to be:

■ settled, though for fast-moving anticyclones or ridges the settled weather may last only for a day or so; quiet, with light winds
■ dry, though thin stratus clouds may produce a few spots of drizzle
■ variable in sunshine amounts: depending on humidity and wind direction, anticyclones may

Table 3.5 The contrasting features of anticyclones and depressions

Feature	Anticyclone	Depression
Surface pressure	High	Low
Wind direction	Anticyclone (clockwise*)	Cyclonic (anticlockwise*)
Airflow	Diverges at surface (converges aloft)	Converges at surface (diverges aloft)
Vertical air motion	Subsides	Rises
Wind speed	Weak	Moderate to strong
Precipitation	Generally dry	Wet
Cloudiness	Stratus or no cloud	Cloudy
Stability	Stable air, with a subsidence inversion aloft	May be unstable
Temperature gradient	Little temperature contrast across the high	Strong temperature contrasts, especially at the fronts
Speed of movement	Slow moving or stagnant	Generally mobile, moving west–east

* in the northern hemisphere

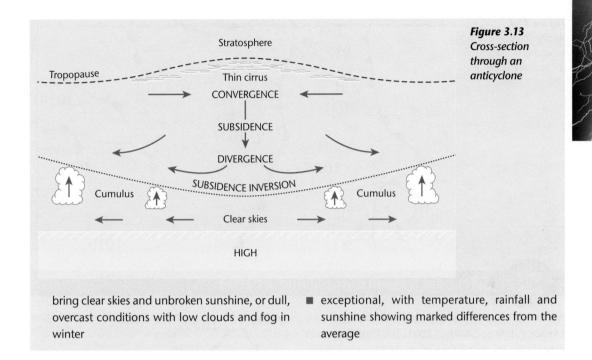

Figure 3.13
Cross-section through an anticyclone

bring clear skies and unbroken sunshine, or dull, overcast conditions with low clouds and fog in winter

■ exceptional, with temperature, rainfall and sunshine showing marked differences from the average

Anticyclonic blocking

Blocking is a common synoptic situation in western Europe. It occurs when a large, slow-moving anticyclone becomes established over the continent, disrupting the normal westerly circulation (Figure 3.14, p. 100). Blocking anticyclones force mild and humid Atlantic air further north or south of its usual track and may persist for several days or weeks. With blocking, the airflow becomes more meridional, with northerly or southerly airstreams often bringing extreme temperatures. Prolonged northerly flows introduce polar and arctic airmasses, and give below-average temperatures at all seasons. A southerly flow, on the other hand, brings tropical continental airmasses from north Africa and above-average temperatures. Summer heat waves are often caused in this way. With blocking, other aspects of weather are likely to be extreme. Droughts may develop, especially in summer, and sunshine amounts can be either unusually high or low.

Figure 3.14 shows a typical blocking situation in western Europe in winter. In this example blocking lasted for 2 weeks. During this period very little rainfall was recorded. Frontal systems and milder Atlantic air (e.g. low 'L' in Figure 3.14) were pushed north over Iceland and south into the Mediterranean. The block produced a prolonged cold spell. Maximum temperatures were just 2.2 °C at Credenhill (Herefordshire) on 22 January and 1.2 °C at Woburn (Bedfordshire) on 24 January. Nights were cold with some very sharp frosts: −8.7 °C at Redhill (Surrey) on the 25 January and −7.5 °C at Shap Fell (Cumbria) on 29 January. Freezing fog was widespread. In Staffordshire temperatures remained below freezing all day on 1 February, with a 24-hour maximum of just −2.3 °C.

Figure 3.14
Anticyclonic blocking, 27 January 2006

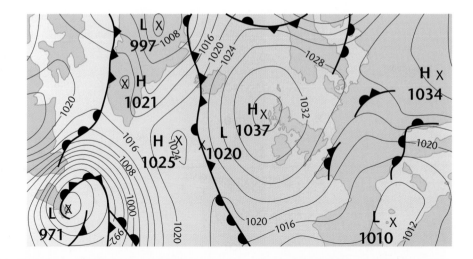

An exceptional and prolonged heat wave struck Europe in July and August 2003. The heat wave was caused by an anticyclone anchored over northern France. For 20 days it blocked Atlantic air masses and drew in hot dry air from north Africa (Figure 3.15).

Extreme heat affected southern England and the Midlands. On 10 August the highest-ever maximum temperature — 38.5 °C — was recorded in the UK. Indeed, around Greater London most stations recorded temperatures around 38 °C. At Gatwick in southeast England daily maximum temperatures exceeded 25 °C on 10 successive days between 3 and 13 August (Figure 3.16). Average temperatures also hit record levels on the continent. In France and Italy temperatures soared to 40 °C and remained unusually high for 2 weeks. In southern Spain temperatures in excess of 40°C were recorded in most cities, and peaked at 46.2 °C in Cordoba and 45.2 °C in Seville.

Impact

Western Europe was unprepared for the 2003 heat wave. In the past, heat waves have never been considered significant natural hazards in Europe. The 2003 heat wave changed all that. While central heating is almost universal in western European homes, few homes have air conditioning. Extreme heat, especially in large urban areas, created a major health crisis. At the same time the combination of

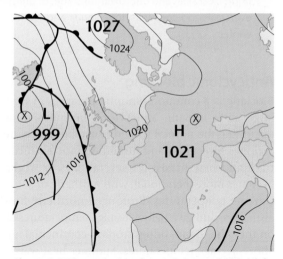

Figure 3.15 *Synoptic situation on 9 August 2003. High pressure covers the whole of western Europe and winds are light everywhere*

excessive heat and drought had severe effects on economic activities, especially agriculture.

Thirty-five thousand deaths, most of them elderly, were attributed to the 2003 heat wave. Worst hit was France with 15000 deaths. The big heat also claimed 7000 lives in Germany, 2000 in the UK and 1400 in the Netherlands. Mortality was highest in large urban areas where heat-absorbent surfaces and sparse vegetation cover amplify temperatures, especially at night (Box 3.7). In France, the highest mortality rates

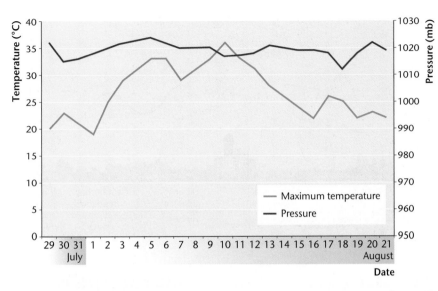

Figure 3.16
Maximum daily temperatures and average daily pressure at Gatwick, 29 July–21 August 2003

were in the major cities. Around one-third of the excessively high French death toll was in the Paris region, and 80% of the victims were aged 75 and over.

The heat wave, accompanied in many parts of Europe by prolonged drought, seriously reduced crop yields. Wheat was badly affected, yields being down by 20% in France, 13% in Italy and 12% in the UK. In eastern Europe the effects were more severe: the Ukraine had a 75% reduction in its wheat harvest, and in Moldova the decline was 80%. Low river levels meant that shipping was suspended on the Elbe and Danube and melting glaciers caused avalanches and flash floods in Switzerland. Portugal experienced massive wildfires which destroyed 10% of the forest area and killed 18 people.

Box 3.7 Killer heat waves and cities

Heat waves mainly affect the elderly, the young and the chronically ill and urban dwellers.

- Normal body temperature is 37 °C.
- When ambient temperatures rise, the human body maintains its ideal temperature by perspiring and varying blood circulation.
- When the internal body temperature rises above 40 °C, internal organs are at risk: if the body temperature is not reduced, death follows.
- High humidity (a feature of western Europe's climate) makes extreme heat even more dangerous. With little or no evaporation to cool the body, perspiration becomes ineffective.
- Urban dwellers are most at risk during heat waves. Urban surfaces with low albedos absorb the heat and create a 'heat island' (Figure 3.17). This is particularly evident at night when heat stored by the urban fabric during the day is released.
- Urban areas also produce heat through domestic heating, factories and vehicles.
- The lack of cooling vegetation in urban areas adds to the high temperatures.
- On some days in summer the difference in temperature between a large city such as London and the surrounding countryside can be as much as 10 degrees.
- Lack of moisture in cities also reduces evaporation and cooling, and gives more energy to heat the atmosphere.
- Apart from heat, people's bodies may be stressed by a pollution 'dome' which settles over cities during anticyclonic weather.

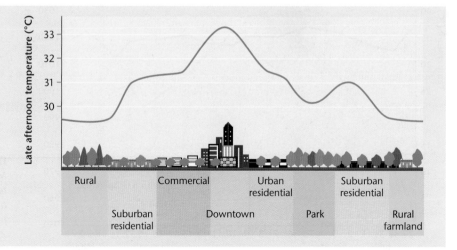

Figure 3.17 Sketch of an urban heat-island profile

Airmasses, heavy snowfalls and cold spells

Heavy snowfalls in the British Isles usually occur during spells of unusually cold weather. Three synoptic situations are most likely to bring snow:

➤ Unstable arctic maritime air moving across the country on a southerly track.

➤ Unstable polar continental air invading the country on a westerly track from the continent.

➤ An Atlantic depression with active fronts moving slowly from west to east following a prolonged spell of cold weather.

Table 3.6 Arctic maritime and polar maritime airmasses in winter

Airmass	Stability	Direction of approach	Winter weather
Arctic maritime	Unstable	Northerly airstream	Arctic maritime air is extremely cold in its source region. As it tracks south across the Norwegian Sea it is warmed and becomes unstable. Wintry showers develop over the sea and over the land in northern Britain. Showers are most frequent on north-facing coasts and on high ground but tend to die out inland. Very low night-time temperatures feature in areas where there is a snow cover (−5 to −10 °C). Low temperatures may result in significant snow accumulations. Arctic maritime air brings the most severe winter weather.
Polar continental	Unstable	Easterly airstream	Polar continental air is very cold in its source region but is warmed as it moves west across the North Sea. (Between January and March sea surface temperatures range from 6 to 9 °C). Warming results in instability and the development of deep cumuliform clouds over the sea. Wintry showers of snow and sleet occur along the North Sea coast and in eastern Britain. Due to low day-time temperatures (0 to 3 °C maximum) significant accumulations of snow may occur. Instability dies out as the airstream moves to the west. Clear skies often give cold but sunny conditions.

Box 3.8 Cold airmasses

Airmasses are large bodies of air covering thousands of square kilometres, with uniform temperature, humidity and lapse rates. Five main airmasses affect the weather and climate of the British Isles: they are shown in Figure 3.18. Some airmasses bring extreme weather conditions. When tropical continental air (Tc) from north Africa invades northern Europe it often results in summer heat waves. Extreme cold and significant snowfalls are associated with arctic maritime (Am) and polar continental (Pc) air.

Cold airmasses develop in source regions of permanent or semi-permanent high pressure. Am air has its source region well inside the Arctic Circle around Svalbad (80°N). There, cold dense air forms a permanent anticyclone with temperatures down to −40 °C in winter. Pc air originates in Siberia, where an intense anticyclone develops in winter, causing temperatures to plunge to −50 °C.

Once an arctic or polar airmass leaves its source region it undergoes changes of temperature and humidity. To reach the British Isles, both arctic and polar air has to cross expanses of sea and ocean. This maritime track modifies the airmasses in two ways:

■ evaporation from the sea surface increases their humidity
■ in winter when the oceans and seas are much warmer than the land, the airmasses are heated from below

Heating through contact with the sea surface makes the airmass unstable, causing it to rise freely through the atmosphere. This process results in the formation of deep convective clouds and wintry showers.

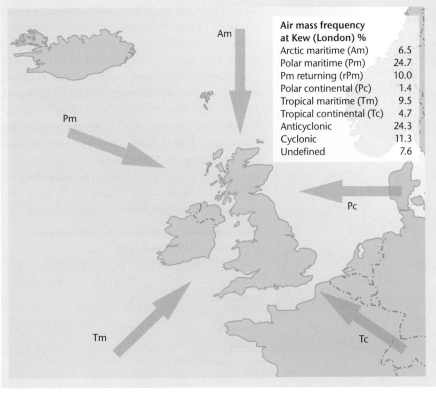

Air mass frequency at Kew (London) %	
Arctic maritime (Am)	6.5
Polar maritime (Pm)	24.7
Pm returning (rPm)	10.0
Polar continental (Pc)	1.4
Tropical maritime (Tm)	9.5
Tropical continental (Tc)	4.7
Anticyclonic	24.3
Cyclonic	11.3
Undefined	7.6

Figure 3.18 Air masses affecting weather and climate in the British Isles

A prolonged cold spell and record snowfalls brought chaos to northern Scotland between 27 February and 7 March 2006 (Table 3.7). Low pressure over Scandinavia fed arctic maritime air southwards across Britain (Figure 3.19). Warmed through contact with the sea, this unstable airmass swept south and brought showers of sleet and snow to northern Scotland. Several polar 'lows' formed in the airstream giving heavy snowfalls in northeast Scotland on 2 and 3 March. Heavy snow was also recorded in the coastal areas of eastern England and across Norfolk. Inland the snow showers died away as the airmass cooled in contact with the cold ground surface. Thus most of central and southern England was dry with clear skies, long sunny spells and night frost.

Table 3.7 *Deepest snow cover recorded between 27 February and 7 March 2006*

Station	Date	Snow depth (cm)
Glenlivet, Banffshire	03.03.06	29
Aberdeen	03.03.06	26
Wick (Caithness)	06.03.06	25
Kirkwall (Orkney)	06.03.06	16
Aviemore	03.03.06	13

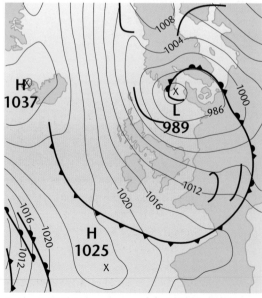

Figure 3.19 *Weather chart, 1 March 2006*

However, on the snowfields of Scotland, clear night skies produced some extremely low temperatures (Table 3.8).

Impact of severe winter weather in northern Scotland

Scotland bore the brunt of the prolonged cold spell in late February and early March 2006. Four successive days of blizzards caused severe disruption to transport and brought much of northern Scotland to a standstill. Roads were affected by deep drifts. In Shetland there were drifts up to 2 m deep. By Friday 3 March falling snow was outpacing efforts to clear it as the snow reached record depths at Aberdeen. Hundreds of motorists were stranded and their vehicles abandoned on the A96 between Inverness and Aberdeen. Snow closed the A98 between Fraserburgh and Banff, and the A981 from Stichen to Memsie on 6 March and caused hundreds of minor accidents. Central Aberdeen and Inverness were gridlocked on 3 March. Disruption to road transport meant that domestic refuse collection had to be suspended in Aberdeen; shops and banks closed early. The snow also affected rail and air transport. Several trains became stuck in deep drifts on the Aberdeen to Dundee line. Inverness airport was closed and flights from Aberdeen airport were severely disrupted. Throughout northern Scotland hundreds of schools closed. Worst hit were Shetland, where all schools were closed for 4 days, and Aberdeenshire, where over 300 schools closed.

Table 3.8 *Lowest temperatures recorded between 27 February and 7 March 2006*

Station	Date	Minimum temperature °C
Altnaharra (Sutherland)	02.03.06	−16.4
Kinbrace (Sutherland)	02.03.06	−14.7
Loch Glascarnoch (W. Ross)	02.03.06	−14.1
Braemar (Aberdeenshire)	02.03.06	−12.7

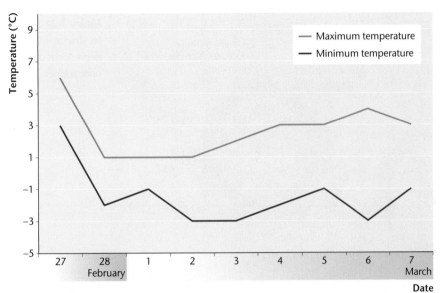

Figure 3.20 *Maximum and minimum temperatures, Aberdeen, 27 February–7 March 2006*

Although most Scottish football fixtures were postponed, the snow was welcomed by the Scottish skiing industry. Conditions were the best for 10 years with record numbers of skiers to the slopes at Cairn Gorm, Nevis, Lecht and Glenshee during the weekend 4–5 March.

Depressions

Depressions are large, travelling low-pressure systems found in middle and high latitudes. They are part of the atmosphere's general circulation, transferring warm airmasses from the tropics towards the polar regions. Depressions bring stormy, wet and changeable conditions, and dominate the weather in middle and high latitudes.

Box 3.9 How depressions form

Depressions are areas of low pressure, up to 3000 km in diameter, which develop on the polar front jet stream. On weather charts they are identified by a roughly circular pattern of isobars and frontal systems. A simplified sequence of events leading to their formation in the northern hemisphere is as follows.

■ Downwind of a trough the jet stream accelerates. This is due to the anticlockwise curvature of the jet stream, which complements the anticlockwise rotation of the Earth (Figure 3.21).

■ Acceleration leads to upper level divergence.

■ At the surface, air converges to compensate for the upper level divergence.

■ As the surface air converges it (a) sucks in warmer tropical air from the south (b) rises vertically through the lower atmosphere (troposphere).

■ Because divergence aloft is greater than convergence at the surface, an area of low pressure (depression) develops.

■ Surface depressions migrate across the Atlantic, steered by the polar front jet stream.

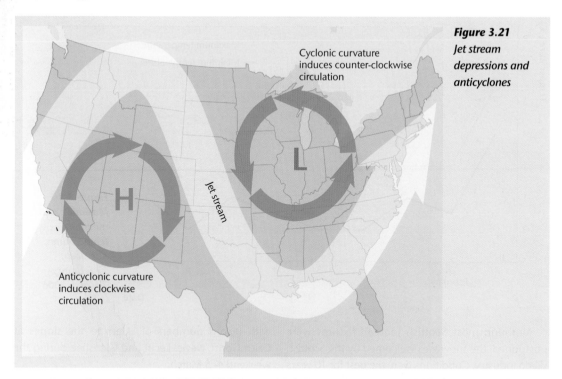

Figure 3.21
Jet stream
depressions and
anticyclones

Cyclonic curvature
induces counter-clockwise
circulation

Anticyclonic curvature
induces clockwise
circulation

Frontal systems

Depressions form as **waves** along the polar front where cold and warm air meet. As the wave develops, the warm air is squeezed into a narrow wedge known as the **warm sector** (Figure 3.22). Because airmasses don't mix easily, sharp boundaries known as **fronts** separate the cold and warm airmasses. The boundary forming the leading edge of the warm sector is the **warm front**. There cold air is replaced by warm. The trailing edge of the warm sector is the **cold front** where warm air is replaced by cold air. Higher wind speeds behind the cold front cause it to move faster than the warm front. As it advances it narrows the warm sector and eventually lifts it off the ground creating an **occlusion**.

The life cycle of a typical depression takes around 4 or 5 days. Starting as a wave on the polar front, as pressure falls the wave becomes more pronounced, until a clearly defined warm sector develops. Thereafter the depression quickly occludes and fills, and disappears from weather charts.

The divergence of air in the jet stream results in a compensating convergence at the surface. As a result air in depressions rises throughout the troposphere. This rising air explains a great deal

Figure 3.22
A typical depression

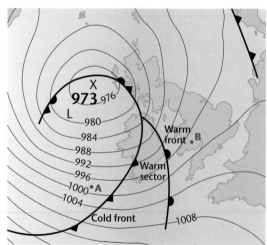

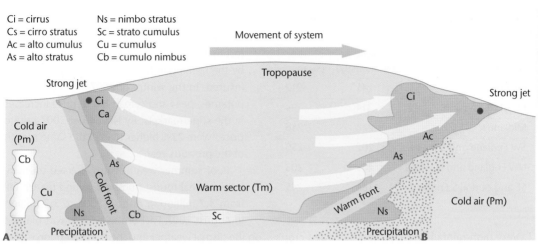

Ci = cirrus   Ns = nimbo stratus
Cs = cirro stratus   Sc = strato cumulus
Ac = alto cumulus   Cu = cumulus
As = alto stratus   Cb = cumulo nimbus

Movement of system

Tropopause

Strong jet

Ci
Ca

Cold air
(Pm)

Cb

Cu

As

Cold front

Ns   Cb

Warm sector (Tm)

Sc

Ci

Ac

As

Warm front

Ns

Cold air (Pm)

Strong jet

Precipitation

Precipitation

A   B

Figure 3.23 *Section through a depression (A to B in Figure 3.22)*

about the weather. As it rises the air cools, condenses, and forms clouds and precipitation. At the warm front, less dense tropical air rises as it slides above colder polar air. At the same time the jet stream acts like a conveyor, drawing the warmer air aloft (Figure 3.24).

At the cold front warm air is being undercut by the advancing polar air. This, together with the jet stream, results in a rapid rise of air and extensive cloud development. Unstable conditions at the cold front often lead to thunder and intense downpours.

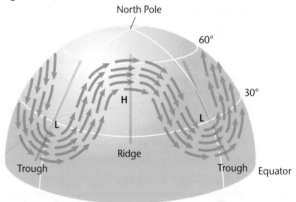

North Pole

60°

30°

H

L

L

Ridge

Trough

Trough   Equator

Figure 3.24 *The polar front jet stream forms a series of waves in the upper troposphere*

Case study   **Record rainfall in the UK: summer 2007**

In June and July 2007, the UK's weather was dominated by a continuous succession of Atlantic depressions. The cause was the persistent location of the jet stream across central Britain, well to the south of its normal position in summer. The jet stream, a fast-moving ribbon of air 7–8 km above the ground, controls the formation and movement of depressions. Normally high pressure from the Azores spreads northward across the UK in the summer, giving fairly settled weather conditions. This failed to happen in 2007.

As a result the summer of 2007 in the UK was the wettest since records began in 1766. With the exception of northern Scotland, all regions had above-average rainfall. In June, rainfall totals in some regions (notably Yorkshire) were three times the monthly average; and in Worcestershire in July, rainfall was four times the monthly average! (Table 3.9).

The economic impact of extreme rainfall

We saw in Chapter 1 how the extreme rainfall event of summer 2007 caused serious flooding in the Midlands, southern England and Yorkshire. This same event also had a major impact on two other economic activities: farming and tourism.

Table 3.9 *Rainfall in selected regions (% anomaly), June and July 2007*

	June (% anomaly)	July (% anomaly)
England	241	212
E and NE England	314	194
Midlands	278	256
SW England and S Wales	202	230
NW England and N Wales	209	203
SE and central S England	186	245

Source: Met Office

Very high rainfall and flooding damaged crops and disrupted farming in many parts of the UK. Heavy rains alone meant that harvesting vining peas was impossible in areas such as North Yorkshire and the East Riding. There, up to 60% of the crop was destroyed. Waterlogged soils led to potato blight and made harvesting impossible. Much of the potato crop simply rotted in the ground.

Flooding caused even bigger problems, affecting 42 000 ha of farmland. Thirty-seven per cent of the flooded area was grassland with arable and fodder crops occupying most of the remainder. Flooded grasslands reduced the silage crop for winter live-stock feed, with wheat being the most badly affected arable crop. The cost of lost production (estimated at £11–24 million) was mainly borne by the farming industry as most crops were not insured. In the winter of 2007–08 shortages of potatoes, peas and cereals led to price increases in the supermarkets. By November 2007 potato prices were 22% higher than in the same month of the previous year.

Poor summer weather also affected tourism. International tourist numbers visiting the UK fell from 3.7 million in August 2006 to 3.2 million in August 2007. Part of this decline was blamed on the dismal weather and the misperception earlier in the summer that much of England was under-water. However, some regions were badly hit. In Gloucestershire and Worcestershire, flooding closed large tracts of the countryside, seriously reducing the number of tourists and damaging the local economy. Tewkesbury Abbey had barely one-quarter of its expected visitation, and both the cricket ground and racecourse at Worcester were closed for several weeks. Many British families booked 'last-minute' holidays to southern Europe to escape the rains and inevitably tourism in traditional British seaside resorts like Skegness and Scarborough suffered.

Global warming and climate change

Key ideas

> Human activities may impact on the global climate to create particular climate hazards.
> The causes of global warming and global dimming are related to human activities.
> Acid rain has adverse environmental impacts.

Global warming

There is conclusive evidence that the Earth's climate has warmed in the past 150 years. Moreover, warming seems to have accelerated since the 1960s (Figure 3.25). Globally, nine of the ten warmest years in the period 1880 to 2005 occurred

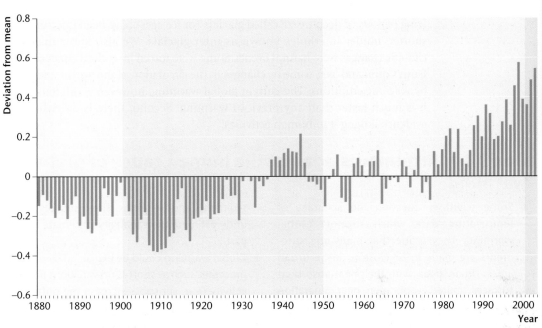

Figure 3.25 *Global temperatures 1880–2005: deviations from the mean*

between 1995 and 2005, and four of the five warmest were 2002, 2003, 2004 and 2005. In the UK temperature records were consistently broken between 2003 and 2006. The highest-ever temperature in the UK (38.5 °C) occurred in August 2003; the highest July temperature (36.1 °C) was recorded in 2006; the summer of 2006 was the third warmest on record; and September 2006 was, by a whopping 3.5 degrees, the warmest ever (Figure 3.26).

Although most scientists now accept the reality of global warming, one key question remains. Is global warming a natural trend or is it due to human activities? We know that the world's climate has fluctuated enormously in the past.

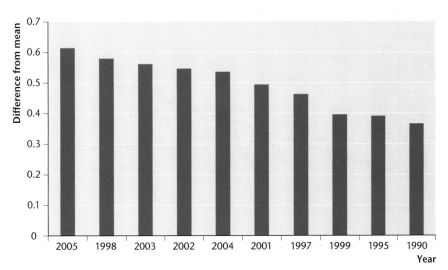

Figure 3.26
Average global temperatures, the ten warmest years, 1880–2005

Long periods of deep freeze called **glacials** (or ice ages) have been interrupted by shorter, milder interludes known as **inter-glacials**. We also know that these climatic changes were natural events. Some were forced by cyclical changes in the Earth's orbit and axis, some by changes in the circulation of the oceans and others by volcanic eruptions. The current global warming, however, is different. First, it is much faster than any previous warming. Second, there is overwhelming evidence linking it to human activities.

Box 3.10 Arguments against the human cause of global warming

■ Some scientists question the accuracy of temperature data which support global warming. They argue that many measurements are made in or close to large urban areas. Urban areas, with their heat-absorbent surfaces, limited evaporation, heat generation and air pollution, are known to be warmer than surrounding rural areas.

■ Climate records for earlier times depend on information derived from ice cores, sea sediments and tree rings. These sources often underestimate the variability of climate in the past.

■ Global warming could be explained by natural processes such as short-term variations in solar activity (e.g. sunspots increase the output of solar energy) and the changing frequency of volcanic eruptions (volcanic eruptions pump sulphur dioxide and ash into the atmosphere, which have a cooling effect).

The natural greenhouse effect

There is a strong correlation between the rise in average global temperatures during the past 60 years and the volume of carbon dioxide in the atmosphere (Figures 3.27 and 3.28). Before 1800 and the beginning of **industrialisation**, average carbon dioxide concentrations were around 270 ppm. Today's carbon dioxide concentrations are 387 ppm (2008) and rising rapidly.

*Figure 3.27
Mean global
temperatures,
1950–2004*

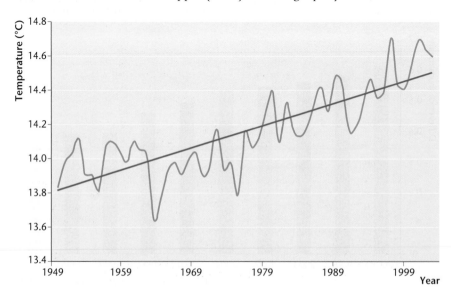

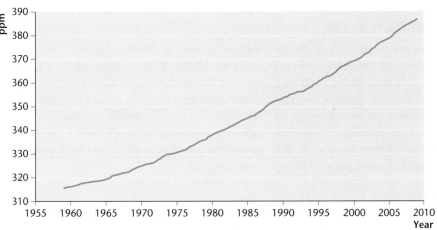

Figure 3.28
Average carbon dioxide concentrations at Mauna Loa, Hawaii, 1959–2008

The so-called greenhouse effect explains the link between global temperatures and carbon dioxide levels. **Greenhouse gases** (GHGs) such as water vapour, carbon dioxide and methane occur naturally in the atmosphere (Figure 3.29). They absorb and re-radiate around 95% of long-wave radiation emitted by the Earth. In this way they are like a giant blanket keeping the Earth warm. Carbon dioxide alone raises average global temperatures by 7 degrees. Without the greenhouse effect most of the planet would be uninhabitable.

However, any significant increase in carbon dioxide and other GHGs means more absorption of long-wave radiation by the atmosphere, causing the planet to warm. This is precisely what has happened in the past 200 years. Industrialisation and **economic development** have been powered by the energy of **fossil fuels** and, at the same time, have been accompanied by massive deforestation and the draining of wetlands. These processes, which have released huge volumes of GHGs into the atmosphere, are thought to be responsible for global warming due to an enhanced greenhouse effect.

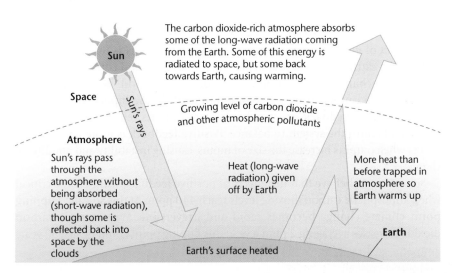

Figure 3.29 The greenhouse effect

Box 3.11 Carbon cycle

Carbon dioxide is part of the carbon cycle (Figure 3.30). Carbon is transferred between stores (or sinks) such as rock strata (e.g. limestone, coal), soil, peat, sea-floor sediments, ocean waters and the atmosphere. Human activities such as burning fossil fuels and deforestation release 6.7 billion tonnes of carbon dioxide to the atmosphere every year. Forty-two per cent of this carbon dioxide is absorbed within the carbon cycle by plants in photosynthesis and by the oceans. The remaining 58%, however, remains in the atmosphere, where it has a residence time of nearly a century. Hence the steady rise in atmospheric carbon dioxide, which creates an enhanced greenhouse effect and leads to global warming.

Figure 3.30
The carbon cycle

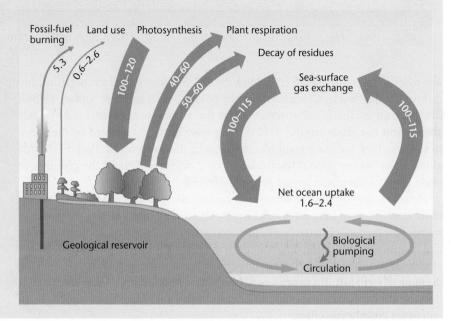

Climate change and positive and negative feedback

The impact of global warming on environmental systems is uncertain. This is because the earth–atmosphere system is highly complex and contains numerous feedback mechanisms that at best are poorly understood. **Feedback** is what happens when outputs from a system return to affect the inputs. There are two types. **Negative feedback** occurs when system outputs reduce the strength of inputs and return the system to balance. **Positive feedback** is more damaging. It occurs when outputs increase the size of inputs, causing instability and amplifying change.

Some experts believe that the effects of positive feedback will become critical when atmospheric carbon dioxide levels reach 440 ppm. At this so-called **tipping point** climate change becomes rapid and irreversible. With current carbon dioxide increases averaging 2 ppm a year, this tipping point could be just 30 years away.

Negative feedback effects

Negative feedback effects are as follows:

➤ Global warming increases evaporation, which in turn increases cloud cover. More cloud cover lowers temperatures, which return temperatures to normal.

➤ Increased burning of fossil fuels releases tiny airborne particles in the atmosphere. Absorption and reflection of solar radiation by these particles reduces the amount of sunlight and should lower temperatures. This process is called **global dimming** (see page 120).

Positive feedback effects

Positive feedback effects are as follows:

➤ A rise in global temperatures causes photosynthesis to slow down and reduces the capacity of the oceans to absorb carbon dioxide. The means more carbon dioxide in the atmosphere, more global warming, further reductions in photosynthesis and so on.

➤ Global warming is fastest in polar regions. Snow and ice normally reflect 90% of incident solar radiation. As the ice melts, however, there is less reflection and more absorption by land and ocean surfaces (the ocean reflects only 4% of insolation). Rising temperatures then lead to even more rapid melting.

➤ Higher temperatures cause more evaporation and increase the amount of water vapour in the atmosphere. Water vapour is an extremely effective greenhouse gas so any increase causes a further rise in temperature. However, an increase in water vapour is double-edged: more water vapour produces more clouds and more reflection, which should in theory reduce temperatures (negative feedback).

➤ 450 billion tonnes of GHGs are stored in the permafrost of Siberia and northern Canada. Rising temperatures could melt the permafrost, releasing huge quantities of methane, a greenhouse gas 60 times more effective than carbon dioxide.

➤ Vegetation grows faster in a warmer world, soaking up more carbon dioxide. Continued warming eventually reduces the ability of plants to absorb carbon dioxide, changing negative feedback into a positive feedback.

➤ Recent research suggests that in a warmer world, soils will dry out, releasing their stocks of carbon and driving up temperatures. Higher temperatures lead to further increases in carbon emissions. Up to 170 billion tonnes of carbon could be released from the land between 2050 and 2100.

➤ Huge amounts of methane are stored as methane hydrates on the ocean floor. Rising temperatures could trigger the release of this methane, creating runaway global warming with disastrous consequences.

The impact of global warming

Climate change

Climate change is the most direct effect of global warming. Powerful computer models give us some idea of the changes expected in the next 100 years (Figures 3.31(a) and 3.31(b)). Major disruption to regional rainfall is forecast: changes that

Figure 3.31(a)
Forecast changes in global rainfall June–August with a doubling of carbon dioxide

Wetter

Drier

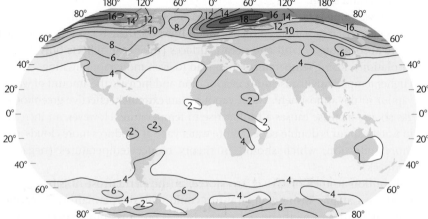

Figure 3.31(b)
Forecast increases in global temperatures in December–February with a doubling of atmospheric carbon dioxide

will affect millions of people. Some regions will get wetter, but large parts of North America, South America, southern Europe, Africa, the Middle East and central Asia will experience lower rainfall and more frequent droughts (Figure 3.31(a)).

Drought in Portugal and Spain in 2004 and 2005 has been linked to global warming. The hot dry summer of 2005 followed an exceptionally dry winter. In Portugal, 97% of the country was hit by extreme drought — the most severe since 1940. Wildfires burned out of control and destroyed an estimated 2400 km² of forest and farmland.

Research by the Intergovernmental Panel on Climate Change (IPCC) suggests an average rise in global temperatures of around 3 degrees is most likely by the end of the century. However, continued intensive use of fossil fuels could see global temperatures rising by as much as 5 degrees. Levels of warming will increase from the equator to the poles. Temperatures in the Arctic and sub-Arctic in winter could increase by 10–18 degrees. Such increases would have massive knock-on effects on the melting of ice sheets and glaciers, sea levels, and arctic ecosystems.

In mid-latitudes higher temperatures will speed up the atmospheric circulation. Severe storms will become more frequent, increasing rates of coastal erosion

and coastal flooding in low-lying coastal areas. Meanwhile, warmer conditions will intensify the water cycle. This will mean more evaporation, more intense rainstorms and more river flooding. In the tropics and sub-tropics, warmer ocean waters will generate more powerful hurricanes and tropical storms. Already there has been a significant increase in the number of category 4 and 5 hurricanes (the most severe storms) in the past 30 years. In the USA and the Caribbean, 2005 was the worst hurricane season on record. It included Hurricane Katrina, the costliest natural disaster in US history (see page 87).

Water resources and farming

Sixteen per cent of the world's population and one-quarter of global economic output could be hit by water shortages caused by climate change. With 98% of the world's glaciers currently retreating, areas that rely on meltwater are uniquely vulnerable (Figure 3.32). Both rich and poor regions are at risk: from California, dependent on melting snow in the Sierra Nevada, to Peru and Ecuador which rely on glacier meltwater from the high Andes.

Computer forecasts for the 2080s suggest that global warming will reduce summer rainfall by up to 40% in southern Britain. Water resources would be further reduced by a possible 3-degree temperature rise, which would increase evaporation and reduce runoff in southeast England to half current levels. This is particularly worrying for a region which is the driest and most densely populated in the UK, and where water resources are already stretched to the limit.

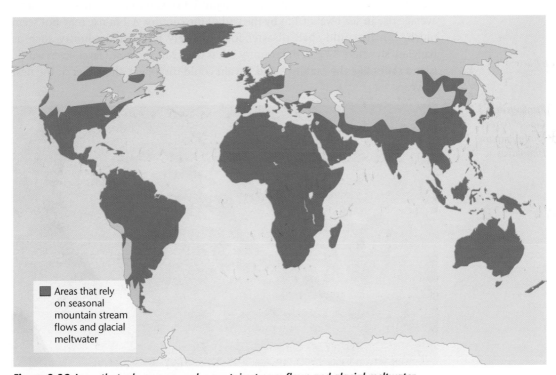

Areas that rely on seasonal mountain stream flows and glacial meltwater

Figure 3.32 Areas that rely on seasonal mountain stream flows and glacial meltwater

Drylands such as southern Europe and north Africa are already marginal for farming. There, any significant decrease in rainfall could lead to desertification. Farming, without irrigation, would become unsustainable. Other regions likely to be affected by drier conditions include the Prairies in the USA and Canada, and the Pampas in Argentina. Today, both are prime agricultural areas. But as drier conditions take hold, cereal production will slump. Some experts believe that production could drop by as much as 400 million tonnes y^{-1}, leading to global food shortages.

Shrinking glaciers and rising sea level

Ninety-eight per cent of the world's glaciers are retreating (Photograph 3.7). The fastest retreat is in the Himalaya, the Arctic, the Alps, the Rockies and the Andes. For example, since 1976 the Huascarin glacier in the Andes has lost 40% of its ice mass, while the O'Higgins glacier in Chile has shrunk by 15 km in the past 100 years. One-fifth of Antarctica's sea ice melted between 1950 and 2000. In 2002 the Larsen B ice shelf in Antarctica provided a dramatic illustration of the rate of change: over 200 m thick and covering 3250 km², it broke up in less than a month. Sea ice in the Arctic in September 2005 was the lowest ever recorded. Indeed, should present trends continue, the Arctic Ocean will be ice-free in summer by the end of the century.

Melting glaciers and ice sheets, together with the expansion of the oceans as their surface waters heat up, are responsible for rising sea levels. Sea level rose by nearly 20 cm between 1900 and 2000 (Figure 3.33). Computer models forecast an average rise in sea level of 1 m by the end of the century. A 1 m rise may not seem much, but it would spell disaster for a densely populated country such as Bangladesh where 37% of the country is less than 3 m above sea level. Even worse, island states like the Maldives and Tuvalu could disappear altogether in the next 50 years.

Photograph 3.7
Glacier retreat:
Khumbu in the
Himalayas

TopFoto

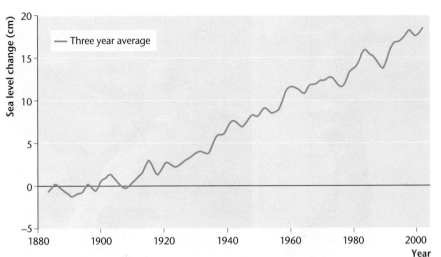

Figure 3.33 Recent sea level rise

In the UK rising sea level will lead to more coastal flooding. A modest 70 cm rise will increase the flood risk in eastern England seventeen times, and if London's sea defences were breached it could cause damage up to £25 billion. Sea level rise and stormier conditions also threaten the UK's coastal defences. In future the costs of maintaining sea walls and other coastal defence structures will be unsustainable. Along some stretches of coast, hard defences will be abandoned and nature left to take its course. Elsewhere defences will be deliberately breached or dismantled as part of a policy of **managed realignment**. Either way, large tracts of reclaimed farmland along the coast will revert to saltmarsh and mudflat.

Ecological effects of climate change

Global warming appears to be altering the timing of the seasons. Compared to the early 1970s spring in the UK now arrives 6 days earlier, and 2 weeks earlier in Spain. Meanwhile autumn has been delayed by an average of 3 days in the past 30 years.

Many plants and animals will be unable to adapt to rapid climate change. In northern Britain, arctic-alpine species, which have survived in 'island' mountain habitats since the last ice age, will disappear. However, a warmer climate will provide opportunities for new species to colonise Britain from the Continent (Photograph 3.8). Changes are already taking place. Some British songbirds which previously spent winter in southern Europe and north Africa (e.g. chiffchaffs, blackcaps) now overwinter in southern England. In the seas around the British Isles warm water species such as swordfish, tuna and sunfish are becoming more common. At the same time, cold water species such as cod and haddock are moving further north.

Biodiversity will decline as a result of global warming. More than half the world's forests, which support hundreds of thousands of species, will be lost if global temperatures rise by more than 3 degrees. If this isn't bad enough, deforestation is likely to accelerate global warming as trees and other plants become net producers of carbon dioxide at higher temperatures.

Photograph 3.8
Hoopoe and bee-eater: two species that could colonise Britain from the Continent due to a warmer climate

In the tropics rising sea temperatures are already causing the death of coral — a phenomenon known as bleaching (Photograph 3.9). Bleaching greatly reduces coral reef biodiversity as well as the economic value of reefs for fishing and tourism.

Photograph 3.9
Bleached coral, Fiji

Ocean currents

Ocean currents move surplus heat from the tropics to high latitudes and help to maintain the global energy balance. However, there is concern that global warming could disrupt the **thermohaline** circulation of the oceans. If this were to happen, the climate of northwest Europe could plunge into deep freeze, with winters as severe as those in eastern Canada today.

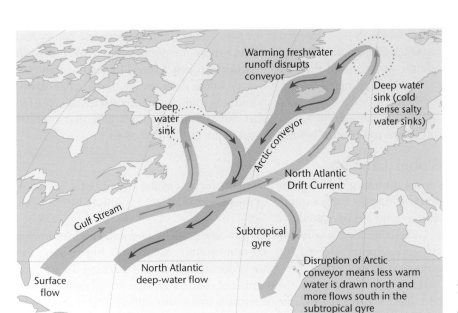

Warming freshwater
runoff disrupts
conveyor

Deep water
sink (cold
dense salty
water sinks)

Deep
water
sink

Arctic conveyor

North Atlantic
Drift Current

Gulf Stream

Subtropical
gyre

Surface
flow

North Atlantic
deep-water flow

Disruption of Arctic
conveyor means less warm
water is drawn north and
more flows south in the
subtropical gyre

Figure 3.34
Thermohaline
circulation in the
North Atlantic

For its latitude, northwest Europe has a singularly mild climate. This is due to the North Atlantic Drift. It transfers warm water from the Gulf of Mexico north-eastwards across the Atlantic Ocean towards Iceland, Norway and the British Isles. The North Atlantic Drift is a natural conveyor, delivering huge amounts of heat energy (equal to one million power stations) to northwest Europe. It keeps the coast of northwest Europe ice-free throughout the winter and maintains winter temperatures 10–15 degrees higher than average for the latitude.

The ocean circulation in the North Atlantic is driven by the **downwelling** of dense, saline water off the coast of Iceland and Greenland (Figure 3.34). As the warm surface waters drift northeast across the Atlantic they cool and become denser. Evaporation also increases water density by raising salinity levels. Eventually, this dense water sinks to the deep ocean floor and returns south as a deep-water current. Thus downwelling acts like a giant pump, powering the entire thermohaline circulation in the North Atlantic.

However, we know that the volume of water carried by the conveyor has dropped by 30% in the past two or three decades. This suggests that downwelling is getting weaker. Why? There are two reasons. The first is the rapid melting of the Greenland ice sheet, releasing huge volumes of fresh water into the North Atlantic. The second is the increased discharge of Siberian rivers such as the Yenisey, Lena and Ob, swollen by melting permafrost and higher rainfall.

This input of fresh water dilutes the surface ocean waters, reducing their salinity and density and weakening the pumping action of downwelling. Eventually a tipping point will be reached and the pump will switch off. The impact on northwest Europe could be disastrous. Without the warming influence of the North Atlantic current, the region will face much harsher winters and a shorter growing season.

Similar events have occurred in the past. Twelve thousand years ago Europe had just emerged from the last ice age. Then, as now, meltwater flooded into the North Atlantic and reduced the ocean's salinity. In just a few decades the conveyor switched off, plunging northern Europe into a mini ice age. The Younger Dryas cool-down lasted a thousand years and was cold enough for glaciers to return to Scotland, Wales and the Lake District. Some climatologists believe that a similar cool-down could occur before the end of the twenty-first century.

Global dimming

Global dimming describes the gradual reduction in the amount of solar radiation reaching the Earth's surface. In the period 1960 to 1991, this reduction averaged around 3% per decade.

Global dimming is caused by tiny airborne particles (aerosols) of dust, smoke, ash and sulphur released into the atmosphere. Solar radiation striking the aerosols is reflected back into space, reducing the amount reaching the surface.

Human activity, through the burning of coal, oil and gas for energy and transport, has increased the volume of aerosols in the atmosphere, and is thought to be the main driver behind global dimming. However, global dimming is also a natural process. Large volcanic eruptions pump huge quantities of ash and sulphur into the atmosphere, which can temporarily reduce the amount of solar radiation received at the Earth's surface. This happened in the 1990s. The Pinatubo eruption in 1991 (the largest in the twentieth century) led to a brief period of global cooling and a sharp increase in the concentration of aerosols in the atmosphere.

The effects of global dimming could be both positive and negative. On the positive side, any reduction in solar radiation will help to offset the greenhouse effect and global warming. If this has happened, though, then the predicted temperature rises in the twenty-first century due to global warming could have been underestimated. The negative effects of global dimming are less well understood. In theory, global dimming could reduce photosynthesis and plant growth. Although this is unlikely in the humid tropics, where limits to plant growth are related to water availability and carbon dioxide rather than sunshine, in cloudier mid- and high-latitude climates it could have some effect. In these areas it is possible that global dimming could reduce crop yields. Some scientists have also suggested that there may be links with the droughts in sub-Saharan Africa in the 1970s and 1980s and global dimming. It is argued that global dimming could reduce evaporation and disrupt the hydrological cycle.

In recent years fears of global dimming have receded as aerosol concentrations in the atmosphere have declined. This is explained by reductions in air pollution in Europe and North America due to legislation and a move away from electricity generated by coal-burning power stations to cleaner fuels such as gas and nuclear energy. Meanwhile, coal consumption, as a result of the rapid industrialisation of China and India, is at an all-time high. Solar dimming is already high in these countries and could once again become a global problem in future.

Acid rain

Acid rain pollution

Causes

Air pollution caused by emissions of sulphur dioxide, nitrogen oxides and ammonia is responsible for acid rain (Photograph 3.10). In the atmosphere these pollutants combine with water droplets to form sulphuric acid and nitric acid. Eventually the chemicals reach the ground in rain and snow, or as dry depositions.

Acid rain is an unwanted side-effect of industrial development, and specifically the burning of fossil fuels. Man-made emissions of sulphur rose sharply from 1945 to the early 1970s. Coal-fired power stations and heavy processing industries such as iron and steel produce large amounts of sulphur dioxide. More than half of all nitrogen oxide emissions come from exhaust gases from motor vehicles. Ammonia is largely derived from intensive livestock farming and organic fertilisers.

The impact of acid rain

Like global warming, acid rain is a major international environmental problem. Because it is dispersed by wind, its effects are transnational. The main adverse effects of acid rain are:

➤ the acidification of lakes, streams and soil

Photograph 3.10 *Air pollution from smokestacks*

Photograph 3.11 *Forests damaged by acid rain*

> the destruction of forests and wildlife (in aquatic habitats)
> the corrosion of buildings and stone monuments, especially those of limestone and sandstone

When soils become acidified essential nutrients are leached out and toxic metals such as aluminium threaten wildlife and enter food chains. For example, dissolved aluminium and acid waters kill aquatic invertebrates such as water snails, mayfly larvae and dragonflies that support birds, fish and aquatic mammals. Forests are also extensively damaged (Photograph 3.11). In the 1970s and 1980 in Europe, almost a quarter of all trees showed some damage due to acid rain. The environmental problems of acid rain were most severe in uplands with high rainfall and in soil and rocks with little free calcium to neutralise the acidity. In the UK upland environments such as Snowdonia and the Lake District were badly affected.

Acid rain in Europe

Acid rain was only recognised as a global problem in 1979 when the Convention on Long-Range Transboundary Air Pollution was signed. In Europe, Norway and Sweden were badly affected. They were net importers of acid rain originating in neighbouring states such as Germany, the UK and Poland. Around 14 000 lakes in Sweden were so badly affected that sensitive organisms could no longer survive in them. Increases in soil acidity disrupted soil chemistry and nutrient cycles, and leached out essential plant nutrients such as calcium and magnesium. These processes caused forests to die.

Responding to the acid rain problem

In Europe concerted action by governments to tackle the problem of acid rain began in the mid-1980s. Agreements signed in 1985, 1988 and 1994 committed countries to make significant reductions in sulphur emissions. Binding emissions ceilings were set in the Göteborg Protocol of 2001 and were to be achieved by each EU state by 2010. They covered the three pollutants mainly responsible for acid rain: sulphur dioxide, nitrogen oxides and ammonia.

Box 3.12 Critical loads

Critical loads are the maximum amount of pollutants that ecosystems can tolerate without being damaged. The concept of critical load — the limit that nature can tolerate — has been used to set targets for emissions reductions in Europe since the mid-1990s. Exposure above the critical load results in harmful environmental effects. In 1990, 34% of the natural environment in Europe was affected by acidic deposition that exceeded the critical load. By 2000 this had shrunk to 11%. In the same year, 20% of forests in EU25 (25 countries that formed the EU in 2004) received acid deposition above critical loads — a figure which should fall to 12% by 2020.

In order to halt acidification processes, **target loads** need to be set for individual states. In Europe in 1990 around 93 million ha of land were affected by acid deposition that exceeded the critical load. To achieve the desired limits and reduce the damage caused by acid rain, it was necessary to reduce acidifying pollution in parts of Europe by 80–90% compared to 1990 levels.

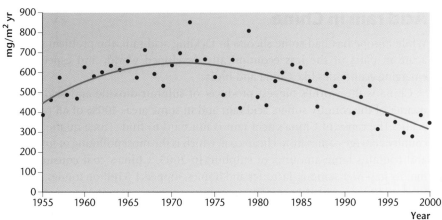

Figure 3.35
Sulphur dioxide concentrations in Sweden peaked in the early 1970s and declined to one-quarter of their peak by end of the century

Europe achieved remarkable success in tackling the acid rain problem (see Figure 3.35). Between 1980 and 2003 emissions from land-based sources in Europe fell by almost 75%. In 1990, 34% of the natural environment in Europe was affected by acidic deposition that exceeded the critical load. By 2000 this had shrunk to 11%.

UK emissions of chemicals that can cause acid rain fell by 52% between 1990 and 2004 (Figure 3.36). Many of the UK's most acidified upland lakes and streams have begun to recover from the effects of acid rain. As acidity declined wildlife started to reappear with sensitive indicator species such as brown trout making a comeback.

Liming acidified lakes to raise their pH levels is a short-term solution to excessive acidity which been successful in Scandinavia. Finely ground limestone is regularly added to 7500 lakes and 11 000 km of waterways in Sweden. Soils are also limed to counter acidification. An input of 3–5 tonnes of lime per hectare protects soils from acidification for 20–30 years.

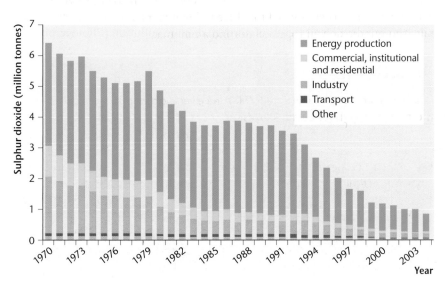

Figure 3.36
Changes in sulphur dioxide emissions in the UK, 1970–2003

123

Acid rain in China

While Europe has had some success in tackling acid rain, the problem remains acute in parts of the less economically developed world, and especially in emerging economies like China and India.

China is the world's biggest producer of sulphur dioxide and acid rain. A quarter of the country suffers acid rain and in some areas 100% of all rainfall is acidic. The cause of China's acid rain is not hard to find. Three-quarters of the country's energy comes from cheap coal, which is the most polluting of fossil fuels and contains large amounts of sulphur. In 2005, China's coal consumption, mainly in power stations, factories and homes, topped 1.8 billion tonnes. As a by-product China emitted 25.8 million tonnes of sulphur dioxide. Meanwhile coal production continues to break all records. It doubled between 1998 and 2005 and is forecast to reach 2.4 billion tonnes by 2010 (Table 3.10). China has plans to build hundreds of new coal-fired power stations. So in the short term pollution will get worse.

Table 3.10 *Coal production in China (million tonnes): 1993–2003*

1998	1999	2000	2001	2002	2003	2004	2005
1151	1280	1299	1382	1455	1722	1992	2190

Acid rain is part of the environmental cost of China's soaring economic growth. The speed of China's industrialisation has simply outpaced environmental protection. The economic and environmental costs are considerable: an estimated US$13 billion a year or 3% of GDP. Acid rain also damages soils, threatens food safety and adversely affects human health.

In many regions acid rain has reached or passed the critical load. This is the case in the south and southwest region where 62% of cities suffer from acid rain pollution.

The rapid growth in numbers of motor vehicles has also contributed to acid rain. With over 2.5 million vehicles in Beijing and the number rising rapidly, the city has the world's worst levels of nitrogen dioxide pollution (Photograph 3.12).

Photograph 3.12
With the number of motor vehicles rising rapidly, Beijing has the world's worst levels of nitrogen dioxide pollution

Focus China/Alamy

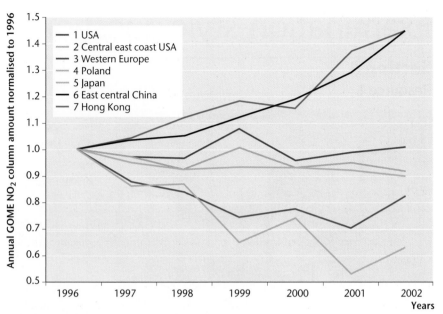

Figure 3.37
Nitrogen dioxide concentrations: contrast between China and other industrialised regions

Meanwhile 70% of Shanghai's 1 million cars do not even reach the oldest European emission standards (Figure 3.37).

Tackling acid rain pollution

China accepts that acid rain pollution is an urgent environmental problem. Too often, however, local governments have failed to enforce environmental standards, fearing they might hinder economic growth. Since 1996 the United Nations Development Programme has provided US$3.6 million to fight acid rain in Guiyang in southwest China, and nitrogen oxides and smog in south China's Guangzhou province.

Environmental authorities have recommended that central government controls emissions from major polluters such as thermal power stations, coke works and oil refineries. This could be done by withholding planning approvals and loans, and raising emissions-control standards.

In Guangdong province in south China, 17 cities, mostly in the Pearl River Delta, are badly affected by acid rain. Guangdong is attempting to control its sulphur dioxide emissions, the main cause of acid rain. Desulphurisation work on 10 coal-fired power stations has begun. Although expensive — US$725 million — it is cost-effective: acid rain results in economic losses of more than US$483 million a year in the province. In addition, coal-fired power stations account for two-thirds of the sulphur dioxide emissions.

Policies for dealing with pollution include charging polluters for sulphur dioxide emissions, setting up special funds for desulphurisation, burning better quality coal and buying electricity from plants that have installed desulphurisation equipment.

Examination-style questions

Section A
Resource 1

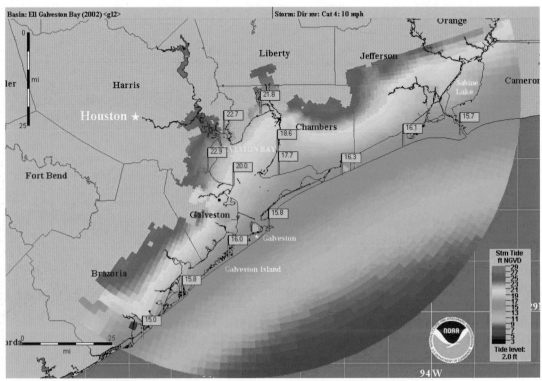

Louisiana hurricane storm surge potential

1 Resource 1 relates to a hurricane hazard on the Gulf coast of the southern USA. Outline an issue indicated and suggest appropriate management. **(10 marks)**

Section B

2 In hurricane hazards, 'storm surges pose the greatest threat to life and property', (Federal Emergency Management Agency). Discuss the validity of this statement. **(30 marks)**

3 Why, and to what extent, are populations in LEDCs more vulnerable to hurricane hazards than those living in MEDCs? **(30 marks)**

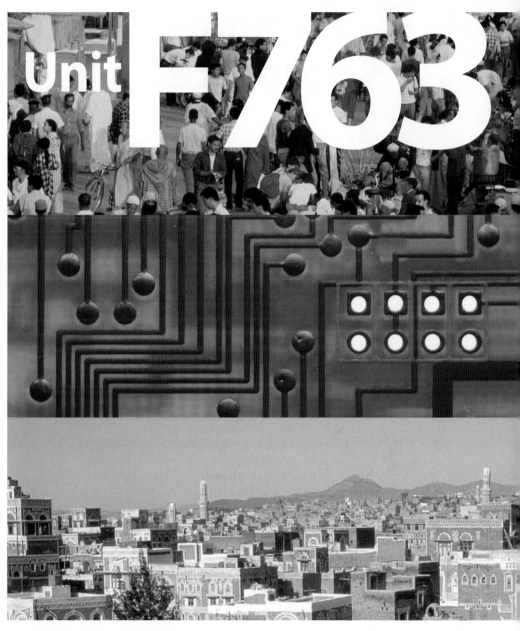

Unit F763

Global Issues

Section B Economic Issues

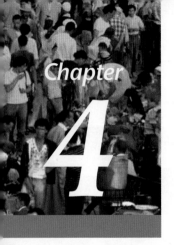

Population and resources

Population change over time

Key ideas
➤ How and why population growth varies over time and space.
➤ Population is dynamic and responds to demographic, social, economic and political factors that vary from place to place.
➤ Populations grow over time by natural increase and net migration.
➤ There are global contrasts in population growth.
➤ The rate of global population growth is changing over time.
➤ Population growth is related to concepts of overpopulation and underpopulation

At the global scale two variables influence population change: births and deaths. If births outnumber deaths the global population expands. This is **natural increase**. Of course, the opposite situation, where deaths exceed births, leads to population decline or **natural decrease**.

At continental, national, regional and local scales a third factor, **migration**, influences population change. The following equation summarises population change at these scales:

population change = (births − deaths) +/− migration

The figures in Table 4.1 show that in 2006 Stockholm experienced both natural population growth and a net migrational gain. As a result its population grew by over 28 000. Jämtland had a more mixed experience. There, deaths outnumbered births giving natural population decrease. However, this was compensated by a

Table 4.1 *Population change in three Swedish counties in 2006*

	Total population	Births	Deaths	Natural change	In-migration	Out-migration	Net migration change	Total population change
Stockholm	1 918 104	26 983	15 658	+11 325	63 419	46 461	+16 958	+28 283
Jämtland	127 020	1295	1584	−289	4407	4117	+290	+1
Västerbotten	257 581	2827	2553	+274	7745	8067	−322	−48

Source: SCB

net migrational gain to give an overall population increase in 2006 of just one person! Västerbotten's experience was almost the reverse of Jämtland's. Its population recorded a healthy natural increase but a heavy net migrational loss. The outcome was an overall population decline or **depopulation** in Västerbotten in 2006.

World population growth

In the past 2000 years or so the world's population has experienced extraordinary change. At the start of the period the UN estimate the total global population to have been around 300 million. For the next millennium the population hardly changed. In fact, it took nearly 1600 years for the world's population to double. By 1800 the global population had reached nearly 800 million; it then doubled in the course of the nineteenth century. It was the twentieth century, however, that witnessed the most extraordinary growth. The world's population almost quadrupled between 1900 and 2000, from 1650 million to just over 6000 million (Figure 4.1). Although this phase of runaway growth has ended, growth continues today: in 2008 the global population stood at 6679 million and by 2050 it will rise to 9400 million.

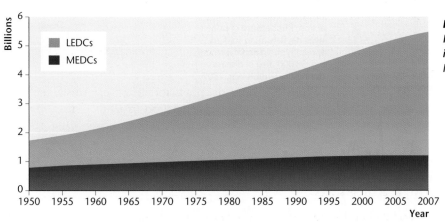

Figure 4.1
Population change in LEDCs and MEDCs, 1950–2007

Box 4.1 Fertility and mortality

The term fertility describes the occurrence of live births. It is accurately measured by the **total fertility rate (TFR)** — the average number of children that a woman gives birth to in her lifetime. The TFR ranges from around 1.5 in eastern Europe to more than 6 in several sub-Saharan and Middle East countries. Mortality is the occurrence of death. **Life expectancy** at birth is a common measure of mortality. A more detailed measure is **age-specific mortality** — the number of deaths of persons of a given age divided by the population in the same age category. **Infant mortality** is the number of deaths of children in their first year, per 1000 live births.

Vital rates

Crude birth rates (CBRs) and **crude death rates (CDRs)** are known as vital rates. Both are insensitive measures of fertility and mortality because they are strongly affected by the age structure. The CBR is the ratio of births to the total population. It is usually expressed per 1000 of the population. In Table 4.1 Stockholm's CBR is:

$$(26\,983 \div 1\,918\,104) \times 1000 = 14.1$$

The CDR is the number of deaths per 1000 of the population. The CDR for Stockholm therefore is:

$$(15\,658 \div 1\,919\,104) \times 1000 = 8.2$$

Natural population change is the difference between the CBR and the CDR. As it is usually expressed as a percentage per year, the difference between the CBR and CDR is divided by 10. Thus, Stockholm's natural population change for 2006 is:

$$(14.1 - 8.2) \div 100 = +0.06\%$$

The **doubling time** for a population is approximated by dividing 70 by the percentage growth rate. At a constant annual growth rate of 0.06% Stockholm's population will double in 70 ÷ 0.06 = 117 years. In comparison, the world's natural increase rate in 2008 was 1.16% which suggests a doubling in just over 60 years.

Case study | Population change at the national scale: Sweden 1750–2008

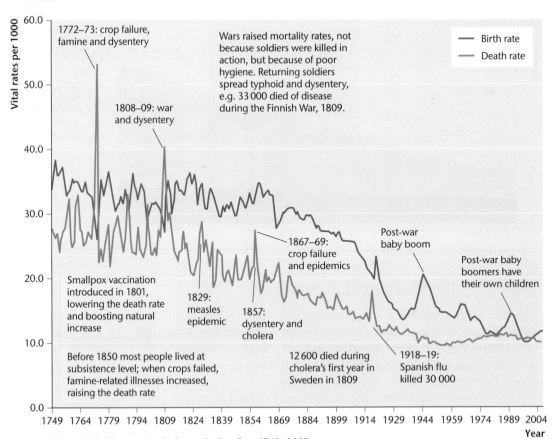

Figure 4.2 *Changes in vital rates in Sweden, 1749–2007*

Accurate population statistics in Sweden extend back to the mid-eighteenth century — longer than for any other country. Figures 4.2 and 4.3 tell us how and why Sweden's population changed during the past 250 years. Between 1749 when records began and the early nineteenth century, the CBR exceeded the CDR in most years. From time to time, years of exceptionally high mortality such as 1772–73 and 1808–09 cancelled out much of the previous years' natural increase. As a result, overall rates of population growth were small.

The early nineteenth century signalled a remarkable change. Mortality began to decline as medical breakthroughs such as the development of the smallpox vaccination, fewer famines and food shortages took effect. By 1880, the CDR had fallen to just 17; meanwhile the CBR remained high at around 30. A combination of falling mortality and high fertility in the nineteenth century led to high rates of natural increase and rapid population growth. Sweden's total population, which stood at 2.35 million in 1800, more than doubled to 5.14 million by 1900.

Towards the end of the nineteenth century, rising standards of living, further improvements in medical technology and most importantly the increasing availability of artificial contraception, led to a steady decline in fertility. The last year when the CDR exceeded 20 was 1875. By 1918 the CBR had fallen to 20.3 and by 1935 to just 13.7. Although mortality continued to decline, the overall rates of natural increase slowed. For a few years after the Second World War there was a resurgence of fertility — the so-called 'baby boom' — but generally, the second half of the twentieth century was a period of low fertility, low mortality and slow population growth. Indeed, between 1997 and 2001, Sweden's low fertility (in 2000 total fertility was just 1.5 children per woman) and ageing population resulted in natural population decrease: the first time this had happened since 1809. Since the 1990s, Sweden's population growth has been sustained by international immigration.

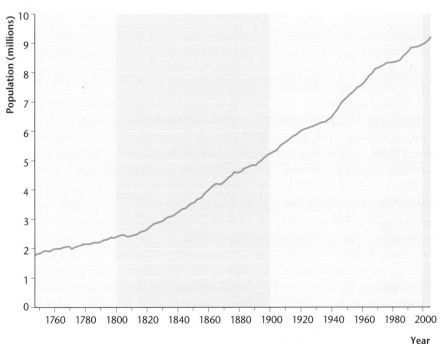

Figure 4.3
Population growth in Sweden, 1749–2007

Box 4.2 The demographic transition model

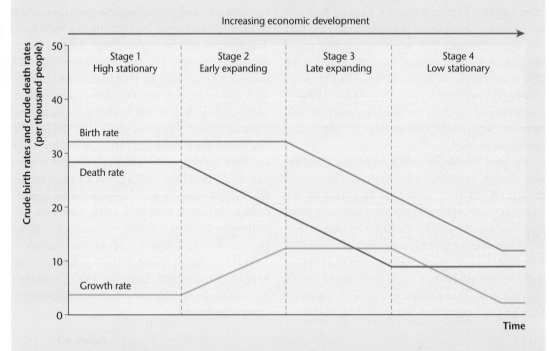

The demographic transition model (DTM) describes the changes in vital rates and population growth that occur with economic development. Stage 1 describes a pre-industrial society with high vital rates and a stable population. Stages 2 and 3 correspond to industrialisation, with falling vital rates and rapid population growth. Finally, in stage 4 (the post-industrial period) demographic stability returns, with low vital rates and little population growth. The key periods in the DTM are stages 2 and 3. In stage 2 mortality falls steeply due to improved diet, sanitation, housing and medical technology, while fertility remains high. The result is rapid population growth. This growth continues in stage 3 but at a lower rate owing to the widespread adoption of contraception and family planning.

The DTM has limited value as a universal description of the demographic changes that accompany economic development. There are several reasons for this:

■ The DTM was based on the demographic experience of a few countries in northwest Europe between 1800 and 1950. Little wonder that the model bears a striking resemblance to Sweden's demographic history during this period (Figure 4.3).

■ Population growth in many LEDCs is not associated with economic development.

■ The decline in mortality in LEDCs is due more to imported Western medical technology than improvements in living conditions.

■ Modern medical technology is transferred from MEDCs to LEDCs.

■ Modern contraceptive methods are widely available in LEDCs.

■ Culture, society and values in LEDCs are both diverse and very different from those in nineteenth-century northwest Europe.

■ Many governments influence population change through their population policies.

■ International migration has an increasing influence on population change in MEDCs and LEDCs.

Population change over space
Global contrasts in population growth

There are huge spatial contrasts in population growth at the global scale. Most obvious is the contrast between rich and poor countries. In 2007 the rate of natural increase in the economically less developed world (ELDW) was 24 times higher than in the economically more developed world (EMDW) (Table 4.2). With a high rate of growth and a population four-and-a-half times bigger than the EMDW, the ELDW accounted for all but 1 million of the world's 78 million population increase in 2007.

Other contrasts appear when we examine the spatial patterns of population growth at the regional scale. Within the ELDW, sub-Saharan Africa and the Middle East have exceptionally high rates of natural growth. In sub-Saharan Africa this is due to high rates of fertility and relatively low mortality rates. However, as a result of AIDS, mortality is much higher in Africa than in any other region in the ELDW. Natural increase is also high in the Middle East, but for different reasons. There, low death rates (as in North Africa and Latin America) stem from the region's youthful age structure.

Asia's population is dominated by China and India. In both countries fertility is falling rapidly and rates of natural increase are in decline. Similar patterns prevail in Latin America and the Caribbean.

In the EMDW rates of natural population change are low. The lowest rates are in the Baltics, eastern Europe and Russia. For several years low fertility and an ageing population structure have led to natural decrease. North America, with its more youthful age structure, has the highest natural growth in the EMDW.

Table 4.2 shows the effect of international migration on population change. Many MEDCs have experienced substantial net migration gains in recent years, which have driven population growth. In contrast, most LEDCs have suffered net migration losses, especially in North Africa, Asia and Latin America.

Table 4.2 *Global contrasts in vital rates, natural increase and population growth, 2008*

	CBR	CDR	% natural change	% population change
LEDCs	22.0	7.8	1.41	1.37
MEDCs	11.0	10.4	0.06	0.22
Sub-Saharan Africa	37.7	14.8	2.29	2.30
North Africa	20.7	5.0	1.56	1.53
Middle East	24.8	5.2	1.96	1.97
Asia (excluding Middle East)	18.6	7.0	1.16	1.12
Latin America and the Caribbean	18.9	5.9	1.30	1.16
Western Europe	10.0	9.9	0.01	0.20
Eastern Europe	10.3	10.8	−0.05	−0.06
Baltics	9.4	12.3	−0.29	−0.46
Commonwealth of Independent States	13.7	13.6	0.01	−0.04
North America	13.8	8.2	0.56	0.88
Oceania	16.2	7.3	2.5	1.12

Factors influencing population change

Population is dynamic: change at national and regional scales is influenced by a combination of demographic, social, economic and political factors.

Demographic factors

Age-sex structure is an important driver of population change. Figure 4.4 shows population pyramids for Afghanistan and Canada. Afghanistan's population is youthful: 44% are children under 15 years and only 2% are aged 65 years and over. In contrast, Canada has a much older population, with 17% being children and 13% old people. Afghanistan's youthful population is partly responsible for its high birth rate (45.8 per 1000 in 2008) and its rapid rate of natural increase of 2.6% a year. Meanwhile, Canada's older population influences its low birth rate (10.7) and a natural increase of only 0.28% a year.

Figure 4.4
Population pyramids for Afghanistan and Canada

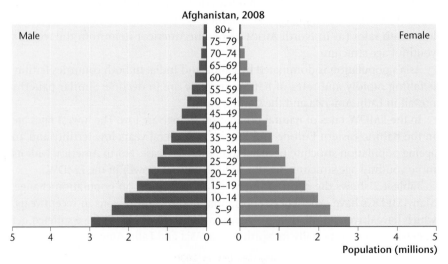

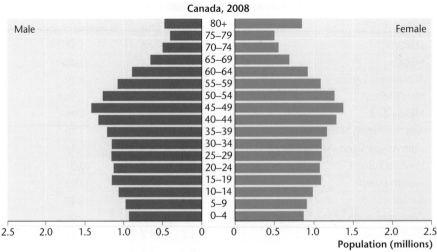

At regional and local scales migration is often the major influence on population change (Figure 4.5). The population pyramid for Grant County in North Dakota shows the effects of out-migration. Out-migration, driven by a lack of employment and educational opportunities for young people, mainly affects the 20–35-year age group. As a result in Grant County young women aged 20 to 35 years comprise just 4.3% of the population. The county's ageing population lowers the birth rate and increases the death rate (Table 4.3). Thus out-migration not only causes depopulation: because it is age selective it also contributes to natural population decrease.

In contrast, Orange County in Florida has experienced a large net migrational gain in recent years. Twelve per cent of the population are young women aged 20

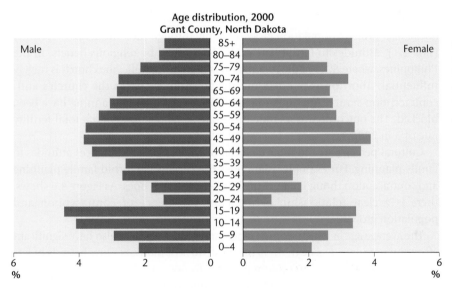

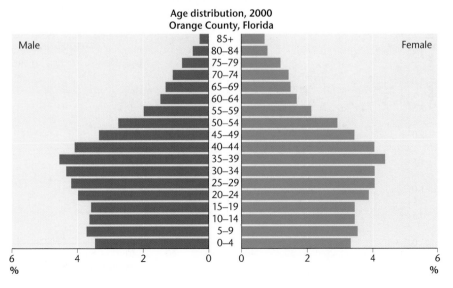

Figure 4.5 Age distribution in Grant County, North Dakota and Orange County, California, 2000

Table 4.3 *Population change in Grant County, North Dakota and Orange County, Florida, 2006*

	CBR	CDR	% natural change pa	Population 1990	Population 2006	% population change 1990–2006
Grant County	7.0	13.7	−0.067	3549	2615	−26.3
Orange County	14.5	6.1	+0.084	677500	1087 00	+60.4

to 35 years. Given its youthful population, the natural increase in Orange County's population is high. Even so, most of its population growth — 75% — was due to in-migration.

Social factors

Social factors affect population growth mainly through their influence on fertility (Box 4.1). Attitudes to fertility are often determined by religious beliefs. In the Philippines, where 80% of the population is Roman Catholic, the church is hugely influential. Abortion is banned and the government backs the church's anti-contraception stance. Attempts to pass laws to fund family planning have been blocked. The outcome was a crude birth rate of 24 per 1000 and a total fertility rate of 3 in 2008.

Cultural perception and interpretation of religion often influences attitudes to family planning. For example, Islam does not specifically forbid family planning and contraception though many Muslims believe that it does. As Figure 4.6 shows, there is a clear relationship between the prevalence of contraception and population growth.

The average age at which women marry and gender equality also have significant effects on population growth. In Bangladesh 46% of marriages involve girls of less than 18 years. In Niger, the figure is closer to 60%. Early marriage means that women in such countries spend a large proportion of their reproductive lives

Figure 4.6
Contraceptive prevalence and population growth in LEDCs

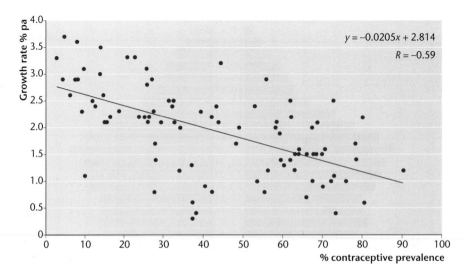

$y = -0.0205x + 2.814$

$R = -0.59$

married, and are therefore likely to have larger families. It is well known that in societies where there is gender equality and where women are better educated and empowered, families are smaller and population growth rates drastically reduced. In contrast, in most MEDCs the average age of marriage and first-time motherhood has increased. In the UK for example, there are now more first-time mothers in the 30–34 age group than in the 25–29 age group.

Economic factors

Economic factors exert a major influence on population growth. Rising wealth is closely associated with lower levels of fertility. Figure 4.7 shows the differences in total fertility and economic wellbeing between the countries of south Asia and northwest Europe. Although total fertility (Box 4.1) is falling in south Asia, it still averages 3.8 compared to 1.7 in northwest Europe. One reason for this difference is the economic value of children. In south Asia, and especially in rural communities, children are often an economic asset.

Photograph 4.1
A child marriage in India

They are able to work to contribute to family incomes at an early age. As a result larger families are often better off than smaller ones. Moreover, in countries where there are no state pensions and welfare payments, children are needed to look after their parents in old age.

In northwest Europe and throughout the EMDW the economic advantages of children are negligible. Children often remain dependent on their parents until their early twenties and the state and occupational pension schemes provide security in old age. In the UK, the average cost of bringing up a child is around £250 000. This imposes considerable **opportunity costs** on parents, who may prefer to spend the money on houses, holidays, cars and lifestyle.

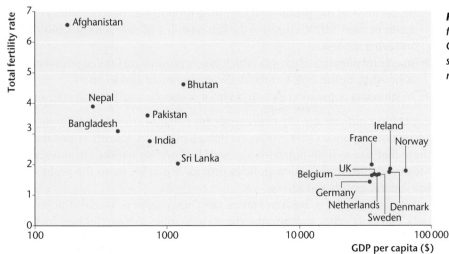

Figure 4.7 *Total fertility rates and GDP per capita, south Asia and northwest Europe*

Table 4.4 *Life expectancy and infant mortality in south Asia and northwest Europe, 2008*

	Average life expectancy (years)	Infant mortality (per 1000)		Average life expectancy (years)	Infant mortality (per 1000)
Belgium	75.9	4.5	Afghanistan	44.2	154.7
Denmark	78.1	4.4	Bangladesh	63.2	57.5
France	80.9	3.4	Bhutan	55.6	94.3
Germany	79.1	4.0	India	69.2	32.3
Ireland	78.1	5.1	Nepal	60.9	62.0
Netherlands	79.2	4.8	Pakistan	64.1	67.0
Norway	79.8	3.6	Sri Lanka	75.0	19.0
Sweden	80.7	2.8			
UK	78.8	4.9			

Many women in MEDCs opt to pursue their careers for economic reasons and postpone having children until their mid to late thirties. However, the ability of women to conceive declines steeply in their thirties, and, with relatively few reproductive years remaining, fertility levels decline.

Economic factors also have a significant effect on mortality. Average life expectancy is on average 15 years more in MEDCs than in LEDCs (Table 4.4). Infant mortality is even more sensitive to economic conditions. High rates of infant mortality in south Asia are intimately related to poverty and inadequate health care. Poverty is associated with contaminated drinking water, poor nutrition, a lack of proper sanitation and sub-standard housing. None the less, mortality continues to fall in LEDCs, and the gap between births and deaths is large enough to sustain annual population growth rates of over 1.5%.

Political factors

Governments seek to influence population growth for a number of reasons.

➤ To resolve economic problems created by ageing populations: rapidly rising proportions of old people and declining proportions of economically active adults in many MEDCs threaten the sustainability of state pensions, health care and other services.

➤ To control population growth, which places pressure on limited resources such as housing, health care, farmland, the environment and so on.

➤ To stimulate population growth both for economic and political reasons.

Population policies usually concentrate on two areas: fertility and migration. Expansionist policies that aim to encourage births are known as **pro-natalist**; those that aim to limit population growth by lowering fertility are **anti-natalist**. Meanwhile pro-immigration policies provide a quicker fix to the problems of low natural growth and ageing.

Several countries in western Europe currently pursue pro-natalist population policies. France offers a range of incentives to families to have children, including tax breaks, cash payments, subsidised child care and paid maternity leave. In addition, large families pay less tax and get concessionary fares on public transport and free admission to public amenities like swimming pools. These policies, together with immigration, have helped to give France the highest fertility rate in Europe — an average 1.98 children per woman — though this falls short of the 2.1 needed to replace the population.

Russia's population is currently declining by 700 000 a year, due largely to natural decrease caused by low fertility and relatively high mortality. In 2006 the government introduced financial incentives worth US$9000 a year (equivalent to two years' average income in Russia) to women who have more than one child. However, this policy alone is not enough to reverse Russia's demographic decline, which could see its population fall from 140 million in 2008, to 110 million by 2050.

China's one-child policy is the most widely publicised anti-natalist programme. Concerned about declining population–resource ratios and the adverse effects of population growth on economic development, in 1979 the Chinese leader, Deng Xiaoping, took drastic steps to slow China's population growth (Figure 4.8). The government's policy limited families to one child. Although the policy was strictly enforced in its early years, it was always interpreted more liberally in rural areas, where two or three children per family were common. Local governments also have some discretion in how they apply the policy. For example, Beijing takes a hard line: mothers applying for a second child can only do so if they are under 28 years old and there is at least a four-year interval since the birth of their first child. Shanghai, faced with a rapidly ageing population, has removed the four-year rule.

The effect of China's population policy was dramatic. Whereas the country's population grew by 73% between 1950 and 1979, growth fell to 37% between 1979 and 2008. Today, one-third of all Chinese families are single-child families: some estimates claim that the policy has been responsible for 400 million fewer births. The latest forecasts suggest that zero population growth will be achieved in the mid-2030s.

Finally, policies towards international migration are often used to manipulate a country's population. For the past 30 years or so the Filipino government has encouraged international emigration. Many young Filipino women either work or live permanently overseas, helping to reduce population growth in the Philippines. Meanwhile the country's economy benefits from remittances sent home.

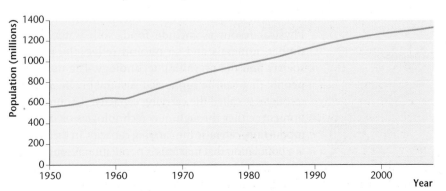

Figure 4.8 China's population growth, 1950–2008

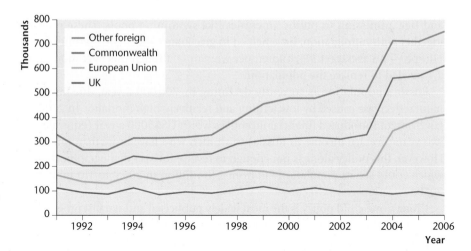

Figure 4.9
International immigration to the UK, 1991–2006

In western Europe, international immigration is seen by many governments as the solution to the problems of ageing populations. In the UK record immigration fuelled the biggest rise in population for almost 50 years (Figure 4.9). The net migrational gain in 2006 alone was nearly 200 000. By 2031 the population is forecast to rise from 61 million in 2008 to over 70 million. At least 70% of this growth will be attributable to immigration. This is the fastest rate of growth since the post-war baby boom over 50 years ago. Because foreign immigrants are mainly young adults, they are helping to push up UK levels of fertility.

Immigration into the UK soared following enlargement of the EU in 2004 and a massive influx of workers from eastern Europe. By 2007, foreign-born workers made up 12.5% of the labour force and accounted for one in four babies born in the UK. Although many EU migrants will eventually return home, the scale of immigration sparked a vigorous debate on the economic benefits of immigration and whether the advantages of migrant skills and cheap labour offset the extra costs of education, health care and social benefits.

Population growth and the concepts of overpopulation and underpopulation

The terms 'overpopulation' and 'underpopulation' are relative ones: they refer to the relationship between the size of a population and available physical resources. Physical resources include food, soil, water, energy, timber, minerals and so on and reflect the needs of society and the prevailing technology. The number of people that can be supported sustainably by available resources is called the **carrying capacity**. Resource development, either through new technologies or increased production, can raise the carrying capacity. In theory there is a population that maximises population:resource ratios at a sustainable level. This is the **optimum population** (Figure 4.10).

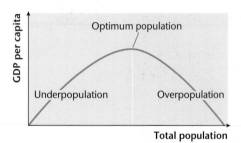

Figure 4.10 *Optimum population diagram*

Box 4.3 The problem with overpopulation and underpopulation

The concepts of overpopulation and underpopulation are often confused with population density and overcrowding. 'High density' no more suggests overpopulation than 'low density' implies underpopulation. Some of the richest countries (e.g. Japan and the Netherlands) have average densities in excess of 300 persons per km². Singapore, despite an average density of 6750 persons km² has a GDP per capita that is higher than Spain's and New Zealand's.

The real problem with overpopulation and underpopulation is that they are only meaningful when applied to societies that depend on local resources. For example, a society based on subsistence agriculture must rely on local resources such as soil, water, wildlife and timber. In the absence of technological change, population growth in such a society will put pressure on local resources which may result in declining crop yields, food shortages and land degradation. Such a society could reasonably be thought of as overpopulated.

However, problems arise when we try to apply the concept of overpopulation to urban societies. In these societies population densities have no relationship to local resources. The resources needed to sustain these populations are garnered worldwide. Their impact on environments and resources is real enough, but too diffuse to be clearly defined geographically. The outcome is societies living at extreme high densities with high standards of living and enjoying rising levels of resource use.

If resource availability fails to keep pace with population growth, resources per person decline. Resources will be overexploited and degraded. This is the situation of **overpopulation**. **Underpopulation** is the opposite situation. It occurs when there are too few people to develop resources fully. This means that resources per capita are less than the theoretical maximum. Thus any increase in population should allow further resource development and create increased resources per capita.

Population growth beyond the optimum level does not always result in overpopulation and declining resources per capita. Pressure on resources caused by rising population can stimulate innovation, summed up by the aphorism 'necessity is the mother of invention' (Figure 4.11). Thousands of years ago, the shift from human hunter-gatherer economies to sedentary agricultural societies was based on the discovery of agriculture, which greatly expanded food supplies

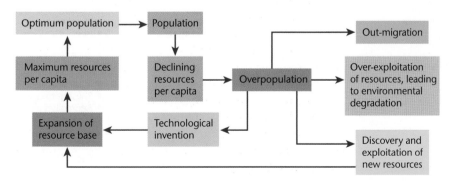

Figure 4.11
Population growth and resources

and allowed population growth. New technology expands the resource base, allowing the exploitation of previously unused resources or the more efficient use of existing ones. An example is the green revolution in south Asia in the 1970s and 1980s, when the introduction of new high-yielding varieties of wheat and rice greatly increased food production.

Definition and classification of natural resources

Key ideas
➤ Resources can be classified in a number of different ways, including source, use and renewability.
➤ There are important differences between renewable, non-renewable, flow and semi-renewable resources.
➤ Changes in technology and society may result in changes in the definition of resources.

Natural resources can be defined as 'stocks of physical assets that are not produced goods, and that are valuable to humans' (*The African Development Report 2007*, OUP). However, the concept of a resource is elusive and there is no single agreed definition. There are similar problems in classifying natural resources: resources can be classified by source, use, extent and renewability (Figure 4.12).

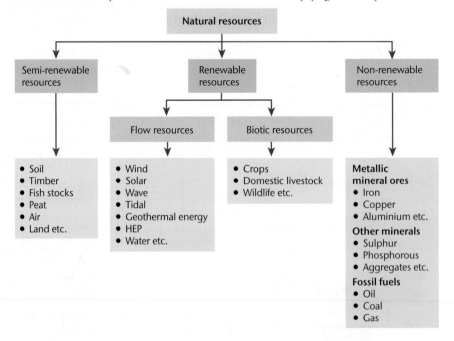

Figure 4.12
A classification of natural resources

Classification of natural resources

Source

Some natural resources can be classified by their source. For example: most fish stocks, shellfish and crustacea are derived from marine sources; minerals are sourced from the Earth's crust, in deep mines and surface quarries; HEP derives from rivers; crops are sourced from farmland; timber comes from forests; geothermal energy from volcanically active areas and so on. However, it is difficult to allocate all resources to broad source categories, which makes the source classification unsatisfactory.

Use

An alternative approach is to classify resources according to their use. We commonly use labels such as food resources, recreational resources, energy and industrial resources. Although this is convenient shorthand, there is the problem that many resources have more than one use. Peat, for example, is used as a fuel and by gardeners and horticulturalists. Wheat, used primarily for food, also provides straw for thatching, building and fuel.

Extent

Resources can be grouped according to the characteristics of their geographical distribution. Point resources are concentrated in small geographical areas. The availability of metallic minerals such as gold and copper is restricted to small areas both globally and regionally. Diamond production is also highly localised (Figure 4.13). Four countries — Russia, Botswana, Angola and the Democratic Republic of Congo — account for nearly three-quarters of global output. In contrast, diffuse resources, such as forests, are geographically widespread. Excluding Antarctica, forests occupy nearly 30% of Earth's land surface (Figure 4.14). Unfortunately not all resources fall conveniently into point and diffuse categories. An example is crude oil. Although oil deposits often have point locations, oilfields may extend over considerable areas such as the Persian Gulf and the northern North Sea. Clearly, the geographical factor in resource classification is strongly dependent on scale.

Renewability

The most useful classification of natural resources is based on their renewability (Figure 4.12). Renewable resources regenerate on human

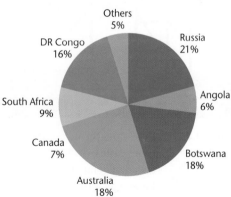

Figure 4.13 World production of diamonds

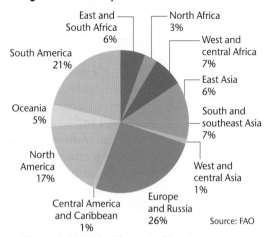

Figure 4.14 Regional extent of forest cover (% of world total)

Photograph 4.2
Examples of
alternative energy:
(a) a solar-powered
furnace in Odeillo,
France, (b) hydro-
electric power, Glen
Canyon dam, USA,
(c) offshore wind
power in the Baltic
Sea

timescales through ecological cycles. Annual and fast-growing plants and crops are renewables. So too are domestic livestock and wild animals. Resources which also regenerate but over longer, intermediate timescales (e.g. 100–1000 years) are known as semi-renewables. They include forests, fish stocks and soils.

A feature of renewable resources is their linkage within ecosystems. They are often connected to other renewable resources. For instance, wildlife and forests rely on water and soil for their renewal. Currently, the key challenge concerning renewable resources is their sustainable management. To achieve this, consumption must not exceed rates of regeneration. For environmental resources such as water, air and land, the main area of concern is pollution and the resources' declining quality.

Flow resources are a separate group of renewables. They have a permanent character and do not need regeneration. All forms of alternative energy, like wind, solar and hydroelectric power, are flow resources (Figure 4.12). Although flow resources cannot be depleted their exploitation depends on other natural resources such as energy, materials and space for construction.

Non-renewable resources are finite on human timescales. Renewability of fossil fuels, metal ores and minerals such as gypsum and limestone is either zero or will occur only over tens of millions of years. Once used, the world's reserves are steadily depleted, though in the case of metals such as steel and copper, recycling can prolong their availability.

Technology and the changing definition of resources

Resources are defined by technology and societal values. Materials only become resources when the technology exists to find, exploit, process and use them. Ten thousand years ago Palaeolithic hunter-gathers in Europe had a simple technology that relied on resources such as wild animals and wild plants, flint and wood. Without the technology to extract and smelt metal ores, it would be several thousand years before iron, copper and tin became recognised as resources.

The development of uranium as a resource

Uranium is a heavy, dense metal. Today uranium is a valuable resource worth over US\$200 kg^{-1} on the world market. Yet until 1789 uranium was undiscovered. For a century or more after its discovery its main use was for colouring glass and providing glazes for ceramics and porcelain. Although the radioactive properties of uranium were known by the start of the twentieth century, uranium remained an element with limited uses until the development of nuclear technology.

In the 1930s research showed that the uranium isotope U-235 was fissile (could be split) and in the process of nuclear fission, huge amounts of energy could be released. Uranium thus became an extremely valuable resource, providing the raw material for nuclear weapons. Later technological breakthroughs made it possible to control fission inside a nuclear reactor and generate electricity from nuclear power. By 2008 there were 435 nuclear reactors worldwide in 30 countries producing 17% of the world's electricity.

Although uranium is diffused widely within the Earth's crust, there are relatively few places where it is concentrated and can be mined economically. This makes uranium a point resource. In 2006, just three countries, Canada, Australia and Kazakhstan, accounted for nearly 60% of the world's uranium production (Photograph 4.3).

Photograph 4.3
Uranium ore mining in Kakadu National Park, Australia

Peter Bowater/Alamy

The supply and use of resources

Key ideas

➤ The supply and use of resources is determined by a combination of physical and socio-economic factors.

➤ The factors which influence the supply and use of resources change with time.

➤ Changes in the supply and use of resources are influenced by technology, economics and societal values.

In this section we shall focus on the supply and use of two resources: tin and wind power. Tin is a non-renewable but recyclable resource; wind power is a renewable flow resource. The supply and use of both resources have undergone considerable change in the past 20 years or so.

Broadly speaking the principal factor that influences the supply and demand for a natural resource is technology (Figure 4.15). This includes the technology to find, extract, transport to market and use a resource. There is, however, one other important influence: economics. A resource will only be exploited if its development is profitable. For example, when the world price for tin is high, it becomes profitable to mine tin in Cornwall. When prices plummet it is not worth digging the ore out of the ground and tin mines close.

Favourable economic conditions (e.g. high prices) which make resource development profitable

Resource development

Natural resources with technology available to find, extract, transport and utilise

Figure 4.15 Factors influencing resource development

Tin

Tin is a heavy metal found in veins in igneous rocks and in alluvial deposits. It is usually mined as the mineral cassiterite and is non-renewable, though recyclable. In some parts of the world such as Cornwall, tin has been mined for thousands of years. Bronze, an alloy of tin and copper, was the first metal to be smelted and was the basis of the technology of human groups after the new stone (neolithic) age.

Large deposits of recoverable tin ore are relatively scarce, and so tin is classed as a point resource. Two-thirds of the world's production is concentrated in two countries: China and Indonesia (Figure 4.16).

In 2005, world output was just over 260 000 tonnes. The main uses of tin are for tin-plating food cans, as a coating (with lead) on zinc and iron to prevent corrosion, for soldering in the electronics industry, for automotive parts and in construction.

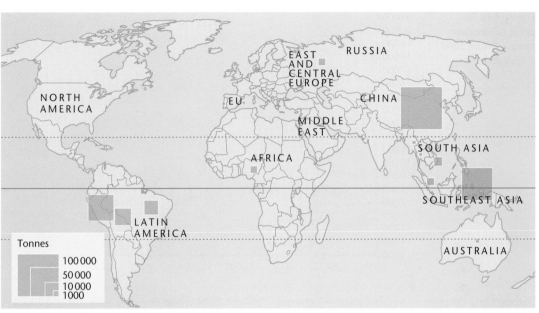

Figure 4.16 *World tin production map*

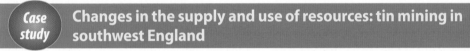

Case study **Changes in the supply and use of resources: tin mining in southwest England**

Decline

Tin occurs in veins or lodes in granite intrusions in Cornwall and south Devon. In fact southwest England has one of the world's biggest reserves of tin. Tin mining in this region has a long history stretching back over 3000 years. Production peaked in the nineteenth century and for most of the last century mining was in decline. Finally, in 1998,

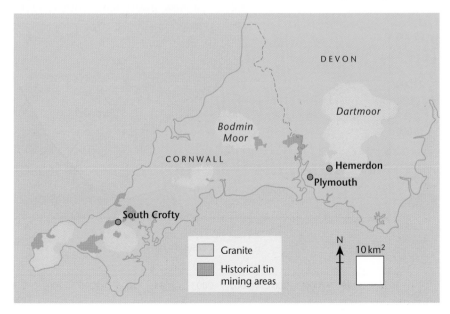

Figure 4.17
Map of tin mining in southwest England

147

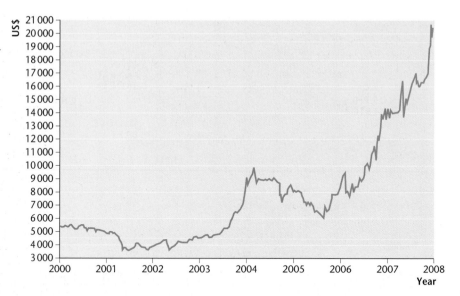

Figure 4.18 *Tin prices (dollars per tonne), 7 April 2000– 7 April 2008*

Europe's last tin mine — South Crofty — between Camborne and Redruth in Cornwall, closed (Figure 4.17). The high costs of recovering tin ore coupled with low world prices had made Cornish tin unprofitable. As a result of falling prices Cornwall's tin deposits lost their status as **reserves** and became part of the general **resource stock** (Box 4.4).

Revival

The situation changed dramatically in the early twenty-first century.

In April 2004 world tin prices were just US$9000 t^{-1}; 4 years later they had soared to over US$20 000 t^{-1} (Figures 4.18 and 4.19). This surge in world prices was driven by demand from the rapidly industrialising economies of China and India. Once again southwest England's tin deposits became economic and attracted the interest of international mining companies.

In 2007, South Crofty was re-opened, with the new owners, Western United Mines, pledging £50 million of new investment. With reserves

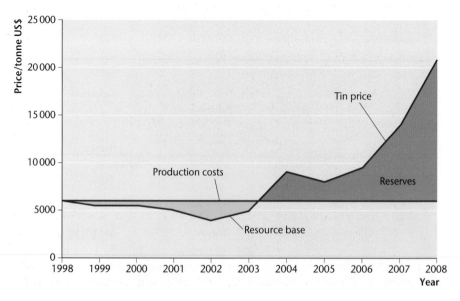

Figure 4.19 *Model showing tin production costs and process*

estimated to last for 80 years, South Crofty will create 250 skilled jobs and help regenerate one of England's poorest regions. It will also stimulate demand for new mining machinery provided by local businesses. Production will be completely mechanised, with no hand-held machinery, and mine tunnels 4 m wide. Ore will be milled on the surface and spoil will be stored underground to fill old mine workings.

Late in 2007, the Australian mining company, Wolf Minerals, confirmed the revival of tin mining in southwest England. It announced plans to reopen the Hemerdon tin and tungsten mine near Plymouth which had closed in 1944 (Figure 4.17). Mining will be open-cast, could create 500 jobs and inject £20 million a year into the local economy. Recoverable reserves of tin and tungsten are estimated at 40 million tonnes and should last for 20–40 years.

Photograph 4.4 *The South Crofty tin mine before re-opening*

Box 4.4 Mineral resources: terminology

Economists use three separate terms to describe resource concepts: resource base, resources and reserves (Figure 4.20).

The **resource base** (or total stock) comprises all occurrences of a mineral in or on the Earth's crust that would become resources if they could be extracted.

Resources are the proportion of the total stock of a mineral that can be extracted under prevailing technological and economic conditions.

Reserves are that part of the resource base which could be economically extracted or produced. The term need not indicate that extraction facilities are in place and operative (Figure 4.19). Reserves include only recoverable resources given prevailing technological, economic and social conditions.

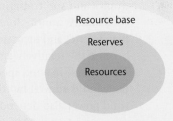

Figure 4.20 *Resource concepts*

Wind energy

Energy supply

Wind energy is a renewable resource with a long history. The power of the wind has been harnessed for millennia as a means of transport, pumping water and milling grain.

Thanks to global warming and climate change, wind power has experienced a renaissance in the past few years. Since 1997 the global generating capacity for

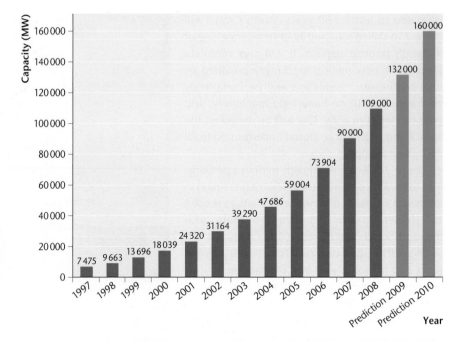

Figure 4.21 World wind energy: total installed capacity (MW), 1997–2007

wind power has increased exponentially (Figure 4.21). Modern wind turbines create electricity without releasing the greenhouse gases responsible for climate change. In theory, the planet has more than enough wind energy to meet present-day global electricity consumption 40 times over.

At the global scale the best locations for generating wind power are in the middle to high latitudes zone of westerly winds, and the trade wind belt in the tropics and sub-tropics. Winds in these latitudes are not only strong, but fairly constant. At a more local level, wind energy is generally higher in coastal areas than inland, and increases with altitude. Stronger winds tend to blow on the coast because the relatively smooth sea surface exerts little frictional drag on air flow. The increase in wind speed with altitude is known as wind shear. Near the ground the wind is slowed by friction, caused by the roughness of the surface. However, wind power also depends on air density, which decreases with height.

Wind resources in Europe

Wind energy potential in Europe, both over the continent and sea, is relatively high (Figures 4.22 and 4.23). Wind speeds are generally higher over the sea than over the mainland, especially along the Atlantic coast. Over the continent, wind energy potential decreases in a southwesterly direction away from the British Isles. The main exceptions to this pattern are deep valleys such as the Rhône in France and the Ebro in Spain which connect to high mountain ranges. Local mountain winds such as the mistral explain the high wind energy potential of southern France, which extends offshore into the Mediterranean. In the eastern Mediterranean high temperatures promote atmospheric mixing that produces high wind energy between Turkey and Greece.

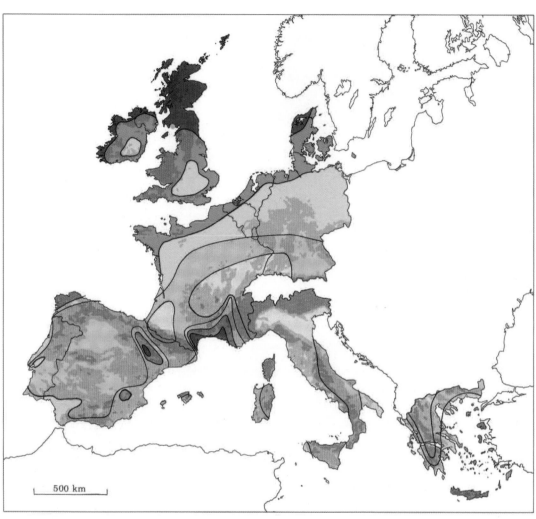

Figure 4.22
Potential wind resources over mainland Europe

Wind resources at 50 metres above ground level for five different topographic conditions									
Sheltered terrain		Open plain		At a sea coast		Open sea		Hills and ridges	
$m\,s^{-1}$	Wm^{-2}	$m\,s^{-1}$	Wm^{-2}	$m\,s^{-1}$	Wm^{-2}	$m\,s^{-1}$	Wm^{-2}	$m\,s^{-1}$	Wm^{-2}
> 6.0	> 250	> 7.5	> 500	> 8.5	> 700	> 9.0	> 800	> 11.5	> 1800
5.0-6.0	150-250	6.5-7.5	300-500	7.0-8.5	400-700	8.0-9.0	600-800	10.0-11.5	1200-1800
4.5-5.0	100-150	5.5-6.5	200-300	6.0-7.0	250-400	7.0-8.0	400-600	8.5-10.0	700-1200
3.5-4.5	50-100	4.5-5.5	100-200	5.0-6.0	150-250	5.5-7.0	200-400	7.0- 8.5	400- 700
< 3.5	< 50	< 4.5	< 100	< 5.0	< 150	< 5.5	< 200	< 7.0	< 400

Wind energy generation in Europe

The generation of wind energy depends on economic, political and physical factors. European governments and the EU promote wind energy because it is:

➤ carbon neutral and does not contribute to global warming

➤ as a flow resource, it is renewable

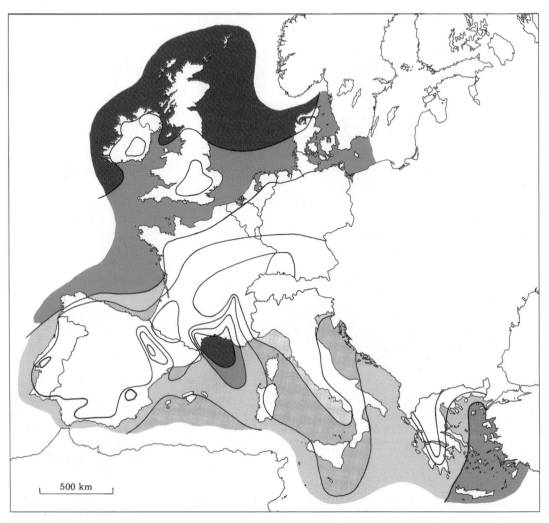

Wind resources over open sea (more than 10 km offshore) for five standard heights									
10 m		25 m		50 m		100 m		200 m	
m s^{-1}	Wm^{-2}	m s^{-1}	Wm^{-2}	m s^{-1}	Wm^{-2}	m s^{-1}	Wm^{-2}	m s^{-1}	Wm^{-2}
> 8.0	> 600	> 8.5	> 700	> 9.0	> 800	> 10.0	> 1100	> 11.0	> 1500
7.0-8.0	350-600	7.5-8.5	450-700	8.0-9.0	600-800	8.5-10.0	650-1100	9.5-11.0	900-1500
6.0-7.0	250-300	6.5-7.5	300-450	7.0-8.0	400-600	7.5- 8.5	450- 650	8.0- 9.5	600- 900
4.5-6.0	100-250	5.0-6.5	150-300	5.5-7.0	200-400	6.0- 7.5	250- 450	6.5- 8.0	300- 600
< 4.5	< 100	< 5.0	< 150	< 5.5	< 200	< 6.0	< 250	< 6.5	< 300

Reproduced by permission of the *European Wind Atlas*, © 1989 by Risø National Laboratory, Roskilde, Denmark

Figure 4.23
Potential wind resources over the sea in Europe

Most European governments have obligations under international treaty to reduce carbon emissions. The Kyoto Protocol, signed by all EU countries, set targets for reductions in carbon emissions. The UK's target is a 12.5% reduction of carbon emissions below 1990 levels by 2012. One way to achieve these targets is to increase the proportion of electricity from renewables. However, wind energy is not entirely carbon-free. The manufacture of turbines, their transport, on-site

construction and disruption of moorland ecosystems consumes energy and/or releases carbon dioxide. The UK has pledged to increase its electricity production from renewables to 15% by 2015, although this target now seems unrealistic.

At the end of 2007 the EU's total wind-generating capacity was 56 535 MW. Germany led the field with nearly 40% of EU production, followed by Spain with 27% (Figure 4.24). Despite its massive resources, only 1.8% of the UK's electricity production was from wind power.

Public opinion has slowed the development of wind power in the UK. Proposed wind farms often meet strong opposition from local people and conservationists. On the mainland, the sites with the greatest potential are often coasts and uplands of high environmental and amenity value. The resulting conflicts and prolonged planning enquiries explain why between 2004 and 2007, of the 282 wind farm schemes submitted, only 57% were approved (Figures 4.25 and 4.26).

Recently the response by the industry has been to site new wind farms offshore, in the Thames estuary, around the Wash and in northwest England. A new generation of giant wind turbines, with blades up to 150 m in diameter and a capacity of 7.5 MW, will be sited several kilometres offshore where they are less visually intrusive. None the less, there are objections. The RSPB argues that offshore wind turbines are responsible for large-scale mortality among migrating birds; meanwhile their impact on marine ecosystems is largely unknown.

The UK government encourages investment in wind power and other types of renewable energy through its Renewable Obligation (RO) policy. This obliges electricity suppliers to provide an increasing proportion of electricity from renewable resources generated in the UK. In 2006–07 the RO was 6.7%.

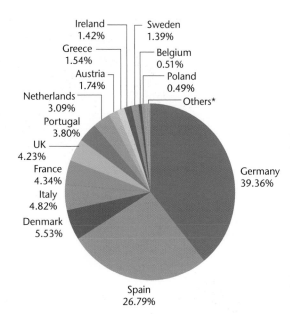

* Czech Republic, Finland, Bulgaria, Hungary, Estonia, Latvia, Romania and Slovakia represent less than 0.5% of the EU cumulative capacity

Cyprus, Malta and Slovenia have no wind power installed

Figure 4.24 *Wind power production in the EU*

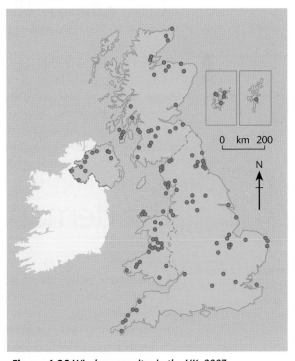

Figure 4.25 *Wind energy sites in the UK, 2007*

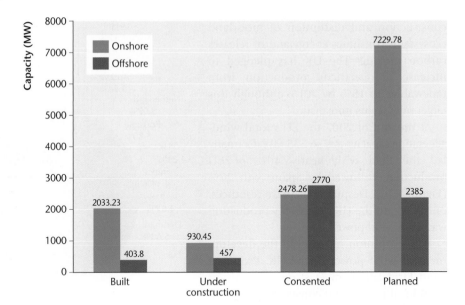

Figure 4.26 *Wind energy capacity (MW) in the UK, 2007*

Change with time

The importance of wind as an energy resource has changed significantly in the past 15 to 20 years. The attraction of wind power derives from its renewability and carbon-free quality. Finite energy resources such as oil and gas, which may well be exhausted by the mid-twenty-first century, have stimulated huge interest in renewables such as wind power. At the same time, potentially calamitous climate change caused by the consumption of fossil fuels, has boosted wind power and other renewables.

Other factors have also led to a reappraisal of wind power. Global political instability has underlined the need for countries to depend less on imported energy such as oil and gas. Diversification of a country's energy mix and greater reliance on domestic energy resources improve energy security. Finally, nervousness about the safety of nuclear energy, following the world's worst nuclear accident at Chernobyl in the Ukraine in 1986, has boosted the attractiveness of wind power and other renewable energy resources.

The demand for resources

Key ideas

➤ The demand for resources varies with time and location.

➤ Demand in terms of quantity and type of resources varies with time and development.

➤ The demand for resources is influenced by population growth and standards of living.

➤ The different patterns of resource demand in MEDCs, LEDCs and NICs change with population growth and rate of development.

In this section we focus on the demand for resources. A range of factors determine levels of resource demand. They include population size, standards of living, types of economy and economic development. Each of these factors can change over time. We shall consider these factors through case studies of three countries at varying stages of economic development: China, the Democratic Republic of Congo and Japan.

Case study — China: demand for resources

Since the turn of the century, China has experienced remarkable economic growth. The Chinese economy is now the second largest in the world, and will almost certainly surpass the world's largest, the USA, sometime in the 2020s. However, most of China's economic growth has occurred within the past 10 years. In terms of standards of living, literacy, urbanisation and infrastructure, China still lags a long way behind North America and western Europe (Table 4.5). For this reason China is classed as a newly industrialising country (NIC).

China's economic growth, based on rapid industrialisation, has created an enormous demand for mineral resources and energy (Figure 4.27). This demand is fuelled by high levels of foreign investment, exports, urbanisation and rising standards of

Table 4.5 Economic and development statistics, China and USA, 2007

	China	USA
GDP	US$2.6 trillion	US$13.2 trillion
GDP per capita	US$4660	US$44 070
Per capita energy use	1316 kg oil equivalent per year	7893 kg oil equivalent per year
Secondary school enrolment	75.5%	94.1%
Improved water supply	76%	100%

Source: World Bank

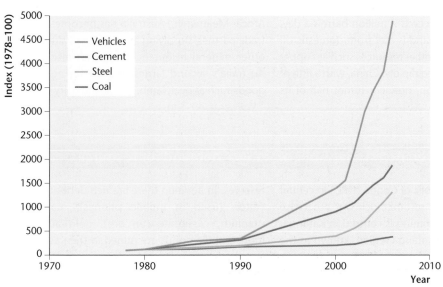

Figure 4.27 Growth of industrial output in China, 1978–2006

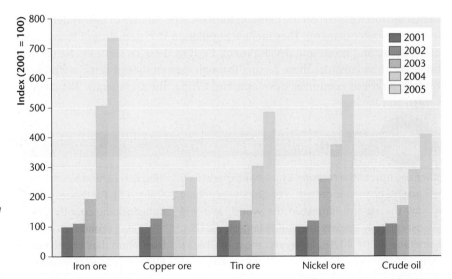

Figure 4.28 *Growth of raw material imports to China, 2001–2005*

living. In 2004 China was responsible for half of the total worldwide growth in metal demand and for one-third of the global increase in the demand for oil. Although China is a huge country with a rich resource base, economic growth on this scale can only be sustained by importing foreign resources (Figure 4.28).

For example, although China is the world's largest producer of iron ore, in 2007 it still imported 375 million tonnes of iron ore; a figure that could rise to 900 million tonnes by 2014. Meanwhile, oil consumption, which in 1990 averaged 2.4 million barrels a day, now exceeds 7 million barrels a day. Only half of this demand is met from domestic oil reserves. Demand for other resources such as copper and oil is also increasing rapidly. China, with a fifth of the world's population, now consumes half of its

cement, a third of its steel and a quarter of its aluminium (*The Economist*, 15 March 2008). Growing demand for resources is being driven by rising prosperity among millions of Chinese. Evidence of this is the growth of private car ownership. Between 2000 and 2006 the number of new cars sold in China grew by an average of 37% a year.

In an effort to secure vital mineral and energy resources, China has developed trading links with suppliers worldwide. Chinese mining and oil firms have invested billions in poor but mineral-rich countries such as the DRC, Angola and the Sudan in Africa. Meanwhile, Australia has become a leading trade partner, supplying iron ore, coal, alumina and other mineral resources. China has also become Australia's second largest market for agricultural goods such as beef, lamb, wheat and dairy products.

Case study

The Democratic Republic of Congo: demand for resources

The Democratic Republic of Congo (DRC) in central equatorial Africa is a resource-rich but otherwise poor LEDC. Mineral mining is centred in Katanga, Kivu and Kasai. The Katanga region, known as the 'copper belt', contains around 10% of the world's copper reserves and 34% of the world's cobalt

reserves. In addition there are rich deposits of zinc, colton (used in mobile phones), manganese, uranium, cassiterite (tin ore), gold and silver. Industrial diamonds are mined in the Kasai region close to the Angolan border. There are major offshore oil deposits at the mouth of the Congo River. The

Photograph 4.5
An open pit copper mine in the Democratic Republic of Congo

Congo, which is the world's second largest river, also has huge HEP potential. At Inga, 150 km upstream from the river's mouth, the river falls 100 m in just 12 km. The proposed Grand Inga Dam could generate 40 000 MW — twice as much electricity as the Three Gorges Dam in China.

Despite its huge reserves of minerals, oil, timber and HEP, the DRC is one of the poorest countries in the world (Figure 4.29). In 2006 average gross income per person was just US$270, life expectancy was 46 years and infant mortality at 129 per 1000 was one of the highest in the world. Development of the country's mineral wealth has been hindered by poor government and the anarchy of civil war between 1998 and 2003. Moreover, smuggling and corruption have, in the past, siphoned off most of the profits from mining. Against this background, international mining companies have been reluctant to invest in the DRC.

The Congo's export earnings — just US$2.6 billion for a population of 60 million people — are not only small, but depend entirely on primary products, especially copper and diamonds. In 2006 copper made up 56% of the value of all exports. This reliance on primary products makes the DRC's economy highly vulnerable to fluctuations in commodity prices on world markets. At the same time, the

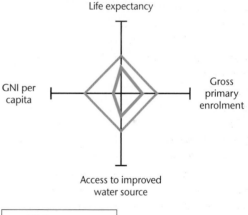

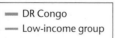

Figure 4.29 *Level of development in the DRC*

country's limited economic development, and the poverty of the Congolese people, mean that domestic demand for raw materials is negligible.

As the political situation stabilised in 2006–07, the DRC's mineral wealth attracted renewed interest from Chinese, American, Canadian, European and Australian mining companies. China has been most active in investing in the DRC in recent years. Investment will bring much-needed trade, economic growth, improvements in roads and railways and hopefully, rising standards of living for the people.

Some mining contracts are linked to infrastructural projects and investment will be a partnership between the state-owned mining company and foreign companies. Agreements include processing and enriching mineral ores before export, which will add value and create badly needed jobs.

Case study — Japan: demand for resources

Japan is at the opposite end of the development spectrum to the Democratic Republic of Congo. Although Japan is resource-poor, it is one of the wealthiest countries in the world. In 2006 its gross domestic product per person was US$38 326 and its human development index was the eighth highest in the world. Modern Japan owes its prosperity to human resources, namely its highly educated and highly skilled workforce.

Japanese industrialisation began with the restoration of the Meiji dynasty in 1867 and the symbolic move of the capital from Kyoto to Tokyo. Defeat in the Second World War proved only a temporary setback as massive foreign investment and economic aid rebuilt the Japanese economy in the 1950s. Powered by manufacturing exports, by 1990 Japan's economy was the second largest in the world.

Japan's economic success has been achieved in spite of its poor natural resource base. Japan has no iron ore, copper or bauxite, and imports most of its coal and three-quarters of its crude oil. Most of the country is mountainous: 65% is covered in forest and only 25% of Japan's land area is suitable for agriculture. Imported raw materials and energy sustain its manufacturing sector and imports provide over half of basic foodstuffs.

Japan's economy has now entered a post-industrial phase (Figure 4.30). Employment and wealth generation depends increasingly on the tertiary sector and producer services like banking, accounting and advertising as well as research, development and design. In 2005 the tertiary sector contributed 69% of the total value of national output. This compares to just 30% from manufacturing industry (Figure 4.31).

Even so, Japan retains a large and thriving manufacturing sector. Thanks to capital-intensive industries, manufacturing output has risen steadily in value, even though manufacturing employs less than 20% of the workforce today. Heavy export-oriented

Figure 4.30
Employment changes in manufacturing and services in Japan, 1960–2007

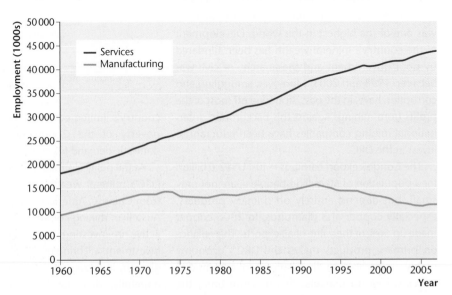

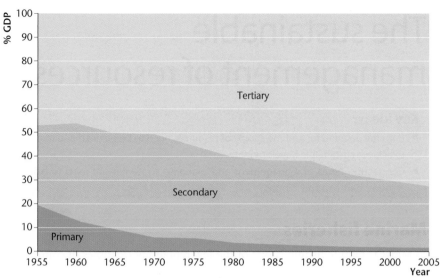

Figure 4.31
Changes in the contribution of economic sectors to Japanese GDP, 1955–2005

industries like steel and shipbuilding, which flourished in the 1960s and 1970s, are being replaced by knowledge-based industries such as telecoms and electronics. Meanwhile, since the mid-1980s, many Japanese transnational companies have located the production of cars and domestic electronic goods offshore, in Europe, North America and Asia. All of these trends explain why the value of Japan's raw material imports fell by 12% between 1993 and 2003.

However, demand for one particular resource continues to rise. Crude oil is easily Japan's biggest single import item by value. Like other MEDCs, Japan's economy and high standard of living is only sustained by the intensive consumption of energy. In fact Japan's energy use rose by 35% between 1990 and 2005 (Figure 4.32). This was driven by the general rise in living standards and the expansion of the economy (GDP grew by 25%) rather than any significant increase in population.

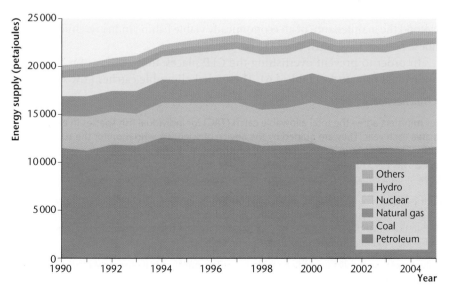

Figure 4.32 Total *primary energy supply for Japan, 1990–2005*

The sustainable management of resources

Key ideas
➤ Both the demand for and the supply of resources need to be planned and managed to achieve sustainable development.
➤ Contrasting types of management and planning strategies are used to balance resource demand and supply.

Marine fisheries

In MEDCs, marine fishing is one of the few remaining examples of commercial hunting, where wild animal populations are exploited directly. Unlike farmers, fishermen have little or no control over production and the ecosystem which supports fisheries. Furthermore, fish are a common resource: no one owns fish until they are caught and every fisherman is vulnerable to the actions of others. For these reasons fish stocks are easily overexploited.

The Common Fisheries Policy

Since 1983, the Common Fisheries Policy (CFP) has been the instrument used to manage the fishing industry and related economic activities in the EU. It aims to create a sustainable fishing industry from an environmental, economic and social point of view. However, by tradition fish have always been a common resource and the CFP gives member states equal access to fishing grounds in EU waters (though coastal waters are reserved for local fishermen). The CFP has two main pillars: first, the conservation of fish stocks and prevention of overfishing; and second the maintenance of an economically viable fishing industry. Unfortunately these policies have often conflicted.

In order to prevent overfishing the CFP places annual limits on catches of individual fish stocks (Table 4.6). These total allowable catches (TACs) are then

Table 4.6 *The Common Fisheries Policy*

TACs and quotas	Fisheries ministers agree the total allowable catch (TAC) for individual fish species in each fishing area each year. They are guided by the advice of scientists who monitor the status of fish stocks. For example, in 2007 the cod TAC for the North Sea was 19 957 tonnes and the UK's quota was 7773 tonnes. If stocks are below safe biological limits (e.g. as herring was in the North Sea in the 1980s), TACs may be zero, or the fishery may be closed until stocks recover.
Fishing effort	To limit the amount of fish caught, restrictions are placed on the number of days that vessels can fish and on net sizes. In 2006 the Scottish fleet was allowed to fish for cod and other whitefish in the North Sea only for 13.6 days per month. The CFP has a fleet management policy designed to limit the fishing capacity of the EU fleet.
Minimum landing size	Only fish of a certain minimum size can be landed. The purpose is to conserve immature fish and allow them to spawn.

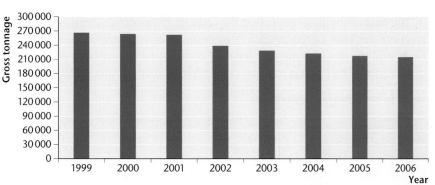

Figure 4.33
Changes in the UK's fishing fleet (gross tonnage), 1999–2006

shared out as quotas among EU states. However, TACs and quotas alone are not enough to conserve fish stocks. Limits on the fishing effort (i.e. number of days at sea, net sizes, size of fish caught etc.) are also imposed. Fishing fleet reduction is a further policy designed to reduce the fishing effort, with EU governments funding the decommissioning of fishing vessels (Figure 4.33). However, reducing the fishing effort in this way has proved difficult. Improved technology in fish detection, more powerful vessels and developments in gear may have made it easier to catch fish. This situation has been made worse by EU grants which encourage fleet modernisation.

Problems in achieving sustainable fisheries

Although the primary purpose of the CFP is to create a sustainable fishing industry, success has been elusive. Overfishing continues and most fish stocks suffer long-term decline (Figure 4.34). Some, such as cod, hake and sand eels are below safe biological limits. The International Council for the Exploration of the Sea (ICES) advises the EU on its annual round of TACs. Its recommendations, based on what is biologically sustainable, are often ignored. For example, despite ICES recommending zero catches of cod in the North Sea fishery every year from 2003 to 2007, TACs were actually set between 23 050 tonnes and 27 000 tonnes. Similarly while ICES recommended a maximum catch for North Sea plaice in 2007 of 32 000 tonnes, the TAC was set at 50 621 tonnes.

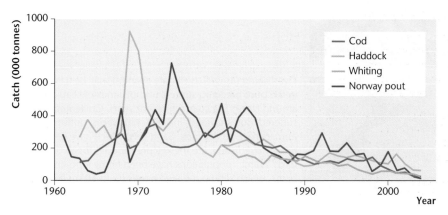

Figure 4.34
The decline of some North Sea fish stocks, 1963–2005

The crux of the problem is that the capacity to catch fish greatly exceeds the regeneration rates of fish stocks. Improvements in equipment, more powerful boats and the use of seine nets have all contributed to increased efficiency in catching fish. The result is massive overexploitation of resources (Figure 4.35).

Figure 4.35 *Problems caused by overfishing in the North Sea*

Cod		Stocks of North Sea cod have been close to collapse for several years and the ICES has recommended zero catches. In 1963 the spawning stock biomass was 157 000 tonnes; by 2004 this had been reduced to just 46 000 tonnes. ICES says there are no clear signs that cod are making a recovery.
Hake	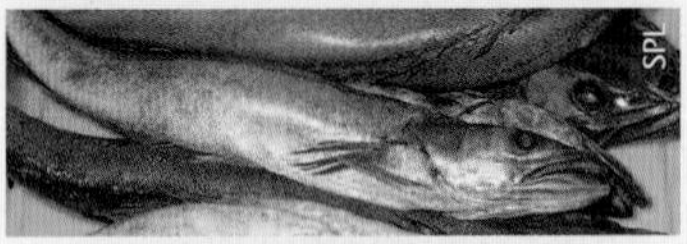	The hake stock in the southern North Sea is as low as 10 200 tonnes. ICES recommended zero catches in 2007 but the TAC was set at 6128 tonnes.
Sand eel		An important species for predation, both for other fish and seabirds, and therefore a vital part of the ecosystem. The North Sea sand eel stock is estimated to have fallen to a historic low level of 325 000 tonnes. In the early 1990s catches of sand eel (the largest industrial fishery) exceeded 1 million tonnes.
Mammals		Both seals and cetaceans (dolphins and porpoises) are caught accidently by fishing gear. These bycatches threaten dolphin and porpoise populations. It is estimated that 7000 harbour porpoises are killed annually by fishing gear in the North Sea.
Discards		800 000 tonnes of dead fish are discarded into the North Sea every yer. Some of the discards are fish that are worthless; some are too small; and some are discarded because fishermen have already achieved their quota for a particular species and do not want to break CFP rules.
Seabirds		Overfishing (as well as climate change) may be a factor in the poor breeding success of thousands of seabirds around North Sea coasts in recent years. Guillemots suffered food shortages in 2004. Kittiwakes, puffins and fulmars have all declined. Sand eels, which have been hugely overfished, are the key prey species for all these birds. Fulmar populations have been hit by long-liner boats, which send out baited hooks up to 50 km long.

The issue faced by fisheries ministers is to balance the long-term health of fish stocks with the short-term demand of the fishing industry and related economic activities. Not only does the fishing industry directly employ thousands of workers, it also supports indirectly a range of onshore economic activities including fish processing, packing, marketing, boat building and boat maintenance. So far the outcome has been unsatisfactory: most fish stocks are dwindling with only 13 species currently being fished sustainably, and 28 fished outside safe biological limits. The future of the fishing industry is in doubt.

Box 4.5 The tragedy of the commons

In 1968, Garrett Hardin proposed the idea that common resources such as seas, oceans and the atmosphere, being subject to increasing human pressure, will inevitably degrade. He referred to this as the 'tragedy of the commons'. In many ways the overexploitation of marine resources in Europe is a modern example this tragedy.

Hardin pointed out the logic to the misuse of common resources. In Europe the sea was one of the last commons, with marine resources such as fish and whales available to all. Rising demand for fish and shellfish, and improvements in catching technology, however, have led to massive depletion of fish stocks, threatening some species with extinction. At the same time parts of the continental shelf like the southern North Sea have been used as 'sinks' for industrial and domestic waste. The problem is this: the resources of commons are by definition unregulated. As a result there is no incentive for individuals or nations (other than conscience) to withdraw unilaterally from their exploitation. To do so merely allows other parties to claim those resources. This process has a remorseless logic: continued exploitation of the commons; their eventual destruction; and ruin to all.

Viewed in this light, the CFP can be seen as an attempt to regulate the marine commons around the EU and avoid this tragedy. It causes resentment because fishermen and governments have traditionally been free to exploit the marine commons. Despite the CFP's aim to create a sustainable resource, the policy still supports the notion that the marine commons should be open to all EU countries. However, the continued decline of fish stocks and overexploitation of resources suggests that the policy is contradictory and therefore unworkable. Elsewhere in Europe, notably in Iceland, the government has exclusive control of marine resources in a 200-mile zone around the country. For the past 30 years, because Iceland has been able to regulate use of its marine resources, it has been able to create a sustainable fishery.

Ecosystem approach to management

Without human interference the North Sea ecosystem would be self-supporting and self-regulating, with energy flows, nutrient cycles and food webs. Today there is a growing awareness that the only effective way to guarantee sustainable harvests of fish and shellfish from the North Sea, is to maintain the health and integrity of the entire ecosystem. However, past exploitation of North Sea fisheries has done quite the opposite. The ecosystem has been degraded by:
➤ inputs of chemicals such as nitrates and phosphates from agricultural runoff causing nutrient enrichment, algal blooms and eutrophication
➤ dumping industrial and domestic wastes, exposing fish, seabirds, marine mammals and invertebrates to toxins such as polychlorinated biphenyls (PCBs), dioxins and heavy metals

➤ overfishing of target species like sand eel (an important prey species) and cod (a top predator), leading to the collapse of fish stocks at both ends of the food chain

➤ trawling which has ruined large areas of the sea bed, destroying the rich and complex ecosystem that supports bottom-dwelling species

➤ burning of fossil fuels which has increased carbon dioxide concentrations and the acidity of the sea water

The ecosystem approach to marine resource management was accepted in principle by the European Commission when the CFP was reformed in 2003. This new approach offers the best way to harvest fish stocks and other marine resources sustainably in future. It aims to consider all aspects of the North Sea ecosystem — its wildlife, its habitats, its pollution as well as its commercial fisheries — in order to protect vulnerable habitats and species, prevent disruption to food chains, maintain key ecosystem processes, and create a healthy marine environment. In this way, the EU is best able to support a prosperous and sustainable fishing industry.

So far, however, the move towards integrated management of the North Sea ecosystem has been slow. The policy remains at odds with the current TACs and quota system. Meanwhile scientific advice on fish stocks and sustainable fishing, for economic and political reasons, is often ignored. Without management based on sound ecological principles, the North Sea's fisheries will be yet another example of the 'tragedy of the commons'.

Forestry in Finland

Figure 4.36 Finnish timber industry statistics

Timber is a renewable raw material and energy resource. The world's largest forest biome is the boreal coniferous forest that extends in a belt around the northern hemisphere between 50°N and 65°N. Finland, in northern Europe, occupies the westernmost part of this belt. Over three-quarters of its land area — around

(a) Tree species

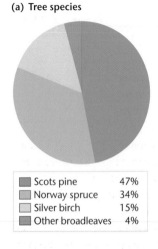

Scots pine	47%
Norway spruce	34%
Silver birch	15%
Other broadleaves	4%

(b) Forest ownership

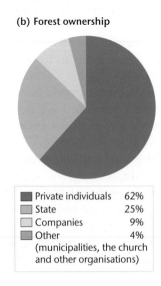

Private individuals	62%
State	25%
Companies	9%
Other	4%
(municipalities, the church and other organisations)	

(c) Annual increment versus annual cut

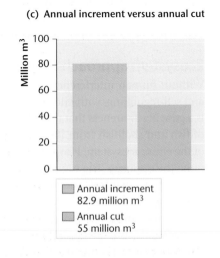

Annual increment
82.9 million m³

Annual cut
55 million m³

23 000 km² — is under forest cover, dominated by three species: Scots pine, Norway spruce and silver birch (Figure 4.36). Compared to more continental locations in Russia and Canada, Finland's climate is relatively mild and more favourable for tree growth. However, productivity declines northwards as the growing season shortens and temperatures become more severe (Figure 4.37).

Forest products are crucial to Finland's economy. They account for 30% of exports and 8% of GDP. Most exports are pulp and paper products with much higher value added than unprocessed logs and sawn timber. Forestry, pulp, paper and related industries such as furniture-making, packaging and printing employ around 200 000 people in Finland. Most Finnish forests are privately owned, the majority on small estates averaging only 26 ha (Figure 4.36).

Sustainable production

The economic importance of Finland's forests and forest products dictates that forestry must be sustainable. In fact sustainable forestry in Finland has a long history that goes back to the end of the Second World War. Sustainable production has been achieved through forestry planning and national forestry programmes (Box 4.6).

The success of sustainable production is clear when we look at the budget of annual timber growth and harvesting. In 2006, for example, timber growth in Finland's forests was 82.9 million m³ compared to a cut of 55 million m³ (Figure 4.36). Indeed for the past 40 years, tree growth has exceeded tree cutting by 20–30%. So successful has the forestry policy been that the current stock growing in Finland's forests is greater than at any time since the foundation of the Finnish state in 1917.

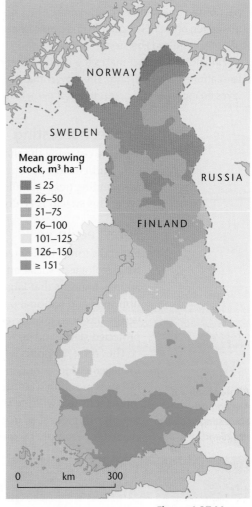

Mean growing stock, m³ ha⁻¹

■ ≤ 25
■ 26–50
■ 51–75
□ 76–100
□ 101–125
■ 126–150
■ ≥ 151

Figure 4.37 Mean growing stock volumes on forest land

Box 4.6 Finland's forest programme

The principal objective of Finland's national forest policy is to achieve sustainability. Finland's National Forest Programme (NFP), approved by the government in 1999, is the main instrument of policy. It aims to:

■ secure employment and the livelihoods of workers in the forestry industry
■ maintain forest habitats and ecosystems, and

enhance their biodiversity and vitality
■ protect the traditional role of forests in Finnish society and culture by creating opportunities for forest-based recreation, including camping, hiking, picking berries and fungi, and hunting.

The Finnish government approved the first NFP in 1999, and since 2000 it has been implemented as part of the government programme. The implementation of the NFP is coordinated by the Ministry of Agriculture and Forestry.

Finland's Forest Act makes it a legal obligation to reafforest after cutting. The government also gives financial aid and grants to forest owners who practise sound management methods which achieve sustainable timber production, maintain forest diversity and the effective management of young forests. Forest associations help owners to improve forest management as well as providing advice on the timber trade and planning.

Timber harvesting

Trees are cut using the shortwood method. The trunks are stripped of branches in situ, and cut to appropriate length. This method causes minimal damage to surrounding trees and allows the branches to decompose and enrich the nutrient cycle. This system is ecologically sustainable (Photograph 4.6).

Forest ecology

Finland's forest policy recognises that its forests are multi-functional: that they have ecological, social and cultural, as well as commercial value. This ecological approach means that large areas of forest are protected by legislation as conservation areas and national parks. In the past few decades forest protection and biodiversity has been given even greater priority. Today 7.6% of Finland's forests have protected status and 10.6% are either protected or have restricted forestry use.

The Forest Act protects habitats of special importance which require sustainable management to maintain their biodiversity. Nature management in commercial forests is monitored constantly, both in private and in state forests. In commercial forests sensitive wildlife sites are normally left undisturbed. Most trees do just as well in commercial as in protected forests, where natural habitats and processes, created for example by rotten timber or burnt trees, are left undisturbed.

Photograph 4.6
Mechanical harvesting of timber in Finland

Reino Hanninen/Alamy

Trees are normally cut in the winter when the ground is frozen and snow-covered, minimising damage caused by heavy machinery and logging. Pollution of surface streams is prevented by leaving protected belts of trees along water-courses and prohibiting the use of fertilisers in groundwater basins.

Finland's forest policy allows only native Finnish tree species to be grown. This safeguards the integrity of the forests, maintains biodiversity and the delicate food webs that rely on native species. No exotic trees, such as Sitka spruce and Douglas fir, which are grown widely in the UK, are planted. Meanwhile the majority of reafforestation is through natural succession, not by planting and re-seeding. Again this helps to maintain the natural appearance, structure and processes of the forest ecosystem.

Examination-style questions

Section A
Resource 1

Table 1 *Water resources (m³ per person per year)*

	1988–92	1993–97	1998–2002	2003–07
China	2364	2251	2165	2125
Egypt	31.1	28.3	25.7	24.3
India	1426	1299	1196	1142
Mexico	4668	4277	3973	3821
Pakistan	468	415	370	348
Uzbekistan	760	690	642	614

1 Resource 1 relates to changes in water resource availability in selected countries between 1988 and 2007. Outline an issue indicated and suggest appropriate management. (10 marks)

Section B

2 To what extent is the rapid growth of population in LEDCs responsible for the widespread degradation of environmental resources? (30 marks)
3 How successful have governments been in their efforts to manage renewable resources sustainably? (30 marks)

5

Globalisation

What is globalisation?

Key ideas
➤ There are marked advantages for economic activity in working at a global rather than a local scale.
➤ Globalisation has both economic and cultural dimensions.
➤ A range of factors is responsible for current globalisation and possible future trends.

There is no simple definition of globalisation. As a process, globalisation has economic, social and cultural meaning. In economic terms, globalisation is about the increasing flows of ideas, people, goods, services and capital. These flows have led to increased integration of the world economy, and the development of ever-closer economic ties between countries. These ties involve the production and marketing of manufactured goods and services worldwide. However, globalisation is not a new process: it has operated since the 1950s. What is different today is its speed and scale, embracing more industries and more countries (Figure 5.1).

For instance, a sportswear manufacturer such as Adidas might design its products in Europe, make them in China or Indonesia, and sell them in the USA. Meanwhile its accounts might be outsourced to a company in India and it might raise capital for new investments in Tokyo or London.

Globalisation means:
➤ More manufactured goods are produced by transnational corporations (TNCs) and the volume of international trade in goods increases.
➤ Flows of raw materials, as part of an international supply chain, increase.
➤ More services such as IT, billing and customer care are outsourced from MEDCs to NICs and LEDCs.
➤ The global economic system becomes increasingly dependent on the global financial system controlled by major world cities such as New York, London and Tokyo.
➤ There is freer movement of capital and people between countries.

Globalisation also has a cultural dimension. It is often said that globalisation by US transnational corporations such as McDonald's and Starbucks transmits American consumer values and a Western lifestyle. People in LEDCs aspire to Western consumerism, undermining traditional values and lifestyles, and creating more homogenised societies.

The causes of globalisation

Globalisation is driven by a combination of factors. The main ones are shown in Figure 5.1.

Liberalisation of trade and finance

The World Trade Organization (WTO), with 152 member states in 2008, provides a forum for discussion on reducing international trade barriers. The WTO has been instrumental in promoting free trade between member countries and has therefore played a crucial role in economic globalisation and the expansion of world trade. Similar liberalisation of finance and other services by removing controls on international capital movement and discrimination in favour of domestic service providers has, in the past 10 years, given globalisation even greater impetus.

Liberalisation of trade and finance

Improvements in transport and telecommunications

Increasing global prosperity and new markets

Out-sourcing of production and services to exploit skills and lower wages

Globalisation

Growth of transnational corporations (TNCs)

Avoiding tariffs and other barriers to trade

Figure 5.1
Factors driving globalisation

Improvements in transport

There have been significant reductions in the costs of transporting raw materials and manufactured goods, and huge advances in the use of information technology and telecommunications in the past 30 years or so. Both trends have helped to stimulate globalisation. Shipping costs have fallen as ever larger vessels achieve **economies of scale** (Figure 5.2). **Containerisation** has done most to reduce the costs of transporting manufactured goods (Photograph 5.1). For example, thanks to containerisation, it costs just US$10 to transport a television set from China to the UK, and 10 cents to ship a bottle of wine from Australia to the USA. The size of container ships is measured by the number of containers they can carry. The

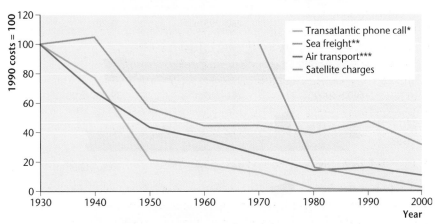

Figure 5.2 *Falling transport and communication costs*

Legend:
— Transatlantic phone call*
— Sea freight**
— Air transport***
— Satellite charges

Y-axis: 1990 costs = 100
X-axis: Year (1930–2000)

* Cost of 3-minute telephone call from New York to London
** Average ocean freight and port charges per tonne of import and export cargo
*** Average air transport revenue per passenger mile

Photograph 5.1
A modern container port

current generation of ships can carry up to 8700 units, but the next generation could be 50% larger (see Figure 5.3). Bulk carriers, designed to carry raw materials such as crude oil, iron ore and coal, have also grown enormously in size. The largest ships weigh over 350 000 tonnes and are nearly 350 metres long. Again, increasing size has been driven by scale economies and lower transport costs. Iron can be shipped from Brazil to China at a cost of US\$20–30 t^{-1}; and from western Australia to China for just US\$11 t^{-1}.

Figure 5.3
Evolution of container ships

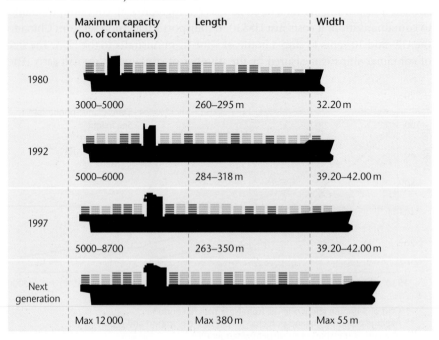

	Maximum capacity (no. of containers)	Length	Width
1980	3000–5000	260–295 m	32.20 m
1992	5000–6000	284–318 m	39.20–42.00 m
1997	5000–8700	263–350 m	39.20–42.00 m
Next generation	Max 12 000	Max 380 m	Max 55 m

Improvements in communications

In the past it was thought that only goods could be traded internationally. The internet has changed all that. Indeed the fastest-growing international trade is in services. This gives another dimension and a huge boost to globalisation. Increasing numbers of large companies in MEDCs are transferring company functions such as accounting, booking, customer care and billing to firms overseas — a process known as international **outsourcing**. India has been most successful in capturing this trade, which is now worth over US$25 billion a year to the Indian economy. India has also become the centre for global IT services, a function which depends entirely on internet access and data communications links. Today, 500 companies have IT operations in the southern city of Bangalore, including IBM, Dell, Hewlett-Packard, HSBC, Virgin and BT. Media services such as news agencies and financial journalism have also relocated successfully in India. Thanks to the internet and telecommunications, world news can be covered just as effectively, and more cheaply, from India as from London or Los Angeles.

Labour costs and skills

The growth of the emerging economies of China and India on the world stage has provided a major impetus to globalisation. These countries have attracted major inward investment from TNCs based in North America, Europe and Japan because of the lower labour costs and, in some sectors, the high skill levels of the workforce. In the past 10 years or so, foreign investment has made India the centre of the global IT industry. India has two major advantages. First, it has a highly educated workforce, with 2 million English-speaking graduates entering the labour market every year. Second, it has low wages, averaging between one-quarter and one-tenth of those for IT workers in Europe and the USA.

Textiles and clothing are examples of labour-intensive industries where profitability is greatly influenced by labour costs. Typical wage rates for workers in the clothing industry in the Yangtse delta region of eastern China are just US$1.40 h^{-1}. This compares with the minimum wage of US$11.20 h^{-1} in the UK. Elsewhere in east Asia wages are even lower. As China's wage levels rise, production will be outsourced to lower-cost neighbouring countries such as Laos and Cambodia. In addition to wages, labour costs in MEDCs are inflated by employers' social contributions to cover pensions, sickness pay, training and so on to each worker they employ. Overall, this adds between 15% and 20% to labour costs in the UK.

Proximity to markets

Many large TNCs have globalised production by locating manufacturing plants overseas. Since the 1980s, Japanese and South Korean TNCs, especially in the motor-vehicle and electronics sectors, have invested heavily in production facilities in North America and Europe. In the process, companies such as Toyota, Sony, Samsung and Hyundai have become truly globalised, with research, design and marketing, as well as production, transferred overseas.

Foreign direct investment (FDI) of this type has two major advantages. By locating close to markets, companies can avoid trade barriers such as import tariffs and quotas. At the same time they are better able to respond to local market preferences and tastes in design. In the case of motor vehicles, investments by TNCs in assembly plants have also attracted clusters of foreign parts manufacturers. They need proximity to assemblers to supply parts 'just-in-time' and to enable them to work closely together.

Chinese manufacturing companies are also set to expand production in markets overseas. For example, Haier, which makes refrigerators, air conditioning and washing machines, is expanding overseas. Other companies have acquired foreign manufacturers as the easiest way of expanding. Shanghai Automotive now owns the Korean firm Ssangyong, and Nanjing Motors bought MG Rover.

Issues surrounding globalisation

Key ideas
➤ The globalisation of economic activity brings advantages and disadvantages to countries and areas.
➤ Globalisation has environmental, economic, social and political impacts.
➤ Globalisation has brought environmental, economic, social and political benefits and problems to NICs and MEDCs.
➤ Globalisation may increase or narrow the development gap between rich and poor countries.

Globalisation has environmental, economic, social and political effects. Some of these effects are positive: others create significant problems. In this section we shall look at the impact of globalisation in two countries: China, and the UK.

Globalisation and its impact in China

In the past three decades China has experienced spectacular economic growth. To understand this growth we must first look at the economic reforms introduced by the Chinese government from 1978 onwards. These reforms opened China to trade and foreign investment and encouraged the development of a market economy (Box 5.1). Economic growth on the scale we have seen in the past three decades could not have happened without them.

Globalisation in Guangdong province
Nowhere has the impact of globalisation in China between greater than in the southern province of Guangdong. Guangdong, with a population of 94.5 million, is China's second-most populous region. It covers an area slightly bigger than England and Wales and has an average population density of 486 persons per km^2.

Box 5.1 China's economic reforms

In the past three decades, China's drive to economic development has had a major influence on globalisation. Change began in 1978 when the Chinese government, led by Deng Xiaoping, aimed to raise standards of living by gradually moving away from a command economy, to a more market-based one. As a result China was opened to international trade and to foreign direct investment (FDI).

Initially economic liberalisation was a step-by-step process. In 1980 a number of special economic zones in the south were established, including three in Guangdong province (Shenzhen, Zhuhai and Shantou) (Figure 5.4). Four years later 14 coastal cities were given similar status and opened to trade and FDI; among them was Guangdong's largest city, Guangzhou (see Figure 5.5). In 1985, China extended its open coastal areas by creating five open economic zones. One, the Pearl River Delta (PRD) adjacent to Hong Kong, has become the powerhouse of China's export-led industrial growth. Regions like the PRD have become prosperous by making goods such as electronic equipment, clothing, shoes and toys for the export market. Further reforms in the 1990s opened the Shanghai region (including river cities in the Yangtse valley) to overseas investment. Investment also went to border cities and provincial capitals. In addition free trade, economic and technological and high-tech zones have been created in several large and medium-sized cities.

These reforms have proved so successful that today, the private sector generates 70% of China's GDP. Economic success is also evident in China's impressive economic growth (exceeding 10% a year), the rising living standards of its people and significant reductions in poverty.

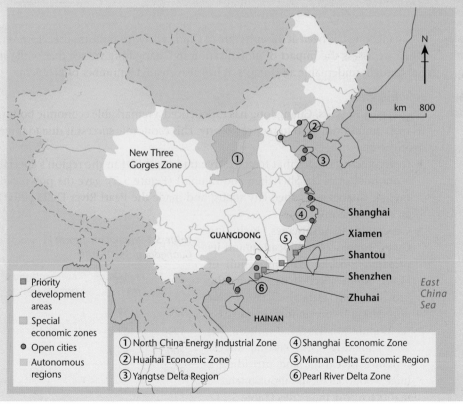

Figure 5.4 *Special economic zones in China*

① North China Energy Industrial Zone ④ Shanghai Economic Zone
② Huaihai Economic Zone ⑤ Minnan Delta Economic Region
③ Yangtse Delta Region ⑥ Pearl River Delta Zone

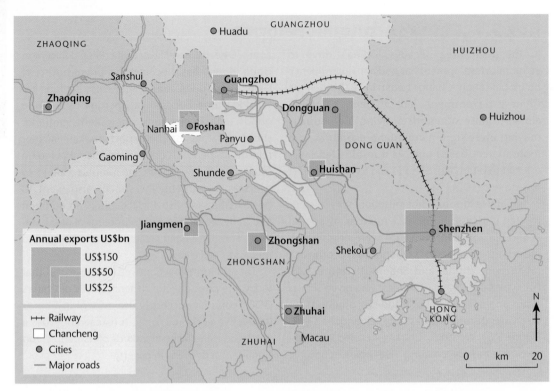

Figure 5.5 Location of the Pearl River Delta region in Guangdong province, and the principal manufacturing centres

Guangdong has been at the epicentre of China's drive to industrialise. However, when we assess the impact of globalisation in Guangdong we see that while it has brought undeniable advantages, it has also created a number of problems.

Advantages

For the past 30 years, Guangdong has experienced a remarkable economic boom. Its main impact has been to reduce poverty. This economic success is due to three main factors:

➤ Government policies that fostered free trade and FDI in the region's special economic zones (in Shenzhen and Zhuhai) (Figure 5.5); gave the provincial capital, Guangzhou, open city status; and made the Pearl River Delta (PRD) an open economic zone.

➤ Geographical advantages, including Guangdong's coastal location and its proximity to the economic hub of Hong Kong. Both have made the province an attractive target for domestic and foreign investment.

➤ Its population of 94.5 million (in 2006) making it the second largest province in China, and providing a huge workforce for its labour-intensive manufacturing industries (Table 5.1).

Table 5.1 Population growth in Guangdong, 1982–2010

	Population (m)	Average annual growth (m)
1982	59.3	
1990	62.8	0.45
2000	85.2	2.24
2006	94.5	1.56
2010	98.0	0.88

Hong Kong is the major investor in Guangdong, followed by Taiwan, Japan, South Korea, Singapore and the USA. Many of the world's leading TNCs such as IBM, Intel, Hitachi, Samsung, Nokia, Sony, Siemens, Panasonic, Bosch, Nestlé, Pepsi, Coca-Cola, Toyota and Mitsubishi have located production in Guangdong. Economic progress has brought employment and rising prosperity to the region as a whole, and especially to the PRD. GDP per capita in the PRD was US$5144 or almost two- and-a-half times the provincial average. In 2006 the PRD accounted for 82% of Guangdong's GDP (Figure 5.5).

Environmental problems

Economic success has been at some cost. Massive urban growth has brought particular problems for Guangdong. Guangdong is China's most urbanised province, with just over 60% of its population living in towns and cities. This proportion rises to 77% in the industrial heartland of the PRD and is likely to top 85% by 2020.

Despite its large population, Guangdong's industrial growth has brought a flood of migrants from the surrounding countryside and from other provinces. The attraction is economic: in 2000, disposable incomes in Shenzhen were four times greater than in rural districts. Urbanisation, fuelled by rural-urban migration, is currently running at between 5% and 6% a year. This has caused serious environmental problems including water and air pollution.

The provision of sewage and industrial waste treatment has not kept pace with urban and economic growth. Three-quarters of Guangdong's cities have no sewage treatment plants, compromising water quality in rivers and threatening water supplies in the PRD. The Pearl River is so grossly polluted downstream from Guangzhou that it is now lifeless. However, since 2005 cleaning up the PRD's rivers has been given greater priority: the cities of Guangzhou and Foshan are currently spending large sums to improve water quality.

Air pollution is also a major concern for city authorities. It peaks in the winter months and is highest in the northwestern parts of the PRD. Sulphur dioxide, emitted by power stations and manufacturing industries, rises above safe levels in Foshan and Guangzhou for several months of the year (Figure 5.6). Pollution from nitrogen oxide from the exhausts of motor vehicles, ozone and fine

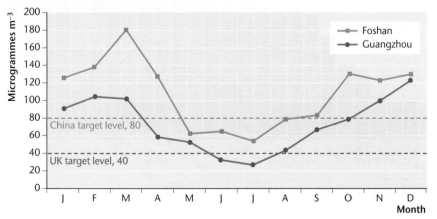

Figure 5.6 *Monthly average sulphur dioxide levels in Guangzhou and Fosham, 2006*

particulate matter follows a similar pattern. Guangzhou is affected by brown smog from the city's motor vehicles for on average 130 days a year. Meanwhile, acid rain, caused by air pollution, is widespread.

Economic problems

In China, serious economic problems stem from globalisation. Average wages are very low (Figure 5.7). Without overtime, it is not unusual for factory employers to pay the minimum monthly wage — US$107 — for an 8-hour day, 5 days a week. Workers often sleep in dormitories attached to the factories and work in conditions that are damaging to their health and would not be tolerated in MEDCs (Figure 5.8).

However, production costs are rising rapidly in response to labour shortages, pressure on employers to improve working conditions and benefits to employees, and more stringent environment-protection laws. The PRD is experiencing acute labour shortages as economic development in western provinces reduces the supply of young migrant workers. As costs rise, globalisation dictates that capital moves elsewhere to lower-cost locations. Today, the attraction of China and the PRD as low-cost manufacturing locations is fast disappearing. The supply chains of major international companies are increasingly shifting overseas to lower-cost locations such as Bangladesh, Vietnam, Indonesia and Cambodia.

The future

As labour-intensive industries are offshored to neighbouring states a period of economic adjustment with higher rates of unemployment may follow. China, however, is already planning for change. Its political leaders know that the country has no long-term future as a low-cost manufacturer. Already it is beginning to

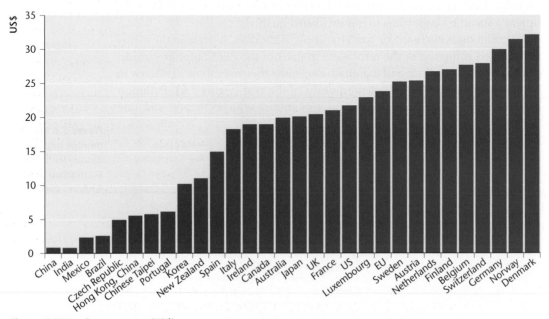

***Figure 5.7** Hourly wage rates (US$)*

Shop until they drop:

UK stores shocked by conditions in their Chinese factories

Clothes and toys on sale in Britain's high streets are made by Chinese workers forced to endure illegal, exhausting and dangerous conditions, according to a new study. It will increase the pressure on retailers to monitor the conditions in which their products are made.

A three-year investigation into booming export factories for companies such as Marks & Spencer and Ikea discovered the human cost of China's "economic miracle". It found an army of powerless rural migrants toiling up to 14 hours a day, almost every day. Many were allowed just one day off a month and paid less than £50 a month for shifts that breached Chinese law and International Labour Organisation rules. Despite evidence of the shocking working conditions, cheap clothes, toys and increasingly electronic goods from the sweatshops are on sale in British shops with household names, including those with ethical buying policies.

Companies are attracted to doing business in the People's Republic of China because of its low-tax development zones, cut-price abundant workforce, and totalitarianism. Independent trade unions are banned by the Communist Party. Assembly-line personnel in free-trade zones in south China operate machinery without safety guards and spray paint with inadequate face masks. They often die in industrial accidents or from gulaosi, the Chinese term for death from overwork. Workplace death rates in China are at least 12 times those of Britain and 13 factory workers a day lose a finger or an arm in the boom city of Shenzhen. In a sign of official disquiet, the state-owned China Daily reported in November that a 30-year-old woman, He Chunmei, died from exhaustion after working 24-hours non-stop at a handicraft factory.

The International Textile, Garment and Leather Workers Union fears that multinationals are in a "race to the bottom" in workers' conditions. Neil Kearney, its general secretary, said: "There's no such thing as cheap clothing because...the main people paying the price are the people producing it." Of a factory visit two months ago, he recalled: "There were about 700 workers in this factory. Those workers appeared dirty, raggedly clothed and malnourished. If you had taken some black-and-white pictures they would have fitted not too badly into Dickensian scenes.

"They were sharing 12 men to a room. Literally they had a box to themselves, like the boxes you see in the films of the concentration camps. The washing facilities were a cold water tap on a balcony. The wages were something like ... £1 a day."

Such miserable conditions allow China to undercut developing countries by up to 60 per cent. It now supplies 90 per cent of the world's toys and one-fifth of Europe's clothes, though textile exports are soaring. With explosive annual growth of 9 per cent, China overtook the UK last month as the world's fourth largest economy and is forecast to pass Germany by 2010. Its transformation from peasant economy to industrial marvel has drawn 100 million peasants to the cities — the largest human movement of people in history. Most of the workers end up in the free-trade factories of the Pearl River Delta. Little publicity emerges about these factories because they are privately run and in Guangdong province, which is 1,500 miles from foreign correspondents in Beijing.

© Independent

Source: Martin Hickman, *Independent*, 14 January 2006

Figure 5.8 *Newspaper report on working conditions in China*

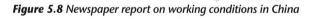

follow the path of South Korea, Taiwan and other NICs, moving away from low-tech, labour-intensive industries like clothing and leather goods and into high-tech industry, software and services.

A pointer to the future is the Xian high-tech industries development zone in Shaanxi province in northeast China. It covers 35 km², includes one of China's biggest technology parks, houses 7500 companies, and is supported by more than 100 universities which produce 120 000 graduates a year, half in computer sciences alone. It is also the centre of China's aerospace industry and the birthplace of the country's space programme.

Impact of globalisation in the UK

The impact of globalisation in the UK has, arguably, been greater than in any other MEDC. However, as we have seen in the example of China, globalisation has brought both benefits and problems.

Benefits
Economic restructuring

Globalisation increases the openness of national economies to international trade and therefore sharpens competition. In the UK, one result has been to restructure the British economy, with services becoming increasingly important, largely at the expense of manufacturing. Today, financial services and business services alone account for one-third of UK exports. Meanwhile absolute employment in manufacturing has declined steeply and manufacturing's share of total economic output has declined. Low-wage economies such as China and India, and advances in communication and transport technology, have been major drivers of change.

Many British manufacturing firms have exploited the advantages of globalisation by transferring production offshore. **Offshoring** allows them to focus on higher value and high-skilled activities such as research, product design, product development and marketing — areas where emerging economies are less competitive. Apart from lower costs, offshoring gives access to larger markets and provides higher productivity and higher value chains.

Globalisation has forced many firms to specialise in areas where they have a **comparative advantage**. In manufacturing this means specialist high-tech industries, pharmaceuticals, aircraft parts, scientific instruments and so on. These industries rely on highly qualified workers, innovation, and world-class research and development. It is only in these manufacturing activities that UK and other MEDCs can out-compete the emerging economies of China and India.

Globalisation has also driven the export of knowledge-intensive services. In 2006 the UK was responsible for 25% of the world's financial services exports and 14% of computer services exports. This success has only been made possible by advances in communications technology. The contribution of knowledge-intensive services such as financial and legal services to the UK economy is greater than in any other country apart from the USA.

Foreign direct investment

Europe and North America top the league of inward and outward foreign investment (Table 5.2). At the national scale, the UK is the second most attractive country in the world for foreign direct investment (FDI). Most of this investment

Table 5.2 *UK inward and outward direct investment (£ billion), 2006*

	Inward investment 2006	Global total inward investment, 2006	Outward investment 2006	Global total outward investment, 2006
Europe	47.6	321.7	16.0	393.8
The Americas	18.9	207.5	21.2	259.7
Asia	11.8	39.5	8.3	53.0
Australia and Oceania	1.8	7.3	3.6	12.6
Africa	0.1	0.5	0.3	15.5
Total	80.3	576.6	49.4	734.7

is by transnational corporations (TNCs). This investment is particularly valuable because foreign TNCs are more productive and faster growing than domestic firms. And in addition to providing employment and value added, they also transfer technology, skills and innovation to the UK. In 2006 foreign TNCs accounted for 35% of the total turnover of manufacturing firms in the UK and employed 20% of the workforce. FDI is particularly important in the UK's automotive industry. The globalisation of Ford's operations explains why, for example, one quarter of its car engines are sourced from Dagenham in Essex. Meanwhile Nissan's Sunderland car plant is the most productive assembly plant in Europe, and Toyota (Derby) and Honda (Swindon) are in Europe's top 10.

International migration

International migration is an intrinsic part of the globalisation process. The expansion of the EU in 2004 and the open-border policy of the UK led to a flood of immigrants from eastern Europe (Figure 4.9, page 140).

In 2006, 12.5% of the UK's workforce was foreign-born, compared to 7.4% 10 years earlier. Migrants have two advantages for the economy. First, they reduce the costs of low-skilled labour; second, they provide additional higher skills. Most studies conclude that immigrants bring substantial economic gains. This is mainly because a large proportion of immigrants are of working age and therefore contribute significantly to GDP. This in turn increases the attractiveness of the UK as an investment location.

Migration is most common among younger adult age groups. In 2003 the 15–24 and the 25–44 age groups together accounted for the large majority of both in-migrants (84%) and out-migrants (75%).

Problems

Globalisation has created problems as well as benefits for the UK. The problems are primarily economic, but they also have social and environmental dimensions.

Economic

Globalisation creates economic problems when firms (both British and non-British) close production and disinvest in the UK. This process creates direct job losses, which often have knock-on effects on local businesses. The problems are most acute in areas which depend heavily on just one or two major employers.

Offshoring also affects service industries. Recent examples include the transfer of many back-office and customer-service jobs to India by leading UK companies such as Norwich Union, Tesco, British Airways and Abbey. In 2005, around 100 000 people in India worked in outsourced customer services. Average salaries vary from £95 to £170 a month. There is also concern that high-value service jobs will be offshored. This is already happening in the IT industry, which in India directly employs over 1.5 million workers.

Loss of control

Globalisation means that business decisions on investment and disinvestment, affecting the lives of thousands of people in the UK, increasingly take place outside the country. The British government has limited power to influence decisions made by foreign TNCs on relocation and offshoring, which often have adverse economic and social consequences.

During the 1970s and 1980s there was significant investment by Japanese, Korean and US TNCs in new manufacturing plants in northern England, Scotland and Wales. These investments gave companies such as Nissan, Samsung and Sony a platform to access the UK and the EU market. However, a common complaint was that this investment supported only low-skilled operations like assembly, while high-value and highly skilled jobs in research, development and design remained overseas. Regions such as northeast England and south Wales, which received large investments in these so-called 'branch plants' were highly vulnerable to changes in costs and therefore to closure.

Today, branch plants are increasingly located in Asia and eastern Europe, with higher-value operations often based in the UK. For example, Ford's small and medium-sized cars are all designed at Dunton in Essex and Cologne in Germany. Dunton, now the UK's largest automotive centre, employs 5000 engineers and support staff.

Immigration and social problems

Globalisation has increased the mobility of workers and has stimulated international migration. Although this migration brings economic benefits, it can also create social problems. In 2004, the enlargement of the EU brought an unexpectedly large influx of migrants from Poland and from other east European states to the UK. Unofficial figures suggest that around 600 000 people migrated to the UK from eastern Europe between 2004 and 2006 alone. This placed enormous strains on public services in some parts of the country and especially in small towns and rural areas. In Boston in Lincolnshire, one in six of the population is foreign born. Other towns and cities with above-average levels include Slough (14%) and Peterborough (13%). Problems of social cohesion have also appeared in small market towns like Thetford in Norfolk which has absorbed large numbers of Portuguese immigrants in recent years.

Environmental problems

Massive deindustrialisation in the 1970s and 1980s, as traditional heavy industries collapsed under foreign competition, led to vast swathes of inner-city and urban waterfront areas in the UK becoming derelict (Photograph 5.2). The result was

geogphotos/Alamy

Photograph 5.2
*Urban dereliction,
London's Docklands*

massive environmental dereliction in areas like the Don Valley in Sheffield, London's Docklands and the Black Country in the west Midlands. Over the years, most of these sites have been reclaimed. However, the closure of a large manufacturing plant such as Ryton near Coventry in 2006 (see p. 189), covering 53 ha, creates significant environmental as well as economic problems.

Transnational corporations and globalisation

Key ideas
> Transnational corporations (TNCs) are large companies whose production of goods, services and sales are organised on a global scale.
> TNCs may have both positive and negative impacts on LEDCs and MEDCs.
> TNCs often have contrasting spatial and organisational structures.

TNCs have a major influence on the global economy, in manufacturing, services and international trade. In this section we investigate two contrasting TNCs — IKEA and Toyota — in terms of their organisation and their spatial structures. We also consider the impact of TNCs on countries at opposite ends of the development scale.

IKEA

Development
IKEA is the Swedish furniture company, famed for supplying low-cost, stylish flatpack furniture. Today it is the world's largest furniture retailer. The company was founded by Ingvar Kamprad in 1943 in Älmhult, southern Sweden. Its first

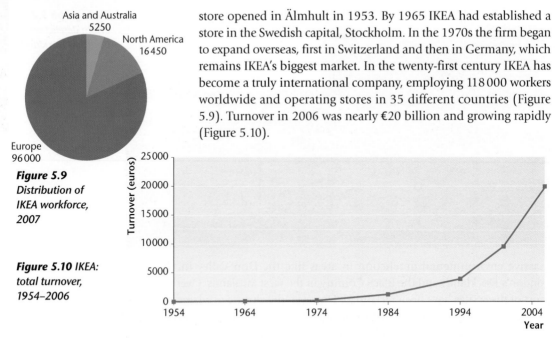

Asia and Australia
5250

North America
16450

Europe
96000

Figure 5.9
*Distribution of
IKEA workforce,
2007*

Figure 5.10 *IKEA:
total turnover,
1954–2006*

store opened in Älmhult in 1953. By 1965 IKEA had established a store in the Swedish capital, Stockholm. In the 1970s the firm began to expand overseas, first in Switzerland and then in Germany, which remains IKEA's biggest market. In the twenty-first century IKEA has become a truly international company, employing 118000 workers worldwide and operating stores in 35 different countries (Figure 5.9). Turnover in 2006 was nearly €20 billion and growing rapidly (Figure 5.10).

Organisation

IKEA has become a global organisation (Figure 5.11). Financial control and strategic decision-making is centred in the Dutch town of Leiden, close to Amsterdam. Amsterdam is an ideal location: as a major city it provides access to high-quality services such as management consulting and advertising, and it is a global transport and communications hub. Älmhult, the birthplace of IKEA, has a key role as the company's design headquarters.

Figure 5.11 *Organisation of IKEA*

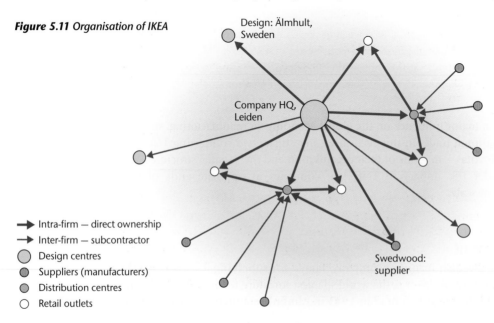

Design: Älmhult,
Sweden

Company HQ,
Leiden

Swedwood:
supplier

→ Intra-firm — direct ownership
→ Inter-firm — subcontractor
◯ Design centres
◯ Suppliers (manufacturers)
◯ Distribution centres
◯ Retail outlets

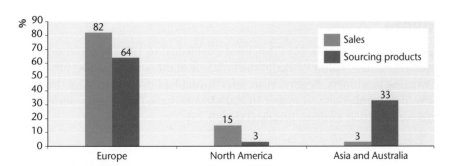

Figure 5.12
Percentage of IKEA sales and sourcing of products by region, 2007

IKEA's headquarters control a complex network of around 1350 suppliers spread across 50 countries. Nearly two-thirds of suppliers are located in Europe, close to its main market. Most of the remainder are in Asia and Australia (Figure 5.12). There is close relationship between the company and its suppliers. Most suppliers source their materials — particularly timber — locally. The company sets strict environmental standards on the sourcing of timber, and its suppliers do not use timber from tropical rainforests.

Suppliers transport finished products direct to IKEA's 31 distribution centres. In order to minimise environmental impact, the company encourages the use of rail transport and has its own rail operations. Because furniture is bulky and expensive to transport, IKEA pioneered self-assembly flatpack furniture which greatly reduces transport costs. Transport by road, rail and sea is by container.

To remain competitive IKEA has to be very price conscious. 'Just-in-time' (JIT) delivery provides goods to retail stores and distribution centres as they are needed and eliminates costly stocks. IT systems record sales in IKEA stores and this information is transmitted to distribution centres and triggers deliveries. A similar system operates between distribution centres and suppliers, with delivery times down to 15 days. Economies of scale in production and sales, and the standardisation of products (same products are sold globally), are critical in keeping costs down.

Although the bulk of IKEA's workforce is in retailing, 13 000 people work in IKEA's own furniture manufacturing company — Swedwood — in nine countries. Swedwood operates 38 factories, with around half of its employees in Poland. A typical factory making pine office furniture in Poland sources all materials within 60 km of the factory and is located close to the main source of timber.

The need to be close to materials is evident in the location of plants in Finland and Russia. The decision to build a factory in the USA gives access both to materials and to the large US market where there are 37 stores.

Impact

Any audit of IKEA's activities would suggest that its worldwide economic and environmental impact is generally positive. The company sets stringent rules for its suppliers, proscribing child labour; it also tries to ensure that its sub-contractors pay fair wages, encourages the use of eco-friendly railways rather than road transport, and sets environmental standards for the production of sustainable timber and forest management. Globally, IKEA directly employs 118 000 co-workers, with thousands of others in supplying companies.

Toyota

Japan's Toyota Motor Co. Ltd (TMC) was established in 1937 as a spin-off from Toyoda Automatic Loom Works, at the time one of the world's leading producers of weaving machinery. Seventy years later Toyota had overtaken GM to become the world's number one car maker. In 2006 Toyota made 7.5 million vehicles, and employed 300 000 workers directly (Figure 5.13).

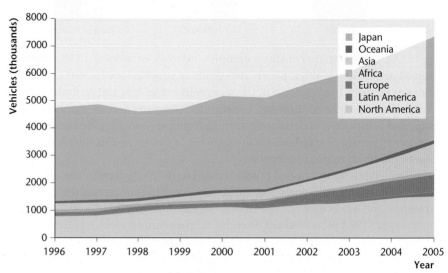

Figure 5.13 *Toyota sales by region, 1996–2005*

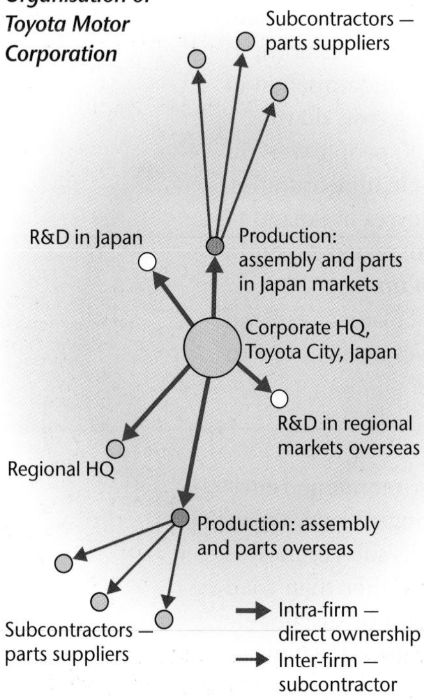

Figure 5.14 Organisation of Toyota Motor Corporation

Organisation

TMC's headquarters are in Toyota City in Japan (Figure 5.14). This is the nerve centre of the company's global operations, making key decisions and exerting financial control. Some control is devolved to regional headquarters which make local decisions that affect operations in North America, Europe, Asia and so on.

Research and development (R&D) remains strongest in Japan, with advanced research into engines, electronic systems, prototypes and the planning and design of new models. However, there are seven R&D centres outside Japan. These are geared to regional markets and with lower-order research functions including vehicle development and collecting technological information.

Production of cars and major parts such as engines and transmissions is geographically dispersed. Toyota operates 52 production units in 27 different countries (Figure 5.15). Until the 1970s Toyota was based in Japan and exported vehicles to overseas markets, mainly in North America and Europe. The globalisation of production began in North America in the 1980s and in Europe in the 1990s. In the 2000s Asia became the main focus for expansion and

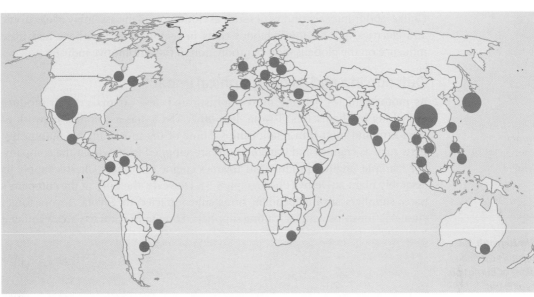

Figure 5.15 Toyota assembly plants

Table 5.3 Reasons for the location of Toyota in the UK at Burnaston, near Derby, and Chester

Tradition	Long tradition of automotive manufacture in the UK.
Market	A large domestic market in the UK and the EU. Easy access to continental Europe.
Language	English: the second language in Japan.
Transport and access to suppliers	Good road transport links: e.g. Derby (A38, A50, M1) and Chester (M56, M6), giving fast access to over 230 British and European suppliers.
Labour	Skilled workforce, with a tradition of engineering in both regions, and flexible working practices.
Government	Supportive attitude of the UK government and local authorities which were eager to attract inward investment and new jobs.
Site	Large, flat sites of a suitable shape with space for expansion. Burnaston covers nearly 250 ha, with an effective infrastructure (i.e. gas electricity, water).

investment. Now globalisation has gone so far that North America has become Toyota's biggest market, accounting for one-third of total sales (see Figure 5.16).

Impetus for globalisation

The drivers behind Toyota's globalisation are:

➤ Lowering unit costs by accessing global markets: this provides savings through economies of scale and allowing the firm to compete more effectively in world markets.

➤ Avoiding trade barriers by locating production in regional markets rather than serving these markets by exports from Japan.

➤ Meeting the specific needs of customers by locating in regional markets (Table 5.3).

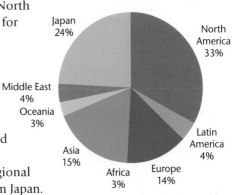

Figure 5.16 Toyota: regional vehicle production, 2005

Unlike labour-intensive industries such as clothing, and the assembly of electronic and electrical goods, lower labour costs in regional markets have had little influence on the globalisation of production in the automotive industry.

Outsourcing and its geographical impact

As motor vehicles become more sophisticated, few car makers can produce everything by themselves. Toyota, like other TNCs, has a complex network of intra-firm and inter-firm relationships. Some of the most valuable automotive parts such as engines and transmissions are supplied from within the company. For example, engines produced at Toyota's engine plant near Chester supply its assembly plant at Derby (Photograph 5.3). However, the bulk of the company's parts' suppliers are independent firms subcontracted to Toyota. Toyota forges close relationships with its leading suppliers. Long-term contracts are negotiated

Photograph 5.3
Toyota's assembly plant at Burnaston, near Derby

David Wootton/Alamy

Table 5.4 *Comparison of IKEA and Toyota*

	IKEA	Toyota
Headquarters	Leiden, close to Amsterdam. Amsterdam is a major urban centre with excellent communication and transport links.	Toyota City, Japan. There is easy access to Tokyo with its financial market and excellent communication and transport links. Regional HQs are based in all the main markets, with power to make local decisions.
Research, development (R&D), design	Älmhult in southern Sweden is the main design centre. Design is also outsourced, mainly to Sweden.	R&D and design are concentrated within the company and are strongest in Japan. There are seven R&D units outside Japan, in the main regional markets.
Production	Most production is outsourced. Subcontractors are located worldwide in 50 different countries. IKEA has its own production arm — Swedwood — employing 13 000 people, mainly in Poland.	Production in Toyota's own assembly plants and parts' factories is located in Japan, Asia, Europe, North America, South America, Africa and Oceania. Toyota 'buys-in' a large proportion of automotive parts from subcontractors.

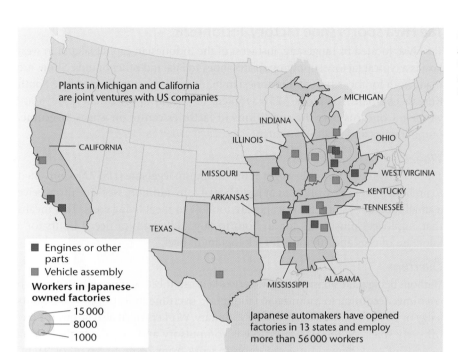

Figure 5.17
Japanese automotive suppliers in the USA

Plants in Michigan and California are joint ventures with US companies

MICHIGAN

INDIANA

ILLINOIS

OHIO

CALIFORNIA

MISSOURI

WEST VIRGINIA

KENTUCKY

ARKANSAS

TENNESSEE

TEXAS

■ Engines or other parts
■ Vehicle assembly

Workers in Japanese-owned factories

15 000
8000
1000

MISSISSIPPI

ALABAMA

Japanese automakers have opened factories in 13 states and employ more than 56 000 workers

and suppliers are often involved in design and product development as well as manufacturing.

One geographical effect of outsourcing, where hundreds of firms supply parts to assembly plants, is the emergence of automotive clusters. The tightly knit relationship between parts' suppliers and Toyota (and other Japanese car companies such as Honda and Nissan), led to a wave of Japanese automotive parts firms locating in the USA close to Toyota's and other new assembly plants in the 1980s. The main cluster was in the mid-west, from Chicago to Kentucky and Tennessee (Figure 5.17). Clustering and access to fast inter-state highways was essential for JIT deliveries of parts to assembly plants. It also helped to promote contact and the flow of information between Toyota and its subcontractors.

Fila Korea Ltd

Fila is a South Korean TNC and a leading brand in sports shoes and other sportswear. Its headquarters are in Seoul. Like other leading sportswear companies, Fila does no manufacturing of its own. Production is subcontracted to manufacturing companies mainly in Asia, Latin America and eastern Europe.

Sportswear manufacture is a labour-intensive process. Therefore, to minimise production costs manufacturing is invariably outsourced to countries with low-wage economies. However, the drive to reduce costs often comes at the expense of the working conditions of employees. Meanwhile, TNCs like Fila push their suppliers for shorter delivery times and lower unit costs. If these are not achieved contracts may be cancelled and suppliers may relocate, threatening workers with redundancy.

Tae Hwa sports shoe factory, Indonesia

Tae Hwa, located in Tangerang, just west of the Indonesian capital Jakarta in west Java is a typical factory supplying sports shoes to Fila and other brands. Shoes are made both for the export and Indonesian markets. The factory, owned by a South Korean company, employs 5250 workers of whom approximately 80% are women. Concerns over the conditions in factories centre on wages, overtime, output targets and health and safety.

Wages

Tae Hwa pays basic monthly wages at the minimum legal rate (US$72). Converted to an hourly rate this works out at just US$0.42. In addition, workers also receive a small food allowance. Basic wages are too low to meet living costs. This means that employees must work for an hour to buy a kilogram of rice, 2 hours for a kilogram of eggs and 10 hours for a kilogram of beef.

Overtime

Without being paid a basic living wage, workers can meet their needs only through overtime. According to Indonesian labour law, overtime must not exceed 3 hours a day or 14 hours a week and must be voluntary. Workers must also be given 1 day off every week. At Tae Hwa overtime is compulsory and illegally high. During periods of peak demand it is common to work from 7 a.m. to 8 p.m. or 9 p.m. Occasionally workers have to work for 32 hours, from 7 a.m. to 3 p.m. the next day, and work for a whole month without a day off. Not only is overtime compulsory: workers refusing to do overtime can be demoted and even sacked.

Output targets

In the sewing department where all the workers are women, management sets impossibly high targets for the number of shoes they must complete in a day. Usually it is impossible to complete the target in a single shift. Routinely the women work a couple of extra hours a day (for which they are not paid), to meet their target. Workers complain that the rare occasions when they fulfil their target, the management then increases it. Workers also complain of sexual harassment by the Korean managers and verbal abuse. Unions are weak and often collude with management and it is alleged that workers have been sacked and blacklisted for union involvement.

Health and safety

Workers complain of needle-stick injuries and backache caused by long hours of repetitive strain. Many workers get sick from chemicals used in the factory, which lead to respiratory problems and allergic reactions.

PSA Peugeot Citroën in the UK

The PSA Peugeot Citroën group is a French TNC and Europe's second largest vehicle manufacturer. In 2007 it produced nearly 3.5 million cars and vans, two-thirds in western Europe and the rest in Slovakia, Brazil and Argentina. It owns and operates 11 assembly plants and 14 plants that manufacture components, and has several joint ventures with companies in China, Italy and the Czech Republic.

In recent years there has been little growth in the 'mature' market for cars and light commercial vehicles in western Europe. Increasingly, the company is looking for opportunities to expand production in emerging markets such as eastern Europe, China and South America where growth is strong. The closure of the Peugeot assembly plant at Ryton near Coventry at the end of 2006 was in part the outcome of this policy (Figure 5.18).

Peugeot to close Ryton with 2,300 job losses

The UK motor industry was dealt another devastating blow yesterday after the French car maker Peugeot announced that its Ryton plant in Coventry is to close with the loss of 2,300 jobs, angering ministers and union leaders alike.

Peugeot's unions immediately vowed to fight the closure and, in a thinly veiled attack, the Secretary of State for Trade and Industry Alan Johnson said he was "extremely disappointed" at the decision, which came despite substantial quality and productivity improvements at Ryton and the offer of government financial aid for production of future models.

The closure of the plant after 60 years of car production follows hard on the heels of the shutdown of the nearby Jaguar factory in Coventry and the collapse a year ago of MG Rover with 6,000 job losses at Longbridge in Birmingham.

The future of Ryton has been hanging by a thread since 2004 after it failed to be selected as a production site for the 206's successor, the 207. Peugeot said Ryton's high production costs, coupled with a slowdown in the European car market, left it with no option but to close the plant.

But unions claimed the company would never have dared to treat French workers in the same way and attacked the lack of consultation, describing the announcement as a "fait accompli". Mass meetings will be held today at Ryton to gauge the strength of feeling among the workforce and the appetite for industrial action over the planned closure.

Last night Jean Martin Folz, the chief executive of PSA Peugeot Citroen, stressed there was no question of the decision being reversed and defended the company's failure to consult the UK Government and trade unions before the announcement. "There was nothing to negotiate and nothing to discuss, it was an economic necessity," he said, adding that any industrial action might only hasten Ryton's closure.

In addition to the 2,300 direct job losses, thousands more jobs in supply companies will be threatened when Ryton closes and 206 production is limited to Peugeot's Poissy and Mulhouse plants in France.

M. Folz said Ryton's high production and logistical costs made it the most expensive of all the company's plants, meaning that the group was unable to justify the investment needed to produce future models.

A Peugeot spokeswoman said the cost of building a 206 at Ryton was €415 (£287) greater than at Poissy because of higher wages, energy costs and the need to import most of the components from the Continent. Only 25 per cent of the parts used in the cars built at Ryton are sourced from UK suppliers.

She added that it would cost €255m to bring Ryton up to the standards of Peugeot's modern plants on the Continent and even then it would still be a much more expensive production site.

Derek Simpson, the general secretary of the engineering union Amicus, said: "It is inconceivable that French workers at Peugeot would be laid off on this magnitude. Weak UK labour laws are allowing skilled British workers to be sacrificed on the altar of a flexible labour market."

Source: Michael Harrison, *Independent*, 19 April 2006

 © Independent

***Figure 5.18** Newspaper report on the closure of Peugeot's Ryton car plant in 2006*

Closure meant the loss of 2300 jobs and had an immediate impact on the local economy. Similar decisions by other TNCs in the automotive industry led to the closure of assembly plants at Coventry (Jaguar Ford), Dagenham (Ford) and Luton (Vauxhall). Ryton's assembly lines were transferred to the Czech Republic and Slovakia where the new 207 model was to be built. In addition to location in eastern Europe's expanding market, other factors influencing the closure decision were lower labour costs in eastern Europe (less than a fifth of those in the UK) and the proximity of the assembly plant to continental parts' suppliers.

Although closure of a large industrial plant like Ryton hit Coventry hard (unions argued that every job at Ryton supported three service jobs locally), a year later all but around 100 of those made redundant had either found new jobs or were in re-training programmes. However, those in work earned significantly less in their new employment. Whereas the average earnings at the Ryton plant in 2006 were £22 000–23 000, a year later most ex-workers were earning between £15 000 and £20 000.

Table 5.5 *The advantages and disadvantages of TNC operations to countries*

Advantages	Disadvantages
Provide inward investment and create jobs for local people.	Exploitation of workforce, especially in LEDCs, with poor working conditions, low wages etc.
Increase incomes and raise living standards among employees.	Environmental pollution (in LEDCs) which governments tolerate to attract investment.
Boost exports and help the trade balance.	Lack of security, with closure of operations as lower-cost locations attract investment elsewhere.
Develop and improve skill levels and expertise among the workforce, and technology and process systems among local firms.	In many LEDCs jobs are mainly low skilled in labour-intensive industries (e.g electronics, clothing).
Increase spending and create a multiplier effect within local economies.	In MEDCs, capital-intensive, foreign enterprises may offer few higher-paid managerial, development, design and marketing opportunities.
May attract related investment by suppliers and create clusters of economic activity.	Lack of control, with key decisions which have important economic implications for a country taken overseas at company HQ.
	Competition could lead to the closure of domestic firms.

International trade and aid

Key ideas

➤ The influence of international trade and aid on global patterns of production.

➤ There are contrasts in the structure, direction and impact of trade in LEDCs, NICs and MEDCs.

➤ International trade is influenced by trade negotiations and agreements.

International trade

There has been a massive increase in world trade both in merchandise and **producer services** (financial, insurance, legal, real estate) in the past 20 years or so. Between 1996 and 2006 world exports of merchandise increased from US$5402–12 083 billion (Figure 5.19). In the same period, the value of exports of producer services also more than doubled, from US$1271–2756 billion.

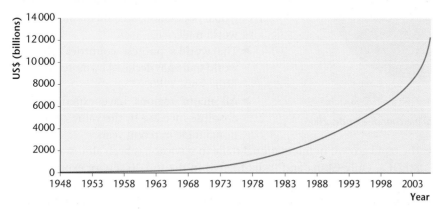

Figure 5.19
Growth of world merchandise exports, 1948–2006

Apart from rapid growth, international trade has a number of other features:
➤ Most international trade is intra-regional. For example, in 2006 74% of international trade in Europe was between European countries, and 54% of North America's trade took place within North America (Figure 5.20).

Figure 5.20 *Inter- and intra-regional merchandise trade, 2006*

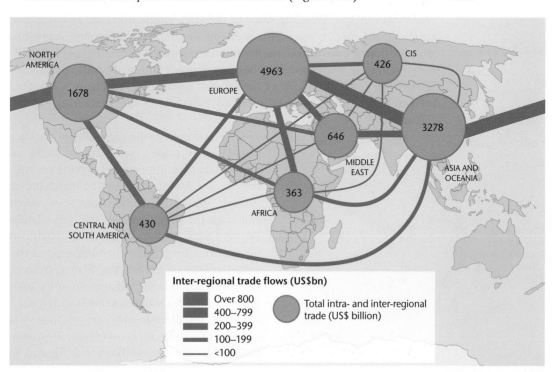

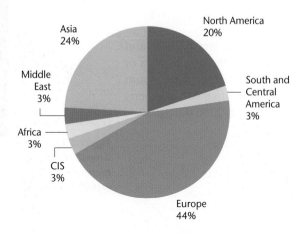

Figure 5.21 *International merchandise trade, 2006*

➤ Most inter-regional trade is between Europe, North America and Asia.

➤ International trade in merchandise is dominated by MEDCs in Europe, North America and Japan, and by emerging economies such as China (Figure 5.21). The poorest 49 countries, comprising 10% of the global population, account for only 0.4% of world trade.

➤ The world's poorest countries' share of world trade has declined by more than two-fifths since 1980.

➤ All major regions have experienced an absolute increase in the value of international trade in recent years.

➤ The rapid growth in international trade in services has been almost entirely in MEDCs. Only China and India figured in the top 20 service exporters and importers in 2006.

➤ World trade is dominated by the top 500 TNCs. In total they account for 70% of world trade.

Trade patterns in contrasting economies

UK: a MEDC

Like most other MEDCs, the value of the UK's international trade has grown rapidly in the past 20 years. This is due to sustained global economic growth, globalisation of the world economy and the expansion of free trade. For the UK, the growth in service exports has been particularly strong. By 2007 commercial services accounted for 38.5% of the value of British exports (Figure 5.22). This increase has helped to offset the relative decline in manufacturing exports (Figure 5.23).

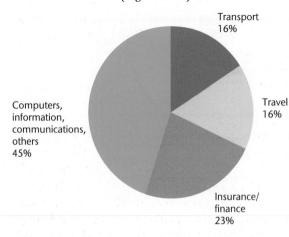

Figure 5.22 *UK exports of commercial services, 2006*

MEDCs dominate the geography of the UK's international trade. For example, 60% of UK merchandise imports and exports are with the EU. Meanwhile 53% of UK merchandise imports by value come from just seven countries: the USA, Germany, the Netherlands, France, China, Belgium and Norway. The main destinations for UK merchandise exports (by value) are the USA, Germany, France, Ireland, the Netherlands and Belgium. In sum, two-thirds of the UK's trade by value is with just 13 countries; and of these, only one — China — is not a MEDC. The main items of trade are manufactured goods, with similar goods figuring as both exports and imports (Table 5.6).

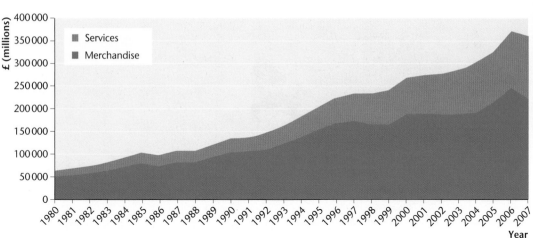

Figure 5.23 *Growth in international trade in merchandise and services, UK, 1980–2007*

Table 5.6 *Leading international trade commodities (% value of exports and imports), UK, 2007*

Exports	Cumulative %	Imports	Cumulative %
Oil	10.3	Vehicles	11.8
Vehicles	19.9	Oil	20.3
Pharmaceuticals	26.5	Miscellaneous manufactured goods	25.5
Miscellaneous manufactured goods	32.5	Telecoms	30.8
Power generating equipment	38.6	Office machinery	35.4
Electrical machinery	42.9	Electrical machinery	39.8
General industrial machinery	47.0	Clothing	43.8
Other transport equipment	50.8	General industrial machinery	47.2
Organic chemicals	54.3	Pharmaceuticals	50.5
Office machinery	57.7	Power generating equipment	53.6

Box 5.2 Regional trade blocs

Within specific geographical areas groups of countries combine to form regional trade blocs. Most countries are members of a trade bloc. The largest are the EU, the North American Free Trade Agreement (NAFTA), the Association of South East Asian Nations (ASEAN) and the Mercado Commun del Sur (MERCOSUR) (Figure 5.24). One-third of the world's trade takes place within trade blocs, while the EU and NAFTA alone make up 53% of world merchandise exports.

Trade blocs promote the interests of member states by:

■ encouraging free trade between them (e.g. by removing or reducing tariff duties)

■ protecting their industries and services from foreign competition by using tariffs, quotas and subsidies

The EU is the largest and most integrated of the regional trade blocs. Two-thirds of the EU's exports are between its 27 member states. Within the EU there is free movement of goods, services, capital and people. While there are no tariffs, customs duties or taxes on the flow of goods within the EU, foreign goods entering the internal market pay a common external tariff. In addition some EU industries such as agriculture and coal are heavily protected from foreign imports by price subsidies.

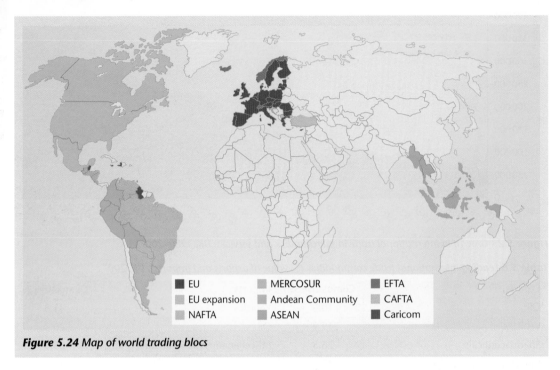

EU   MERCOSUR   EFTA
EU expansion   Andean Community   CAFTA
NAFTA   ASEAN   Caricom

Figure 5.24 *Map of world trading blocs*

Brazil: a NIC

Brazil has the tenth largest economy in the world and is the economic powerhouse of South America. In 2005 its GDP per capita was US$8402 and economic growth in the 2000s averaged 4–5%. However, there is massive income inequality within the country. According to the UN just over one-fifth of the population lives in poverty, surviving on less than US$2 a day. Income inequality, measured by the Gini coefficient (see p. 287), is 56.7, compared with 34 in the UK.

Nearly three-quarters of Brazil's exports and 60% of imports were with South and Central America, North America and Europe. South and Central America is Brazil's most important export market for manufactured goods. Trade with Brazil's neighbours is promoted by membership of the MERCOSUR (Box 5.2). The long-term aim of MERCOSUR is to create a free-trade zone among its members similar to the EU.

Figure 5.25
International trade, Brazil, 2006

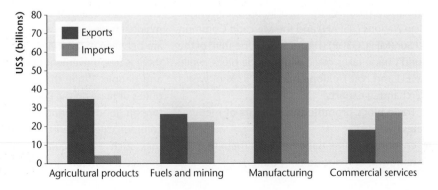

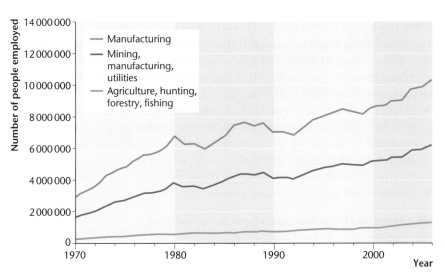

Figure 5.26 Growth of leading economic sectors, Brazil, 1970–2006

Primary products such as foodstuffs and mineral ores, with little added value, comprised 47% of all exports in 2007 — a proportion far higher than in MEDCs (Figures 5.25 and 5.26). The main markets for Brazil's primary products are Europe and North America.

Compared to the UK, exports of commercial services are small, amounting to just 11.5% of all exports by value (2006). In fact Brazil is a net importer of commercial services, which accounted for one-fifth of the total value of imports in 2006.

Burundi: a LEDC

Many LEDCs depend heavily on a narrow range of primary commodities for their export earnings. Burundi, a small LEDC in east Africa, is no exception: landlocked and resource poor, 90% of its population depend on subsistence agriculture. On the UN's human development index, Burundi ranks 170th out of 177 countries.

The country's economy is based on the export of coffee and tea, which account for 90% of foreign exchange earnings (Figure 5.27). Over half of Burundi's exports go to the EU which provides privileged market access. Meanwhile, Burundi's manufacturing sector is largely undeveloped. Poor access overland and reliance on Kenya's ports are two factors which deter foreign investment and industrial development.

Burundi's export performance depends on the success of the annual harvest and prices on world markets. World prices for primary commodities fluctuate more than prices for manufactured goods, creating severe economic problems during periods of oversupply and low demand. Diversification into new primary export products would strengthen the country's economic situation. Better still would be diversification into manufactured goods. Manufacturing provides higher and more stable export earnings, as well as jobs, new skills and vital infrastructure.

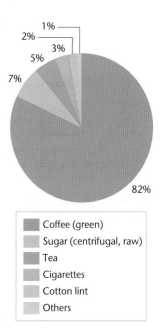

Figure 5.27 Exports, Burundi, 2007

International trade negotiations and agreements

The World Trade Organization (WTO) is the international body that deals with the rules of trade at the global level. Currently the WTO is made up of 152 member countries. (Its promotion of free trade has been an important driver of globalisation.) The WTO has several purposes:

➤ To liberalise trade by removing or reducing obstacles such as tariffs and subsidies. This aim is founded on the belief that ultimately, free trade benefits everyone. However, the WTO recognises that trade liberalisation can have undesirable side-effects, especially on the weaker economies, and there are circumstances when it is necessary to retain protective trade barriers.

➤ To settle trade disputes between member states.

Table 5.7 Trade agreements between the EU and New Zealand, and the EU and the ACP

EU and New Zealand bilateral trade agreement in agricultural products	
Background	**Agreement**
Before the UK joined the EU in 1973, New Zealand had a special trade relationship with the UK: 90% of New Zealand's meat and dairy products were exported to the UK. Special trading arrangements were negotiated between the EU and New Zealand to secure the latter's main export market. Although New Zealand's major export markets have increasingly shifted to Asia and the Pacific rim, the EU remains New Zealand's second largest trading partner (for sheepmeat, dairy produce and wine). The UK remains New Zealand's most important trading partner within the EU.	Initially the EU imposed a common external tariff of 20% on New Zealand imports. This was later reduced to 10% and then to 0% with a voluntary limit on the volume of New Zealand exports. The Uruguay round of WTO negotiations in the 1990s changed this arrangement and introduced Tariff Rate Quotas (TRQs). New Zealand's lamb exports to the EU were allocated a tariff-free quota of 227 000 t year^{-1}. Any imports exceeding the quota attracted a 12.8% tariff. New Zealand has, none the less, complained that trade in lamb is unfair. Whereas New Zealand sheep farmers receive no government subsidies, EU farmers can lower their prices because they get a ewe subsidy of €21 per head.
EU and bilateral trade agreement with ACP banana growers	
Background	**Agreement**
There is a long-running dispute between the EU, ACP banana growers, Latin American banana growers and the WTO. The UK and France have close political, historic and economic ties with many small countries in Africa, the Caribbean and the Pacific (ACP) which depend heavily on banana exports. The special trade agreements concluded between the UK, France and the ACP banana growers were adopted by the EU. Meanwhile, other banana exporters, especially in Latin America (e.g. Ecuador, Nicaragua, Mexico) complained that these arrangements were unfair. They argued that they should have the same access to the EU market as ACP growers. However, growing conditions in Latin America are more favourable, the scale of production is much greater (with large plantations owned by US TNCs) and therefore costs are low. Free trade would mean that ACP growers could not compete and that most would go out of business.	The 2000 Cotonou trade agreement between the EU and ACP provided a 775 000 tonne tariff-free quota for ACP bananas. At the same time Latin American producers faced a €230 t^{-1} tariff for their banana exports to the EU. In 2007 WTO ruled that this agreement violated global trade rules, giving an unfair advantage to ACP growers. Although the tariff for Latin American bananas was reduced to €175 t^{-1} the WTO insists that the revised trade arrangements remain unacceptable. By the end of 2008 the dispute was still unresolved.

➤ To negotiate trade agreements signed by the bulk of the world's trading nations. These agreements provide the legal ground rules for international trade. Their purpose is to ease the international flow of goods and services and at the same time allow governments to meet their social and environmental objectives.

Bilateral trade agreements

Bilateral trade agreements are negotiated between two territories. They are legally binding between these territories only and have a significant impact on trade patterns. Table 5.7 outlines the bilateral trade agreements between the EU and New Zealand, and the EU and the small banana producers of Africa, the Caribbean and the Pacific (ACP) region.

International aid

International aid describes money or resources that are transferred from economically developed to economically less developed countries. Crucially the donor countries (or organisations) do not expect full or direct repayment.

Donor and recipient countries

Donor countries are predominantly rich countries and belong to the Organisation for Economic Cooperation and Development (OECD). Despite the commitment made to the UN (1970) to give international aid equal to 0.7% of their GDP, few countries achieve this target (Figure 5.28). Although in absolute terms

Figure 5.28
Development aid as percentage of GNI in OECD countries, 2007

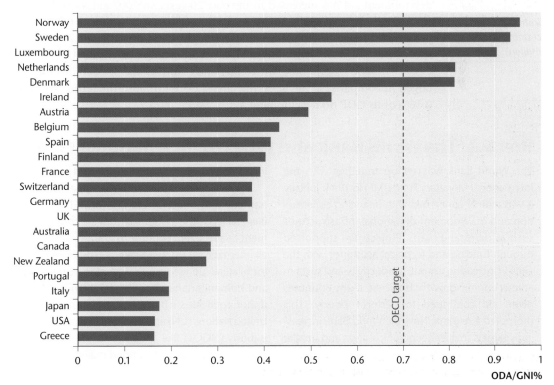

ODA/GNI%

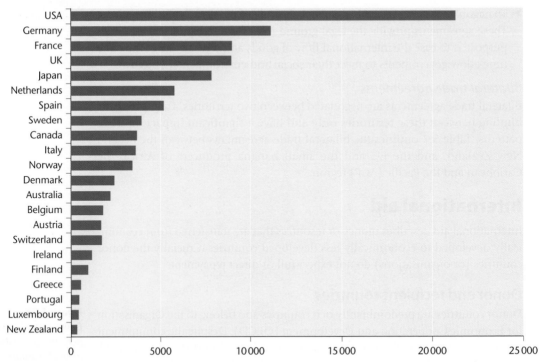

Figure 5.29
Development aid from OECD countries (US$ million), 2007

development aid has increased in the past 20 years, in 2007 aid from 22 OECD countries dropped 8.4% to US$103.7 billion (Figure 5.29). Meanwhile, aid as a percentage of donors' GDP continued its sharp decline. In 2007 the 27 EU nations spent 0.38% of their GDP on development aid, compared with 0.41% in 2006. Only Denmark, Luxembourg, the Netherlands, Norway and Sweden met the 0.7% target. In comparison, the USA, the largest donor in absolute terms, spent just 0.16% of its GDP on development aid.

Box 5.3 The World Bank and types of international trade

The World Bank was set up together with the International Monetary Fund (IMF) in 1944. Initially it was mainly concerned with financing construction and development of national infrastructures such as dams and roads. Projects are supported through funding and technical assistance with the aims of increasing output, productivity and sustainable economic growth. However, many countries given aid continued to perform poorly. This prompted a re-think. Now the World Bank increasingly targets smaller geographical areas and smaller projects. Aims include raising the incomes of peasant farmers, increasing food production,

improving education, water supply and health care.

There are two fundamental types of international aid: **bilateral aid** and **multilateral aid**. Bilateral aid is the assistance from a donor government to a recipient country. In 2007, nearly 70% of all international aid was bilateral. The main targets for bilateral aid are technical assistance, debt relief and humanitarian aid. Multilateral aid is through donor agencies such as the World Bank, IMF, the United Nations (UN) and non-governmental organisations (NGOs) like Oxfam and the Red Cross. These organisations are funded mainly by the rich OECD countries.

Official development assistance (ODA) from Organisation for Economic Cooperation and Development (OECD) countries

Net ODA	2005	2006	2007
Current (US$m)	107 099	104 421	103 654
ODA/GNI	0.33%	0.31%	0.28%
Bilateral share	77%	74%	69%

Top ten recipients of gross ODA (US$ million)

1	Iraq	15 182
2	Nigeria	8 747
3	China	2 535
4	Indonesia	2 392
5	Afghanistan	2 286
6	India	1 672
7	Sudan	1 492
8	Vietnam	1 417
9	Zambia	1 348
10	DR Congo	1 293

Recipients of ODA by (a) region (US$ million) and (b) economic sector

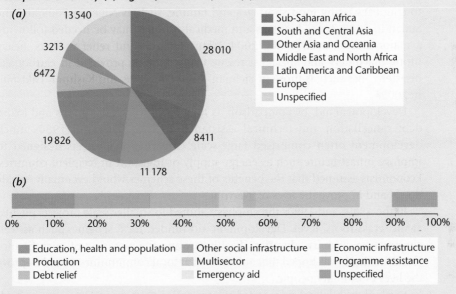

Figure 5.30 *Bilateral and multilateral overseas development aid from OECD countries, 2005–07*

Why countries give international aid

Rich countries in the OECD give international aid for economic, political and ethical reasons. Economic aid provides a number of benefits to recipient countries. It:

➤ increases foreign investment
➤ helps payment of interest on foreign debt
➤ provides foreign exchange to pay for imports
➤ assists the development of infrastructure such as ports, airports, roads, energy supply and so on
➤ provides additional income to the government

International aid is also given for political reasons. Donor countries may have an economic interest in maintaining the existing government in power, however corrupt or undemocratic. This is particularly the case in recipient countries like the Sudan or the Democratic Republic of Congo, which have rich natural resource bases.

Finally aid is given for ethical reasons. Most obvious are simple humanitarian reasons such as assisting poor people and helping them to achieve a decent quality of life. In the nineteenth century many LEDCs were exploited by European colonial powers like the UK, France and Belgium. International aid is one avenue these countries can use to repay the debt they owe LEDCs for past colonial exploitation.

Emergency aid and development aid

Emergency aid is the short-term assistance given to countries facing disasters which pose an immediate threat to life. For example, food supplies are air-lifted to countries facing food shortages and famine, such as Niger in 2005 and the Sudan in 2008. Tents, blankets and medical supplies may be needed following a major disaster such as the 2004 Asian tsunami; and relief workers, heavy lifting machinery and specialist rescue teams may be provided in earthquake disaster zones such as those in Sichuan, China, in 2008 and Kashmir, Pakistan, in 2005.

Development aid, by comparison, is long term; it includes grants and loans, debt cancellation and technical assistance. In the 1970s and 1980s much development often comprised large-scale construction projects designed to improve infrastructure such as energy supply or transport in recipient countries. Economists assumed that the benefits of these schemes would eventually 'trickle down' and improve the lives of everyone.

In the 1980s and 1990s the emphasis shifted to smaller-scale projects pitched at the 'grass-roots' level. Development aid funded local schemes such as well construction, primary education, health care and the provision of microfinance (local credit). It was hoped that aid directed at local communities would improve the lives of ordinary people.

Much of the bilateral aid targeted at large-scale infrastructural projects was 'tied'. In other words grants and loans invariably came with conditions concerning how the money could be spent. This usually meant importing resources, machinery and technical assistance from the donor country rather than shopping around for the best deal. Arguably 'tied' aid benefits the donor country as much as the recipient. However, donor countries argue that 'tied' aid is essential to counter inefficient corrupt officials in recipient countries, and to prevent the diversion of aid to military spending and extravagant projects such as presidential palaces and lavish parliamentary buildings.

Increasingly, multilateral aid channelled through organisations like the World Bank and IMF is 'tied'. Often aid is granted subject to strict conditions, such as structural adjustment programmes aimed at creating an economic environment that fosters growth. This might mean, for example, placing limits on public spending in the donor country, even though this might result in cut-backs in welfare and educational programmes, and unemployment.

Case study — Emergency aid and the Cyclone Nargis disaster in Myanmar

Cyclone Nargis devastated the Irrawaddy Delta region of southern Myanmar (Burma) on 2 and 3 May 2008 (Figure 5.31). A storm surge (see p. 85) killed at least 140 000 people, destroyed 450 000 homes and damaged 350 000 others. In the worst affected areas such as Bogale and Labutta townships, 77–85% of houses were destroyed. Overall, an estimated 2.4 million people were severely affected by the disaster.

Emergency aid had two objectives. The first was to provide urgent humanitarian assistance in the form of food, shelter, clean water and medical supplies (Photograph 5.4). Initially the flow of international aid was obstructed by the Myanmar government, which for political reasons refused to allow aid agencies and aid workers access to the country. For example, in June the government would not allow ten helicopters from the UN World Food Programme to fly relief missions, while four US warships, packed with food supplies, were refused permission to off-load their cargoes. Although by July, 13 UN agencies and 23 NGOs were working in the disaster area, delays caused by the government meant that barely half of those severely affected by the disaster had received any humanitarian assistance.

The second objective was to rebuild damaged infrastructure such as roads, bridges, schools and hospitals, and restore livelihoods. The last involved reclaiming the 2000 km^2 of rice fields damaged by saltwater. The cost of economic recovery over 3 years is estimated at US$1 billion and will require long-term financial support from the international community.

The UN's initial appeal for international aid raised just US$95 million in the three months following the disaster. Although this figure was well below

Figure 5.31 *Myanmar and the Cyclone Nargis disaster*

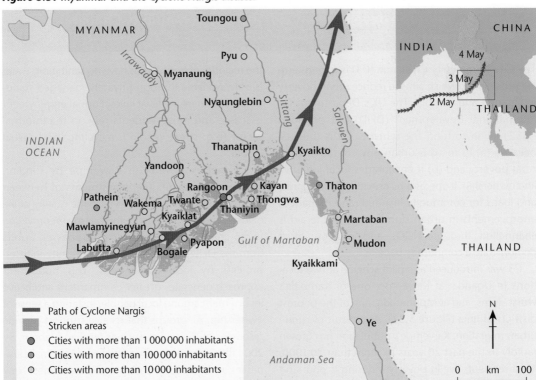

Photograph 5.4
A relief camp for Cyclone Nargis victims, southern Myanmar

Eddie Gerald/Alamy

expectations, emergency aid was sufficient to ensure that none of the cyclone victims died of starvation. A revised UN appeal covering the period from August 2008 and April 2009 aimed to raise nearly US$500 million. Food security was the most urgent problem. The delta region provides two-thirds of Myanmar's rice crop. With damage to farmland, lack of seed and the loss of farm animals, it was clear that Myanmar's rice crop in 2009 would fall well short of the country's needs. In the short to medium term, Myanmar will have to rely on food imports paid for in part by international aid.

Case study: Long-term development aid: the City Community Challenge in Uganda

The City Community Challenge (C3) is a long-term aid programme which aims to reduce urban poverty in Uganda and Zambia. The UK's Department for International Development (DFID) has provided US$2 million to fund the scheme. C3 is unusual because (a) its focus is urban poverty rather than rural poverty and (b) it encourages local initiative and ownership. It operates by providing small grants and loans for community-inspired (and managed) improvements in urban slums. Most of the aid is channelled through NGOs and projects must demonstrate a community benefit.

C3 was introduced as a pilot scheme at two locations in Uganda: at Kawempe, one of Kampala's worst slums, and at Mpumudde, one of the poorest districts of Jinja (Figure 5.32). As a result of rural–urban migration, Kawempe's population has grown rapidly in the past 20 years to more than 300 000. Most residents live in poverty; housing is poor and crime is rising; HIV prevalence is around 25%; the majority of households have no sanitation; water is only available through privately managed standpipes, and there are few clinics. Formal employment is scarce and most residents rely on the informal sector (e.g. street vending, recycling) and casual labour.

C3 tackles poverty in Kawempe by funding small improvements (i.e. investments of between US$100–1000 per project) to raise the quality of life of local residents. In practice this has meant providing micro-credit to fund individual businesses. Funds from the DFID are allocated to community-initiated projects by local committees. This bottom-up approach generates greater commitment and active involvement among local people, fostering a sense of ownership. All groups that receive support provide resources of their own, such as land and labour. By 2004 the C3 fund had supported over 140 small businesses and helped to set up many new ones. New businesses included retailing, fish farming, charcoal

making, broom making, carpentry, water supply, maize trading and many others. As well as raising incomes, new businesses provide jobs for local people. Financial backing has also been given to training programmes and improvements in water supply and sanitation.

In Mpumudde the emphasis has been on housing development. Shelter was identified by local people as the main priority need. An initial scheme aimed to build 74 low-cost houses, with a target of 286 in the long term. Grants of US$2400 per household were available from the C3 fund, with a further US$400 loan for income generation. In addition, grants are available to develop practical skills such as bricklaying and plastering. The C3 initiative at Jinja has attracted significant external resources, including a 14-classroom primary school built by the International Methodist Church and a transit centre for homeless street children. However, though the private sector has provided subsidised building materials and planning advice, its involvement has so far been limited.

Figure 5.32 *Map showing Kampala and Jinja, locations for the C3 pilot schemes*

Evaluating the impact of globalisation

Key ideas

➤ Governments vary in their response to globalisation and are increasingly looking to reduce the harmful impacts.

➤ The impact of globalisation can be measured and evaluated in different ways.

➤ Some countries manage the impact of globalisation on their economy and society.

As we have seen in this chapter, globalisation has many positive effects: it has stimulated economic growth, expanded world trade, created jobs, boosted investment and reduced the costs of goods and services. However, globalisation also has a downside. The international movement of capital has often resulted in the contraction of employment; and free trade has exposed the fragile economies of the least developed countries to aggressive competition from more efficient producers. Meanwhile the advance of technology, and its diffusion through globalisation, has created a demand for higher skill levels leading to increased inequality between socio-economic groups, countries and regions.

Chapter 5

Thus the overall impact of globalisation at the national scale has been highly variable. In economic terms most MEDCs and emerging economies have probably enjoyed a net benefit. The situation in many LEDCs is less clear. Within countries, globalisation creates winners and losers. It favours better-off, better educated and skilled groups. Often it is lower-income, poorly educated and less-skilled groups who have been the losers.

Managing the impacts of globalisation in the UK

While on balance the UK has benefited from the globalisation of the world economy, globalisation has also brought a number of problems. Governments need to manage these problems to minimise their impact on economy and society. Among the problems linked to globalisation that affect the UK are:

➤ increased competition from foreign industries and services as a result of trade liberalisation, advances in communications and transport, and foreign direct investment (FDI). This development threatens domestic economic activities and employment.
➤ large increases in international immigration, which put pressure on the job market (especially for lower-skilled workers), housing, education, health services and so on
➤ increased dependence on FDI by powerful TNCs, with related problems of loss of control of decision-making and potential disinvestment
➤ increased personal and spatial inequality, with a widening gap between rich and poor

The UK government, in cooperation with the EU, has responded to these problems in a number of ways. They include: restrictions on international trade; controls on international immigration; subsidies to industries; grants to regions and locations hit hardest by foreign competition; and income redistribution from richer to poorer regions and individuals.

Trade barriers

Despite the global advance of free trade, restrictions on the international movement of some goods, especially agricultural products, textiles and clothing, remain in place. Many agricultural products entering the EU (e.g. dairy produce, beef) are subject to a common external tariff. The purpose of the tariff is to protect the livelihoods of EU farmers, promote the economic health of rural communities which depend on farming and strengthen national food security. In a bid to protect the textile and clothing industries, the EU imposes an average common tariff of 8% on imports. However, tariffs and quotas are variable, and there are special agreements for neighbouring non-EU countries, as well as many emerging and developing economies.

Protection for UK and EU industries is also achieved through domestic price support and export subsidies. Agriculture in the UK and the EU is protected by

both. Farmers get fixed area payments for wheat, sugar beet and oil seed and other crops. Similar subsidies are given to livestock farmers for sheep and cattle. These subsidies give domestic producers a significant price advantage over food imports from outside the EU.

Subsidies are not confined to agriculture. Airbus, the EU manufacturer of commercial aircraft, receives support from the EU for research and development and preferential loans from the European Investment Bank. Boeing, its main rival in the global commercial aircraft industry, complains that this financial help amounts to unfair competition.

Some economic activities, such as the dairy industry, receive export subsidies from the EU. Dairy exporters get refunds on butter, cheese and powdered milk, which help to secure jobs in the dairy industry and allow farmers to compete in world markets.

International immigration

Globalisation has resulted in the freer movement of people, as well as goods, services and capital. International migration doubled between 1975 and 2005. Today 3% of the world's population live outside their country of birth.

The UK has experienced unparalleled international immigration since 1997. Before 1997 net migrational change was virtually zero (Figures 5.33 and 5.34). In other words the number of people entering the country was roughly equal to the number leaving. Since then, net international migration has been running at around 200 000 a year. Immigration was given a massive boost in 2004 with the enlargement of the EU and the UK government's decision to allow unrestricted entry to migrants from the ten new member countries (Photograph 5.5). Such has been the recent scale of immigration, that current projections suggest a total UK population of 73 million by 2046.

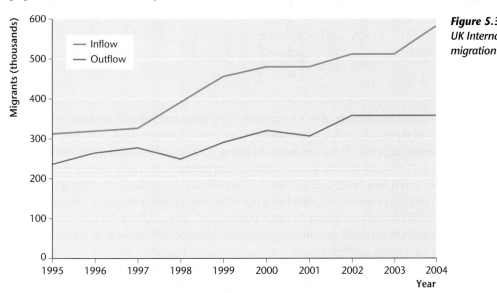

Figure 5.33
UK International migration

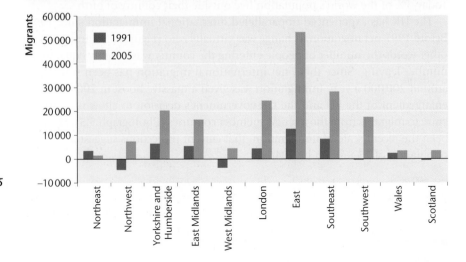

Photograph 5.5
Migrant workers from eastern Europe planting lettuces on a farm in Suffolk

Figure 5.34 UK *international migration by region, 1990–2005*

Population growth of this magnitude represents a significant problem to the UK, and especially to the overcrowded southeast where the majority of immigrants settle. Already there are huge housing shortages in this region. Add to this problems of traffic congestion, inadequate public transport infrastructure and loss of green belt land, and the need to accommodate perhaps another 13 million people in the next 40 years becomes extremely problematical.

The overall economic benefits of immigration are debatable. While there is no doubt that highly qualified immigrants or those with skills that are in demand (e.g. nurses, teachers) contribute more in taxes than they gain through tax credits and benefits, the economic case for unskilled immigrants is far from clear. Unskilled immigrants compete with unskilled Britons for jobs, keep wages at minimum levels and may add to unemployment.

Table 5.8 *The UK's new policy for international immigration assesses the economic value of potential immigrants using a points system*

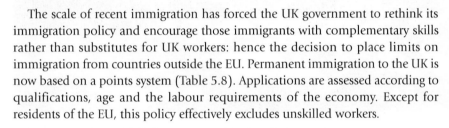

Tier 1: highly skilled migrants	Migrants able to contribute to growth and productivity. Workers in this category will have the greatest opportunities to settle for good because they have the most potential for generating wealth, e.g. by setting up companies and creating jobs.
Tier 2: skilled migrants	Available to migrants from outside the EU. Qualification based on a points system which includes sponsorship from an employer, qualifications, income and English language ability. Applications need a minimum of 70 points to qualify for residence.
Tier 3: low-skilled migrants	Limited numbers of low-skilled workers needed to fill temporary labour shortages. Until recently, the government allowed temporary migration to jobs in hospitality, food processing and agriculture from all over the world. Now this policy applies only to workers from the EU, who do not need prior permission to work in the UK.
Tiers 4 and 5: students and temporary workers	Foreign students wanting to study in the UK. Temporary workers allowed to work in the UK for a limited period of time to satisfy primarily non-economic objectives.

The scale of recent immigration has forced the UK government to rethink its immigration policy and encourage those immigrants with complementary skills rather than substitutes for UK workers: hence the decision to place limits on immigration from countries outside the EU. Permanent immigration to the UK is now based on a points system (Table 5.8). Applications are assessed according to qualifications, age and the labour requirements of the economy. Except for residents of the EU, this policy effectively excludes unskilled workers.

Inward foreign direct investment (FDI)

The UK has been highly successful in attracting inward FDI. Inward FDI has been higher than in any other MEDC apart from the USA. This investment has raised productivity, created thousands of jobs, and encouraged innovation, new technologies and new skills. However, despite its obvious benefits FDI can be problematic. For example, foreign firms may compete directly with indigenous firms. In addition, FDI tends to be concentrated disproportionately in London and the southeast, attracted by the transport infrastructure, clusters of related economic activities, producer services and skilled labour.

In the 1980s and 1990s, successive governments attempted to tackle these problems and exert some control on FDI. Japanese car manufacturers such as Toyota and Nissan had to agree to source 60–65% of parts locally. Foreign manufacturing companies were also given financial incentives to locate production outside the more prosperous areas of the UK, in regions like the northeast and south Wales that had high levels of unemployment and had suffered severe deindustrialisation.

Inequality

Globalisation has led to a widening of inequality both in a personal and spatial sense. An example is the financial globalisation of the City of London since the early 1990s. For the City's highly skilled workforce this development brought huge salary increases. However, for the majority of UK workers, it merely increased

John Sturrock/Alamy

Photograph 5.6
Deindustrialisation in the UK: a derelict engineering factory in Sheffield

personal disparities in wealth. Inequality in incomes in the UK (measured by the Gini coefficient) increased from 28 to 35 between 1980 and 2007 though some of this change was due to the effects of technology which tend to boost the incomes of the more highly educated and skilled workers.

We have seen that globalisation increases spatial inequality. Inner London is the UK's (and EU's) richest region with an average income 303% higher than the EU average. Wales, with an average of 92.2%, is the UK's poorest region. Prosperous regions like London and the southeast became magnets for inward FDI. Meanwhile, traditional economic activities such as manufacturing and mining, heavily concentrated in peripheral regions like Wales and northern England, suffered severe international competition and deindustrialisation (Photograph 5.6).

Examination-style questions

Section A

Resource 1

India's garment industry stained with sweat and tears

In southern India's Tirupur town, young girls are lured to work in the garment industry with a promise of a 'golden opportunity' to earn their own dowry at the end of a three-year apprentice period. Known as 'camp coolies', they instead end up working in deplorable conditions for years getting virtually nothing.

While NGOs say labour laws are not stringent enough, Tirupur Exporters say that flexible labour laws favourable to entrepreneurs are needed if India is to compete with China, whose market share of the garment exports industry is 25–27% as opposed to India's 3.5%.

According to a Tirupur People's Forum (TPF) study these girls are paid between 70 and 95 cents a day. Every month, US$9.5 to US$11.5 are deducted for boarding and lodging. According to the NGO SAVE, these girls are almost like prisoners in their hostels, which are usually in the same compound as their workplace, and can only step outside the gates escorted by a warden.

Highlighting the deplorable housing conditions of these workers, the TPF study says: 'Sumangali scheme workers are kept in an abandoned poultry farm. Approximately 50 to 60 women workers sleep in a 25×6 square metre area which is dusty and dingy. There is no space for privacy and there are only four toilets.' Many suffer severe nutritional deficiencies as well.

1 **Resource 1 provides information on some aspects of globalisation.**
   Outline an issue indicated and suggest appropriate management. (10 marks)

Section B

2 **Discuss the view that the impact of inward investment by transnational corporations on an area is often more harmful than beneficial.** (30 marks)
3 **How and with what success have governments managed the harmful economic, social and environmental effects of globalisation?** (30 marks)

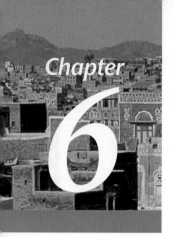

6

Development and inequalities

Key ideas

➤ Levels of economic development and quality of life can be assessed both quantitatively and qualitatively.

➤ Countries vary in their levels of economic development.

➤ Levels of development influence the quality of life and standard of living.

➤ Levels of economic development and quality of life vary geographically at a global scale.

➤ There are significant contrasts in levels of development and quality of life between MEDCs, NICs and LEDCs.

Economic development and quality of life

It is apparent that we live in a world where huge differences exist between countries in levels of economic development and quality of life. However, before we explore these differences and the reasons for them we need to define the terms 'economic development' and 'quality of life'.

Economic development is the process of creating wealth by mobilising human and natural resources to produce saleable commodities, manufactured goods and services. By generating wealth, economic development has a direct impact on the standard of living and quality of life. Providing wealth is distributed equitably within a country, economic development should create jobs, raise incomes and give most people a better standard of living. In practice this means two things: improvements in the consumption of material resources such as food, clean water, clothing and housing; and better access to essential services like education and health care.

Yet an increase in the standard of living is not the same thing as an improvement in the quality of life. For millions of people in LEDCs economic development and accompanying urbanisation in recent years has indeed brought increased material wealth. None the less economic development has a downside. For many people economic development has meant longer hours, being away from home and family for long periods, and living in overcrowded cities that suffer chronic pollution and high levels of crime. Meanwhile, for a significant minority in the population, economic development brings few gains and often only serves to increase inequality in society.

Measures of economic development and quality of life

Quantitative measurements

The most widely used measure of economic development is **gross domestic product (GDP) per capita** in US$ (Table 6.1). GDP per capita is the total market value of all final goods and services produced in a country in a given year divided by its population. To take account of geographical variations in the cost of living, GDP per capita is adjusted for each country with purchasing power parity (PPP).

GDP is a basic economic growth indicator and measures economic output. It does not, however, include the social and economic costs of production and is therefore a poor indicator of quality of life and well-being.

An alternative to GDP per capita is **gross national income (GNI) per capita**. This measure is widely used by the World Bank and is the dollar value of a country's annual income divided by its population. Unlike GDP per capita, GNI per capita also includes flows of income from overseas.

There is a close correlation between annual energy consumption per capita and economic development. Energy is a key factor in industrial growth and in supporting essential services that influence the quality of life. The high material standards of living enjoyed by most people in MEDCs are sustained by the lavish consumption of oil, gas, coal and nuclear energy.

Table 6.2 ranks the top and bottom ten countries by **energy consumption per capita**. While energy consumption correlates closely with economic development, there are anomalies. For instance, Table 6.2 excludes small oil-producing countries such as the United Arab Emirates with

Table 6.1 *GDP per capita (PPP), richest and poorest countries, 2006*

10 richest countries		10 poorest countries	
	US$		US$
Luxembourg	65 994	Yemen	846
Ireland	40 087	Niger	832
USA	39 319	Madagascar	817
Norway	38 196	Guinea-Bissau	782
Switzerland	33 062	Ethiopia	778
Iceland	32 338	Sierra Leone	754
Austria	31 900	Tanzania	657
Denmark	31 768	Burundi	635
Netherlands	31 749	DRC	633
Belgium	31 131	Malawi	555

Table 6.2 *Primary energy consumption per capita, 2006*

Top 10 countries		Bottom 10 countries	
	Mbtu per capita		Mbtu per capita
Iceland	489.6	Burkina Faso	1.4
Singapore	457.1	Rwanda	1.3
Norway	455.7	Central African Republic	1.3
Canada	436.2	Ethiopia	1.2
Luxembourg	431.2	Somalia	1.2
USA	340.5	Mali	1.0
Australia	273.4	Burundi	1.0
Sweden	259.9	Afghanistan	0.6
Netherlands	258.5	Cambodia	0.6
Belgium	249.2	Chad	0.3

Box 6.1 Human Development Index (HDI)

The UN's Human development index (HDI) is a measure of development based on economic and social indicators. UN member states are ranked each year from 1st to 177th. The index ranges from 1 (most developed) to 0 (least developed). In 2007–08 there were 70 countries with a high index of 0.8 and above, 76 countries with a medium index of 0.5 to 0.79, and 21 countries with a low index of less than 0.5. Iceland was ranked 1st and Sierra Leone was 177th.

The HDI is a composite measure of health, knowledge and standard of living. It combines data on life expectancy, adult literacy and school enrolment, and GDP per capita (PPP in US$).

The HDI shows the huge inequalities in well-being and life chances between countries. By looking at both economic and social aspects of people's lives, it provides a much more complete picture of a country's development than other indicators, such as GDP per capita. Introduced in 1990, it also provides a comparative measure of progress in economic and social development over the past two decades.

Table 6.3 GDP per capita and infant mortality rate (IMR) in a random sample of 50 countries

	GDP per capita	IMR		GDP per capita	IMR
Afghanistan	175	157	Liberia	161	133
Angola	2058	132	Luxembourg	79851	5
Australia	36045	4	Mali	392	129
Bahrain	17773	11	Mauritania	598	63
Belgium	35388	4	Mongolia	820	40
Bolivia	1028	46	Myanmar	1506	66
Bulgaria	3512	12	Netherlands	38248	5
Cameroon	1033	88	Nicaragua	953	21
Chad	603	119	Norway	63918	3
Colombia	2696	19	Panama	4791	18
Costa Rica	4615	10	Philippines	1184	23
Cyprus	20841	6	Qatar	52239	8
Denmark	47768	4	Romania	4568	15
Egypt	1211	29	Saudi Arabia	13399	15
Estonia	10213	7	Singapore	26876	3
France	34935	4	Somalia	565	116
Gambia	304	74	Sudan	769	65
Greece	20281	7	Switzerland	49351	4
Guatemala	2517	30	Macedonia	2834	15
Haiti	517	49	Tanzania	328	73
India	736	55	Trinidad }	12417	12
Ireland	48524	5	Tobago		
Jamaica	3671	14	Uganda	302	77
Kenya	560	64	Uzbekistan	558	55
Laos	486	51	Yemen	798	93

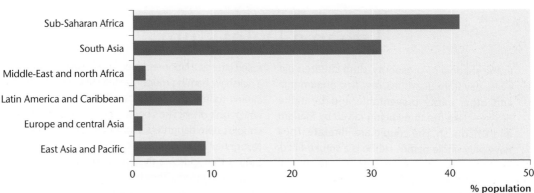

Figure 6.1
Percentage of population living in absolute poverty

exceptionally high levels of energy consumption. Energy consumption statistics also understate the use of energy in many of the world's poorest countries that rely heavily on local biofuels such as firewood and animal dung.

A variety of other quantitative indicators are used to measure economic development and quality of life. **Infant mortality** is highly sensitive to economic and environmental conditions, being influenced, among other things, by the health of mothers, diet, the availability of clean drinking water, sanitation, housing and health care. **Life expectancy**, another summative measure of well-being, is affected by similar factors. Meanwhile, the World Bank defines absolute poverty as living on less than US$1 a day. Using this criterion, sub-Saharan Africa and south Asia have the highest poverty levels (Table 6.3). Indeed in 2005, there were seven countries in sub-Saharan Africa where more than 60% of the population were living in absolute poverty (Figure 6.1).

Qualitative approaches

Literal descriptions of the lives of poor people provide us with a vivid and person-alised view of what poverty really means. By comparison, the pictures painted by statistical measures such as GDP per capita and infant mortality are objective and bland: they fail utterly to convey the suffering and daily struggle of hundreds of millions of people, especially in LEDCs. The newspaper article in Figure 6.2 (p. 214) provides us with an insight into life in a Delhi slum. There lack of employment and low wages condemn thousands of families to absolute poverty. Living on a dollar a day means that slum people cannot afford decent housing, have no proper sanitation or mains water and have insufficient food. The result of poverty is disease, which as part of a vicious cycle, reproduces poverty.

Global contrasts in development and quality of life

There are huge global contrasts in levels of development and quality of life (Figure 6.3, p. 215). The rich developed world consists of western Europe, North America, Japan and Australasia. At the opposite end of the development spectrum are the

Life in a Delhi slum

In the shadow of prosperity, slum children die every day from diarrhoea, measles, pneumonia and other easily preventable and treatable diseases. Like the three being raised by Mariam and Dharmesh. The couple are illiterate. They have only single names. Home is a smoke-filled, 8-foot-by-8-foot hut. A dim light bulb the hue of a harvest moon hangs over a burlap-covered bed fashioned from a steamer trunk. There is no toilet, no sink. For this, the couple pays 850 rupees a month in rent — about $17, half their income.

Mariam and Dharmesh came here from a village in eastern India, where, they said, people were even more impoverished.

"In Orissa, we didn't have enough food to eat," Dharmesh said.

A few years ago, he was stricken with tuberculosis. Although the government supposedly provides free TB treatment, Mariam said it is impossible to get into the clinic and get medications unless you first pay a fee. A social worker with a private charity helped them raise the money, effectively saving Dharmesh's life.

He first found work in Delhi as a ragpicker — combing through trash for scraps of clothing. He toiled later as a labourer. Lately, he's been pedaling a rickshaw, earning roughly a dollar a day. Mariam cleans toilets when she can find the work — which isn't often. She's been home, caring for the couple's twin daughters. The infants, Reshma and Noorjeham, have blank eyes and the distended bellies that indicate dysenteric diarrhoea — a major killer in India. They have been sick for weeks, but their parents can't afford to get a true diagnosis, let alone buy medicine.

"When we can afford it, we give them milk," Mariam said. "When we have no money, we give them sugar water."

Five-year-old Arshad recently got kicked out of school for poor attendance, adding to the family's woes. Because of the twins' illnesses, Mariam needed her son to help at home. Their plight illustrates the cycle of disease and poverty. Illness undermines opportunity — income. Poverty begets more illness, which begets more poverty. It's a process of erosion.

"I have hope that one day we will get out of here," Mariam said. She forced a smile and looked away, bringing an arm across her face to hide the tears.

"We are always in God's hands."

Figure 6.2 A vivid picture of absolute poverty in India

Source: Tom Paulson, *Seattle Post-Intelligencer*, 8 December 2003

LEDCs of sub-Saharan Africa, south Asia and parts of Central America. However, between these extremes there are many middle-income countries. Some of these countries are currently undergoing rapid economic development through industrialisation. As a group, these countries are often called **newly industrialising countries (NICs)**, though 'emerging economies' is the term increasingly used. China and India are the outstanding examples of emerging economies; others include Brazil, Argentina, Thailand and Malaysia.

The World Bank divides countries into three groups:
- low-income countries, which have a GNI per capita per year of less than US$935
- middle-income countries, with a GNI per capita per year of between US$936 and US$11 456
- high-income countries with more than US$11 456 GNI per capita per year

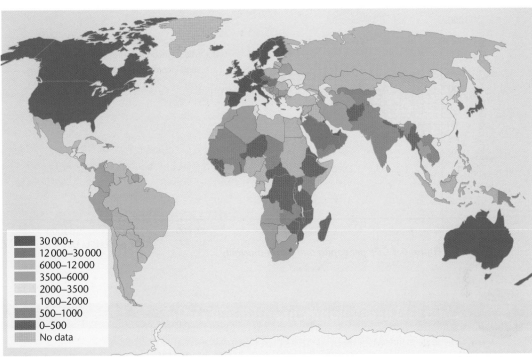

Figure 6.3 *Global GDP per capita, 2007*

The uneven distribution of wealth at a global scale is evident if we compare the incomes and populations of these three groups of countries. The 49 low-income countries defined by the World Bank contain 20% of the world's population but account for only 1.5% of the world's annual income. Compare this with the high-income group: they have 16% of the world's population but 74% of the world's annual income. Meanwhile the average GNI per capita in high-income countries is 50 times higher than in low-income countries.

Box 6.2 Statistical analysis of development and quality of life

The data in Table 6.3 are a systematically chosen sample of 50 countries with indicators of economic development and quality of life. GDP per capita represents levels of economic development, and infant mortality is a surrogate measure for quality of life. These two variables can be used to classify countries according to their level of development. Figure 6.4, p. 216 shows the data plotted as a scatter chart. This does two things:

■ The plot reveals that the variables are closely related (in this instance the relationship is log-log).

■ By delimiting (subjectively) breaks in the distribution, it is possible to define three distinct groups of countries: low income/least developed; middle income/less developed; and high income/more developed.

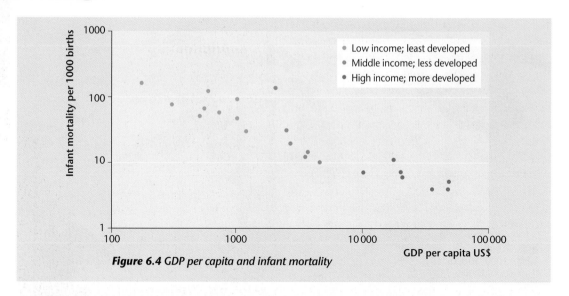

Figure 6.4 GDP per capita and infant mortality

Legend:
- Low income; least developed
- Middle income; less developed
- High income; more developed

Axes: Infant mortality per 1000 births (vertical); GDP per capita US$ (horizontal)

Case study Contrasts in development and quality of life

Afghanistan

Afghanistan, a small landlocked country in south-west Asia, is one of the poorest and least developed nations in the world. An estimated 53% of the population lives below the poverty line — a proportion rarely found outside sub-Saharan Africa. Over half of all older children are not in school, public health is poor, and much of the population suffers shortages of housing, clean water, health care and jobs (Photograph 6.1).

Agriculture is the mainstay of the Afghan economy, supporting 80% of the population. However, the country depends heavily on foreign aid and on the illicit production and trade in opium. Lack

Photograph 6.1
A family in the refugee camp at Buthhak, Afghanistan

Vario images GmbH & Co.KG/Alamy

of economic development in the past 40 years has been due in large measure to the country's political instability. The Soviets invaded Afghanistan in 1979, only for the communist regime in Kabul to collapse in 1992. There followed a period of anarchy before the Taliban captured most of the country and installed a fundamentalist Islamic government. They in turn were overthrown following invasion by the USA and its allies in 2001. Today, a guerrilla war is being fought in the southern provinces between a resurgent Taliban and the allies.

There is no doubt that war and civil unrest have contributed to the nation's poverty and have held back economic progress. According to the UN there are 130 000 long-term displaced Afghans in the country, plus thousands of refugees from neighbouring Pakistan and Iran (Photograph 6.1). Other obstacles to development include government corruption and a poorly educated and largely unskilled workforce.

Discrimination against women and girls has greatly reduced Afghanistan's economic potential. Gender inequality means that only one-third of children in school are girls and traditionally women have been banned from public life. Inequality is evident in mortality statistics: rates of maternal mortality in the poorest districts (up to 6.5 mothers for every 100 live births) are the highest in the world.

South Korea

In economic terms, South Korea is classed as a newly industrialising country or NIC. Its economic development since the 1960s has been spectacular. Four decades ago South Korea's GDP per capita was comparable with poorer countries in Africa and Asia. By 2007, South Korea had risen to 49th in the GDP league table of 205 countries.

Economic growth and prosperity is due to industrialisation. Sponsored and directed by the government, industrial development focused on export industries: first light industries in the 1960s; then heavier industries such as shipbuilding, steel and chemicals in the 1970s and 1980s; and most recently motor vehicles and consumer electronics. At the heart

Travel Pix/Alamy

Photograph 6.2 *The Samsung building and Rodin Gallery, Seoul, South Korea*

of this industrialisation have been a handful of huge transnational Korean companies such as Samsung, LG and Hyundai (Photograph 6.2). Increasingly South Korea is moving to a more knowledge-based economy, relying on its highly educated workforce.

Annual economic growth rates have been especially high in recent years with GDP per capita increasing from US$11 568 in 2002 to US$18 164 in 2006 (Figure 6.5). Moreover, rising average incomes have not been at the expense of equality. Korea's Gini coefficient is comparable to most west European countries, while men and women have fairly equal status (Table 6.4).

Denmark

Denmark is a small, prosperous country in northwest Europe with a vibrant market economy. Its GDP per capita and the material standard of living of its people are among the highest in the world. The country's economic success is founded on good

Table 6.4 *Contrasts in development and quality of life: Denmark, South Korea and Afghanistan*

	GDP per capita (US$)	Total fertility rate	Adult literacy rate (%)		Life expectancy (years)		Adult economic activity rates (%)	
			Men	Women	Men	Women	Men	Women
Denmark	51 074	1.8	100	100	76	81	69	59
South Korea	18 164	1.2	100	100	75	82	74	50
Afghanistan	319	7.1	51	18	44	44	88	40

Figure 6.5 *Growth of GDP in South Korea, 1983–2007*

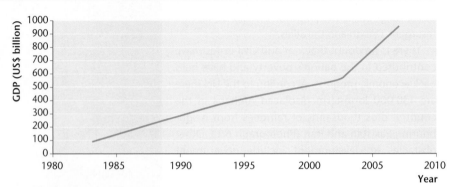

governance and its human capital, in particular its highly educated and highly skilled workforce. Denmark's economic success centres on high-tech agriculture and thousands of small businesses enterprises which emphasise design and quality. Leading exports include machinery, instruments, farm products, chemicals, furniture and wind turbines.

The social and political circumstances of the country also give its citizens a high quality of life. In the UN's 2007–08 human development index, Denmark was ranked 14th. Denmark is a stable social democracy with a commitment to equality. A generous welfare system and a redistributive tax system have effectively eliminated poverty. Indeed, the average difference between the most prosperous and least prosperous Danes (measured by the Gini coefficient) is the lowest in the world (Photograph 6.3).

Photograph 6.3 *High living standards in Denmark: business people walk past a luxury yacht moored at Copenhagen harbour*

Paul Maguire/Alamy

Explaining levels of economic development and inequalities

Key ideas

➤ Physical, economic, social, political and historical factors influence the relative levels of development of countries and lead to inequalities.

➤ Economic development can increase as well as decrease inequalities between and within countries.

Factors influencing economic development

A range of factors influence relative levels of development that in turn lead to inequalities:

➤ Physical: natural resources (energy, minerals, soil, climate etc.) and location/accessibility.

➤ Historical: time and the legacy of past economic, social and political events.

➤ Political: the quality of governance and political stability.

➤ Social: education, workforce skills, population growth, gender inequality and disease.

➤ Economic: foreign inward investment, infrastructure and trade.

However, a single factor rarely explains differences in development and inequality between and within countries. More often these differences result from a combination of physical, historical, political, social and economic factors.

Physical

Physical advantages such as mineral and energy resources, while desirable, are not essential for economic development. Although some MEDCs do have vast natural resource wealth (e.g. USA, Canada, Russia, Australia), many others such as the Netherlands and Switzerland have a minimal natural resource base. Climate is an important natural resource that has a direct effect on some economic activities such as farming and tourism. Many MEDCs have climatic conditions that contribute to development and support productive agriculture (e.g. France, Italy) and mass tourism (e.g. Spain, Greece). Equally, a harsh physical environment need not be a handicap to development. For instance, Finland and Canada, despite their cold climates, rugged relief and high latitude, are two of the richest countries in the world.

Access to the oceans for trade and new technologies has played a pivotal role in economic development. Most MEDCs have direct access to the oceans, although there are exceptions, such as Switzerland and Austria in western Europe.

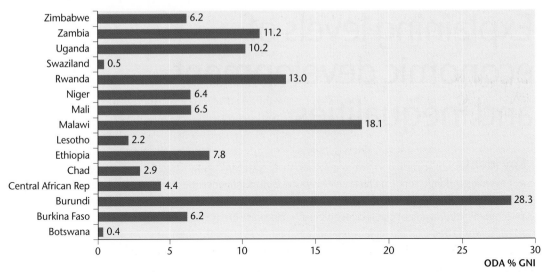

Zimbabwe — 6.2
Zambia — 11.2
Uganda — 10.2
Swaziland — 0.5
Rwanda — 13.0
Niger — 6.4
Mali — 6.5
Malawi — 18.1
Lesotho — 2.2
Ethiopia — 7.8
Chad — 2.9
Central African Rep — 4.4
Burundi — 28.3
Burkina Faso — 6.2
Botswana — 0.4

ODA % GNI

Figure 6.6 *Overseas development aid as a percentage of GNI in landlocked African countries, 2006*

However in western Europe, even **landlocked** countries are generally no more than a few hundred kilometres from the coast, and those that are often have good access to inland waterways.

None the less, landlocked countries have a relative disadvantage in terms of development. They have to rely on the cooperation of neighbouring states with coastlines for international trade. This can be a problem in parts of the world that are politically unstable or in the centre of a continental landmass thousands of kilometres from the coast.

Africa has 15 landlocked countries. In some of these countries, geographical isolation has contributed to low levels of economic development (Figure 6.6). Seven of Africa's landlocked countries are among the 15 poorest in the world. It is perhaps no coincidence that the two landlocked countries in South America — Paraguay and Bolivia — are also the continent's poorest.

Historical

The timescale of economic development can influence a country's economic status. Most countries in western Europe have a long history of economic development stretching back two centuries or more. These countries have had time to become fully settled, exploit their natural resources, and build up infrastructure and human capital. Contrast this with economic development in much of Africa, Asia and Latin America that only started in the twentieth century.

Many countries in the economically developing world are still struggling with the legacy of colonialism. Nineteenth-century colonialism by European superpowers such as Britain and France was exploitative. Colonies supplied food products and minerals for the benefit of the colonial power. Economic development was only encouraged where it facilitated resource exploitation (e.g. through the building of ports and railways). Meanwhile, many modern LEDCs created by colonial powers are artificial states that fail to recognise tribal and national differences. In the past half century, this legacy of colonialism has fuelled political instability and civil wars in many African countries, such as Kenya, Nigeria, Sudan and Rwanda.

Political

Governments can both promote and deter economic development. Modern Japan is an example of the former. Until the late nineteenth century Japan was a feudal society. For hundreds of years Japan had followed an isolationist policy with minimum contact with the outside world. All this changed in 1868 with the restoration of the imperial Meiji dynasty. Japan embarked on a policy of modernisation and industrialisation, open to new technologies and trade with the rest of the world. By 1912 the Japanese economy had been transformed. The country had a well-developed transport and communications infrastructure, an educated and skilled population, a fast-growing industrial sector based on new technology, and a powerful army and navy. Government policy laid the foundations for an economy that was to become one the most dynamic in the twentieth century.

Social

Human capital

Human capital includes the education and skills of the workforce. It is a major driver of economic development. In modern knowledge-based economies, where service activities account for 80% of employment, high literacy and skill levels are of key importance. The world's most advanced economies rely on human capital as their principal resource (Figure 6.7). Human capital has been equally important to the recent success of emerging economies such as India, Taiwan and Singapore.

Of course, low levels of literacy and skill are a consequence as well as a cause of lack of development. Pre-industrial economies in Africa and Asia based on labour-intensive agriculture create little demand for a highly educated workforce. With limited productivity and little engagement in international trade, GDP per capita levels are inevitably low in these economies.

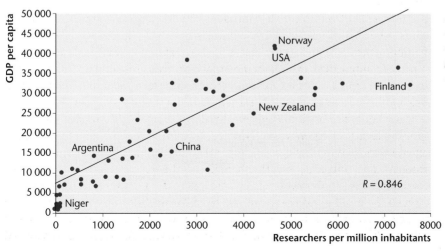

Figure 6.7
Relationship between GDP per capita and researchers, 2005

Gender inequality

In many poor countries women are denied equal access to education, employment and personal development. The effect is to neutralise a large part of the potential workforce, reduce productivity and hold back economic development. Gender inequality is most pronounced in sub-Saharan Africa, south and west Asia and Arab states (Figure 6.8). Sub-Saharan Africa's poorest countries — Niger, Chad, and the Central African Republic — also have the highest gender inequality. However, the most extreme inequality is found in two Islamic states: Afghanistan (gender parity index 0.56) and Yemen (0.64).

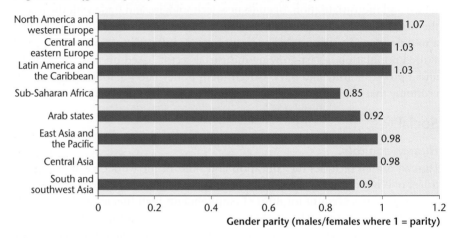

Figure 6.8 Gender parity in education: primary to tertiary, 2006

Population growth

Rapid population growth by itself does not retard economic development, and in some circumstances may stimulate economic growth. However, many of the world's poorest countries have rapidly expanding populations (Figure 6.9). Several countries in sub-Saharan Africa have population growth rates that outstrip economic growth. The result is high rates of dependency, poverty and little evidence of economic progress in per capita terms.

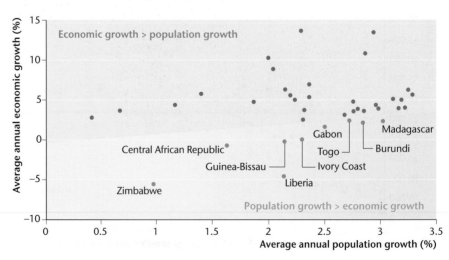

Figure 6.9 Population growth and economic growth in sub-Saharan Africa, 2001–05

Tropical diseases

Poor health and the prevalence of disease check economic development. At the same time, poor health and disease are symptoms of poverty and inadequate health care. The most serious tropical diseases are malaria, tuberculosis, dengue, schistosomiasis and trypanosomiasis. Disease has its greatest impact in the humid tropics of Africa, Asia and Latin America where one in six of the population is affected.

Malaria

Malaria is the most important tropical disease (Box 6.3, p. 224). Found in over 90 countries, it affects between 300 and 500 million people (Figure 6.10). According to the World Health Organisation (WHO) more than 1 million people die of malaria every year, mostly infants, young children and pregnant women, the majority of them in sub-Saharan Africa.

The social and economic costs of malaria are huge. WHO estimates that in the worst-affected countries malaria accounts for an average 1.3% loss in economic growth. This has led to substantial differences in GDP between countries with and without malaria. As a chronic, debilitating illness malaria greatly reduces workers' efficiency and output. It also affects school attendance and impairs the performance of children at school. Both individual households and the public health sector spend a substantial part of their incomes on prevention and treatment, which further increases poverty.

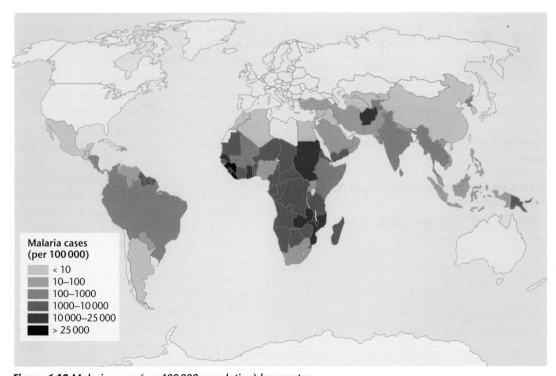

Malaria cases
(per 100 000)

   < 10
   10–100
   100–1000
   1000–10 000
   10 000–25 000
   > 25 000

Figure 6.10 *Malaria cases (per 100 000 population) by country*

Box 6.3 Malaria: infection and transmission

Malaria is caused by parasites of the species *Plasmodium* that are spread from person to person through the bites of infected mosquitoes. The common first symptoms — fever, headache, chills and vomiting — appear 10–15 days after a person is infected. If not treated promptly with effective medicines, malaria can cause severe illness that is often fatal.

Malaria transmission depends on local factors such as rainfall patterns, proximity of mosquito breeding sites and mosquito species. Some regions have a fairly constant number of cases throughout the year — these are **malaria endemic** — whereas in other areas there are 'malaria' seasons, usually coinciding with the rainy season.

Large and devastating epidemics can occur in areas where people have had little contact with the malaria parasite, and therefore have little or no immunity. These epidemics can be triggered by weather conditions and made worse by food shortages, political conflicts and natural disasters.

Source: WHO

Economic

The main economic factors that influence levels of development are FDI, international trade and infrastructure.

FDI is essential to economic development: it generates jobs that input money to national economies; stimulates economic growth; and attracts new skills and new technologies. It all helps to finance essential transport infrastructure (Figure 6.11).

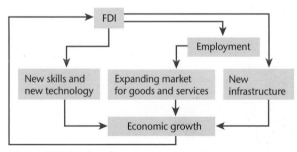

Figure 6.11 *Foreign direct investment and economic growth*

Table 6.5 *Global shares of population and FDI by region/country, 2006*

Region/ country	% share global population	% share global inward FDI
EU	7.6	46.0
USA	4.6	10.9
Africa	14.2	3.4
Latin America	8.6	11.3
Asia	60.5	21.8
MEDCs	18.5	59.2
LEDCs	81.5	36.5

There are, however, large global inequalities in FDI (Figure 6.12). The EU, with just 7.6% of the world's population, takes 46% of all FDI. Africa on the other hand, receives only 3.4% of global FDI despite having 14% of the world's population (Table 6.5). These inequalities reflect differences in existing levels of economic development between the EU and Africa, and the more attractive investment opportunities in the EU (Figure 6.12).

A close correlation exists between international trade and economic development (see Chapter 5). International trade is dominated by MEDCs and contributes significantly to prosperity in countries like the USA, Germany and Japan (Figure 6.13). In contrast many countries in Africa and Asia have little involvement in world trade, adding to their poverty and lack of development. Yet we should be cautious when examining the influence of trade on development: after all, the volume of trade of any country is as much a consequence as a cause of its development.

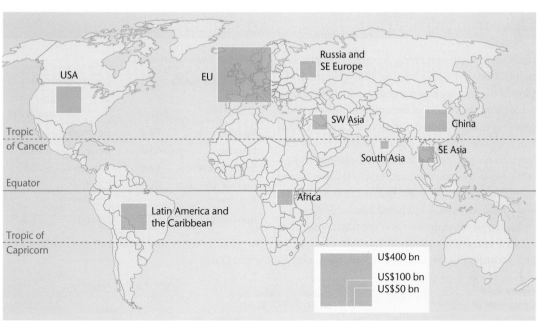

Figure 6.12 *Principal FDI inflows by country and region*

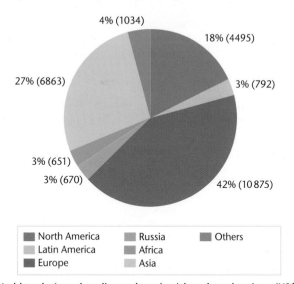

Figure 6.13 *World trade (merchandise and services) by selected regions (US$ billion), 2006*

One important pre-requisite for successful economic development is a modern transport infrastructure. International tourism requires airports capable of handling large jet aeroplanes; international trade in commodities and manufactured goods relies on deep-water ports; manufacturing industries need efficient roads and railways; and most industries (and especially service activities) depend on telecommunications networks such as broadband internet. An effective infrastructure is therefore essential to attract FDI.

Namibia, in southwest Africa, according to UN definition is a lower-middle income state (Figure 6.14). Most of the country is arid and semi-arid. Its economy is based on the export of mineral ores, fishing and a growing tourism industry. GDP per capita in 2006 was just under US$7000, making Namibia one of sub-Saharan Africa's more prosperous countries (Figure 6.15). None the less, this prosperity is relative. Nearly two-fifths of Namibians live below the poverty line, and unemployment is estimated around 35%.

Economic development over the past century has created massive inequality in Namibian society: in fact according to the Gini coefficient, inequality in Namibia is higher than in any other country in the world (Table 6.6).

Table 6.6 *Global inequalities*

Highest inequality		Lowest inequality	
	Gini coefficient		Gini coefficient
Namibia	74.3	Denmark	24.7
Lesotho	63.2	Japan	24.9
Sierra Leone	62.9	Sweden	25.0
Central African Republic	61.3	Czech Republic	25.4
Botswana	60.5	Slovakia	25.8

Figure 6.14
Geography of Namibia: percentage living below the poverty line

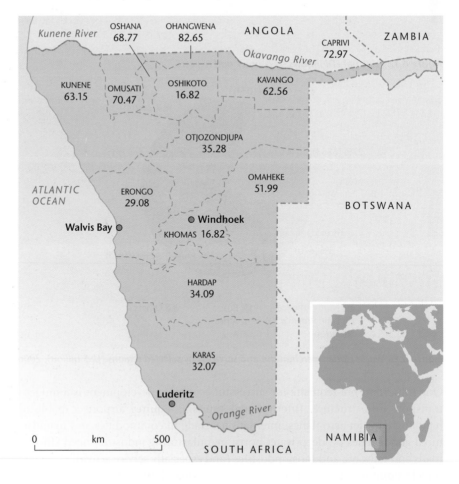

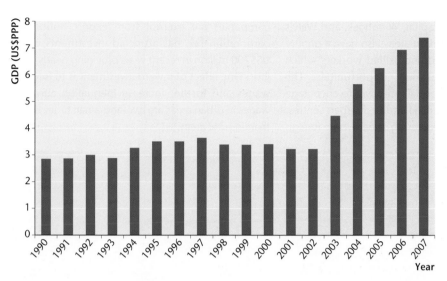

Figure 6.15
Namibia: GDP growth, 1990–2007

In theory economic growth should benefit the poor and reduce poverty (Figure 6.16). However, it could be argued that economic development has actually increased the gap between rich and poor in Namibia. For example, Figure 6.16 shows that the incidence of poverty in Namibia is greater than might be expected, given its GDP per capita. Indeed the poorest 20% of the population account for only 2.5% of total expenditure. Poverty is driven by high unemployment, insufficient economic growth and the HIV/AIDS epidemic which affects over a fifth of the population. There is a huge income gap between white and black Namibians. Although whites comprise only 5% of Namibia's 2-million population, they own most of the land, farms and other businesses. Commercial farm incomes (most commercial farms are operated by whites) are eight times higher than non-commercial operations. Much of this social and economic inequality in Namibia is a legacy of apartheid and the colonial era.

Economic development has also given rise to spatial inequality (Figure 6.14). Investment in infrastructure, public services, and commercial services (e.g. tourism, retailing) is concentrated in urban

Box 6.4 Namibia: historical background

Namibia only became a sovereign state in 1990 following a prolonged war of independence. European colonisation began in the late nineteenth century when the territory became German South West Africa following the Conference of Berlin (1883). However, the Germans were never fully in control and there were numerous conflicts and rebellions between 1890 and 1908. In 1915 Germany surrendered administration of the territory to South Africa. Namibia effectively became the fifth South African province. In 1948 South Africa's apartheid system (separate development) was imposed and Windhoek, the capital city, became a 'whites only' area (Photograph 6.4). In the 1960s a separatist movement led by the South West Africa People's Organisation (SWAPO) emerged, which aimed to achieve independence. South Africa, determined to retain Namibia's mineral wealth (diamonds, uranium, vanadium), resisted this movement, and fought a long military campaign in Angola and Zambia as well as Namibia. However, the eventual collapse of the apartheid regime in South Africa led to Namibian independence in 1990.

areas, especially the capital, Windhoek, and Walvis Bay, the main port. Urban areas also have a pool of more highly educated and skilled workers which provides better investment opportunities. The government offers financial incentives to encourage FDI which is polarised in a handful of urban centres. Walvis Bay's export processing zone, where foreign companies are exempt from export duties and corporation tax, has attracted investments worth US$700 million in recent years providing nearly 7000 jobs. One effect of inward investment is to force up wages and further increase inequality: currently wages in urban areas are two-and-a-half times higher than in rural areas.

Photograph 6.4
Prosperous Windhoek

Figure 6.16
Economic development and poverty in sub-Saharan Africa

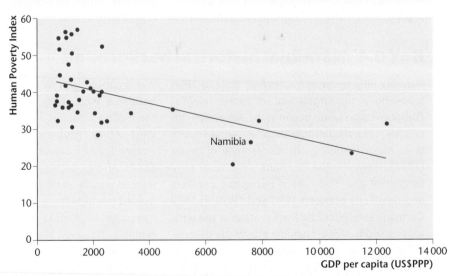

The development gap

Key ideas

➤ The development gap is the difference in prosperity and well-being between rich and poor countries.

➤ In the poorest regions of the world the development gap is widening; elsewhere there is evidence that the gap is narrowing.

➤ Economic models such as cumulative causation (Myrdal and Friedmann) and Rostow's model attempt to explain the development gap.

➤ A range of factors, including physical, economic, social and political issues, explain why the development gap is widening in some regions and narrowing in others.

The development gap refers to the difference in wealth between rich and poor countries. Figure 6.17 shows changes in GDP per capita in the world's richest and poorest regions between 1970 and 2006. It shows not only a huge gap between rich and poor, but that the gap has widened massively over the past four decades.

The economic performance of Africa, and especially sub-Saharan Africa (i.e. the whole of Africa excluding north Africa), is striking. Growth has been very slow throughout all sub-Saharan Africa. Although GDP per capita increased in all parts of this region between 1970 and 2006, this improvement was from a very low base. For example, in 1970 GDP per capita in east Africa was US$141; by 2006 this had risen to US$200. The people of east Africa and sub-Saharan Africa in general are, on average, better off today than in 1970, but they are still poor. Another way of looking at this is to compare the GDP per capita in sub-Saharan Africa with that of North America over the same period. In 1970 GDP per capita in North America

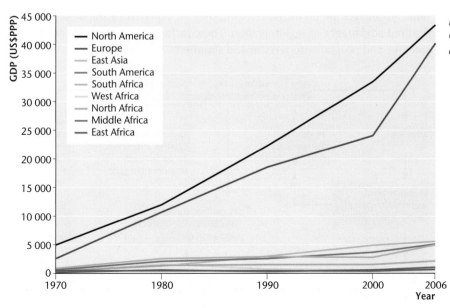

Figure 6.17
Changes in GDP per capita by region, 1970–2006

was 40 times greater than that of east Africa. By 2006 the multiple had increased to 125 times greater. While slow improvement is occurring in the world's poorest regions, MEDCs in North America and Europe are soaring ahead, widening even further the development gap.

An exception to this trend — one where the development gap is narrowing — is east Asia, which includes Japan and emerging economies such as China. In 1970 much of east Asia was as poor as Africa and GDP per capita was just one-fifteenth that of North America. However, the 16-fold increase in GDP per capita that occurred in east Asia between 1970 and 2006 (outstripping growth in North America and even in northern Europe) has narrowed the development gap. Today GDP per capita is one-eighth that of North America.

Theoretical models of spatially uneven development

A number of theoretical models provide some general explanation of uneven development at global and national scales.

Circular and cumulative causation models
Myrdal's model
Gunnar Myrdal's circular and cumulative causation model proposes that **initial advantages** to economic development in a core region (e.g. natural resources, accessibility) trigger a series of virtuous growth cycles through positive feedback (Figure 6.18). Initial economic growth creates employment, in-migration and the expansion of local markets. The emergence of clusters of firms, with pools of skilled labour, local markets and inter-firm linkages (or **external economies**), attracts further investment leading to another cycle of growth. Eventually the initial advantages are no longer relevant: they are replaced by the more powerful **acquired advantages** of agglomeration. These include economic and social infrastructure, and proximity to services and suppliers.

Figure 6.18 Model of cumulative causation (after Myrdal)

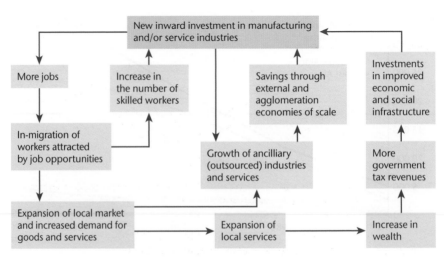

In Myrdal's model, growth in the core is at the expense of the periphery with beneficial 'spread' effects being counteracted by negative 'backwash' effects. The inevitable outcome is geographically uneven development, a situation that is common throughout the economically developing world and in many MEDCs today.

Friedmann's model

John Friedmann's core-periphery model describes four stages of spatial economic development (Figure 6.19).

Figure 6.19
Friedmann's core-periphery model of economic development

Stage 1 Relatively independent local centres; no hierarchy. Typical pre-industrial structure; each city lies at the centre of a small regional enclave.

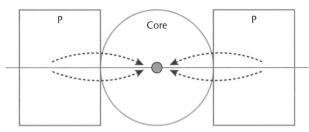

Stage 2 A single strong core. Typical of period of incipient industrialisation; a periphery emerges; potential entrepreneurs and labour move to the core; national economy is virtually reduced to a single metropolitan region.

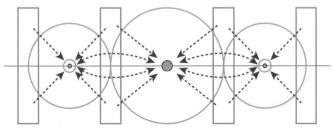

Stage 3 A single national core, strong peripheral sub-cores. During the period of industrial maturity, secondary cores form, thereby reducing the periphery on a national scale to smaller intermetropolitan peripheries.

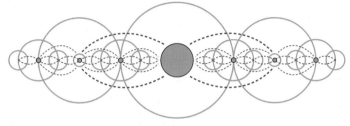

Stage 4 A functional interdependent system of cities. Organised complexity characterised by national integration, efficiency in location, maximum growth potential.

➤ In the pre-industrial stage, stage 1, the geography of economic activity is fairly uniform with small urban centres serving local markets.

➤ By stage 2, early industrialisation has brought big changes: wide regional disparities have developed with the emergence of an economic core and a surrounding periphery. At this stage, the strong economic core supports a single large city that dominates all other centres in the urban hierarchy. Meanwhile the periphery exists in a state of dependency, and its development lags behind the core. Flows of materials and people move from the periphery to the core, fuelling the economic growth of the core and draining the periphery of resources (see Myrdal's 'backwash' effects, above). During stage 2, the economic geography of a country is little more than a single large metropolitan region.

➤ As the economy expands in stage 3, prosperity, as in Myrdal's model, slowly 'spreads' from the core to the periphery. This is explained by excessive demand and congestion in the core forcing up labour, land and other costs. As investment spreads from the core, cities begin to grow in the periphery as economic development takes hold.

➤ Eventually, by stage 4, spatial economic inequalities between core and periphery have largely disappeared and a mature urban hierarchy has been established.

Friedmann's model provides us with a conceptual framework for viewing economic development at global and national scales. Today's global economic core consists of the world's leading financial centres (e.g. New York, London, Tokyo) and their supporting metropolitan regions such as the northeast USA, western Europe and Japan. More generally the economic core can be defined as North America, the EU and Japan.

The present-day relationship between the economic core and the world's poorest peripheral regions such as sub-Saharan Africa and southwest Asia has parallels with stage 2 of the Friedmann model. Many African economies depend heavily on the economic core, exporting agricultural products, minerals, energy and labour. However, these flows of materials and people have 'backwash' effects on the world's poorest countries, hindering their economic development. Moreover, there is little evidence that 'spread' effects, in the form of large-scale inward investment by TNCs, are likely to occur in future.

Friedmann's model also provides an explanation of emerging economies like China and India. High costs and skills shortages in many MEDCs have encouraged outward investment from the core to the periphery by North American, European and Japanese firms. Outsourcing of production and services has stimulated double-digit economic growth in China, India and other emerging economies, which is helping to close the development gap.

Rostow's model of economic development

Walt Rostow's model proposes a five-stage sequence of economic and social development through which all countries should pass (Figure 6.20).

➤ Stage 1: **traditional society** — based on custom and tradition, simple technologies, bartering and a subsistence economy.

➤ Stage 2: **pre-conditions for take-off** — defined by an increase in the rate of

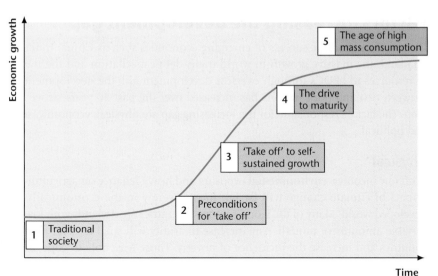

Figure 6.20
Rostow's model
of economic
development

investment, the early development of necessary economic and social infrastructure, a new elite of entrepreneurs, merchants and capitalists, and an effective centralised state.

➤ Stage 3: **take-off into sustained growth** — a period of 10–30 years dominated by rapid economic growth. Investment is concentrated in so-called 'leading sectors' of the economy, especially in manufacturing industry.

➤ Stage 4: **the drive to maturity** — sustained economic growth and diversification into higher-value-added manufacturing industries and service activities.

➤ Stage 5: **age of high mass consumption** — the increasing importance of consumer goods and services and the rise of the welfare state.

Rostow's model explains the development gap by differences between countries in their history of economic growth (Figure 6.20). The earlier a country enters take-off, the more advanced it will be on the development curve. Hence the UK, which started to industrialise over two centuries ago, is in stage 5, whereas many countries in Africa, only recently in stage 1, have made little progress along the path to development. China and India, which began to industrialise in earnest only in the past 30 years or so, have clearly advanced to the stage of 'take-off'.

While the model is a useful description, it has little to tell us about the social, economic, political and environmental factors that influence economic development. Moreover, it assumes that development is controlled by market forces when often it is strongly influenced by government and centralised planning. The recent economic success of South Korea and China show us how important government control is.

The inevitability of development implied by the model is also questionable. Decades after independence, many of the world's poorest countries show only limited signs of economic progress. Thus the development gap between rich and poor countries is actually getting bigger. Indeed, in the past 50 years only a handful of countries have successfully bridged this gap.

Factors increasing the development gap

Despite the economic success of emerging economies such as China, India and Thailand, the massive growth in world trade, debt cancellation and the transfer of resources to LEDCs through overseas development aid, the development gap between rich and poor nations has increased over the past 50 years, as we have seen. The factors responsible for the increasing gap are physical, economic, social and political.

Physical

With low incomes, environmental exposure and heavy reliance on agriculture the impact of climate change will be felt most severely in the economically less developed world. Many of the world's poorest countries are drylands with low and variable amounts of rainfall. Any increase in aridity will spell disaster for these countries and increase the incidence of poverty. Those least able to cope are the poor, who lack the resources to afford higher prices for basic foods.

Already there are signs that climate change is increasing the frequency of drought. Rainfall in the Sahel region of Africa has declined 50–60 mm below the long-term average since the late 1960s (Figure 6.21). Countries such as Ethiopia, Niger and the Sudan have suffered more frequent droughts, causing famine, malnutrition and starvation. In 2005, 3 million people in Niger were hit by famine; 6 months later there were severe food shortages in Malawi, also caused by drought.

Drylands are fragile environments. Falling crop yields puts extra pressure on the land through overcultivation, overgrazing and deforestation, which in turn causes soil erosion, land degradation and desertification. In Africa, 65% of all farmland is affected by soil degradation, condemning millions to poverty in the future and increasing the development gap.

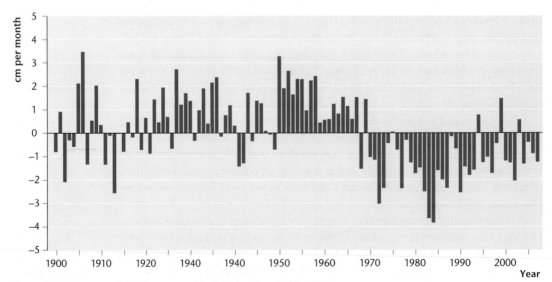

Figure 6.21 *Mean precipitation anomalies, Sahel region, 1900–2007*

TopFoto

Climate change also brings an increased likelihood of extreme rainfall events. The result is severe floods, such as those that affected Mozambique in 2000 and Bangladesh in 2007. The Mozambique floods killed approximately 800 people and 20 000 head of cattle, damaged 1400 km^2 of farmland and destroyed 90% of the country's irrigation infrastructure. Although floods are an annual event in Bangladesh, the 2007 flood was particularly severe, killing over 300 people and making millions homeless. Its economic impact included a 0.2% drop in GDP in 2007, and inflation caused by food shortages. LEDCs recover only slowly from natural disasters of this kind, which may set back development several years. In future, natural hazards like droughts and floods will become more extreme and more frequent, making it even more difficult to close the development gap.

Photograph 6.5
Drought in the
Sahel region

Political

Good governance is essential to any successful bridging of the development gap. It could be argued that the poor economic performance of sub-Saharan Africa in the past 50 years owes as much to poor governance with its attendant corruption, maladministration, political in-fighting, inter-tribal conflicts and wars, as to any other factor.

Case study **Zimbabwe**

No country in recent times illustrates more the importance of good governance to economic development than Zimbabwe. Since 2000, Zimbabwe has suffered economic meltdown. Once the breadbasket of southern Africa, food production declined by nearly one-third between 2000 and 2005. Today 45% of Zimbabweans are malnourished and the country relies heavily on food imports and food aid. Annual inflation in 2008 was running at 11 million per cent, and a loaf of bread which cost Z$5 in 1998 cost Z$1.6 trillion in 2008.

The causes of this economic disaster are almost entirely political. Government land seizures (in which farmland was redistributed to government supporters) destroyed at a stroke the country's highly productive farm sector, hitting food exports, food security and rural incomes. Meanwhile, poor fiscal policies and irresponsible spending led to huge budget deficits. The government responded by printing money that triggered hyperinflation. Zimbabwe's unpopular government maintained its grip on power by the use of violence and intimidation to crush opposition.

The economic fall-out from misgovernance has been widespread. Large numbers of educated and skilled workers such as doctors, nurses and farmers have left Zimbabwe, foreign aid has been suspended and foreign investors have been scared off. As a result economic development in Zimbabwe has gone backwards and poverty has become the norm: now 83% of Zimbabweans live on less than US$2 a day, compared to just 30% in 1999.

Population growth

Rapid population growth is both a cause and a consequence of lack of development. Figure 6.9 (p. 222) shows that between 2001 and 2005, nine countries in sub-Saharan Africa had population growth rates that exceeded economic growth. Rapid population growth in countries such as Madagascar, Togo, Gabon and Burundi has held back economic progress and widened the development gap. Rapid population growth in sub-Saharan Africa has also created youthful populations with high rates of dependency (Table 6.7). Furthermore, even where economies have grown faster than population, economic advance is held back by excessive population growth.

Table 6.7 *Percentage of population aged 0–14 years, 2008*

Sub-Saharan Africa	42.9	Near East	32.8
Asia	26.4	Latin America	28.9
North Africa	30.0	Western Europe	15.7
Eastern Europe	15.6	North America	19.8
Oceania	23.5		

AIDS

Through its impact on the labour force, households and enterprises, AIDS has played a more significant role in the reversal of human development than any other single factor.

Source: *2006 Report on the global AIDS epidemic*, UNAIDS

Acquired Immune Deficiency Syndrome (AIDS) is caused by a virus (human immunodeficiency virus or HIV) that was first isolated in 1983 and has since spread rapidly, especially in many LEDCs. The World Health Organization (WHO) estimated that in 2007, 33.2 million people worldwide were HIV positive, resulting in 2.1 million deaths from AIDS in that year.

Once again, sub-Saharan Africa is the worst-affected region with 22.5 million people living with HIV — two-thirds of the world's total (Figure 6.22 and Table 6.8). An AIDS study in Burkina Faso, Rwanda and Uganda concluded that because of AIDS the proportion of the population living in extreme poverty will increase from 45% in 2000 to 51% in 2015. AIDS has been a major factor contributing to the widening development gap between sub-Saharan Africa and the rest of the world.

The AIDS epidemic has created a huge increase in the demand for health care. In South Africa, AIDS consumes 60–70% of all hospital expenditure. The annual cost of AIDS in southern Africa is now US$30 per person per year compared to overall public health spending in most African countries of just US$10 per person per year (source: AVERT — international AIDS charity).

Table 6.8 *Death rates due to AIDS in southern Africa, 2005*

	Deaths per 100 000 people per year
Botswana	1020
Lesotho	1282
Mozambique	605
South Africa	675
Swaziland	1550
Zambia	840
Zimbabwe	1384

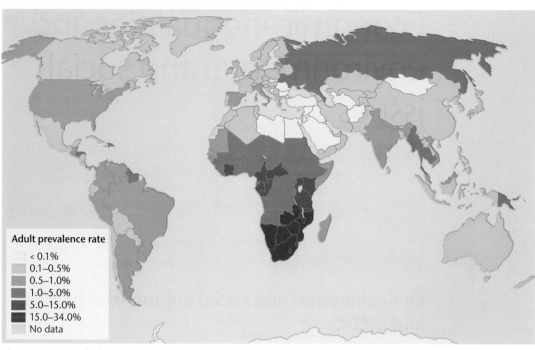

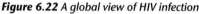

Adult prevalence rate

    < 0.1%
    0.1–0.5%
    0.5–1.0%
    1.0–5.0%
    5.0–15.0%
    15.0–34.0%
    No data

Figure 6.22 *A global view of HIV infection*

AIDS has led to a steep rise in households without income earners as adults become either too ill to work or have to care for sick family members. It has also increased food insecurity, due to a reduction in agricultural output as farm work is neglected or abandoned. In Swaziland and the Central African Republic, school enrolment has fallen by 25–30% because of AIDS: many families can no longer afford school fees and children are either too ill to attend school or have to stay at home to care for sick relatives.

Because most people living with HIV are younger adults (aged 15–49 years) the economic impact on business is particularly severe. Shortages of labour and high absenteeism push up costs, lower productivity and reduce profits. This in turn leads to a fall in tax revenues and inward investment. There is no doubt that AIDS has contributed to the dire economic situation of much of sub-Saharan Africa. The overall economic impact of AIDS amounts to an annual loss of production equal to 1% of GDP in the region — a figure that is likely to increase even more in future.

Economic inequalities and environmental and social issues

Key ideas
➤ Economic inequalities may result in environmental and social conditions also becoming unequal.
➤ There are spatial variations in air, water, noise and solid pollution within NICs and MEDCs.
➤ Economic and social inequalities within cities and regions result from the interaction of economic and social factors.

Environmental and social inequalities in NICs and MEDCs

Economic development exerts a strong influence on environmental and social inequalities between and within countries. In newly industrialising countries (NICs) such as China and Brazil, the priority is economic growth. Rapid industrialisation increases GDP and exports, and provides the jobs and wealth needed to raise incomes and invest in economic and social infrastructure. However, industrialisation and economic growth come at a cost. In particular environmental and social conditions, at least in the short term, often deteriorate. Invariably, the **negative externalities** of industrialisation are distributed unevenly: pollution is concentrated in major cities and regions of heavy industry, and among the poorest groups in society.

The post-industrial economies of MEDCs create fewer environmental and social negative externalities. Moreover, MEDCs can afford to give environmental and social issues, which influence the quality of life, much greater priority. This is not to say that geographical disparities and environmental and social inequalities do not exist in MEDCs, only that they are far less severe than in NICs.

Environmental inequalities in China

Rapid industrialisation has led to spectacular economic growth and urbanisation in China in the past 30 years. However, the pace and scale of China's economic development is environmentally unsustainable: a massive pollution legacy has caused widespread problems, not just in the major cities and industrial zones, but also in many rural areas.

Table 6.9 *Urbanisation in China (% urban population), 1980–2006*

1980	1985	1990	1995	2001	2006
19.4	23.7	26.4	29.0	36.0	43.9

Air pollution

Industrialisation has caused major air pollution problems. Much of this pollution derives from China's coal-based economy and its reliance on electricity generated in coal-fired power stations. The result has been drastic increases in industrial emissions of sulphur dioxide and suspended particulates.

Air pollution is most severe in the heavy industrial regions of northern China such as Shanxi province (Figure 6.23). Shanxi was described by a *New York Times* journalist thus:

> There is a Dickensian feel to much of the region. Roads are covered in coal tar; houses are coated with soot; miners, their faces smeared almost entirely black, haul carts full of coal rocks; the air is thick with the smell of burning coal.

The main reason for air pollution is the concentration of heavy industries, especially coal mines, coke ovens, power stations, and iron, steel and chemical works (Photograph 6.6). However, particulate air pollution in northern China (including Beijing) is exacerbated by frequent dust and sandstorms when winds blow from the semi-arid and desertified interior (Figure 6.24).

Figure 6.23 *Map of Shanxi province, northern China*

Photograph 6.6
Heavy industry and pollution in Shanxi

Dennis Cox/Alamy

Figure 6.24
Air quality levels in cities in China's provinces

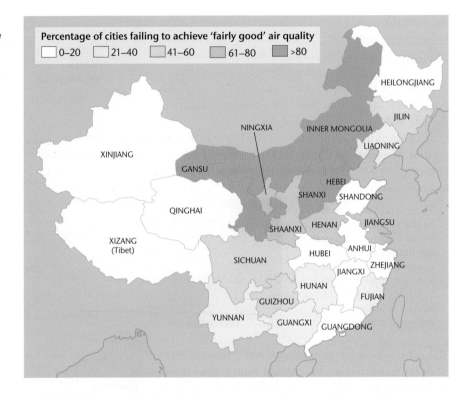

Percentage of cities failing to achieve 'fairly good' air quality
☐ 0–20 ☐ 21–40 ☐ 41–60 ☐ 61–80 ■ >80

Of China's ten most polluted cities, four are in Shanxi province. Datong, the centre of coal mining, is one of the world's most polluted cities. Half of the pollution comes from power stations. Pollution peaks during the winter months, when **temperature inversions** trap the smog. Sometimes the pollution is so bad that motorists drive with their lights on even during the daytime, and residents are advised to stay indoors.

The social costs of air pollution are considerable. High incidences of lung cancer and respiratory diseases are linked directly to air pollution. Linfen city, in Shanxi province, tops China's air pollution charts. People on their way to work wear face masks to protect themselves from the polluted air. Beilu, on the outskirts of the city, is known locally as the 'cancer village'. Out of a total population of approximately 1000, 20 have died recently from cancer, and the death rate could be as much as ten times higher than the average for China. About a kilometre from the village there is a coke works, a coal processing plant, a power station and a pharmaceutical factory. Beilu is located in a natural basin that acts as a sink for polluted air. The local water supply, from shallow wells, is also polluted.

In China as a whole, air pollution causes around 400 000 premature deaths a year. Sadly, conditions are unlikely to improve in future: new coal-fired power stations are being commissioned at a rate of one a week in a desperate attempt to sustain China's economic boom; and, despite efforts by the government, Table 6.10 shows that China has failed to achieve its air pollution targets for cutting sulphur dioxide emissions in its recent Five Year Plan.

Table 6.10 *Environmental targets for China's tenth Five Year Plan (million tonnes)*

	Planned 2005	Actual 2005	Performance (+/–%)
Sulphur dioxide emissions (industry)	14.5	21.7	50
Soot emissions (industry)	8.5	9.5	11
Water (chemical oxygen demand)	13.0	14.1	8

Coal burning and the release of sulphur dioxide is also a major cause of acid rain. Acid rain falls on 30% of the country and is worst in the south and southeast. In 2005 China emitted 28 million tonnes of sulphur, 28% higher than in 2000. Acid rain has a serious environmental impact: crops are poisoned, lakes acidified and forests destroyed up to several hundreds of kilometres from pollution sources. China's acid rain is also exported to neighbouring South Korea and Japan and is therefore a transnational as well as national environmental issue.

Beijing is one of the most polluted capital cities: levels of nitrogen dioxide pollution, which can cause fatal damage to the lungs, are among the highest in the world. Blame rests with an explosive increase in car ownership and the resulting sharp rise in nitrogen oxide emissions. Between 2000 and 2008 the number of vehicles in Beijing more than doubled to reach nearly 3 million.

Water pollution

One of China's most serious environmental problems is water pollution. Surface water quality is worst in the most densely populated and industrialised parts of the country. Every year factories and cities routinely dump 40–60 billion tonnes of wastewater and sewage into lakes and rivers. Accidental spillages of toxic chemicals into rivers and lakes also add to pollution loads.

In 2004, about 25 000 km of China's rivers were too polluted to support aquatic life, and 90% of rivers around urban areas were badly polluted. Pollution of lakes is also a problem with three-quarters suffering **eutrophication**.

A recent survey showed that only two-fifths of river systems had water quality fit for human consumption, and nearly 30% were so polluted they were unsuitable for agricultural use. Polluted drinking water and inadequate water treatment is a severe health risk, especially in rural areas. There, above-average mortality rates from stomach, liver and bladder cancer are linked to contaminated drinking water.

Water scarcity is a problem in China's semi-arid northern and western regions and adds to environmental stress in two ways. First, overexploitation of groundwater has led to a widespread fall in the water table (up to 50 m in some areas); and second, water scarcity often forces farmers to use polluted water (Figure 6.25). Crop irrigation using wastewater is common practice and poses a risk of contamination to the human food chain with heavy metals like cadmium, lead, copper and mercury.

Solid waste pollution

In Shanxi province 'coal-mining operations have damaged waterways and scarred the land. Because of intense underground mining, thousands of acres are prone

Figure 6.25
Groundwater
depletion and
polluted water
supply in China,
2003

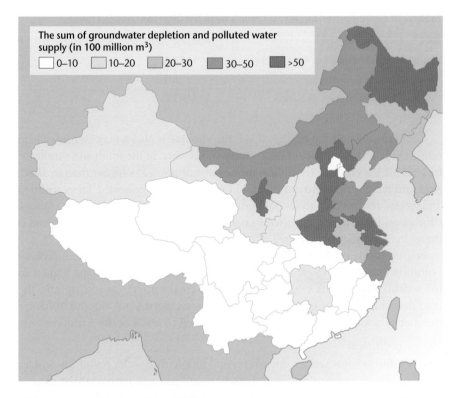

to sinking, and hundreds of villages are blackened with coal waste' (*New York Times*, 11 June 2006). The solid waste from coal mining is a big problem, covering the land in unsightly spoil heaps and contributing to the pollution of air and water. Spoil from China's coal mines covers over 900 km², two-thirds of which is former arable land.

China is the world's largest producer of municipal solid waste, generating 155 million tonnes in 2005. In the same year, China produced 1.3 million tonnes of industrial solid waste. The production of both types of waste is increasingly rapidly, at current rates doubling every 10 years. Eighty per cent of solid waste goes to landfill, the remainder is either incinerated or composted. However, most landfill sites are insanitary and fail to meet international standards.

Solid industrial waste is often hazardous. Its toxic, flammable and corrosive properties pose direct threats to human and environmental health. Forty per cent of China's hazardous solid waste (e.g. alkalis, acids, inorganic fluoride, copper and inorganic cyanide) is produced by the chemical industry. In total, just over 15% of this waste is discharged untreated into the environment.

Noise pollution

According to a recent Chinese government survey, 1% of China's population suffers heavy noise pollution. Thirteen cities (3% of those surveyed) are regarded as heavily polluted by noise. However, noise pollution from motor vehicles, construction sites, markets, bars and entertainment venues has been increasing in the past decade in most major cities. In Beijing more than 1 million residents

suffer excessive noise pollution every day. Average traffic noise in Beijing is 71 decibels (any sound above 70 decibels is unpleasant for humans). Traffic noise is often amplified by the narrow streets in Chinese cities.

Industry is also a major source of noise pollution. Rapid economic development has led to round-the-clock construction in Shanghai, Beijing and other large cities. Problems also arise because with little land-use zoning, residential areas are often located close to factories and other industrial establishments. Noisy surroundings result in earache and lack of sleep for residents. In fact, noise generates more complaints from urban residents than any other form of pollution.

Box 6.5 Air pollution in northern China in winter

The cold winters in northern China exacerbate the problems of air pollution from sulphur dioxide, nitrogen oxide and particulates. Temperature inversions develop as the cold ground surface chills the overlying air (Figure 6.26). Warmer air is then displaced above the cold surface layer to form an inversion. The warm air acts like a 'lid' preventing smoke and other pollutants from dispersing upwards and trapping pollution near the surface. When the pollution mixes with radiation fog it forms a lethal cocktail known as smog.

Warm air

An inversion 'lid' above the smokestack plume prevents the upward dispersal of pollutants

Cold air

Figure 6.26 Air pollution caused by fumigation

 Case study **Social and economic inequalities in Cape Town**

Cape Town has a population of nearly 3.5 million within its metropolitan area, and is South Africa's second largest city (Figure 6.27). Its population could top 4 million by 2021. Like other cities in South Africa, it is divided by huge social and economic inequalities. These inequalities closely follow ethnic lines, and are most pronounced between Black Africans and Whites. There are also sharp inequalities between Whites and the two other main ethnic groups, Coloureds and Asians.

Social and economic inequalities were an intrinsic feature of the apartheid political system that survived in South Africa until the early 1990s.

'Apartheid' means separate development, so the segregation of racial groups was deliberate policy. Blacks, Whites, Coloureds and Asians lived in separate suburbs and had their own schools, transport, clinics and other services. Movement of non-Whites was strictly controlled by the pass laws.

In the post-apartheid period, racial segregation in Cape Town has remained strong and integration has made little progress. In 2004, only eight suburbs had populations made up of at least 20% of each of the three main ethnic groups (Blacks, Whites and Coloureds). The only difference is that today segregation is based on income rather than race.

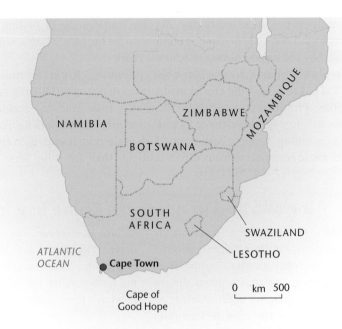

Figure 6.27 *Cape Town, South Africa*

However, as the Whites are the most affluent group (they comprise 19% of the population but own 58% of the wealth) and the Blacks the poorest (32% of the population with 9% of the wealth), in practice segregation continues to follow racial and ethnic divisions.

Poverty and inequality

Inequality in wealth between ethnic groups translates into spatial inequality. Cape Town has its own geography of inequality (Figures 6.28 and 6.29). Black Africans are mainly concentrated on the sandy expanses of the Cape Flats, on the southeast periphery. Prosperous White suburbs are located south of the city centre in the Cape Peninsula (e.g. Constantia), on the Atlantic coast (e.g. Clifton) and in the northern suburbs. Mitchell's Plain, also in the southeast, is dominated by Coloureds.

Ironically, the dismantling of apartheid actually increased poverty among the Black population. With the abolition of the pass laws, non-White groups were able to move freely within the country. This resulted in massive rural–urban migration throughout South Africa. Cape Town became the favoured destination for thousands of Black migrants from the impoverished rural districts of Eastern Province. The vast majority of migrants settled in the sprawling slum townships of Cape Flats such as Nyanga and Khayelitsha. Today these townships are some of the poorest and most deprived suburbs in South Africa.

Causes of poverty and inequality

The main drivers of poverty and inequality are poor housing, unemployment, low skill levels, HIV/AIDS and demographics.

Housing

The scale of in-migration since the early 1990s has overwhelmed the Cape Town authorities, who found it impossible to provide sufficient affordable homes. As a result the number of shacks rose from 28 000 in 1993 to 110 000 in 2004 (Photograph 6.7, p. 247). This meant rapid growth of informal settlements and a backlog of housing, which in 2005 had reached 265 000. Poor housing leaves residents susceptible to extreme winter weather, including floods, strong winds and low temperatures. People living in these conditions suffer poor health and greater risks from disease and epidemics. In addition, fire is a constant danger in the townships due to their high density, use of flammable building materials, and reliance on wood and paraffin for cooking and heating.

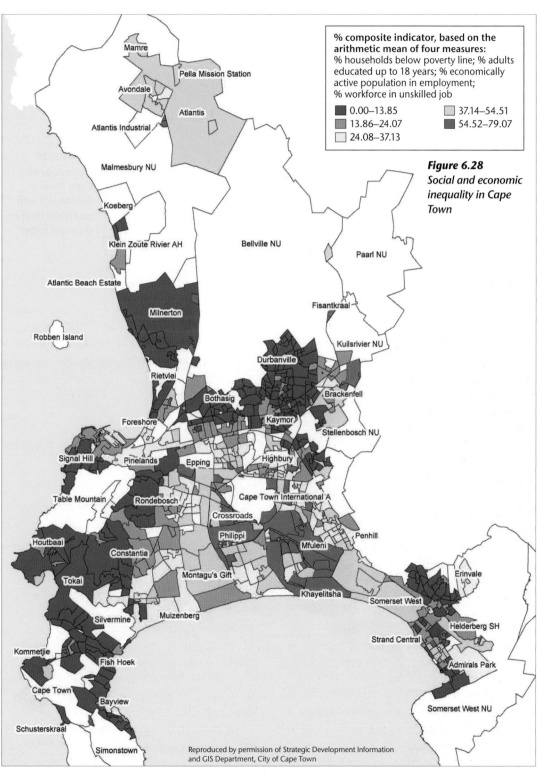

% composite indicator, based on the
arithmetic mean of four measures:
% households below poverty line; % adults
educated up to 18 years; % economically
active population in employment;
% workforce in unskilled job

▪ 0.00–13.85   ▫ 37.14–54.51
▪ 13.86–24.07   ▪ 54.52–79.07
▫ 24.08–37.13

Figure 6.28
*Social and economic
inequality in Cape
Town*

Reproduced by permission of Strategic Development Information
and GIS Department, City of Cape Town

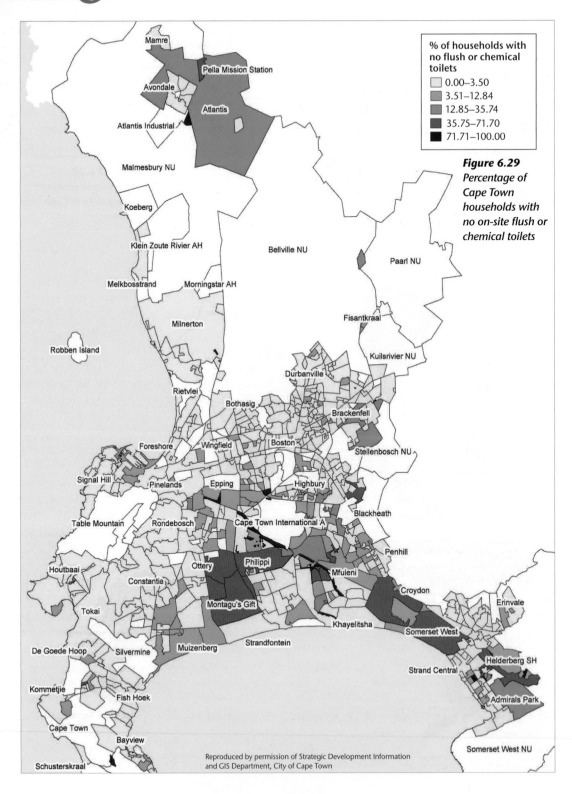

Figure 6.29
Percentage of Cape Town households with no on-site flush or chemical toilets

% of households with no flush or chemical toilets

- 0.00–3.50
- 3.51–12.84
- 12.85–35.74
- 35.75–71.70
- 71.71–100.00

Reproduced by permission of Strategic Development Information and GIS Department, City of Cape Town

Photograph 6.7
Township shacks

Employment

Thirty-two per cent of all households in Cape Town live below the poverty line. Unemployment is the main driver of poverty. Again, unemployment rates reveal sharp differences between racial groups. Whereas 44% of Black males of working age are unemployed, White male unemployment is just over 5%. For Coloured males the unemployment rate is nearly 25%. Given the youthful age structure of Cape Town's Black population, unemployment levels could be even higher in future.

The large influx of poorly educated rural migrants in the past 15 years has increased unemployment rates among the Black population. Because the formal sector cannot absorb the labour demand, the **informal sector** has had to expand. Today it is estimated that more than one-fifth of all employment in Cape Town is in the informal sector. This sector is populated by the unskilled and those who are unemployable in the **formal sector**. Those fortunate to find employment in the formal economy are often badly paid and many have long commutes to the city centre that they can barely afford.

HIV/AIDS and environmental health

Thousands of households have been plunged into poverty by the HIV/AIDS epidemic. HIV/AIDS also reinforces poverty and inequality. Prevalence rates are highest in the poorest parts of the city and rates are increasing. Nyanga and Khayelitsha townships are hardest hit. There, more than one in four of the population is HIV positive.

Poor environmental conditions, including a lack of adequate sanitation, poor water supply, over-crowding and malnutrition, also contribute to poverty by causing ill-health and reducing the productivity of workers.

Reliance on fuelwood and paraffin for cooking and heating contributes to high levels of air pollution in the townships, which increases respiratory illness. Air pollution, emanating largely from the townships, frequently hangs as a brown haze over Cape Town.

Cross Roads and Constantia

Nowhere in Cape Town is the spatial contrast in prosperity more obvious than between the suburbs of Cross Roads and Constantia (Table 6.11). Cross Roads is an impoverished Black township in Nyanga, on Cape Flats. Constantia, south of the city centre, occupies the rolling countryside of the northern Cape Peninsula.

In Cross Roads nearly 80% of households live below the poverty line (i.e. have incomes of less than £1280 a year). Household expenditure is dominated by food (40%) followed by energy (10%), health (9%) and clothing (8%). A high proportion of the poor experience extended periods of food shortage and hunger. Undernutrition and malnutrition are widespread. Less than half of all households have access to water in their properties. Poverty and inequality promote high crime rates: Nyanga is the most dangerous suburb in Cape Town, recording 266 murders and 196 rapes in 2007–08 (Figure 6.30).

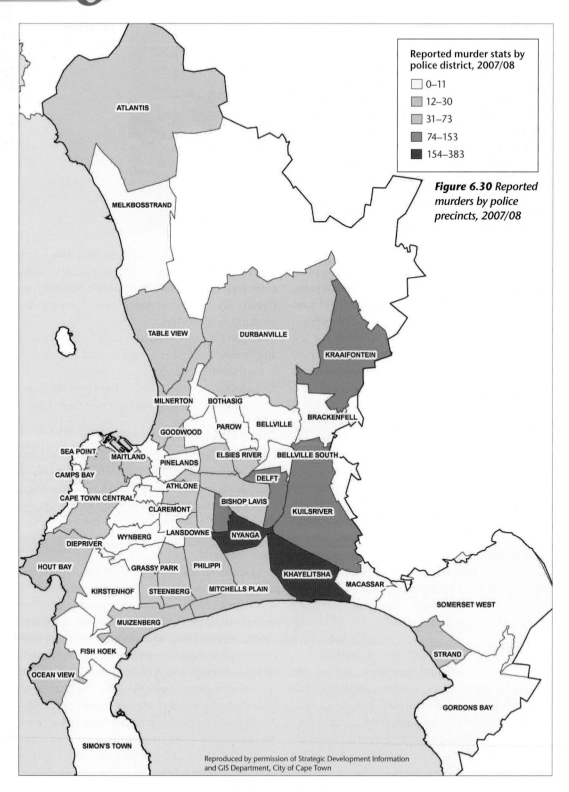

Reported murder stats by police district, 2007/08

- 0–11
- 12–30
- 31–73
- 74–153
- 154–383

Figure 6.30 Reported murders by police precincts, 2007/08

Reproduced by permission of Strategic Development Information and GIS Department, City of Cape Town

		Constantia (% population)	Cross Roads (% population)
Ethnic origin	Black African	5.99	98.26
	Coloured	6.08	1.74
	Indian/Asian	1.13	0
	White	86.80	0
Age (years)	0–17	24.56	36.89
	18–34	16.46	36.90
	35–64	45.29	24.58
	64+	13.68	1.63
University educated		32.49	0.64
Language	English	87.16	0.14
	Afrikaans	6.80	1.86
	Xhosa	2.92	95.47
	Others	3.12	2.5
Informal housing		0.14	43.64
Household income per year (£)	0–1280	9.17	78.79
	1281–5120	13.82	20.01
	5121–20 480	43.80	1.02
	20 481–81 920	28.83	0.08
	>81 920	4.38	0.11
Access to water in dwelling		93.57	45.89
Flush toilets in dwelling		98.92	58.64

Table 6.11
Socio-economic inequalities in Cape Town: Constantia and Cross Roads suburbs

Constantia is one of Cape Town's oldest and most affluent suburbs. Properties are large, densities are low, and the residents enjoy a quality of life comparable to any exclusive suburb in North America and western Europe. Nearly 87% of the population is White and less than 10% of households live below the poverty line.

In contrast to the Black townships, Constantia is one of Cape Town's safest suburbs. Even so, many residents protect their properties with high walls mounted by razor wire, electric fences and window bars.

Many new housing developments are 'gated' communities patrolled by armed security guards.

Reducing social and economic inequalities

Key ideas
➤ Most governments aim to reduce extreme social and economic inequalities.
➤ Various approaches have been used to reduce extreme inequalities with varying degrees of success.
➤ Governments have used a variety of methods to reduce social and economic inequalities, including planning, education, taxation, subsidies and the law.

Features of social and economic inequalities

Social and economic inequalities are found in all countries, though they tend to be most extreme in the poorest LEDCs (see Table 6.6, p. 226). Some of the widest inequalities are in sub-Saharan Africa, the world's poorest region. Meanwhile the most equitable societies are rich countries such as Norway, Denmark and Japan.

Social and economic inequalities often relate to particular groups in society, For instance, race, ethnicity, gender and age are closely associated with inequality and **social exclusion**.

The United Nations, through its development programme, is committed to reducing poverty and inequality. However, these goals are best achieved through national government programmes. Most governments, driven by ideals of social justice and political cohesion, aim to reduce the extremes of poverty and inequality.

Inequalities take a number of different social and economic forms. Some groups are disadvantaged because they have unequal access to health care, education services and the housing market. Others suffer high levels of exposure to crime, anti-social behaviour and lower life expectancies. However, inequality is most obvious in economic terms, where it is often associated with poverty, low incomes, low skills and high levels of unemployment. Many outcomes of inequality are closely interrelated. For example, poor educational attainment often results in low incomes and unemployment, which in turn are more likely to induce physiological and mental ill-health. In other words, the poorest socio-economic groups often suffer **multiple deprivation**.

Table 6.12 Methods used to tackle social and economic inequalities

Taxation	Income tax is often used by governments to redistribute wealth from more prosperous to less prosperous groups, and so create a fairer society. Most governments have progressive tax systems where the better-off pay a larger proportion of their incomes in tax. Essential items such as food may be exempt from tax. This benefits poorer groups that spend a larger percentage of their income on food. This information can be found at **www.investorwords.com**
Subsidies	Governments also try to reduce inequality by giving subsidies to poorer groups. Children in poor families may get free school meals, clothing allowances and help with university fees. Pensioners may get subsidies for fuel and transport. Other subsidies may include free child care for single parents. Low wage earners, unemployed workers and those with long-term disability are entitled to benefits.
Planning	Governments, charities and housing agencies often give priority to upgrading housing and services in the poorest areas. At a local scale this happens in informal slum settlements in cities in LEDCs, as well as in rundown inner-city locations in MEDCs. Planning is often organised geographically and is targeted at the most deprived areas which vary in scale from neighbourhoods to entire regions.
Law	Legislation exists in most MEDCs which outlaws discrimination on racial, ethnic, gender and age criteria and aims to give equal opportunities to all groups. Often in MEDCs the poorest groups of workers are protected by minimum-wage legislation.
Education	Governments often provide funding for training and upgrading skills in order to raise skill levels and qualifications, improve employment prospects and boost economic growth. Education programmes designed to improve personal health (e.g. diet, obesity, smoking) are often targeted at the poorest groups in society.

Inequality also has a spatial dimension, with poverty and social exclusion often having their own distinctive geography. Some places with higher incomes, lower unemployment and faster economic growth are more prosperous than others. Where people live often influences the quality of the health care, education and other services they receive, and even their life chances. The geography of inequality exists at all scales, from global to local, and it is especially evident between urban and rural populations.

Governments use a variety of methods to reduce social and economic inequalities. Table 6.12 outlines the principal ones.

Social and economic inequalities in the UK

Social and economic inequalities are widespread in the UK. The overall distribution of income is highly unequal and has changed little since 1997. For example, the richest 10% have 30% of the total income, while the poorest 10% have just 2%. Despite government promises to eradicate child poverty, it was estimated that in 2008, 3.9 million children in the UK lived in families below the poverty line. Child poverty is most strongly concentrated in London and urban-industrial areas, the English Midlands and northern Britain (Figure 6.31).

Social and economic inequalities have a direct effect on health inequalities. For instance, children living in poverty are ten times more likely to die in infancy than the average, and as adults are fifty times more likely to suffer from diabetes and bronchitis. Average life expectancy for males in Glasgow varies from 82 years in

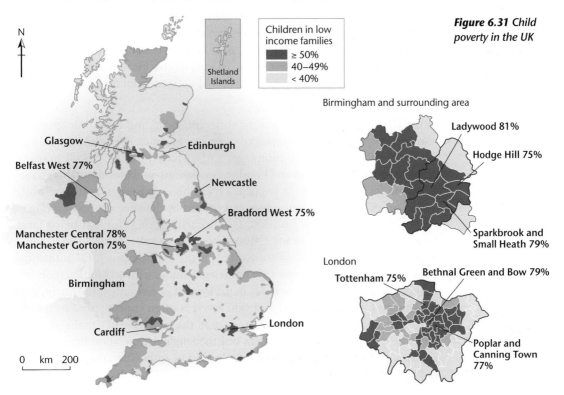

Figure 6.31 *Child poverty in the UK*

the prosperous suburb of Lenzie, to just 54 years in inner-city Calton. In London there is a similar picture: the residents of Hampstead can expect to live 11 years longer than residents in nearby St Pancras. In future, health inequalities are expected to widen between different geographical areas, genders, ethnic communities and socio-economic groups.

Methods used to reduce social and economic inequality
Taxation and subsidies
The UK government supports a range of measures designed to raise incomes of the lowest paid and provide financial support for disadvantaged groups such as poor families, single parents, pensioners and the disabled. In 1999 it introduced a minimum wage. Around 1 million workers benefit from the minimum wage, which by October 2008 had risen to £5.73 per hour for adult workers. Meanwhile unemployed workers aged 25 years and over are eligible for a job seeker's allowance worth £3146 per year.

Tax credits provide additional help to low-paid workers and poorer families with children. For example, a single full-time worker earning £10 000 per year receives an extra £12 a week in tax credit. A family with the same income but with three young children gets an extra £5000 per year in tax credits. On top of tax credits, all families with children receive child benefit worth £978 per year for the oldest child and £653 per year for other children. Tax credits are also available for disabled workers on low incomes.

Value-added tax is payable on most goods and services. However, food, water, clothing and shoes are zero-rated. This assists lower income groups who spend a greater proportion of their income on essential goods. Income support is available for people on low incomes such as carers and the disabled who work for less than 16 hours a week. Children whose parents receive income support, child tax credits and job seeker's allowance are entitled to free school meals.

Local planning
In the UK access to housing among different social and economic groups is unequal. People who are unemployed or on low incomes, or whose jobs are insecure have difficulty getting mortgages to purchase housing. Social housing, supplied by local authorities and housing associations, provides affordable accommodation for these groups. In England 19% of housing is social rented, of which 60% is provided by local authorities and the rest by housing associations (Figure 6.32). Eligibility is based on need, families with young children being given priority. Even so, there are nearly 100 000 homeless households in England, mainly comprising single unemployed men. This is the case, despite local authorities having a legal obligation to provide homeless families with accommodation.

Social and economic deprivation, in the form of poverty, unemployment, poor housing and low educational and skill levels is often concentrated in specific geographical areas. Between 1995 and 2006 the government's main planning instrument for improving these areas was the Single Regeneration Budget (SRB). The SRB was a partnership scheme involved local authorities, the private sector and voluntary organisations.

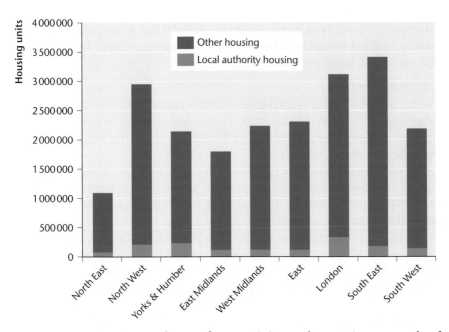

Figure 6.32 Local authority and other housing in English regions

Easington in County Durham, a former mining settlement, is an example of the type of area that the SRB has assisted (Photograph 6.8). Following the closure of the local colliery in 1993, Easington suffered severe social and economic deprivation. Under the SRB scheme, the district has received nearly £45 million. This money has been used to fund a variety of projects that include job creation, raising educational achievement, improving the environment and enhancing quality of life through the provision of services. However, while the SRB has

Photograph 6.8 *Easington, County Durham*

improved the lives of residents in Easington, it has failed to improve the district's relative position in national deprivation league tables. In 2007 Easington was still the seventh most deprived district in England.

Regional planning

The EU is committed to reducing regional inequalities and promoting regional development through its Cohesion Policy. Essentially this policy provides financial support to the poorest regions through a package of grants and subsidies from the EU's structural funds.

The current Cohesion Policy runs from 2007 to 2013. It identifies the poorest regions — known as convergence regions — as having a GDP per capita of less than 75% of the EU average. In total there are 84 convergence regions spread across the 27 countries of the EU.

The UK has two convergence regions: West Wales and the Valleys, and Cornwall and the Scilly Isles. In 2008 these regions had a GDP per capita approximately 80% of the EU average, and lagged well behind the UK's other regions. By comparison, the southeast, the UK's wealthiest region, recorded a GDP per capita that was 23% above the EU average. These differences show the wide regional inequalities that exist in the UK.

West Wales and the Valleys receives the highest level of support from the Cohesion Policy. During the period 2007–13 the structural funds will inject £1.4 billion into the region's economy. This money will be matched by UK government funding, amounting to a total subsidy of £3.2 billion. These subsidies should encourage economic growth in West Wales and the Valleys (and narrow regional inequalities) by:

➤ developing a higher value-added economy by promoting knowledge-based activities and innovation
➤ encouraging new business start-ups
➤ modernising the transport infrastructure
➤ supporting long-term economic and social regeneration among deprived communities
➤ creating 33 000 new jobs and providing financial assistance for 14 000 businesses

Law

Discrimination against certain groups on the basis of ethnicity, race, religion, age, sexual orientation and gender has contributed to social and economic inequalities in the UK. Legislation protects individuals against discrimination, particularly in areas such as employment, housing and education, and reduces inequalities. The main aspects of inequalities legislation are shown in Table 6.13.

Education

One of government's most common strategies for closing the gap between rich and poor is to improve educational opportunities. In 2007, 55% of secondary schools in England and Wales failed to reach the government's own benchmark of 30% of children getting at least five good GCSE passes. Educational under-achievement is closely associated with poverty. For instance, in 2007, nearly half

Table 6.13 *Inequalities: the legal framework*

The Equal Pay Act (1970–74)	Pay and benefits must be the same, regardless of gender, for the same employment.
The Sex Discrimination Act (1975)	Discrimination in recruitment for employment, education etc. is unlawful.
The Race Relations Act (1976)	It is unlawful to discriminate on grounds of colour, race and ethnic origin in areas of employment, housing and education.
The Disability Discrimination Act (1995–2006)	Discrimination against disabled groups is unlawful in recruitment for employment and education.
Employment Equality Regulations (2003)	Discrimination on grounds of sexuality, religion/belief and age in employment, training and adult education is unlawful.

of all 16-year-olds qualifying for free school meals failed to pass any GCSEs at grades higher than D. Despite decades of government effort, educational inequalities between children from the poorest and wealthiest backgrounds remain wide: teenagers from wealthiest families are five times more likely to go to university than those from the poorest.

The Labour government elected in 1997 placed education at the top of its agenda. In the following 10 years spending on education rose steadily, and by 2008 accounted for nearly 6% of the UK's gross domestic product.

Several policy initiatives were taken, aimed at raising standards and providing more equal educational opportunities. Independent but publicly funded schools known as academies were created by Act of Parliament in 2000. These schools, located in areas of low educational attainment, were outside the control of local authorities. By 2010, 243 academies will have been established in England and Wales.

Other developments include increasing the school leaving age to 18 years by 2015; free nursery education for all four-year-olds, with a minimum entitlement of 15 hours per week for 38 weeks a year by 2010; financial incentives for teenage parents to remain in school; and financial support (up to £30 per week) for students aged 16 who opt to stay on in the sixth form.

Examination-style questions

Section A
Resource 1

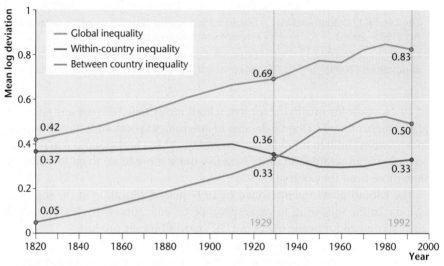

Source: *UN World Development Report*, 2006

Changing inequalities at global, national and regional scales

1 Resource 1 provides information on inequalities at global, national and regional scales. Outline an issue indicated and suggest appropriate management. (10 marks)

Section B

2 Consider the view that economic development increases inequalities both within and between countries. (30 marks)

3 How and to what extent is it possible to reduce social and economic inequalities? (30 marks)

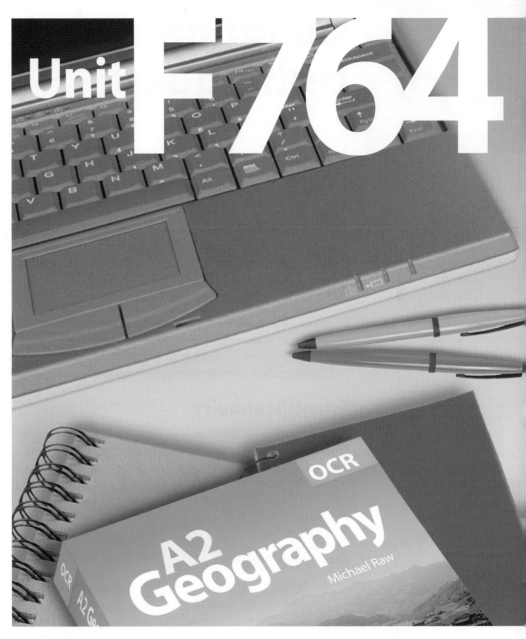

Unit F764

Geographical Skills

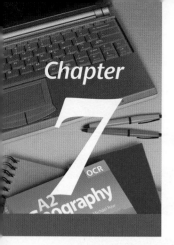
Geographical techniques

Hypothesis testing

Key ideas
➤ Successful geographical investigation depends on identifying a clear geographical question or hypothesis.
➤ The question/hypothesis must be at a suitable scale, capable of research and based on wider geographical theories, ideas or processes.

Unit 2 at A-level requires students to understand and to practise, through fieldwork and classwork, a variety of skills relevant to geographical investigation. They include hypothesis testing, data collection, data presentation, data analysis, and the evaluation of methodology and outcomes.

Scientific enquiry

Geography uses scientific methodology to investigate geographical phenomena (Figure 7.1). This methodology, based on hypothesis testing, is quantitative and, as far as possible, objective. A **hypothesis** is a statement about a presumed relationship or difference between variables. In geography, hypotheses usually take one of two approaches:
➤ Is A different from B?
➤ Is A related to B?

Figure 7.1 Hypothesis testing

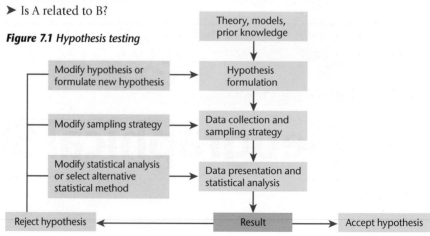

Most hypotheses are usually derived from **theory** and should be testable using scientific methodology. Theory can be defined as a set of statements or principles that have been tested and proved valid (Box 7.1). As a result they are used to make predictions about physical and human phenomena.

Box 7.1 Theory in geography

Theory is a set of statements or principles which have been tested and proved valid. Hypotheses are usually formulated from a coherent body of theory. Below are two examples of theory: equilibrium in fluvial geomorphology and settlement hierarchies.

Equilibrium in fluvial geomorphology

Rivers are energy systems, deriving their energy from discharge and gradient. This energy is expended through flow (i.e. overcoming friction between the channel boundaries), sediment transport and erosion. In the long term, rivers achieve an equilibrium state, having just sufficient energy to transport their water and sediment. However, equilibrium can be disturbed in the short term. For example a surplus of energy will cause erosion, which lowers the channel bed and reduces the gradient. This adjustment removes surplus energy. On the other hand any deficit of energy results in deposition, steepening the channel gradient and giving the additional energy needed for transport. Both adjustments return the fluvial system to equilibrium.

Settlement hierarchies

Settlements are central places that provide services to their own populations and to people in the surrounding area. Thus settlements serve a population that forms a **catchment area** or **trade area**. The rank (or order) of a settlement in the hierarchy depends on the number, range and order of services it provides. High-order centres provide services for large populations. In this way they can meet the **thresholds** needed to make them viable. These centres often serve extensive catchments, and as a result, high-order centres are (a) few in number (b) often widely spaced.

Settlement hierarchies are an efficient vehicle to provide people with the goods and services they need. Goods and services purchased frequently (e.g. food, gyms) are found locally in all service centres. This helps to minimise travel to consumers. The low threshold requirements of these services mean they are available even in the lowest order settlements.

The outcome of these principles is a settlement hierarchy based on the level of service provision. Near the top of the hierarchy are a handful of high-order centres (i.e. cities), offering a full range of services to a large population and an extensive catchment. At each lower level in the hierarchy (e.g. towns, villages, hamlets) there is a progressive decrease in the number and range of services provided, size of catchment and the total population served.

Hypothesis testing: an example

We know that the transport of bedload particles in a river should result in a decrease in their size with distance downstream. We base this assumption on our knowledge of fluvial processes. During transport, abrasion and attrition will reduce the average size of particles, even though this relationship will be complicated by the input of sediment from tributary streams. Thus our hypothesis (H1) will be:

Bedload particles become smaller with increasing distance downstream.

We can test this hypothesis by collecting sediment samples at regular intervals downstream, using either random or systematic sampling methods, and measuring the size of particles. Our aim is to select a sample that represents the statistical **population** (i.e. all sediments in the stream) accurately. Our sample data are then described and analysed using charts and statistical methods. If the outcome shows beyond reasonable doubt that sediments do indeed decrease in size with distance downstream, we accept the hypothesis as proven.

However, should our results fail to confirm the hypothesis, what then?

➤ First we need to consider the possibility that sediments do not decrease in size downstream. This may require us to extend data collection to include sediment inputs from tributary streams and from bank erosion. It might also mean changing our initial hypothesis.

➤ Second, it is possible that sediments do in fact decrease in size downstream, but that our methodology failed to detect it. In this case we could take a number of actions. We might decide to increase the size of our sample; attempt more detailed data collection by measuring three axes of sediments (instead of one); or choose to collect sediment on comparable sites in the channel such as point bars.

➤ Finally, we might review our statistical analysis. A statistical test such as correlation might be too demanding, and a simpler test comparing the differences in sediment between upstream and downstream locations might give us the proof we need.

It is clear that once we reject a hypothesis, hypothesis testing becomes an iterative process, as we revisit each of the main stages of scientific enquiry.

Developing a plan or strategy

Key ideas

➤ A successful geographical investigation requires planning, which balances the need for accuracy against limitations imposed by time and resources.

➤ The data and data sources required to test hypotheses need to be identified.

➤ Strategies for data collection (including sampling) need to be established.

➤ An assessment of potential risks in undertaking research needs to be made.

➤ Methods of minimising risk need to be considered.

The first stage of hypothesis testing is to develop a strategy for the investigation. This involves identifying the data required and their sources, and planning fieldwork.

Sources of data

Primary and secondary data

There are two types of data used in geographical investigation: primary and secondary. **Primary data** are new data, which have not previously been collected or processed. The clearest example is fieldwork data. Students conducting questionnaires, observing urban land use or measuring slope angles in the field are collecting primary data (Photograph 7.1).

Documents (either paper or electronic) such as the census of population, rainfall records, electoral registers, historical maps and so on can also be a source of primary data. Raw data taken from documentary sources (e.g. eighteenth-century baptisms and burials in parish registers), compiled originally for non-geographical purposes, can be classed as primary data. Once extracted, these data can then be processed to show time trends or spatial differences in population change.

Confusion often arises in defining **secondary data**. Let's be clear: all secondary data must come from documentary sources. However, as we have seen, documentary sources can also be a source of primary data. Secondary data usually refers to published documents such as textbooks, articles, maps, charts and diagrams. In other words, secondary data have already been processed, ordered and analysed before publication. For example, an investigation of a river flood, based on a previously published hydrograph, a synoptic chart of the weather conditions at the time, and a newspaper article which described the flood's impact on residents, would be using secondary data.

Photograph 7.1
Questionnaire work

Documentary data sources

Topographic maps

Topographic maps are the basis for most investigative studies in geography (Figure 7.2). They are used in at least three different ways: as sources of information such as relief and drainage, and historical changes in the form and lay-out of settlements; for recording and storing data gathered in the field such as rural and urban land use; and for providing a spatial framework for studies which involve spatial sampling, e.g. households, vegetation types.

Four types of large-scale Ordnance Survey maps are widely used at AS and A-level: 1:50 000 (Landranger), 1:25 000 (Pathfinder), 1:10 000 and 1:2500. Two of these — 1:50 000 and 1:25 000 — are now available in electronic format. These are shown in Figure 7.2, which also lists some of their uses in geographical enquiry. The map chosen for study will depend on the scale of the investigation and on the level of detail required. For example, a survey of land use in a rural area covering 50 km^2 would require a 1:25 000 map. This is the smallest scale that shows field boundaries (the basic unit for plotting rural land use). The larger-scale 1:10 000 map also shows field boundaries but would be impractical to use in the field for anything other than small areas.

Maps at 1:2500 scale are available only for urban areas in the UK. Because of their detail they are particularly useful in small-scale urban studies. For example, a random stratified sample of households could be obtained from a 1:2500 map for a small suburb or estate, using data on street names, house numbers and dwelling type (Figure 7.2 (d)).

The earliest large-scale Ordnance Survey maps date from the mid-nineteenth century and are available at the 6-inch-to-1-mile scale. These maps are useful in investigations of settlement and landscape change. They are available as free downloads for small areas from **www.old-maps.co.uk**.

Geology maps

1:50 000 and 1-inch geology maps, published by the British Geological Society, are available for most of the UK. There are two types: solid geology and drift geology maps. Solid geology maps show surface rocks without surface deposits such as clay, sand, peat and alluvium. Drift geology maps show these surface deposits as well as outcrops of solid rock and areas of mass movement. Newer editions of the maps combine both solid and drift geology.

Geology maps are the starting point for many studies in physical geography. An investigation of runoff in a drainage basin will need detailed information on drainage basin geology. Downstream changes in the composition of a river's bedload will be related to the geology of a river and its tributaries. Both solid and drift geology are important influences on soil development and agricultural land use. Furthermore, in rural areas, geology has a strong control on materials used in traditional buildings.

Goad plans

Goad maps are large-scale plans of shopping centres in the UK and parts of Europe (Figure 7.3). First produced in the 1980s and frequently updated, they provide

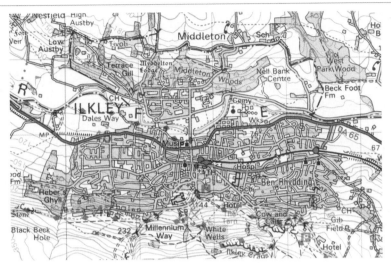

Figure 7.2 *(a) 1:50 000 Landranger Ordnance Survey map*

1:50 000 maps are useful in investigations at a regional scale.
- locating the origins of shoppers interviewed in a service centres
- delimiting small drainage basins
- understanding relief and drainage
- describing and explaining rural settlement patterns
- describing amd explaining the shape and situation of settlements
- describing the distribution of woodland

Electronic versions of the 1:50 000 series published by Anquet allow 3D transformations of the maps and also give complete satellite photo coverage.

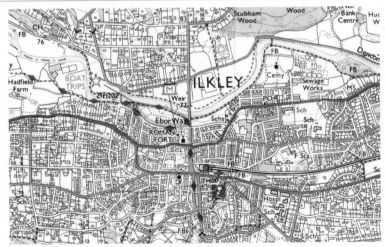

Figure 7.2 *(b) 1:25 000 Pathfinder Ordnance Survey map*

1:25 000 maps are useful in investigations at a sub-regional scale such as:
- describing and explaining the overall internal structure of towns and cities
- describing house types and the layout of suburban areas
- plotting rural land use (1:25 000 maps show field boundaries)
- detailed description of relief (contours are at 5 metre intervals)

Electronic versions of the 1:25 000 series published by Anquet allow 3D transformations of the maps and also give complete satellite photo coverage.

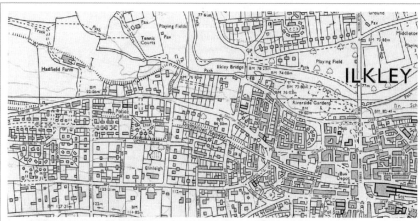

Figure 7.2 *(c) 1:10 000 Ordnance Survey map*

1:10 000 maps are useful in investigations at a local scale such as:
- recording the age of buildings
- recording land use types
- recording types of housing
- delimiting flood hazard areas from spot height data
- settlement site characteristics based on spot heights

Figure 7.2 *(d) 1:2500 Ordnance Survey map*

1:2500 are useful in investigations at the smallest scale to:
- identify individual houses by street name, number and house type (e.g. for spatial sampling exercises)
- record the exact location of shops and other commercial functions in a village, town or city centre
- provide detailed information of physical sites from bench marks (maps do not include contours)
- give detailed information on the functions of buildings

information on retailers, their activity, floorspace and address details. Goad plans are an invaluable source of data on retail change and the spatial distribution of retail types (e.g. service retailers, product retailers, multiple and independent stores) in town centres (see Figure 7.3).

Figure 7.3 *Goad map of part of Norwich*

Land-use maps

The Land Utilisation Survey in the early 1960s produced 1:25 000-scale maps of land use in England and Wales that covered around 10% of the country (see Figure 7.13, p.278). These maps are valuable historical documents. They allow analysis of changes such as urbanisation, land reclamation and the conversion of pastureland to arable land (or vice versa) over the past 50 years. Land-use patterns in relation to soils, geology, slopes, altitude, flooding and distance from urban areas can also be investigated.

Table 7.1
Postcode hierarchy in the UK

LA	LA11	LA11 6	LA11 6RW
Postcode area	Postcode district	Postcode sector	Postcode unit
124 areas in the UK	2934 postcode districts	9903 postcode sectors	1.76 million postcode units each comprising around 15 households
1 map covering the UK	6 regional maps covering the UK	36 maps covering the UK	No maps available

Postcode maps

Many investigations in human geography based on interviews require information on respondents' place of residence. Problems often arise because of scale inconsistency in responses, which range from precise addresses to the names of counties. Postcodes provide alternative and more consistent data. Maps are available from the Ordnance Survey that show the boundaries of postcode areas, districts and sectors.

For local investigations, postcode units are most useful, though as Table 7.1 shows, there are no published maps which show postcode unit boundaries. To some extent this problem can be overcome by accessing the 'up my street' website (www.upmystreet.com). There the geographical centre of individual postcode units is identified, though their boundaries are not defined.

Weather charts

Synoptic weather charts for the North Atlantic and the British Isles are available from several online sites (Table 7.2). The charts produced by the Meteorological Office, issued at noon and midnight, are the most detailed. They show isobaric patterns and frontal systems (Figure 7.4). Synoptic charts are useful in local investigations that focus on extreme weather events such as heavy rainfall, snowfall, heat waves and drought. For example an investigation of local flooding

Table 7.2 *Online sources of synoptic weather charts*

Area coverage	Information shown	Source	Website
North Atlantic and much of northern Europe	Pressure patterns and fronts. Forecast charts for 5 days ahead	BBC	www.bbc.co.uk/weather/coast/pressure
North Atlantic and much of northern Europe	Pressure patterns and fronts	Met Office	www.westwind.ch
North Atlantic and much of northern Europe	Pressure patterns and fronts	Met Office	meteonet.nl/aktueel/brackall.htm
North Atlantic and much of northern Europe	Pressure patterns and fronts	Met Office	www.wetter-zentrale.com
Animated maps of jet stream in North Atlantic	Pressure patterns at high altitude	The weather channel	uk.weather.com
Archive synoptic charts for North Atlantic and western Europe	Pressure patterns and fronts	Met Office	www.wetterzentrale.com

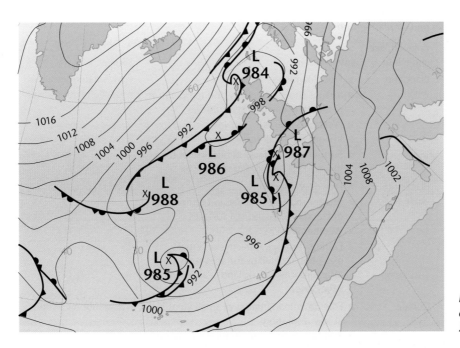

Figure 7.4 Synoptic chart: noon, 22 October 2006

might require a synoptic chart to describe the regional weather conditions which produced the event.

Satellite images/air photographs

Satellite images and aerial photographs contain valuable information on weather systems, land use, the shape and internal layout of settlements, river channels, coastlines and so on (Table 7.3, p. 268). Compared to maps, these images are likely to be more recent (in the case of weather satellite images updates may occur at hourly intervals). Depending on resolution, satellite images and aerial photos are more detailed. However, this can be a two-edged sword because the clutter of detail (or noise) makes photographic images more difficult to interpret.

Census of population

The UK census of population has been taken every 10 years since 1801. Initially the census was little more than a count of heads, but by the mid-nineteenth century its scope had been extended to include occupations, places of birth and the relationship of people to each other within households.

The census is an essential source of information for government planning and the allocation of resources such as housing, education and health care. By law every household in the UK must complete a census questionnaire. Compared to the early censuses, the modern census is far reaching. For example the 2001 census document was 20 pages long. Respondents had to record household occupants on census night. There were questions on household accommodation, as well as 35 separate questions relating to each household member. Among the personal information required was date of birth, gender, educational qualifications, ethnicity, religion and employment.

Table 7.3 *Satellite images and air photographs*

Type	Colour/black and white	Information	Source
Infra-red and visible geostationary weather satellite images; satellite in fixed position 35 800 km above the Equator	Black and white	■ Free downloads ■ Images show reflectivity and temperature of cloud, ocean and sea surfaces ■ Weather systems ■ Images are small scale ■ Further detail is lacking because of the low-angled view of Europe	www.sat.dundee.ac.uk www.wetterzentrale.de
Infra-red and visible weather satellite images from polar orbiting satellites; satellites in low orbit — 870–880 km above the Earth's surface	Black and white	■ Free downloads ■ Images show reflectivity and temperature of cloud, ocean and sea surfaces ■ Weather systems ■ During summer, reflectiveness gives exceptional detail of surfaces such as large urban areas, uplands, large river valleys etc.	www.sat.dundee.ac.uk
Vertical aerial photos of landscape	Colour	■ Free download images of small areas but at low resolution ■ 1:50 000 images are useful for land-use and settlement studies ■ High resolution images available for purchase	www.multi-map.com
Vertical aerial photographs of landscape	Colour	■ Vertical air photographs available with electronic 1:50 000 and 1:25 000 maps ■ Higher resolution than free multi-map images ■ 1:25 000 images useful for land-use and settlement studies	www.anquet.co.uk
Satellite images of landscape	Colour	■ Free download images ■ Resolution is highest for large urban areas and sufficient for detailed investigations of land use, building types and settlement growth at 1:2500 scale ■ Images can be transformed to 3D	earth.google.com
Satellite images of landscape	Colour	■ Free download images ■ Resolution in the UK is less than Google Earth but is useful for studying land use in rural areas ■ Images can be transformed to 3D	worldwind.arc.nasa.gov

Census information for 56 data sets is published for a hierarchy of geographical areas (these data are available online at www.neighbourhood.statistics.uk) (Figure 7.5). In 2001 a new hierarchy of neighbourhood areas was created for England and Wales (Figure 7.6). At the base of the hierarchy are over 175 000 output areas. Data are then aggregated at successive scales and published for super output areas, local authorities (i.e. metropolitan districts, counties, unitary authorities, rural districts), regions (e.g. southwest) and England and Wales (Table 7.4).

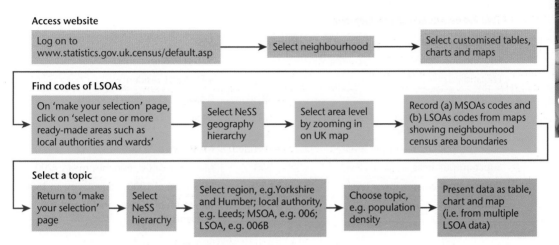

Access website

| Log on to www.statistics.gov.uk.census/default.asp | → | Select neighbourhood | → | Select customised tables, charts and maps |

Find codes of LSOAs

| On 'make your selection' page, click on 'select one or more ready-made areas such as local authorities and wards' | → | Select NeSS geography hierarchy | → | Select area level by zooming in on UK map | → | Record (a) MSOAs codes and (b) LSOAs codes from maps showing neighbourhood census area boundaries |

Select a topic

| Return to 'make your selection' page | → | Select NeSS hierarchy | → | Select region, e.g. Yorkshire and Humber; local authority, e.g. Leeds; MSOA, e.g. 006; LSOA, e.g. 006B | → | Choose topic, e.g. population density | → | Present data as table, chart and map (i.e. from multiple LSOA data) |

Figure 7.5 *Accessing neighbourhood census data at the super output area (lower level) (LSOA)*

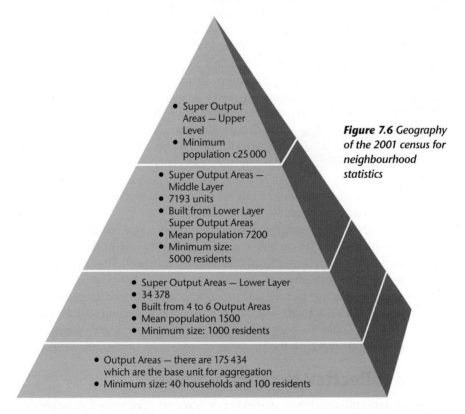

- Super Output Areas — Upper Level
- Minimum population c25 000

- Super Output Areas — Middle Layer
- 7193 units
- Built from Lower Layer Super Output Areas
- Mean population 7200
- Minimum size: 5000 residents

- Super Output Areas — Lower Layer
- 34 378
- Built from 4 to 6 Output Areas
- Mean population 1500
- Minimum size: 1000 residents

- Output Areas — there are 175 434 which are the base unit for aggregation
- Minimum size: 40 households and 100 residents

Figure 7.6 *Geography of the 2001 census for neighbourhood statistics*

At each level in the hierarchy the new census units are approximately equal in population. Most have some geographical significance (e.g. they might cover a single village or a distinctive housing area) and boundaries that will remain largely unchanged between censuses.

Neighbourhood census statistics, available for the smallest areas, are an invaluable source of data for AS and A-level geography studies. Spatial variations in

Table 7.4 Census geography hierarchy

Geographical unit	Number	Size
England and Wales		52 041 916 residents
England		49 138 881 residents
English regions	9	2.515–7.171 million residents
Metropolitan districts, counties, unitary authorities, rural districts	171	34 563– 1 329 718 residents
Super output areas — upper level	To be decided	Minimum c.25 000 residents
Super output areas — middle level	7193	Minimum 5000 residents; mean 7200
Super output areas — lower level	34 378	Minimum of 1000 residents; mean 1500
Output areas	175 434	Minimum of 40 households and 100 residents

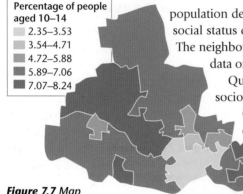

Percentage of people aged 10–14

- 2.35–3.53
- 3.54–4.71
- 4.72–5.88
- 5.89–7.06
- 7.07–8.24

Figure 7.7 Map of age structure in Newcastle-upon-Tyne from 2001 census data

population density, age structure, ethnicity, place of birth, income and social status can be investigated for a single suburb or housing area. The neighbourhood statistics website has the option of mapping the data or presenting them in charts or tables (Figure 7.7).

Questionnaire surveys in geography usually require some socio-economic and/or demographic profile of respondents. Characteristics such as gender, age, income, social status etc. can be related to behaviour such as distances travelled, preferences, goods and services purchased, places visited and so on. However, many profiling characteristics, especially income, employment and social status, are highly personal. Some respondents may be affronted by questions of this nature; some may refuse to answer, while others may answer untruthfully.

The ACORN geodemographic classification offers a way round this problem. It is a classification based on where people live. Every one of the 1.75 million postcode units, comprising 15–20 households, has been allocated to one of 4 geodemographic categories, 14 groups and 56 types (**www.caci.co.uk/acorn/acornmap.asp**). To use the classification, respondents need to provide their postcode unit. This information is far less personal than income, employment or socio-economic status. To determine the geodemographic category, group or type postcode units are input on the 'up my street' web page (**www.upmystreet.com**).

Data collection through fieldwork

Primary data collection through fieldwork relies on observation, measurement and interviews.

Observation

Observation, and the systematic recording of geographical features, is at the core of traditional fieldwork. Data collection through observation uses skills such as field sketching of landscapes, physical features, soil profiles and village sites

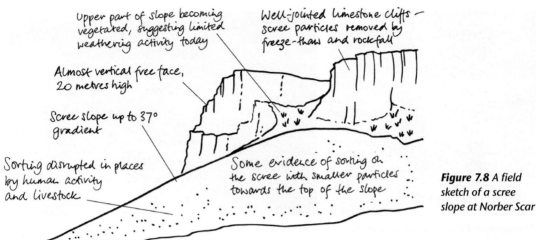

Upper part of slope becoming vegetated, suggesting limited weathering activity today

Well-jointed limestone cliffs – scree particles removed by freeze-thaw and rockfall

Almost vertical free face, 20 metres high

Scree slope up to 37° gradient

Sorting disrupted in places by human activity and livestock

Some evidence of sorting on the scree with smaller particles towards the top of the slope

Figure 7.8 *A field sketch of a scree slope at Norber Scar*

Figure 7.9 (a) Part of a shopping classification recording sheet

Product Retailers	Number	Service Retailers	Number
Convenience outlets		Household services	
Baker	|||	Estate agent	||||
Butcher	||	Solicitor	||
Chemist	||	Financial services	
Confectioner		Accountant	
Tobacconist/newsagent	|||	Bank	||||||
Delicatessen		Building Society	||
Frozen food		Insurer/broker	
General store		Health care services	
Greengrocer/fishmonger		Optician	||||
Off licence			Chiropodist	
Petrol station		Business/government services	
Supermarket		Consumer advice	
Superstore (food)			Employment agency	
Others		Job Centre		
Comparison outlets		Printing/copying	
Clothing & footwear		Leisure services	
Bridal wear		Amusement arcade	
Clothes — general	|||	Cafe	||||

Figure 7.9 (b) Classification of ages of housing

Ages of housing	Code for base map	Description
Pre 1870	1	Use of traditional local building materials (e.g. stone, hand-made brick, timber frames) and architectural styles. Large terraces, town houses, detached with extensive gardens. Houses often well maintained and close to town/city centre.
1870–1919	2	Mostly small terraces in the inner city. High density. Typically 2 rooms downstairs and 2 upstairs. No gardens. Backyards. Back-to-back in some northern cities. Often private rented. Gentrification in some neighbourhoods.
1920–1945	3	Inter-war semi-detached in mature suburbs. Gardens but no garages. Older local authority estates (usually semis) in mature suburbs.
Post 1945	4	Large local authority estates (often on the edge of town) comprising semi-detached, high-rise flats and modern terraces. Owner occupied estates in outer suburbs comprising modern semi-detached, detached and town houses.

(Figure 7.8). Observation may also require students to classify and record shop types, land uses, house types and ages of buildings. Environmental assessment surveys ask students to convert their subjective observations of the quality of the physical and human environments into scores. Pedestrian flows and traffic flows are based on simple counts observed over fixed time intervals. Counts of individual plant species are also used in vegetation surveys that use **quadrat** and **transect** sampling methods.

Except for field sketching, data collection through fieldwork observation requires a recording schedule such as a large-scale map, a classification scheme or a pro-forma. Some examples are shown in Figure 7.9 (a–c).

Measurement

Most aspects of fieldwork in physical geography involve data collection through measurement. Measurements rely on standard apparatus and instruments such as ranging poles, quadrats, metre rulers, tapes, clinometers, current meters,

Figure 7.9 (c) Housing types and tenancy

Code for base map	Housing types	Tenancy
1	Small terrace	a = owner occupied/owned outright
2	Large terrace	b = private rented
3	Semi-detached	c = local authority rented
4	Detached	
5	Apartments and flats	
6	Maisonettes	

Photograph 7.2 *Measuring slope angles with a clinometer*

Photograph 7.3 *Measuring a bankfull channel cross-section*

thermometers and anemometers. A common theme in physical geography investigations is that of relating shape or form to processes. Thus hillslopes may be surveyed using ranging poles, clinometers and tapes in order to relate slope angles to mass movements such as soil creep. Beach profiles may be measured to establish whether beach particle size influences gradient. The width and depth of river channels in cross-section can be measured and their shape related to discharge, sediment coarseness and channel slope (Photographs 7.2 and 7.3).

Questionnaires

Some data, such as the profile of people and businesses, personal behaviour, attitudes and viewpoints, can only be accessed through questionnaires or interviews. There are two approaches to questionnaire surveys. First, there are questionnaires completed privately by respondents at home or in the office. Students deliver and collect the questionnaires either by hand, or by post. Second, there are questionnaire surveys where students are present to record the responses directly. These interviews, for practical reasons, are most often conducted in public spaces (i.e. the street), though on some occasions doorstep interviews are undertaken.

Both postal questionnaires and street interviews have advantages and disadvantages. Postal questionnaires are likely to be more objective, with target populations chosen randomly or systematically from a list of addresses. Responses are also likely to be more measured and considered. However, there are disadvantages. Postal questionnaires, completed in the absence of the researcher, are more challenging to devise, and need to be precise and free from ambiguity. In addition costs of delivering and collecting the questionnaires could be significant (especially if they are posted). Meanwhile response rates for postal questionnaires are often low.

Street interviews are more difficult to control and often result in data which are unrepresentative. Given the circumstances, questionnaire surveys of passers-by have to be fairly brief, with little or no time for considered answers. Their informality and the personal interaction between interviewer and interviewee, however, are definite advantages. Students have the opportunity to explain and prompt respondents, which often produces a much higher success rate than postal questionnaires.

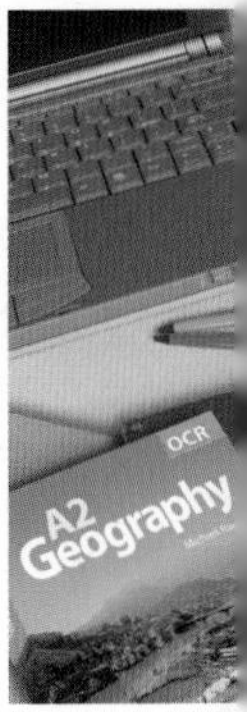

Box 7.2 Designing questionnaires

1 Initial decisions

At the outset you must decide what information is needed, who the respondents (target population) are, and the method of survey (street interviews, postal questionnaires) to be used.

2 Content and types of questions

Because respondents have limited time, and you depend on their goodwill to complete the questionnaires, only those questions that are essential should be included. Questions should be as clear and simple as possible and most should focus on facts (which are easier to collect) rather than attitudes and opinions. Questions that have political and religious connotations or are in any way economically, socially or ethnically offensive must be avoided.

As far as possible questions should be designed to elicit standardised responses so they can later be compared, tabulated and classified. For example, responses to the question 'how often do you shop in this town centre?' can be standardised as 'several times a week', 'once a week' and 'less than once a week'. Multiple-choice questions presented in a tick-box format should be used wherever possible.

Questions dealing with attitudes and opinions generate more information if some form of rating scale is used. For example, a question such as 'do you think that traffic congestion is a problem in this town?' will produce only binary 'yes' or 'no' answers. If, however, the question is modified to read 'to what extent is traffic congestion a problem in this town' then we can use a rating scale such as 'not a problem', 'a minor problem', 'a significant problem', 'a severe problem'. A numerical scale 1 to 6 could be used in place of a nominal scale, where 1 = 'no problem' and 6 = 'a severe problem.' Purely open-ended questions are likely to produce answers which are difficult to analyse and quantify.

3 Layout

Questions should have a logical sequence. In the exemplar shopping questionnaire, the questions on shopping behaviour progress from goods and services purchased and frequency of shopping trips in the centre where the interviews take place, to shopping trips to other centres (Figure 7.10). Questions concerning personal characteristics are generally placed towards the end of a questionnaire. This is because respondents may regard this information as confidential and decline to answer. However, this is less likely if they have already answered the earlier questions; and even if they refuse to answer you will still have some useful information from their earlier responses.

MARKET TOWN QUESTIONNAIRE

This questionnaire should be completed ONLY by people who are shopping AND who shop regularly in the town.

1 What is the name of the settlement where you live?

2 Which of the following goods/services have you bought (or used)/do you intend to buy (or use)?
(tick as appropriate)

- Food and household consumables
- Durable goods (e.g. clothes, shoes, electrical goods)
- Financial and legal services (e.g.banks, building societies, solicitors)
- Other services (e.g. hairdresser, travel agent, café, pub, leisure etc.)

3 How often do you shop in this town centre?
(tick as appropriate)

- Several times a week on average
- Once a week on average
- Less than once a week on average

4 In which town do you normally shop for the following items?

- Shoes and clothing
- Food

5 In which towns (or villages) do the adults in your household work?

- Town/village (1)
- Town/village (2)

6 How often do you use internet shopping to get the goods and services you need?
(tick as appropriate)

- Quite often
- Occasionally
- Never

QUESTION 7 IS ONLY TO BE ANSWERED BY RESPONDENTS WHO LIVE OUTSIDE THE MARKET TOWN.

7 Apart from shopping for goods and services, for what other reasons do you visit this town?
(tick as appropriate)

- Work
- Medical/doctor/dentist
- Visit relatives/friends
- Education/school/library
- Recreation/leisure
- Other

8 What is your full postcode (e.g. LA11 4RW)

Figure 7.10 *Market town questionnaire*

Location				Date	
Potential hazards	Risk present/ absent	Level of risk		Depart time	Return time
		High	Medium	Low	
Urban hazards					Action taken
Roads/Traffic					
Threats from public					
Getting lost					
Toxic wastes					
Others					
Rural hazards					
Rivers					
Rockfall					
Toxic wastes					
Fieldwork equipment					
Tides					
Waves					
Cliffs					
Steep slopes					
Animals					
Exposure to weather					
Getting lost					
Others					
Signed (Student)		Date	Signed (Teacher)	Date	

Figure 7.11* *Fieldwork risk assessment

Risk assessment

Geographical fieldwork, whether in an urban or rural environment, always includes an element of risk. Before undertaking any fieldwork you must do three things. First, identify the potential hazards. Second, assess the risk posed by each hazard. Third, devise a strategy or plan for dealing with the hazard. Usually we formalise this process by completing a risk assessment sheet, which is submitted to a teacher or supervisor for approval (Figure 7.11). The purpose of the risk assessment exercise is to minimise risk to yourself and others in the fieldwork party.

There are a number of general safety guidelines that are common to geographical fieldwork which should be adhered to when undertaking personal investigative studies:

- Always work in groups. Ideally, groups should comprise at least three people. If an accident occurs resulting in injury, one member of the group can get help while the other remains with the injured person.
- Carry a mobile phone. Leave your phone switched on for the duration of the fieldwork and make sure that you have exchanged phone numbers with your teacher or supervisor.
- Wear (or carry in a rucksack) suitable outdoor clothing. This includes waterproofs (jacket and trousers) and several layers of clothing. For river studies wellies or waders are essential, and for work on slopes or in rough terrain, walking boots that provide a good grip and protect your ankles.
- If you are working in a remote rural area you should carry a torch, a survival bag, a whistle and emergency rations.
- Carry a small first aid kit at all times.
- Carry a map at the appropriate scale.
- Leave details of your itinerary with your teacher or supervisor, including your times of departure and return.

Data collection

Key ideas

- A successful geographical investigation is based on thorough methods of data collection and recording.
- Data collection includes both primary and secondary data.
- There are a number of different ways of collecting data to ensure reliability and accuracy.

The second stage of hypothesis testing is the collection of data. Reliable and representative sampling techniques are essential in this process.

Sampling

A sample is a sub-set of items selected from the statistical **population**. In this context, the term 'population' does not mean people. It refers to all the data available. For example, in a study of a shingle beach, the population comprises all the pebbles on the beach. In a survey of household movements in a suburb, the population is all the households that moved into the suburb in the past year.

Most geographical investigations are based on samples rather than the statistical population. However, any investigation is only as good as the sample on which it is based. As a result, it is essential that samples are chosen according to established rules designed to represent a population accurately. A successful sample will enable researchers to make valid inferences about the characteristics of a population from the characteristics of the sampled items.

The alternative to sampling is to investigate the entire statistical population. While this approach would eliminate problems associated with unrepresentative samples, it is impracticable. Most statistical populations are simply too large to study every individual. Moreover, a high level of accuracy, comparable to surveying the entire population, can be achieved from a well-designed sample, and at a fraction of the cost.

Qualities of a good sample

A good sample has the following qualities:
➤ It is unbiased, i.e. estimates of population characteristics such as the mean and standard deviation are neither consistently larger nor consistently smaller than the true values.
➤ It is precise, i.e. it provides an accurate estimate of population characteristics.
➤ It is large enough to provide conclusive results in terms of statistical significance.
➤ It can be collected easily and with the minimum of resources.

Types of sampling

Sampling methods in geographical investigations may be divided into spatial and non-spatial (Figure 7.12).

Non-spatial sampling

There are three types of non-spatial sampling: random, systematic and stratified.

The basic assumption of **random sampling** is that every item in a population has an equal chance of inclusion in the sample. It is often forgotten that the term 'random' has a specific meaning in statistical sampling: it means that samples are selected using random numbers, generated either from a calculator or a random numbers table. Random sampling is most appropriate if there is a listing of the population (e.g. a list of businesses on an industrial estate, or households in the electoral register), allowing samples to be selected by random numbers. Although such lists are not available for most study areas, random sampling is not

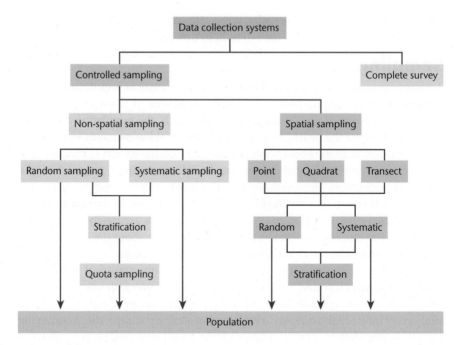

Figure 7.12
Sampling systems

impossible. For example, high-street shoppers could be chosen for interview by generating random numbers between 1 and 9. If, say, 100 random numbers in this range were generated prior to fieldwork, then the sampling process could be implemented quite efficiently.

Systematic sampling is an alternative to random sampling. With systematic sampling items are sampled from a population at regular intervals. The sample interval is usually chosen randomly. Systematic sampling is both quicker and simpler than random sampling. For these reasons it is often preferred in fieldwork investigations.

Both random and systematic sampling methods are often combined with stratification. Many statistical populations are far from homogeneous, consisting of many sub-groups. If some of these sub-groups are relatively small they may be underrepresented by simple random and systematic sampling. Common criteria used to stratify populations include age, gender, socio-economic status, income, ethnicity, employment and so on.

There are two sampling strategies that aim to represent the sub-groups in a statistical population: **stratified random and systematic sampling**; and **quota sampling**. The difference between them relates to the selection of individuals for the sample. Stratified random and systematic methods select sample individuals objectively, whereas in quota sampling a researcher deliberately chooses individuals to fill the quota for each sub-group. As a result quota sampling is less scientific than stratified random and systematic sampling. It is, however, more practical, and given constraints of time and money, may often be the only feasible means of collecting a stratified sample. Box 7.3 describes an example of stratified sampling.

Box 7.3 Stratified and quota sampling

This investigation aims to determine the geographical pattern of retail spending within Preston's CBD in northwest England. Preston's CBD serves a catchment of approximately 250 000. The retail structure of the city's CBD is divided into six areas: Fishergate, Friargate, the Fishergate Mall, the St George's Mall, the St John's Mall and the covered market.

Methodology

Street interviews of shoppers provide data on where they purchase goods and services and how much they spend in each of the six shopping areas. Simple random and systematic sampling is rejected because it is unlikely to produce a representative sample. This is because some groups, such as women and older adults, are more likely to agree to be interviewed than others. A stratified or quota sampling method based on three criteria is used instead.

- A small pilot survey in the city centre shows that: 65% of weekday shoppers are women and 35% are men.
- The same pilot survey gives the following estimated age profile for shoppers: 18–39 years — 40%; 40–65 years — 30%; over 65 years — 25%.
- Preston's 2001 census data give the following

breakdown for housing tenure: owner occupied — 74%; local authority rented — 17%; private rented — 9%.

These criteria are selected because it is assumed that where people shop and how much they spend will be influenced by gender, age and socio-economic status (i.e. housing tenure). In addition, it is feasible to incorporate these criteria into a workable quota sampling system.

Generating quotas

The target sample is 100 shoppers divided, on the basis of gender, age and housing tenure, into the groups shown in Table 7.5.

The table provides the quotas for interviews. For example, our sample will include 21 women aged between 18 and 39 who are owner occupiers, 5 in the same age group who rent from the local authority and so on. Clearly, stratified and quota sampling are more elaborate strategies than simple random or systematic methods. Any decision to use stratified and quota sampling has to balance the desire for accuracy against the extra costs of collecting the data.

Gender	No.	Age groups (years) (no.)			Housing tenure	No.
		18–39	40–65	65+		
Women	65	21	15	12	Owner occupied	48
		5	3	2	Local authority rented	10
		3	2	2	Private rented	7
Men	35	12	3	1	Owner occupied	16
		7	2	1	Local authority rented	10
		7	1	1	Private rented	9

Table 7.5 Sample groups for survey of retail spending

Spatial sampling

Spatial sampling is used where location is an essential feature of the items being studied. It is therefore of particular importance in geographical investigations. Samples are selected from points, areas and lines using random, systematic and stratified sampling strategies.

Spatial sampling procedures using points, areas and lines can be illustrated

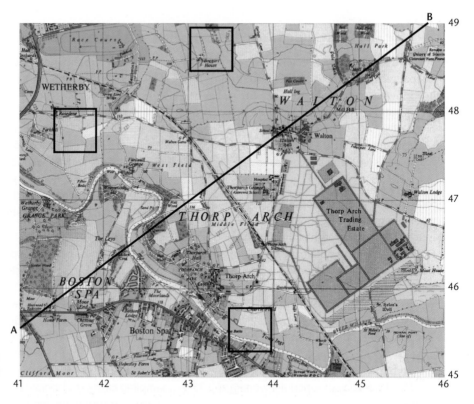

Figure 7.13 Land-use map for Boston Spa, West Yorkshire

with reference to the 1:25 000 land-use map in Figure 7.13 (and see p. 265). We shall assume that the purpose of sampling is to estimate the proportion of arable land, pasture land, woodland and urban land in the area.

Point sampling

We can sample land use at random points on the map by generating random six-figure grid references. This is done by using the random number function on a calculator and combining say 100 three-figure eastings between 410 and 460, with 100 three-figure northings between 450 and 490. Two problems arise with this procedure. First, generating random grid references and locating them on a map is time consuming, especially if large samples are needed. Second, unless a large enough sample is taken, it is possible that the distribution of random points on the map could give rather uneven coverage.

Both problems can be addressed by using systematic, rather than random, point sampling. Systematic point sampling relies on a grid of coordinates placed randomly over the map. In this example, the coordinates of the national grid system can be used. Land use is then sampled at the points of intersection on the grid.

Randomly drawn lines of transect (such as line A–B in Figure 7.13) are a third strategy for generating point samples. Sample points can either be at regular intervals along a transect, or at locations derived from random numbers. In order to collect a large enough sample, several random lines of transect are needed. This raises the problem associated with random point sampling: namely that the transects may give uneven coverage of the map.

Area sampling

Area sampling based on quadrats offers an alternative to point sampling. A quadrat is either a square of standard size on a map, or a metal frame (typically 1 m × 1 m), sub-divided into smaller squares, and used in the field. Quadrats are located in a study area either randomly or systematically. Within quadrats sampled items may be counted, recorded as absent or present, or their areal coverage estimated.

The quadrats in the land-use map in Figure 7.13 have been located randomly. They provide a spatial framework for data collection. Data could be collected in several ways. We could, for example, record the absence or presence of arable land, pastureland, woodland and urban land in each quadrat. More generally we might simply record for each quadrat the dominant land use (i.e. the land use covering the largest area). A more detailed approach would be to estimate the proportion of different land uses in each quadrat.

It is important to know that outcomes from quadrat sampling are strongly influenced by quadrat size. In the land-use example, land use tends to vary by field, and quadrats need to be large enough to cover three or four fields. Quadrat sampling is often used in vegetation surveys. In this context the quadrat should be large enough to accommodate the area occupied by individual plant species.

Quadrat size is also influenced by the geographical distribution of the population. Where populations are highly clustered, small quadrats located randomly or systematically may fail to pick up enough samples. Figure 7.14 shows the sparse and clustered distribution of yellow mountain saxifrage between 300 m and 700 m above sea level. Small quadrats are much less likely to generate sufficient samples to show the influence of altitude on geographic distribution, compared to larger ones.

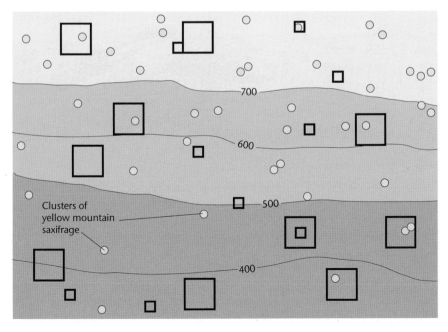

Figure 7.14
Quadrat sampling of distribution of yellow mountain saxifrage (Saxifraga azoides)

Figure 7.15
Stratified spatial sampling using a transect and quadrats to investigate particle size sorting on a talus slope

Line sampling

Many geographical investigations use samples derived from lines or transects. Transects are particularly effective where they cross contrasting areas of relief, geology, land use, soils and so on. Although transects usually follow one or more straight lines, in urban studies they may, for practical reasons, often follow the street pattern.

Sample data are collected at random and systematic intervals, either as points or areas (quadrats), along a line of transect. Figure 7.15 shows a strategy for collecting a sample of scree particles on a talus slope. First a base line is established at the slope foot. Then transects are located randomly and at right angles to the base line to the top of the slope. Finally quadrats are located at systematic intervals (lower, middle, upper) on the slope.

Belt transects are a type of line sample. They are often used when populations are thinly spread across an area and where a line transect would fail to generate a large enough sample. A belt is identified on either side of a random line of transect and sample items are measured and recorded within this zone. The example in Figure 7.16 shows how belt sampling can produce an objective sample of boulders from a field of perched blocks (Photograph 7.4). Once selected, weathering pits on the boulders can be measured to determine rates of surface lowering by weathering processes.

Michael Raw

Photograph 7.4
Perched blocks

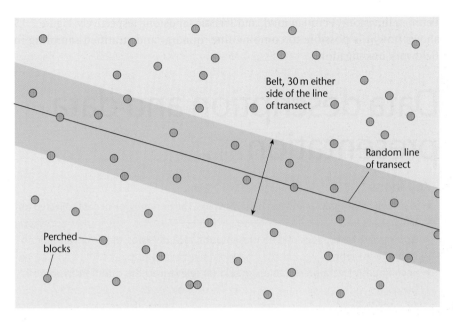

Figure 7.16 *Belt transect, Norber Scar*

Stratified spatial sampling

It is possible that rural land use in the area covered by the Boston Spa land-use map is influenced by the underlying geology (Figure 7.17). If this is so, any attempt to estimate the proportions of different land uses using simple random or systematic sampling methods could result in error. The solution is random stratified sampling, where land use is sampled on the three different rock types in proportion to the area of the map they occupy. Let's assume that 60% of the area is Permian limestone, 35% is Permian marl and 5% is Triassic sandstone. A stratified random sample of 100 would comprise 60, 35 and 5 points on the

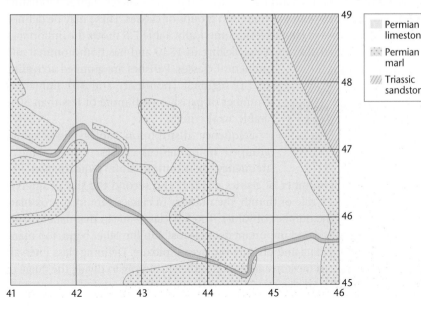

Figure 7.17 *Geology of the area covered by the Boston Spa land-use map (Figure 7.13)*

Permian limestone, Permian marl, and Triassic sandstone respectively. Figure 7.15 shows how it is possible to combine line, quadrat and stratified sampling in fieldwork investigation.

Data description and data presentation

Key ideas

➤ A successful geographical investigation involves the presentation of data collected to a high standard.

➤ Appropriate techniques of data presentation include maps, diagrams, annotated photos and graphs.

➤ Techniques of data presentation should be relevant to the question/hypothesis posed.

The third stage of hypothesis testing is data description and data presentation. Quantitative data, collected by observation, measurement and interviews are processed and presented as tables, charts, maps and descriptive statistics. The purpose of data description and data presentation is to generalise raw data to reveal spatial and temporal patterns and trends. Both are essential steps prior to analysis and interpretation.

Tables

A large number of values may be generalised and represented as tables. Tabulating data usually involves putting values into groups or classes. These may be defined nominally (e.g. types of land use) or numerically. Table 7.6 shows the importance of arable land in parishes in Warwickshire in 1840 and has both nominal and numerical classes. Parishes are grouped according to (a) regional (nominal) and (b) numerical (number of parishes with more or less than 30% arable area) criteria.

Frequency distribution tables show values grouped in numerical classes. Constructing a frequency distribution table requires two key decisions: first, the number of classes needed; and second the size of interval between classes. As a rule of thumb, the number of classes should approximate the square root of the number of values. Too few classes mean that data become excessively generalised and important detail is lost. On the other hand, too many classes fragment the data and obscure the overall picture. Defining class intervals is less problematic. In most instances it is sufficient simply to divide the range of values by the number of classes.

Table 7.6 *Percentage arable area by parish in Warwickshire c.1840*

	No. parishes <30%	No. parishes >30%
Arden and Avon Valley	1	18
Feldon	6	2

Box 7.4 Creating a frequency distribution table

Table 7.7 Random sample of slope angles: Muggleswick Common, County Durham

14	13	12	11	9	16	3	7	10	13	6	9	6	10	10	7
5	5	3	6	6	6	4	6	6	15	9	13	12	17	16	23
16	24	32	17	29	12	21	16	2	18	28	5	5	6	6	6
7	8	7	9	9	8	7	7	9	8	8	7	7	11	8	4
2	4	9	9	6	7	9	7	5	5	8	6	7	5	10	11
15	40	15	40	33	8	6	11	12	6	6	5	5	6	5	4
9	12	11	11	9	12	10	12	12	17	16	16	17	18	21	9
12	6	14	17	24	35	8	10	7	6	7	8	6	8	9	30
6	4	5	5	3	4	4	5	4	4	4	5	4	6	5	4
7	5	2	2	2	2	3	25	7	5	7	7	8	7	6	7
6	5	4	5	4	4	2	4	5	8	35					

Number of values: 171
Number of classes: $\sqrt{171} = 13$
Range of values: $2 - 40 = 38$
Class interval: $38 \div 13 = 3$

Table 7.8 Frequency distribution table of slope angles at Muggleswick Common

Classes	Number of values
1–3	11
4–6	59
7–9	44
10–12	21
13–15	8
16–18	13
19–21	2
22–24	3
25–27	1
28–30	3
31–33	2
34–36	2
37+	2

Types of chart

As a method of data presentation, charts have advantages over tables. They have a greater visual impact, are easier to interpret, and show patterns and trends in data sets with more clarity. In this section we shall look at several types of chart and discuss their suitability for describing different data sets.

Histograms and frequency curves

We represent frequency distribution tables with a type of bar chart known as a **histogram** (Figure 7.18, Box 7.5).

The stepped appearance of a histogram is determined artificially by the choice of class intervals. So a more meaningful way to show the data is to replace the bars with a smooth **frequency distribution curve**.

Although the curve is drawn by eye, the area below the curve should be the same as the area of the histogram; there should be no net transfer of values which might alter the histogram's overall shape; and any smoothing should be confined to adjacent columns.

Frequency curves like the one in Figure 7.18, which are approximately symmetrical and bell-shaped, describe a **normal distribution**. Normal distributions can vary in their degree of sharpness or flatness — a property known as **kurtosis**. However, many data sets in geography are asymmetrical or **skewed**. **Positively skewed** distributions, where the 'tail' of the distribution extends to the right, occur widely (e.g. slope angles, sediment sizes, population densities) (Figure 7.19).

Box 7.5   Drawing a histogram using Excel

Year	Rainfall (mm)	Year	Rainfall (mm)	Year	Rainfall (mm)
1955	1437	1972	1636	1989	1061
1956	1252	1973	1248	1990	1610
1957	1051	1974	1333	1991	1078
1958	1331	1975	1416	1992	1020
1959	1352	1976	1004	1993	903
1960	1268	1977	1280	1994	1262
1961	1462	1978	1118	1995	1275
1962	1296	1979	1189	1996	1511
1963	1207	1980	1257	1997	1647
1964	1317	1981	1342	1998	1337
1965	1016	1982	1356	1999	1647
1966	1290	1983	1452	2000	905
1967	1157	1984	1401	2001	1286
1968	1598	1985	891	2002	1060
1969	1057	1986	1342	2003	1385
1970	1366	1987	995	2004	1068
1971	1434	1988	1112	2005	1277

Table 7.9 Annual rainfall at Olympia, Washington, USA, 1955–2005

1 Enter data in Table 7.9 into an Excel spreadsheet.
2 In 'tools' select 'data analysis'.
3 In 'data analysis' select 'histogram'.
4 In the 'input range box' enter the annual rainfall data (simply select the data with the mouse).
5 Place the cursor in the 'bin range' box and enter the class boundaries chosen, e.g. 900, 1000, 1100, 1200, 1300, 1400, 1500, 1600.
6 Click chart output to get a frequency table and a histogram.

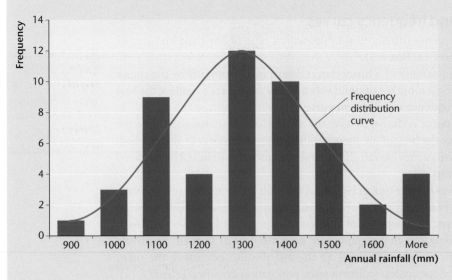

Figure 7.18 Histogram of annual rainfall at Olympia, Washington, USA, 1955–2005

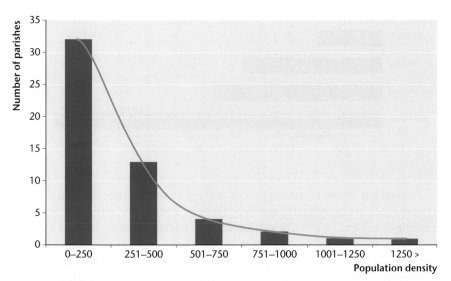

Figure 7.19
Populations of North Yorkshire parishes, 2006: a positively skewed frequency curve

Negatively skewed distributions, where the 'tail' extends to the left, are less common.

Frequency distributions are sometimes plotted as **cumulative frequency curves**. They show the proportion of a data set above or below particular thresholds. For example, Figure 7.20 shows a cumulative frequency curve for mean daily flows on the River Ribble at Salmesbury in Lancashire. It shows, for example, that the flow exceeds 50 cumecs around 20% of the time, but is less than 10 cumecs around 30% of the time.

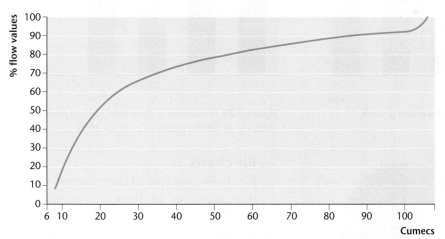

Figure 7.20
Cumulative frequency curve: mean daily flow on the River Ribble at Salmesbury, 2000–05

Bar charts

Bar charts comprise a series of rectangles that are proportional in length and area to the values they represent. They are often used where data relate to discrete places or units of time, for example, the age structures of individual towns or villages, population changes by local authority between two census dates, mean discharge on a river recorded at several gauging stations (Figure 7.21) and so on.

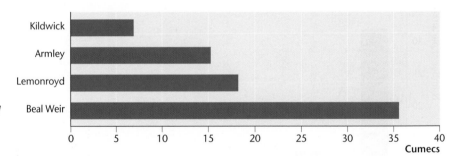

***Figure 7.21** Mean flow on the River Aire at four gauging stations*

Stacked bar charts represent two or more data sets by sub-dividing the bars (Figure 7.22). Where several charts show the same phenomenon (in time or space), shading of sub-groups must be consistent. Stacked bar charts can be used to represent both absolute values and proportions. Figure 7.22 shows graphically the changes in the number of people living in urban areas in MEDCs and LEDCs between 1950 and 2030. It emphasises the huge absolute increase in urban dwellers in LEDCs. Based on the same data, the stacked bar chart in Figure 7.23 gives a better idea of the shifts in the proportion of urban dwellers during this period.

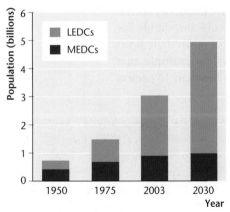

***Figure 7.22** Global urban growth, 1950–2030*

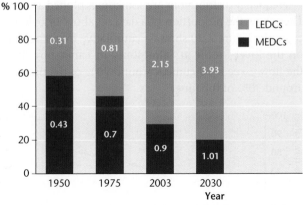

***Figure 7.23** Proportion of the world's urban population (billions) in MEDCs and LEDCs, 1950–2030*

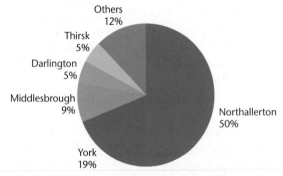

***Figure 7.24** Destination chosen for clothes shopping by Northallerton residents*

Pie charts

Pie charts are a type of circular graph divided into segments to show sub-groups in a population (Figure 7.24). They can be used as an alternative to stacked bar charts. The population is represented by the area of the chart. The first segment in a pie chart normally starts at 12 o'clock. However, the number of sub-groups represented should be limited: with more than seven or eight it becomes difficult to differentiate segmental shading.

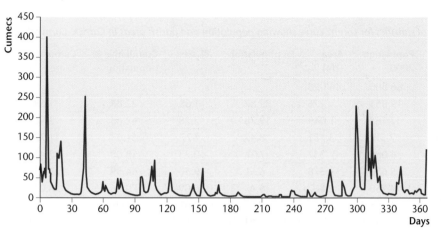

Figure 7.25 Mean daily flow of the River Ribble at Salmesbury, 2005

Line charts

Line charts show continuous changes in variables in time and space, such as population change at yearly intervals and changes in rental values with distance from a city centre. Line charts differ from trend lines because they show actual, rather than average, trends (Figure 7.25).

Lorenz curve

A Lorenz curve describes the inequality in a distribution. Box 7.6 explains how to construct and interpret a Lorenz curve.

Box 7.6 Constructing a Lorenz curve

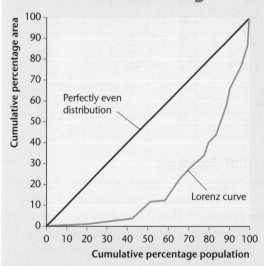

Figure 7.26 Lorenz curve showing population and parish areas in Carrick, Cornwall

Figure 7.26 is a Lorenz curve that plots the population of parishes in the Carrick district in Cornwall, and the area of each parish. Both variables are plotted as cumulative frequencies arranged by the rank order of parish population size. The unevenness of the population distribution is striking. Over half of the district's population occupies just 12% of the land area. The diagonal line in Figure 7.26 represents the situation where there is equality between population and land area (i.e. 10% of the population is found on 10% of the land area, 20% of the population on 20% of the land area and so on). The more the Lorenz curve deviates from the diagonal the greater the unevenness of the population distribution.

The Gini coefficient provides a more precise measure of inequality. It is the ratio of the area between the diagonal and the Lorenz curve, to the total area below the diagonal. The ratio is usually multiplied by 100 and expressed as a percentage. The higher the value of the coefficient the more uneven is the distribution.

Table 7.10 *Derivation of statistics for Lorenz curve showing population and parish areas in Carrick, Cornwall*

Parish	Population 2000	Area (Ha)	% population	% area	Cumulative % population	Cumulative % area
CARRICK DISTRICT	86 800	46 098				
Falmouth	19 855	776	22.87	1.68	22.87	1.68
Truro	17 165	1 049	19.78	2.28	42.65	3.96
St Agnes	7 310	3 581	8.42	7.77	51.07	11.72
Penryn	6 085	337	7.01	0.73	58.08	12.45
Perranzabuloe	5 650	4 378	6.51	9.50	64.59	21.95
Kenwyn	4 750	2 807	5.47	6.09	70.06	28.04
Feock	3 535	1 203	4.07	2.61	74.13	30.65
Mylor	2 545	1 471	2.93	3.19	77.06	33.84
Probus	2 010	2 842	2.32	6.17	79.38	40.01
Perranarworthal	1 630	730	1.88	1.58	81.26	41.59
Chacewater	1 540	1 141	1.77	2.48	83.03	44.07
Ladock	1 525	2 821	1.76	6.12	84.79	50.19
Kea	1 520	2 246	1.75	4.87	86.54	55.06
Gwennap	1 465	1 479	1.69	3.21	88.23	58.27
St Newlyn East	1 465	3 488	1.69	7.57	89.91	65.83
St Clement	1 245	1 298	1.43	2.82	91.35	68.65
Cubert	1 210	1 383	1.39	3.00	92.74	71.65
St Erme	1 200	1 642	1.38	3.56	94.13	75.21
St Just in Roseland	1 130	1 076	1.30	2.33	95.43	77.54
Veryan	950	2 195	1.09	4.76	96.52	82.31
Gerrans	910	1 375	1.05	2.98	97.57	85.29
Tregony	810	717	0.93	1.56	98.50	86.84
St Allen	455	1 480	0.52	3.21	99.03	90.05
Ruanlanihorne	255	927	0.29	2.01	99.32	92.07
St Michael Penkevil	230	1 739	0.26	3.77	99.59	95.84
Cuby	180	936	0.21	2.03	99.79	97.87
Philleigh	175	981	0.20	2.13	100.00	100.00

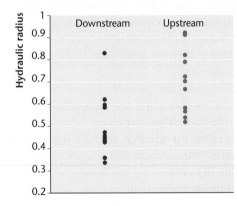

Dispersion diagrams

Dispersion diagrams are single-axis charts which show the distribution of values in small data sets. Figure 7.27 shows the hydraulic radius values at two sites on a small stream in Northumberland. The chart suggests that the stream channel becomes more efficient downstream (i.e. the hydraulic radius increases).

Figure 7.27 *Dispersion diagram showing the hydraulic radius at upstream and downstream sites: Eglingham Burn, Northumberland*

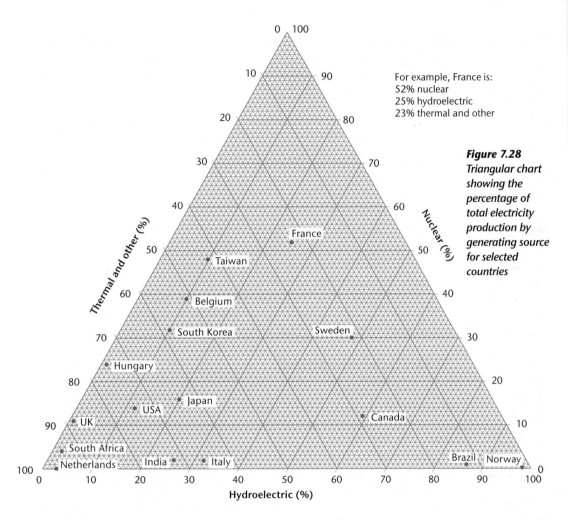

For example, France is:
52% nuclear
25% hydroelectric
23% thermal and other

Figure 7.28
Triangular chart showing the percentage of total electricity production by generating source for selected countries

Triangular charts

Triangular charts are used to plot three percentage values whose sum is 100%. Examples include the proportion of a workforce in primary, secondary and tertiary employment; the proportion of sand, silt and clay in a soil; and the proportion of children, adults and old people in a population. Triangular charts can provide a visual comparison of differences between places (Figure 7.28), as well as changes at a place through time.

Scatter charts

Scatter charts are used to plot two variables, *x* and *y*. Variable *x* is the **independent variable** which causes change in the **dependent variable**, *y*. For example, river discharge can be plotted on a scatter graph against drainage basin area (Figure 7.29). Here, drainage basin area is the independent variable because it influences river discharge. The closer the scatter of points approximates a straight line, the stronger the relationship. In Figure 7.29, the points trend from bottom left to top right

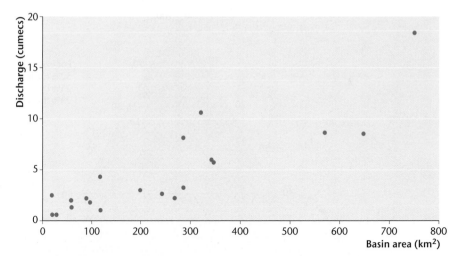

Figure 7.29 Scatter chart showing drainage basin area and river discharge in Northumberland

suggesting that as drainage basin area increases, discharge increases. This is known as a positive relationship. If the points on a scatter chart trend from top left to bottom right, the relationship is negative or inverse. The decline of temperature (y) with altitude (x) is an example of a negative or inverse relationship.

Statistical mapping

Maps are an important means of presenting statistical information. They have particular value because they (a) make it easier to relate data to specific locations, and (b) help to identify geographic trends and patterns more effectively than data tables and charts.

Statistical maps show the spatial distribution of quantitative data. To some extent, however, all statistical maps are a compromise: to achieve visual impact and clarity there is inevitably some loss of detail and accuracy. Effective statistical maps show spatial information clearly and store statistical data that can be retrieved, at least in general form, without undue difficulty.

In this section we shall consider the construction, application and value of five types of statistical map: dot maps, choropleth maps, proportional symbol maps, isoline maps and flow maps.

Figure 7.30 Dot map showing population distribution in mid-Airedale and mid-Wharfedale, 2001 (based on super output areas — middle level)

Dot maps

Dot maps show the location of a given quantity of a variable with a dot of constant size (Figure 7.30).

Dot maps have one great advantage over other statistical maps: they provide information on the distribution of phenomena within areal units. As a result they give us an excellent visual impression of geographical distributions and densities. A further

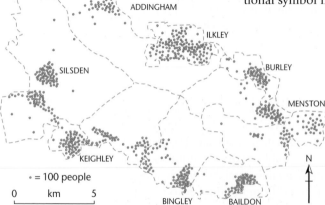

Box 7.7 Constructing dot maps

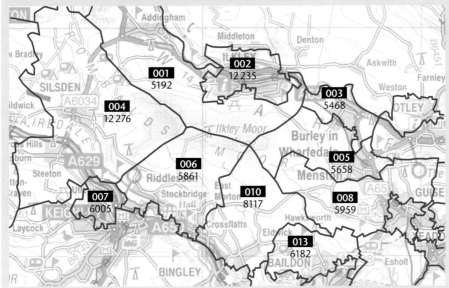

Figure 7.31
Base map for the construction of Figure 7.30, showing the boundaries of super output areas (middle level) and the settlement pattern

1 Source a base map, showing the geographical areal units for which data are aggregated (Figure 7.31). These units could be local authorities, super output areas, wards, parishes etc.
2 Decide on the number of items represented by each dot. Dot values should be small enough to allocate at least a few dots to the areal units of lowest density. In areas of highest density, the dots should just begin to merge.
3 Decide on the size of dots. Dot size will depend partly on the dot value and partly on the scale of the map. If dots are drawn by hand they must be consistent in size and shape.
4 Allocate the appropriate number of dots to each areal unit and plot the dots on the map. The placement of dots must be guided by prior knowledge of the factors that affect the

distribution. For example, a dot map of population distribution will rely heavily on the settlement pattern within areal units. Figure 7.31 shows large spatial variations in population density within some units. In Unit 004, for example, population is largely concentrated in two settlements — Silsden and Steeton. The rest of the area comprises empty moorland.

Care should be taken to place some dots in boundary zones between statistical areas. Within high-density areas such as towns and cities, the dots should be placed randomly (uniform placements should be avoided). In low-density units, the dots should be allocated to areas of known importance.

5 Add a key, title, scale and direction to the map.

advantage is that spatial patterns are not interrupted artificially by the boundaries of areal units. Dot maps are also valuable stores of statistical information. For instance, the approximate populations of the geographical units in Figure 7.30 can be recovered by counting the dots.

However, dot maps also have disadvantages. They are time consuming to draw, partly because a good deal of prior information is needed about the factors that control the geographical distribution. They can also give a misleading impression

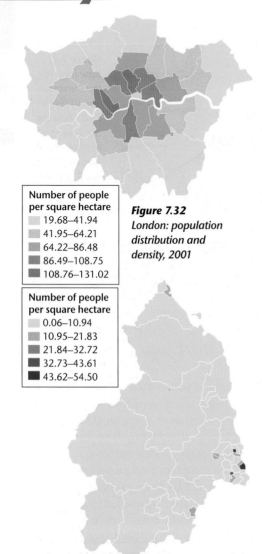

Number of people per square hectare
- 19.68–41.94
- 41.95–64.21
- 64.22–86.48
- 86.49–108.75
- 108.76–131.02

Figure 7.32
London: population distribution and density, 2001

Number of people per square hectare
- 0.06–10.94
- 10.95–21.83
- 21.84–32.72
- 32.73–43.61
- 43.62–54.50

Figure 7.33 Northumberland: population distribution and density, 2001

of accuracy and precision: rarely is the exact location of an occurrence known. Finally, in high-density areas where the dots begin to merge, recovering accurate information may be difficult, while in low-density areas they provide minimal details of the actual distribution.

Choropleth maps

Choropleth maps, also known as proportional shading maps, are the most widely used statistical maps in geography. They show spatial variations in values between areas by colour or shading. Customised choropleth maps are available for the 2001 census for England and Wales at the National Statistics website (www.statistics.gov.uk) (Figure 7.32). Similar customised maps are available for the 2000 US census (www.census.gov) and for the 1999 census of France (www.recensement.insee.fr).

Choropleth maps use standardised data such as ratios, percentages and averages. This is because the number of items in any geographic unit is partly a function of its areal extent. Thus population totals are standardised by area as population densities; age groups are plotted as percentages of the total population; cropland is expressed as a percentage of the total cultivated area; and unemployment as averages.

Choropleth maps are relatively simple to construct and are particularly useful when data are published in bundles for areal units such as super output areas, wards and parishes. Nonetheless, choropleth maps have several weaknesses. First, they tell us nothing about the internal distribution of values within areal units. This is a major limitation, especially where units are large (as in Figure 7.33) and distributions are highly irregular. Second, because areal units often vary enormously in size, large units can have a dominating effect on the appearance of the map (Figure 7.33). Third, the boundaries of areal units often create sudden discontinuities in spatial patterns that are not present in reality. In extreme cases, the distributions shown by choropleth maps may owe more to the arbitrary size and boundaries of areal units than to the actual distributions. In these circumstances choropleth maps are unsatisfactory and you should consider alternative mapping methods.

Proportional symbol maps

The proportional symbols used for mapping are circles, squares, triangles and bars. Proportional symbol maps are based on the principle that the area of each symbol

Box 7.8 Constructing choropleth maps

1 Calculate standardised values (i.e. percentages, densities, averages) for areal units. Record them on a base map which shows the units for which data are available.

2 Divide the data set into classes or groups. A balance between excessive generalisation (too few classes) and too much detail (too many classes) is needed. Too many classes will over-complicate the map and make it difficult to recognise differences in colour or shading. Five or six classes are usually sufficient. However, the final decision may be influenced by factors such as the size and shape of the areal units, and the scale and purpose of the map.

3 Decide on the class intervals. Three methods are available depending on the type of information being mapped: (1) fixed intervals where a data set has meaningful thresholds (e.g. a sex ratio of 1000, zero net migration); (2) intervals designed to reflect natural breaks in the data sets (identified by plotting values as dispersion charts; (3)

fixed intervals based on mathematical relationships (e.g. arithmetic, geometric, logarithmic, percentile, standard deviation). At the simplest level, arithmetic classes are obtained by dividing the range of values by the number of classes. However, this method has problems if the data are skewed: some classes will have large numbers of values and others will have very few. It is important that no single class should occupy too large an area and thus dominate the map (Figure 7.33).

4 Choose a logical system of colouring or shading. Monochrome maps use a gradation of tones from light (low values) to dark (high values). If colours are used, softer colours from the middle part of the spectrum (greens, yellows) represent the lower values, and more striking colours from the opposite ends of the spectrum (reds, purples) represent the higher values.

5 Add a key, title, scale and direction to the map.

is proportional to the value it represents (Figure 7.34). Unlike choropleth maps, proportional symbol maps show absolute (not standardised) values such as population counts, employment and retail floorspace.

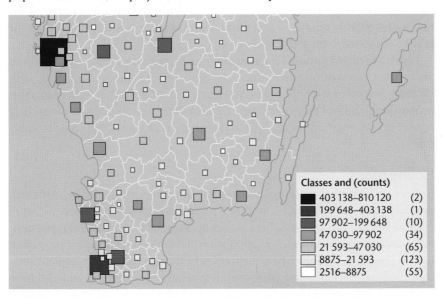

Figure 7.34
Proportional symbol map: population counts by commune in southern Sweden

Classes and (counts)	
403 138–810 120	(2)
199 648–403 138	(1)
97 902–199 648	(10)
47 030–97 902	(34)
21 593–47 030	(65)
8875–21 593	(123)
2516–8875	(55)

Box 7.9 Constructing proportional symbol maps

1 Choose a symbol — a circle, square, triangle or bar.

2 Choose a scale. The largest symbols should not obscure the symbols in adjacent areal units. Overlapping symbols are acceptable in high-density areas, providing their radii (or one side) are visible to allow estimates of values (Figure 7.34). For the population counts for the West Midlands, a scaling factor ($\sqrt{P} \times (10 \div 988.477)$ was used to give the largest circle a radius of 10 mm, and the largest square a 10 mm side.

3 Calculate the area of each symbol. Remember that when proportional circles and squares are used the radius of circles and the sides of the squares vary with the square root of the value represented. Calculations of radii, where the largest circle should be 10 mm in radius, are shown below. If proportional squares are preferred, the sides of the squares are the same as the radii of the circles.

4 Plot the symbols centrally within areal units.

5 Add a key, title, scale and direction to the map.

Metropolitan District	Population (P)	$\sqrt{(P)}$	$\sqrt{(P)} \times (10/988.477)$
Birmingham Metropolitan District	977 087	988.477	10.00 mm
Coventry Metropolitan District	300 848	548.50	5.55 mm
Dudley Metropolitan District	305 155	552.41	5.59 mm
Sandwell Metropolitan District	282 904	531.89	5.38 mm
Solihull Metropolitan District	199 517	446.67	4.52 mm
Walsall Metropolitan District	253 499	505.49	5.11 mm
Wolverhampton Metropolitan District	236 582	486.39	4.92 mm

Proportional symbol maps give an excellent visual impression of geographical distributions. Their impact is clear and immediate. However, the mapping technique has weaknesses. One problem is a tendency to underestimate the values represented by larger symbols. For example, doubling the sides of a square or the radius of a circle increases the area four times, not twice. It is very difficult for the human eye to judge these differences.

Placement of proportional symbols also causes problems when several symbols are concentrated within small areas. The outcome may be overcrowding, with excessive overlap of symbols making interpretation difficult. Finally, because most proportional symbol maps are based on area data, like choropleth maps, they convey no information on the spatial distribution of values within geographic units.

Isoline maps

Isolines (or isopleths) are lines on maps that join places of equal value. Although derived from point measurements, they represent distributions that have a continuous surface. For this reason isolines are not appropriate for representing geographically discrete phenomena such as population and land use. Isolines are most often used in physical geography where they represent surfaces such as atmospheric pressure (isobars), precipitation (isohyets), temperature (isotherms) and elevation (contours). Their use in human geography includes journey times (isochrones)

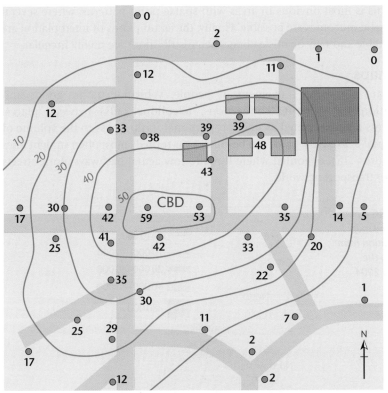

Figure 7.35 *Isoline map of pedestrian densities in a town centre*

and transport costs (isodapanes). In urban geography, land values and rents and pedestrian densities (Figure 7.35) can be represented by isoline maps.

Isoline maps give an excellent overview of spatial patterns, especially for phenomena continuously distributed in space, and where details are not important. However, their construction is more subjective than most other statistical

Box 7.10 Constructing isoline maps

1 The point locations for data sources, or the areal units for data aggregation need to be identified on a base map.

2 Values are plotted as points on the base map.

3 Decide on the number of isolines and their values. Five or six is likely to be sufficient. Larger numbers make drawing impracticable. Generally, the fewer the point values on the map the fewer the isolines. It is conventional to use regular intervals between isolines (e.g. 4-mb intervals between isobars, 10-minute isochrone values). The allocation of values to isolines is

similar to the procedure for defining class boundaries on choropleth maps (see Box 7.8).

4 Fit the isolines by interpolation. Interpolation assumes a constant gradient of change between data point values. For example, if we had to draw a 10 °C isotherm between point values of 11 °C and 9 °C it would pass exactly halfway between them. When drawing isolines you should note that they never cross.

5 Isolines should be numbered and if required, the areas between them layered or shaded.

6 Add a key, title, scale and direction to the map.

maps. This is most obvious in areas with sparse point patterns, where several equally valid outcomes are possible. Finally, the assumptions of interpolation are rarely tenable and may be misleading when distributions are highly irregular.

Flow maps

Flow maps show the movement of people, vehicular traffic, goods and information (e.g. internet connections, telephone calls) between places. Movements are represented as lines proportional in thickness to the volume of flow (Figure 7.36). Flow paths can be either non-routed (most often straight lines as in Figure 7.36), or routed where flows follow actual pathways along streets and other transport networks.

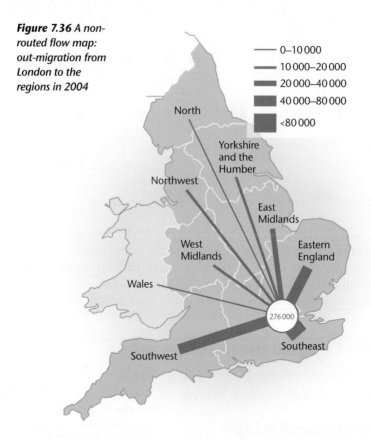

Figure 7.36 *A non-routed flow map: out-migration from London to the regions in 2004*

Flow maps are an effective mapping method for showing the general patterns of movement and interaction between places. However, although visually successful, like other statistical maps, they are highly generalised. Flow categories often cover a wide range of values making it impossible to recover any detailed information. Non-routed flow maps are particularly generalised. Routed flow maps to some extent overcome this problem. For pedestrian and traffic flows the corridors of movement are important. Even so, abrupt changes of flow often occur at count points which may not reflect actual changes on the ground.

Box 7.11 Constructing flow maps

1 A base map is needed showing either the point locations where flows are recorded (e.g. a street plan) or the areal units for data aggregation.

2 Decide on the number of flow classes and the interval between classes. Usually five or six classes are sufficient. Class intervals may be arithmetic or geometric, but must cover all values. Ideally there will be no empty classes (Box 7.8).

3 Select a suitable scale for line widths. Line width will depend on the scale of the map and the flow values. Widths will be proportional to flow volumes. On non-routed maps the need to avoid flows which overlap may also influence line widths.

4 Draw the flows to scale and shade them with a single colour. In order to emphasise the flows, where maps are computer drawn, the base map may be muted.

5 Add a key, title, scale and direction to the map.

Analysis and interpretation of data

Key ideas

➤ A successful geographical investigation involves a variety of analytical approaches.

➤ Patterns and trends in data presentation should be described.

➤ Where appropriate, statistical analysis of data should be undertaken.

➤ Results should be interpreted in relation to original questions/hypotheses.

➤ Explanations of anomalous results should be given.

Statistical methods can be divided into two groups: **descriptive** statistics such as the mean and standard deviation, and **inferential** (analytical) statistics which test difference and correlation.

Descriptive statistics

We have seen how tables and charts can be used to describe data sets. However, we often need to summarise a data set more succinctly with a single numerical value. We can do this by using measures of central tendency and dispersion.

Measures of central tendency

Measures of central tendency represent data sets by a middle value around which the other values cluster. There are three standard measures of central tendency: the arithmetic mean (or average), the median and the principal mode.

Arithmetic mean

The arithmetic mean is the sum of values in a data set divided by the total number of values. In statistical notation the mean is shown thus:

$$\bar{x} = \sum(x) \div n$$

Table 7.11 *Mean monthly rainfall at Oban and Cotonou (Benin)*

Month	Oban	Cotonou
J	146	33
F	109	33
M	83	117
A	90	125
M	72	254
J	87	366
J	120	89
A	116	38
S	141	66
O	169	135
N	146	38
D	172	13
Mean	120.9	108.9
Median	118	63.5

Box 7.12
Statistical notation

Many statistical formulae use the capital sigma symbol, Σ. It means that you should sum the values in a data set. If we need to specify which values we need to sum we attach additional notation to Σ.

$$\sum_{i=1}^{10}(x)$$

The above notation tells us to sum all values of x, starting at the first value ($i = 1$) and finishing at the tenth value. If $i = 1$ were replaced by $i = 3$ then we would start summing from the third value.

where $\bar{x}$ = arithmetic mean; x is a value in a data set; n is the number of values in a data set; and $\sum(x)$ is the instruction to sum all values of x.

The mean is the most widely used measure of central tendency and the only one based on mathematical principles. As we shall see, it figures prominently in many other statistical calculations. However, the mean is not always the most appropriate measure of central tendency. Everything depends on the nature of the data set. Because the mean weights each value according to its magnitude, different distributions can give similar mean values. Table 7.11 shows that Oban (Scotland) and Cotonou (Benin) have similar mean monthly rainfall values. Despite this, the monthly rainfall values are very different, the monthly range of values being more than three times greater at Cotonou.

Generally the mean provides an accurate summary where data have a normal distribution and a narrow range of values. Thus when distributions are skewed by a number of exceptional high or low values, the mean is often unrepresentative of the data set.

Median

The median is the middle value in a data set ranked in order of size. Thus in a data set comprising 21 values the median is the 11th ranked value. Where a data set has an even number of values, the median is the average of the middle two values (in Table 7.11 this would be the sixth and seventh ranked values). Unlike the mean, the median gives equal weight to each value. As a result it is a more representative measure than the mean for data sets that are skewed. However, the median has weaknesses. Even more than the mean, wildly different data sets can give similar median values. Moreover, having no true mathematical properties, the median cannot be used in any further statistical calculations.

Principal mode

The principal mode is the class in a histogram (or frequency table) that contains the most values. It is useful when classes are described nominally. For example,

Powers' roundness chart classifies river sediments into six categories: very angular, angular, sub-angular, sub-rounded, rounded and well-rounded. Changes in sediment roundness can be described by the mode at successive downstream locations.

Overall, the principal mode is the least useful measure of central tendency. Where numerical classes are used, the principal mode has a range of values rather than a single value, while distributions which are bi-modal cause particular confusion. Finally, the value of the principal mode depends entirely on the arbitrary choice of class intervals.

Measures of dispersion

Although measures of central tendency summarise data sets with a single value, they tell us nothing about the dispersion of values. Measures of dispersion, such as the **range**, **inter-quartile range** and the **standard deviation** do this.

Range

The range is the difference between the highest and lowest values in a data set. In Table 7.11, Oban's range of mean monthly rainfall is 100 mm exactly whereas Cotonou's is 353 mm. The main limitation of the range is that it uses just two values in a data set.

Inter-quartile range

The inter-quartile range is more representative, being based on half the values in a data set. It is used alongside the median as a statement of dispersion. To find the inter-quartile range we first arrange the data in rank order of size. The median is defined by dividing the data set in half. Each half is then split into four equal parts known as **quartiles**. The boundary for the upper 25% of values is known as the **upper quartile**: the boundary which marks the lowest 25% of values is the **lower quartile**. The difference between the upper quartile and lower quartile is the inter-quartile range.

Standard deviation

The standard deviation, also known as the root mean square deviation, is the most useful measure of dispersion. Its calculation incorporates all the values in a data set. The standard deviation is also used in many other statistical measures such as the students' *t* test correlation (see p. 305). The formula for the standard deviation is:

$$\sigma = \sqrt{\sum(x - \bar{x})^2 \div n}$$

σ = standard deviation
x = each value in the data set
$\bar{x}$ = mean of data set
n = number of values in the data set

The standard deviation has a precise relationship with data sets which follow a normal frequency distribution. For these distributions 68.27% of the area below the frequency curve (Figure 7.37) lies between plus or minus one standard deviation of the mean. Two standard deviations account for 95.45% of the area below the curve.

Box 7.13 Calculating the standard deviation for discharge of the River Brock, Lancashire

***Table 7.12** Mean annual discharge (cumecs), River Brock, 1979–2005*

Year	x	$x - \bar{x}$	$(x - \bar{x})^2$	Year	x	$x - \bar{x}$	$(x - \bar{x})^2$
1979	0.987	0.128	0.0164	1994	0.849	−0.010	0.0001
1980	1.371	0.512	0.2621	1995	0.554	−0.305	0.0930
1981	1.315	0.456	0.2079	1996	0.488	−0.371	0.1376
1982	0.948	0.089	0.0079	1997	0.72	−0.139	0.0193
1983	0.939	0.080	0.0064	1998	1.005	0.146	0.0213
1984	0.877	0.018	0.0003	1999	0.797	−0.062	0.0038
1985	0.913	0.054	0.0029	2000	1.217	0.358	0.1282
1986	1.027	0.168	0.0282	2001	0.799	−0.060	0.0036
1987	1.002	0.143	0.0204	2002	0.92	0.061	0.0037
1988	0.93	0.071	0.0050	2003	0.592	−0.267	0.0713
1989	0.568	−0.291	0.0847	2004	0.886	0.027	0.0007
1990	0.668	−0.191	0.0365	2005	0.644	−0.215	0.0462
1991	0.655	−0.204	0.0416	mean =	0.859	$\sum(x - \bar{x})^2 =$	1.2811
1992	0.841	−0.018	0.0003			$\sum(x - \bar{x})^2 \div n =$	0.0474
1993	0.682	−0.177	0.0313			$\sqrt{\sum(x - \bar{x})^2 \div n} =$	0.218

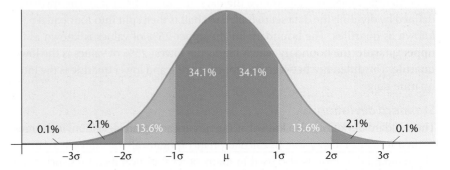

***Figure 7.37** The normal frequency distribution and the standard deviation*

To convert a value into a unit of standard deviation (known as the **standard deviate**) we subtract the mean and then divide by the standard deviation:

standard deviate = (value − mean) ÷ standard deviation

The standard deviate is often represented by 'z' and is referred to as a 'z value'. For example, to estimate the likelihood that the average annual flow on the River Brock in any one year will exceed 1 cumec we first calculate the standard deviate and then find the probability in tables of the normal deviate (Figure 7.38).

standard deviate = (1 − 0.859) ÷ 0.218 = 0.647

According to Figure 7.38, 0.647 (0.65) corresponds to a probability of 0.242 or 24.2%

Table of the standard normal (z) distribution

z	0.00	0.01	0.02	0.03	0.04	0.05	0.06	0.07	0.08	0.09
0.0	0.0000	0.0040	0.0080	0.0120	0.0160	0.0199	0.0239	0.0279	0.0319	0.0359
0.1	0.0398	0.0438	0.0478	0.0517	0.0557	0.0596	0.0636	0.0675	0.0714	0.0753
0.2	0.0793	0.0832	0.0871	0.0910	0.0948	0.0987	0.1026	0.1064	0.1103	0.1141
0.3	0.1179	0.1217	0.1255	0.1293	0.1331	0.1368	0.1406	0.1443	0.1480	0.1517
0.4	0.1554	0.1591	0.1628	0.1664	0.1700	0.1736	0.1772	0.1808	0.1844	0.1879
0.5	0.1915	0.1950	0.1985	0.2019	0.2054	0.2088	0.2123	0.2157	0.2190	0.2224
0.6	0.2257	0.2291	0.2324	0.2357	0.2389	0.2422	0.2454	0.2486	0.2517	0.2549
0.7	0.2580	0.2611	0.2642	0.2673	0.2704	0.2734	0.2764	0.2794	0.2823	0.2852
0.8	0.2881	0.2910	0.2939	0.2967	0.2995	0.3023	0.3051	0.3078	0.3106	0.3133
0.9	0.3159	0.3186	0.3212	0.3238	0.3264	0.3289	0.3315	0.3340	0.3365	0.3389
1.0	0.3413	0.3438	0.3461	0.3485	0.3508	0.3531	0.3554	0.3577	0.3599	0.3621
1.1	0.3643	0.3665	0.3686	0.3708	0.3729	0.3749	0.3770	0.3790	0.3810	0.3830
1.2	0.3849	0.3869	0.3888	0.3907	0.3925	0.3944	0.3962	0.3980	0.3997	0.4015
1.3	0.4032	0.4049	0.4066	0.4082	0.4099	0.4115	0.4131	0.4147	0.4162	0.4177
1.4	0.4192	0.4207	0.4222	0.4236	0.4251	0.4265	0.4279	0.4292	0.4306	0.4319
1.5	0.4332	0.4345	0.4357	0.4370	0.4382	0.4394	0.4406	0.4418	0.4429	0.4441

Figure 7.38
Normal
deviate
tables

Coefficient of variation

The value of the standard deviation is strongly influenced by the magnitude of the mean. This is a problem when comparing dispersion in two different data sets with very different means. We overcome this problem by using the coefficient of variation. This standardised measure expresses the standard deviation as a percentage of the mean.

coefficient of variation = $[\delta \div \bar{x}] \times 100$

For example, in Table 7.13 the River Coquet has a larger standard deviation that the River Brock mainly because it has an average flow that is ten times greater. However, when we use the coefficient of variation, which standardises dispersion against the mean values, we see that the River Brock has a slightly higher flow variability than the River Coquet.

Table 7.13 *Variability of flow of the Rivers Brock and Coquet, 1979–2005*

	Mean flow (cumecs)	Standard deviation (cumecs)	Coefficient of variation (%)
River Brock at Bilsborrow, Lancashire	0.859	0.218	25.38
River Coquet at Morwick, Northumberland	8.587	1.981	23.06

Inferential statistics

Inferential statistics get their name because they are used to infer population values from sample values. This leads us to the concept of **statistical significance** and the probability that the outcomes of investigations based on sample data are due to chance. Normally any outcome which yields a significance level of 0.05 (or 95%) and above is accepted as being statistically significant (Table 7.14).

Table 7.14
*Statistical
significance*

Significance level	% significance	Probability that out-come due to chance	Statistically significant
0.001	99.9	1 in 1000	Significant
0.01	99	1 in 100	
0.025	97.5	1 in 40	
0.05	95	1 in 20	
0.1	90	1 in 10	Not significant
0.2	80	1 in 8	
0.3	70	1 in 7	

In this section we shall look at the following inferential statistics: standard error of the mean, students' *t* test, Mann–Whitney U test, chi-squared test, Spearman rank correlation and simple regression.

Box 7.14 One-tailed and two-tailed significance tests

Tests of statistical significance may be either one-tailed or two-tailed. When a hypothesis states the direction of the difference or relationship, we use a one-tailed test. For example, a one-tailed test would be used to investigate the hypothesis that particles at the foot of a scree slope are larger than particles at the top. This hypothesis predicts the direction of the difference. A two-tailed test would simply investigate the difference in particle sizes at the top and bottom of the slope. The hypothesis is more general and does not state the direction of the difference. Probabilities for one-tailed tests are exactly half the value of probabilities for two-tailed tests.

Standard error of the mean

The standard error is used to assess the value of the population mean from sample data sets. It is defined as the standard deviation of the sampling distribution of the mean.

$$\sigma_M = \frac{\sigma}{\sqrt{n}}$$

where σ_M is the standard deviation of the sample and *n* is the sample size.

The logic of the standard error is that if you took a large number of samples from a population, calculated the mean for each sample and then plotted them as a frequency curve, they would follow a normal distribution. The standard deviation of this **sampling distribution** is known as the **standard error of the mean**.

The standard error enables us to estimate the limits of the population mean. This is because its relationship to the sampling distribution is the same as standard deviation to the normal frequency distribution. In other words, approximately 68% of values lie within one standard error of the mean, 95% are within two standard errors and so on.

An example of the calculation of the standard error of the mean is shown in Table 7.15. Assume that we want to estimate the average size of scree particles on a talus slope from a random sample of 24 particles. The sample mean is 10.77 cm and the sample standard deviation is 5.11 cm.

standard error of sample mean $(\sigma_M) = \dfrac{5.11}{\sqrt{24}} = 1.04\,\text{cm}$

Substituting values in the standard error formula gives us a standard error of the mean of 1.043. We know that at the 95% confidence level the population mean lies between plus and minus two standard errors. Thus with 95% probability the population mean will be 10.77 +/− (2 × 1.043) or between 8.60 cm and 12.84 cm.

It is worth noting that the precision of the standard error is related to the square of the sample size. Thus to double the accuracy of the standard error in our example, from 1.04 cm to 0.502 cm, would require a four-fold increase in sample size. This relationship has an important bearing on decisions concerning sample size and the desired level of precision in estimating the population mean.

Table 7.15 Particle size (cm — median axis): scree slope at Austwick

12	5	5.5	8	11
30	7	10	9	12
16	9.5	12	11	9.5
9	6	15	8	10
13	13	11	6	
Sample mean = 10.77		Sample standard deviation = 5.11		

Standard error of the percentage

The standard error of the percentage is often used when estimating the proportions of land-use types in an area from samples. When analysing percentages or proportions it is necessary to modify the formula for estimating the standard error of the mean. The formula for calculating the standard error of the percentage is:

$$\sqrt{(p\% \times q\%) \div n}$$

where p is the percentage of a given land-use type, q is the remaining percentage (i.e. all other uses), and n is the size of the sample.

Box 7.15 Calculating the standard error of the percentage

A systematic point sample of a 1:25 000 land-use map in the North Downs in Kent gave the following results:

Table 7.16 Results of systematic point sample of 1:25 000 land-use map

Land-use type	% land use (p)	Number of sample points (n)	Standard error %
Grassland	13.8	67	4.21
Arable land	33.5	161	3.72
Woodland	24.4	118	3.95
Market gardening	8.0	39	4.34
Others	20.3	98	4.06

Standard error of the percentage for grassland:

$$\sqrt{(13.8 \times 86.2) \div 67} = 4.21\%$$

Thus with 68% confidence, the actual percentage of grassland in the area is 13.8 +/−4.21%

Testing the differences between data sets

Many hypotheses in geographical investigation focus on the differences between samples. A number of tests are available to determine whether the differences between data sets are statistically significant or simply due to chance. Three widely used tests of difference are the students' t test, the Mann–Whitney U test and the chi-squared test.

Students' t test

The students' t test compares the arithmetic means of two samples to determine the likelihood that any difference could have occurred by chance. Unlike most other inferential tests used in geographical investigation, students' t is a **parametric** test. This means that it should only be applied where samples are derived from populations that have a normal frequency distribution (see Box 7.16).

Mann–Whitney U test

The Mann–Whitney U test, like the t test, measures the difference between two data sets. However, unlike the t test, it is a non-parametric test. This means that it is distribution-free and makes no assumptions about the normality of the population from which sample data are drawn. In geographical investigation, where so many statistical populations are skewed, this flexibility is especially valuable.

The U test has other advantages. It can be applied to small data sets, data measured on an ordinal (or rank order) scale and to data sets containing unequal numbers of values. However, as the non-parametric equivalent of the t test, the U test can only be applied to two data sets (see Box 7.17).

Chi-squared test

Chi-squared is used to determine whether an observed frequency distribution differs significantly from the frequencies that might be expected if the distribution were random. Like the U test, chi-squared is a non-parametric test (see Box 7.18).

There are two versions of the chi-squared test: a one-sample version and a test for two or more sample distributions. Both tests are only appropriate where the following conditions apply:

➤ Data are in frequencies (i.e. counts for individual cells). The test is invalid for values given in percentages or proportions.
➤ There should not be many categories for which expected frequencies are small. For example, when there are more than two categories no more than one-fifth of expected frequencies should have values of less than five, and none should be less than one.

Two-sample chi-squared

The requirements for this version of the chi-squared test are similar to the one-sample version. However, it is important to note that there are few categories where expected values are less than 5. This requirement is often met by merging some categories and accepting a higher level of generalisation. Box 7.19 (page 308) shows the method for calculating the two-sample chi-squared statistic.

Box 7.16 Calculating students' *t*

Hypotheses

1 Birth rates are higher in rural than in urban parishes in Sweden in 1875 (one-tailed test).
2 There were significant differences in birth rates between rural and urban parishes in Sweden in 1975 (two-tailed test).
3 Rural parishes:
   $\bar{x}_r$ (mean) = 31.73
   s_r (standard deviation) = 3.47
   n_r (sample size) = 11
4 Urban parishes:
   $\bar{x}_u$ (mean) = 26.82
   s_u (standard deviation) = 3.97
   n_u (sample size) = 11
5 *t* test formula:
$$t = \bar{x}_r - \bar{x}_u \div \sqrt{(s_r^2 \div n_r) + (s_u^2 \div n_u)}$$
$$t = 31.73 - 26.82 \div \sqrt{(3.42^2 \div 11) + (3.97^2 \div 11)}$$
$$= 3.09$$

Table 7.17 Crude birth rates (per 1000) in central Sweden, c.1875

Rural parishes		Urban parishes	
Härjerad	29	Vänersborg	30
Fyrunga	32	Borås	29
Ving	29	Allingsås	26
Flo	31	Amal	27
Karaby	29	Ulricehamn	23
Längjum	33	Mariestad	23
Frammestad	28	Lidköping	24
Vara	40	Skara	24
Längjum-med-Vessby	34	Skövde	29
Lundby	30	Falköping	36
Bitterna	34	Hjo	24

Reference to statistical tables of the *t* distribution (Figure 7.39) determines the statistical significance of *t* (i.e. the likelihood that the sample difference in birth rates reflects a real difference in the population). The value of *t* (3.09) is checked against an estimate of sample size known as **degrees of freedom**. More specifically, degrees of freedom are the number of observations that are free to vary to produce a known outcome. In this instance the mean birth rate for rural areas has 10 degrees of freedom because the values for ten parishes can vary, but the eleventh is fixed. Thus we have in total $n_r - 1 + n_u - 1 = 20$ degrees of freedom for rural and urban samples. The **critical value** of *t* at the 0.01 level for 20 degrees for a two-tailed test in Figure 7.39 is 2.85. As our *t* value exceeds the critical value, the difference is significant at the 0.01 (i.e. 1 in 100) level. In other words, there is only a 1 in 100 probability that the difference in birth rates between rural and urban parishes is due to chance. (NB: the *t* value is also significant at the 0.01 level for the one-tailed test.)

Degrees of freedom	Significance level (one-tailed)				
	0.05	0.025	0.01	0.005	0.0005
	Significance level (two-tailed)				
	0.10	0.05	0.02	0.01	0.001
1	6.314	12.71	31.82	63.66	636.62
2	2.920	4.303	6.965	9.925	31.599
3	2.353	3.182	4.541	5.841	12.924
4	2.132	2.776	3.747	4.604	8.610
5	2.015	2.571	3.365	4.032	6.869
6	1.943	2.447	3.143	3.707	5.959
7	1.895	2.365	2.998	3.499	5.408
8	1.860	2.306	2.896	3.355	5.041
9	1.833	2.262	2.821	3.250	4.781
10	1.812	2.228	2.764	3.169	4.587
11	1.796	2.201	2.718	3.106	4.437
12	1.782	2.179	2.681	3.055	4.318
13	1.771	2.160	2.650	3.012	4.221
14	1.761	2.145	2.624	2.977	4.140
15	1.753	2.131	2.602	2.947	4.073
16	1.746	2.120	2.583	2.921	4.015
17	1.740	2.110	2.567	2.898	3.965
18	1.734	2.101	2.552	2.878	3.922
19	1.729	2.093	2.539	2.861	3.883
20	1.725	2.086	2.528	2.845	3.850
21	1.721	2.080	2.518	2.831	3.819
22	1.717	2.074	2.508	2.819	3.792
23	1.714	2.069	2.500	2.807	3.768
24	1.711	2.064	2.492	2.797	3.745
25	1.708	2.060	2.485	2.787	3.725
26	1.706	2.056	2.479	2.779	3.707
27	1.703	2.052	2.473	2.771	3.690
28	1.701	2.048	2.467	2.763	3.674
29	1.699	2.045	2.462	2.756	3.659
30	1.697	2.042	2.457	2.750	3.646
40	1.684	2.021	2.423	2.704	3.551
60	1.671	2.000	2.390	2.660	3.460
80	1.664	1.990	2.374	2.639	3.416
100	1.660	1.984	2.364	2.626	3.390

Reject H_0 if calculated value of *t* is **greater than** critical value at chosen significance level.

Figure 7.39 Students' t distribution

Box 7.17 Calculating the U statistic

Hypothesis

There are significant differences in the value of land per acre between larger and smaller farms in Haslingden in 1769 (two-tailed test).

1 Arrange the values in the two data sets in rank order of size for both samples together.
2 Where values are tied the mean ranking is used. For example, if a data set comprises five values – 18, 23, 25, 25, 27 – the rank order would be 1, 2, 3.5, 3.5, 5. If the fifth value were also 25, then the ranking would be 1, 2, 4, 4, 4.
3 Sum the rank values for each of the data sets separately and then calculate the U statistic from the following equations:

Equation 1
$$U = n_x \times n_y + \left(\frac{n_x(n_x + 1)}{2}\right) - \Sigma r_x$$

Equation 2
$$U = n_x \times n_y + \left(\frac{n_y(n_y + 1)}{2}\right) - \Sigma r_y$$

where n_x and n_y are the number of values in data sets x and y, and Σr_x and Σr_y are the sums of the rank values in data sets x and y.

The smaller of the two values for U is used in statistical tables to estimate significance (Figure 7.40). Unlike other inferential tests, U is significant if it is *less than* the critical value listed in the tables. You can check the accuracy of your calculations because the sum of the two U values should equal the product of n_x and n_y.

The value of U value from Equation 1 is:
$$15 \times 15 + \left(\frac{15(15+1)}{2}\right) - 286.5 = 58.5$$

The value of U value from Equation 2 is:
$$15 \times 15 + \left(\frac{15(15+1)}{2}\right) - 178.5 = 166.5$$

To determine the significance of the U value (58.5) in Box 7.17 we refer to U tables (Figure 7.40). These show that the critical value of U at the 0.025 level (for a two-tailed test) when n_x and n_y are both 15, is 64. Because our U value is less than the critical value we conclude that it is statistically significant at the 0.025 level. In other words, we can be 97.5% confident that our sample difference reflects a real difference in the value of farmland on small and large farms in the Haslingden area in 1769.

Sample X: farms >25 acres		Sample Y: farms <25 acres	
	Rank		Rank
1.46	9.5	1.14	22
0.77	27	1.92	3
0.25	29.5	1.21	18
0.84	26	2.05	2
1.31	15	1.44	12
0.74	28	1.81	4
0.25	29.5	1.04	24
1.03	25	1.15	21
1.34	13	1.66	7
1.11	23	1.69	5.5
1.19	19	1.16	20
1.69	5.5	2.12	1
1.46	9.5	1.25	17
1.27	16	1.56	8
1.45	11	1.38	14
	$\Sigma r_x = 286.5$		$\Sigma r_y = 178.5$

Table 7.18 Farm sizes and land values in Haslingden, Lancashire in 1769 (£ per acre)

Statistical table of U values

		n_y													
		2	3	4	5	6	7	8	9	10	11	12	13	14	15
	2	0	0	0	0	0	0	0	0	0	0	1	1	1	1
	3	0	0	0	1	1	2	2	3	3	4	4	5	5
	4	0	0	0	1	2	3	4	4	5	6	7	8	9	10
	5	0	0	1	2	3	5	6	7	8	9	11	12	13	14
	6	0	1	2	3	5	6	8	10	11	13	14	16	17	19
	7	0	1	3	5	6	8	10	12	14	16	18	20	22	24
n_x	8	0	2	4	6	8	10	13	15	17	19	22	24	26	29
	9	0	2	4	7	10	12	15	17	20	23	26	28	31	34
	10	0	3	5	8	11	14	17	20	23	26	29	30	36	39
	11	0	3	6	9	13	16	19	23	26	30	33	37	40	44
	12	1	4	7	11	14	18	22	26	29	33	37	41	45	49
	13	1	4	8	12	16	20	24	28	30	37	41	45	50	54
	14	1	5	9	13	17	22	26	31	36	40	45	50	55	59
	15	1	5	10	14	19	24	29	34	39	44	49	54	59	64

Reject H_0 if calculated value is **less than or equal to** critical value at chosen significance level.

Figure 7.40 Statistical tables of U values

Box 7.18 Calculating a one-sample chi-squared

Hypothesis

The distribution of bracken shows a preference for steeper slopes (one-tailed).

A study of the distribution of bracken on Muggleswick Common, an area of moorland in County Durham, suggested a relationship between slope angle and frequency of occurrence.

The question is whether the distribution of bracken simply reflects frequency of slope angles on the moor, or whether the plant shows a preference for particular slopes. If we assume the distribution is random we can generate an expected distribution based on the frequency of slopes. Thus, 44% of bracken samples (i.e. 14.52) will occur in the slope class 0–6.9°, 12.54 in class 7–13.9°, and 5.94 in the class of more than 13.9°. Our expected distribution looks very different from the observed distribution.

The formula for calculating the chi-squared statistic is:

$$\sum ((O - E)^2 \div E)$$

The final step is to find the significance of the chi-squared from statistical tables (Figure 7.41). Degrees of freedom are obtained by multiplying the number of columns (k) minus one, by the number of rows (r) minus one. In this example,

df	0.10	0.05	0.01	0.005	0.001
1	2.71	3.84	6.63	7.88	10.83
2	4.61	5.99	9.21	10.60	13.82
3	6.25	7.81	11.34	12.84	16.27
4	7.78	9.49	13.23	14.86	18.47
5	9.24	11.07	15.09	16.75	20.51
6	10.64	12.53	16.81	13.55	22.46
7	12.02	14.07	18.48	20.28	24.32
8	13.36	15.51	20.09	21.95	26.12
9	14.68	16.92	21.67	23.59	27.83
10	15.99	18.31	23.21	25.19	29.59
11	17.29	19.68	24.72	26.76	31.26
12	18.55	21.03	26.22	28.30	32.91
13	19.81	22.36	27.69	29.82	34.53
14	21.06	23.68	29.14	31.32	36.12
15	22.31	25.00	30.58	32.80	37.70

Figure 7.41 *Chi-squared tables*

with three columns and two rows there are (3–1)(2–1) or 2 degrees of freedom. The chi-squared tables show that at the 95% confidence level with two degrees of freedom the critical value of chi-squared is 5.99. Our chi-squared value exceeds the critical value, which means that it is statistically significant (in fact it is significant at the 0.001 level). Thus we can assume that bracken is not randomly distributed on the moorland and appears to show a preference for steeper (and therefore better drained) slopes.

Slope classes (°)	% area occupied by each slope category	Number of quadrats dominated by bracken
0–6.9	44	4
7–13.9	38	18
>13.9	18	11

Table 7.19 *Slope angle and bracken distribution on Muggleswick Common*

	0–6.9°	7–13.9°	>13.9°
Observed (O)	4	18	11
Expected (E)	14.52	12.54	5.94
(O – E)	–10.52	5.46	5.06
(O – E)²	110.7	29.8	25.6
(O – E)² ÷ E	7.62	2.38	4.31

$\sum((O - E)^2 \div E) = 7.62 + 2.38 + 4.31 = \mathbf{14.31}$

Table 7.20 *Observed and expected distribution of bracken on Muggleswick Common*

Box 7.19 Calculating the two-sample chi-squared

Most towns and cities grow outwards from their historic core. As a result, the fabric of the urban environment gets newer with distance from the centre. This idea is illustrated in Table 7.21. It shows how in Preston in 1910, the distribution of cotton mills built before and after 1845 varied with distance from the town centre.

Hypothesis
The ages of mills decrease with distance from the town centre

	Age of mills	A 0–1 km	B 1.1–2 km	C 2.1–3 km	Σr
1	Pre 1845	12	26	4	42
2	Post 1845	2	21	18	41
	Σk	14	47	22	83

Table 7.21 Age of cotton mills in Preston in 1910 and distance from the town centre

1 Sum the row values, column values and the total number of values in the data set.
2 Calculate the expected frequencies for each cell by multiplying its row value by its column value and dividing by the total number of values (Table 7.22). For example, the expected value for cell A1 in Table 7.21 is: $(14 \times 42) \div 83 = 7.08$; B1 $= (47 \times 42) \div 83 = 23.78$.
3 Substitute the expected values for each cell in the chi-squared formula and sum the results:

$$\Sigma((O - E)^2 \div E)$$

Table 7.22 Calculating expected frequencies

$(42 \times 14) \div 83 = 7.08$	$(47 \times 42) \div 83 = 23.78$	$(22 \times 42) \div 83 = 11.13$
$(14 \times 41) \div 83 = 6.92$	$(47 \times 41) \div 83 = 23.22$	$(22 \times 41) \div 83 = 10.87$

Chi-squared $= (12 - 7.08)^2 \div 7.08 + (26 - 23.78)^2 \div 23.78 + (4 - 11.13)^2 \div 11.13 + (2 - 6.92)^2 \div 6.92 + (21 - 23.22)^2 \div 23.22 + (1 - 10.87)^2 \div 10.87 = 16.59$.

The significance of the chi-squared value is checked in statistical tables (see Figure 7.41) against $(k{-}1)(r{-}1)$ degrees of freedom — in this example 2 degrees, where k is the number of columns and r is the number of rows. The critical value for chi-squared at the 0.001 level with 2 degrees of freedom is 13.82. As our value exceeds the critical value we accept it as statistically significant. Thus we can accept the hypothesis that the age of mills declines with distance from the centre of Preston in 1910.

Testing relationships between data sets
Correlation

Correlation measures the statistical association between two variables, x and y. It is used to determine how variations in x influence y. Variable x is known as the **independent variable** and is responsible for changes in the **dependent variable**, y.

Although the relationships in Table 7.23 are clear, identifying independent and dependent variables is not always straightforward. For example, does the volume of pedestrian flow in a high street explain the types of shops found there, or do the shops themselves influence flows? Do wave types influence beach gradients or vice versa?

There are several measures of statistical correlation. We shall concentrate on two: Spearman's rank correlation, and Pearson's product moment correlation. Both tests require two variables arranged in paired values and assume that one variable (*x*) influences change in the other variable (*y*). The strength of the relationship between the two variables is measured by a correlation coefficient.

Correlation coefficients

Correlation coefficients measure the strength of a relationship or association between two variables, *x* and *y*. They vary on a scale from +1 to −1, where +1 is a perfect positive correlation and −1 a perfect negative or inverse correlation (Figures 7.42 (a) and (b)). A correlation coefficient close to zero suggests little or no relationship (Figure 7.42 (c)).

Spearman rank correlation

Spearman rank correlation is a non-parametric test. It thus belongs to the same group of statistical tests as chi-squared and the U test and has the advantage of being distribution-free.

Pearson's product moment correlation

Pearson's product moment correlation is an alternative to the Spearman rank correlation test. Its outcome is a coefficient of correlation that has exactly the same properties as the Spearman rank correlation coefficient. Because Pearson's correlation is a parametric test it should only be used when sample data are drawn from a statistical population that has a normal distribution. Calculation of the Pearson product moment coefficient can be lengthy. However, this standard test is available in Excel (see Box 7.21, p. 311).

Table 7.23 *Examples of independent and dependent variable relationships*

Independent variable (*x*)	Dependent variable (*y*)
Altitude	Temperature
Drainage basin area	Stream discharge
Gradient	Velocity of stream flow
Distance	Number of commuters
Types of beach sediment	Beach gradient
Slope angle	Frequency of terracettes

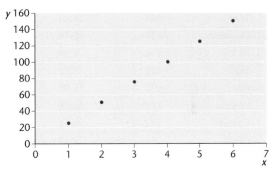

***Figure 7.42** (a) Perfect positive correlation: +1*

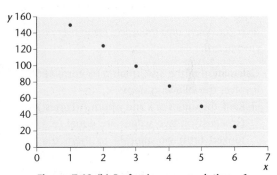

***Figure 7.42** (b) Perfect inverse correlation: −1*

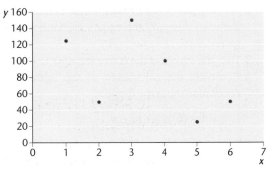

***Figure 7.42** (c) Weak correlation: 0–0.2*

Box 7.20 Calculating the Spearman rank correlation

The Spearman rank correlation, like the U test, is calculated from ordinal rather than ratio or interval data. This means that the original data are arranged in rank order of magnitude and the calculation is based on the rank values.

Table 7.24 *River catchment area and mean river discharge*

River	Catchment area (km²), x	Mean discharge (cumecs), y	Rank x	Rank y	Rank difference (d) between x and y	Difference squared (d^2)
Aln	205	2.42	10	9	1	1
Skerne	250	1.59	9	11	−2	4
Tees	1264	18.84	2	1	1	1
Derwent	1634	16.46	1	2	−1	1
Nidd	516	8.54	4	5	−1	1
Skell	120	1.52	11	12	−1	1
Aire	692	15.07	3	3	0	0
Wharfe	443	13.79	5	4	1	1
Calder	342	8.52	7	6	1	1
Greta	86	2.27	12	10	2	4
Coquet	346	5.68	6	7	−1	1
Wansbeck	287	3.24	8	8	0	0

$$\sum d^2 = 16$$

Hypothesis

River catchment area influences mean river discharge (two-tailed).

Calculation of the Spearman rank correlation (r_s) involves the following steps:

1 Rank the values of x and y from 1 (largest) to 12 (smallest). If two values are equal (e.g. both ranked fifth) we allocate to them the same average ranking (i.e. $(5 + 6) \div 2 = 5.5$). If three values tie as fifth ranking, the revised ranking would be $(5 + 6 + 7) \div 3 = 6$.

2 For each pair of values find the difference in rank between them (d) and square each difference (d^2).

3 Sum the square of the differences ($\sum d^2$).

4 Complete the calculation of the Spearman correlation using the formula:

$$r_s = 1 - (6\sum d^2) \div n^3 - n$$

In the example above the Spearman rank correlation between catchment area (x) and average discharge (y) = $1 - (6 \times 16) \div 1716$

$$r_s = 1 - 0.056 = +0.944$$

The significance of the correlation coefficient is obtained from tables (Figure 7.43). In this example there are 12 pairs of values (i.e. 12 degrees of freedom). The critical value of r_s at 0.01 level is 0.78. Our correlation coefficient **exceeds** the critical value and is therefore statistically significant at this level.

Degrees of freedom	Significance level (one-tailed) 0.025	0.01	0.005
	Significance level (two-tailed) 0.05	0.02	0.01
5	1.000	1.000	
6	0.886	0.943	1.000
7	0.786	0.893	0.929
8	0.738	0.833	0.881
9	0.683	0.783	0.833
10	0.648	0.746	0.794
12	0.591	0.712	0.777
14	0.544	0.645	0.715
16	0.506	0.601	0.665
18	0.475	0.564	0.625
20	0.45	0.534	0.591
22	0.428	0.508	0.562
24	0.409	0.485	0.537
26	0.392	0.465	0.515
28	0.377	0.448	0.496
30	0.364	0.432	0.478

Figure 7.43 *Spearman rank correlation tables*

Coefficient of determination

The coefficient of determination is the product moment correlation coefficient squared, expressed as a percentage. It measures the statistical variation in y 'explained' by x. In the example in Box 7.20, the product moment correlation coefficient of 0.78 gives a coefficient of determination of $0.78^2 \times 100\% = 61\%$. We can therefore say that 61% of the variation in average river discharge is 'explained' by catchment area. This, of course, still leaves 39% unexplained. Other factors which contribute to inter-basin variations in river discharge include mean annual rainfall, rates of evaporation and land use.

Box 7.21 Procedure for calculating Pearson's product moment correlation in Excel

1 Open an Excel document and insert pairs of data for x and y variables.
2 Select 'autosum' on the standard toolbar and click 'more functions'.
3 Select the category 'statistical', scroll down and select 'PEARSON', and click 'OK'. The following screen appears.

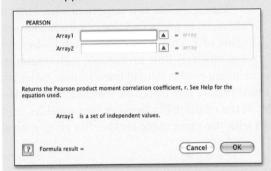

4 Place the cursor in the box 'array 1' and select all the data for variable x in your spreadsheet.
5 Place the cursor in the box 'array 2' and repeat for the dependent variable y in your spreadsheet.
6 The correlation coefficient will appear under formula result in the functions argument box.

Degrees of freedom	Significance level (one-tailed)			
	0.05	0.025	0.01	0.005
	Significance level (two-tailed)			
	0.10	0.05	0.02	0.01
1	0.9877	0.9969	0.9995	0.9999
2	0.900	0.950	0.980	0.990
3	0.805	0.878	0.934	0.959
4	0.729	0.811	0.882	0.917
5	0.669	0.754	0.833	0.874
6	0.622	0.707	0.789	0.834
7	0.582	0.666	0.750	0.798
8	0.549	0.632	0.716	0.765
9	0.521	0.602	0.685	0.735
10	0.497	0.576	0.658	0.708
11	0.476	0.553	0.634	0.684
12	0.458	0.532	0.612	0.661
13	0.441	0.514	0.592	0.641
14	0.426	0.497	0.574	0.628
15	0.412	0.482	0.558	0.606
16	0.400	0.468	0.542	0.590
17	0.389	0.456	0.528	0.575
18	0.378	0.444	0.516	0.561
19	0.369	0.433	0.503	0.549
20	0.360	0.423	0.492	0.537

Figure 7.44 Pearson's product moment correlation tables

The Pearson product moment correlation coefficient for the catchment area and river discharge data in Box 7.20 is +0.85. This compares with +0.94 for the Spearman rank correlation. It suggests that the Pearson correlation is a more demanding test than Spearman's. However, for the two-tailed test (with numbers of pairs minus one degree of freedom) the Pearson correlation coefficient is still statistically significant at the 0.01 level.

Simple linear regression

Simple linear regression, involving two variables, x and y, is a technique for fitting a straight line to points on a scatter chart. The regression line is known as 'least squares' because it minimises the sum of the squares of the deviations

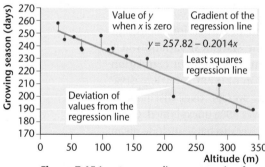

Figure 7.45 Least squares linear regression for growing season and altitude in northern England

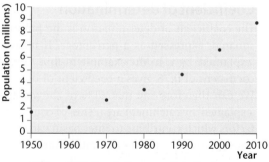

Figure 7.46 Population growth in Benin, 1950–2010

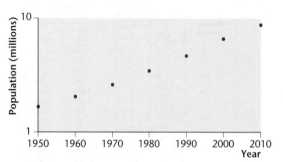

Figure 7.47 Population growth in Benin, 1950–2010, with y-axis transformed to a logarithmic scale

from the line, and is statistically the 'best fit'. Regression lines are expressed in the form of an equation:

$$y = a +/- bx$$

where regression coefficient a is the value of y when x is zero, and b is the gradient of the trend line. An equation with a plus sign describes a positive correlation; a minus sign describes an inverse correlation.

Regression has two important uses. First, it allows us to predict a value of y from a known value of x. This is especially useful when we have plenty of data on variable x, but relatively little on variable y. For example, from a simple regression model we might predict rainfall from altitude, or length of the growing season from altitude (Figure 7.45). Second, a regression equation provides us with precise model of the relationship between two variables, and allows us to make comparisons with the same variables in other geographical locations.

Box 7.22 Fitting a least squares linear regression line using Excel

The simplest way to fit a simple regression line to points on a scatter chart is to use an Excel spreadsheet.

1 Open an Excel document and insert pairs of data for x and y variables.
2 Select the chart wizard.
3 Select scatter chart.
4 Complete the scatter chart with appropriate title and labels for x and y axis and select 'as new

sheet' and then press 'finish'.
5 Select 'chart', then 'add trendline', then 'linear regression'. A trend line will appear on your scatter chart.
6 Under chart options select 'equation' and 'r squared'. The equation for the linear regression line will appear on your chart, as well as the coefficient of determination.

Linear regression models are inappropriate where data trends are curvilinear. Figure 7.46 shows that population growth in Benin in west Africa followed a curvilinear trend between 1950 and 2010. Fitting a linear regression (i.e. straight line) to this trend would be misleading and inaccurate. However, if we transform the *y* axis in Figure 7.46 to a logarithmic scale, the trend becomes a straight line (Figure 7.47). This allows us to fit a linear regression model of the form:

Log $y = a + bx$

Spatial statistics
Index of dissimilarity

The index of dissimilarity is usually applied to the study of segregation among ethnic groups (e.g. Table 7.25). It measures the unevenness with which two groups

Table 7.25
Blackburn:
dissimilarity index

	1	2	3	4	5	6
Ward	Ward population total	Asian (B_i)	White (W_i)	B_i/B	W_i/W	Column 4 – column 5
Audley	8505	4855	3650	0.1710	0.0335	−0.138
Bastwell	7388	5854	1534	0.2062	0.0141	−0.192
Beardwood	5484	512	4972	0.0180	0.0456	−0.028
Corporation Park	6645	2752	3893	0.0969	0.0357	−0.061
Earcroft	4253	88	4165	0.0031	0.0382	−0.035
East Rural	1921	12	1909	0.0004	0.0175	−0.017
Ewood	6592	189	6403	0.0067	0.0587	−0.052
Fernhurst	3953	45	3908	0.0016	0.0358	−0.034
Higher Croft	6961	138	6823	0.0049	0.0625	−0.058
Little Harwood	6182	2311	3871	0.0814	0.0355	−0.046
Livesey with Pleasington	6806	54	6752	0.0019	0.0619	−0.060
Marsh House	6023	118	5905	0.0042	0.0541	−0.050
Meadowhead	5888	79	5809	0.0028	0.0533	−0.050
North Turton with Tockholes	4190	16	4174	0.0006	0.0383	−0.038
Mill Hill	6352	307	6045	0.0108	0.0554	−0.045
Queens Park	5685	2296	3389	0.0809	0.0311	−0.050
Roe Lee	5948	330	5618	0.0116	0.0515	−0.040
Shadsworth	7651	539	7112	0.0190	0.0652	−0.046
Shear Brow	7404	5446	1958	0.1919	0.0179	−0.174
Sudell	6806	272	6534	0.0096	0.0599	−0.050
Sunnyhurst	6342	274	6068	0.0097	0.0556	−0.046
Wensley Fold	6422	1843	4579	0.0649	0.0420	−0.023
Whitehall	4069	56	4013	0.0020	0.0368	−0.035
		28 386	109 084			−1.368
		$B = 28\,386$	$W = 109\,084$			1.368×0.5
					Dissimilarity index =	**0.684**

are distributed within small spatial units such as wards or census tracts, which together make up larger geographical areas such as towns and cities.

The formula for calculating index (D) is:

$$D = 0.5\sum (B_i \div B) - (W_i \div W)$$

where:

B_i = the total population of ethnic group B in the ith ward or census tract

B = the total population of ethnic group B in the larger geographic area (e.g. city)

W_i = the total population of ethnic group W in the ith ward or census tract for which D is calculated

W = the total population of ethnic group B in the larger geographic area (e.g. city) for which D is calculated

The index ranges from 0 to 1. The higher the score the more segregated the groups are. An index of zero means that the proportion of group B's population in each census tract is exactly the same as the proportion of group W's population. The calculation for Blackburn's Asian and White populations are shown in Table 7.25. The index of 0.684 suggests a high level of segregation among the Asian population. However, ethnic segregation is often much higher in American cities. In 2000, the index of dissimilarity for Black versus White groups was 0.837 for New York, and 0.861 for Detroit.

Nearest neighbour analysis

Nearest neighbour analysis is a technique measuring point patterns in space. Although originally devised by ecologists, geographers have most commonly used nearest neighbour analysis to give precise descriptions to rural settlement patterns.

The nearest neighbour index ranges from 0, where all the points form a single cluster, to 2.15 which is a perfectly uniform pattern. Values falling between these two extremes suggest a random pattern. The technique is based on finding the average distance between points and their nearest neighbour. Taking each point in turn, the distance to the nearest neighbouring point is measured.

The index (R) is calculated by dividing the observed mean distance between nearest neighbour points (D_{obs}) by the mean distance expected from a similar number of points distributed randomly in the same area (D_{ran}). D_{ran} is obtained from the formula:

$$(D_{ran}) = \frac{1}{2\sqrt{N \div A}}$$

where N is the total number of points and A is the given area.

Location quotients

Location quotients are most often used to measure the concentration of an economic activity in an area or region compared to the national average.

Box 7.23 Calculating the nearest neighbour index for the settlement pattern around Market Rasen

- Average observed distance between settlements (D_{obs}): 1.7 km
- Area of map (*A*): 615 km^2
- Number of settlements: 79
- Expected distance under assumption of randomness:

$$(D_{ran}) = \frac{1}{2\sqrt{N \div A}}$$

$$(D_{ran}) = \frac{1}{2\sqrt{79 \div 615}} = \frac{1}{2 \times 0.358} = 1.39$$

- Nearest neighbour index (*R*) = (D_{obs}) ÷ (D_{ran}) = 1.7 ÷ 1.39 = 1.22

The index (*R*) shows that the settlement pattern is largely random.

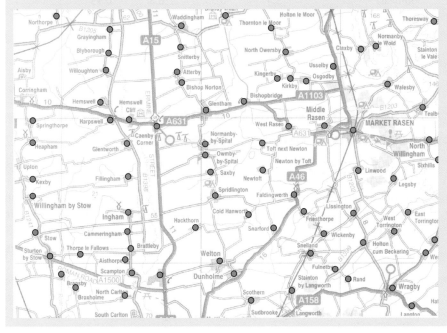

Figure 7.48
Settlement pattern around Market Rasen, Lincolnshire

A location quotient of 1 shows that the activity is represented in exactly the same proportion as nationally. Less than 1 suggests that activity is more important locally than nationally; and more than 1 indicates that the activity is less important locally compared to the national average.

The data in Table 7.26 show the percentage of the workforce engaged in primary and secondary activities in the UK and its regions. The location quotients (LQ) tell us that primary activities are relatively three-and-a-half times more important in Northern Ireland than in the UK as a whole. The regional importance of secondary activities is less variable. Location quotients range from 0.75 (i.e. 25% below the national average) in London, to 1.36 (i.e. 36% above the national average) in the West Midlands.

Table 7.26 *Location quotients (LQ) for primary and secondary industries in the UK*

	Primary		Secondary	
	%	LQ	%	LQ
UK	6.2	Not applicable	7.3	Not applicable
Northeast	5.4	0.87	7.4	1.01
Northwest	4.8	0.77	7.7	1.05
Yorkshire and the Humber	6.3	1.02	8.6	1.18
East Midlands	6.8	1.10	9.7	1.33
West Midlands	6.0	0.97	9.9	1.36
East	5.5	0.89	7.8	1.07
London	0.2	0.03	5.5	0.75
Southeast	3.4	0.55	6.8	0.93
Southwest	9.9	1.60	7.1	0.97
Wales	14.6	2.35	6.6	0.90
Scotland	10.9	1.76	5.9	0.81
Northern Ireland	22.0	3.55	6.1	0.84

Presenting a summary of findings and an evaluation of the investigation

An investigation is completed by (a) providing a summary of the main findings and (b) evaluating the outcomes.

Earlier in this chapter (p.259) we described an investigation into the downstream changes in sediment shape in a river channel. We can use this example to show how to present a summary and evaluation of an investigation.

Figure 7.49 shows the results of the investigation. We can summarise the results as a series of bullet points:

➤ There is a general trend for sediments to become rounder with distance downstream. Well-rounded (WR) and rounded (R) sediments become more frequent downstream than angular (A) and very angular (VA) sediments.

Figure 7.49 *Downstream changes in sediment roundness*

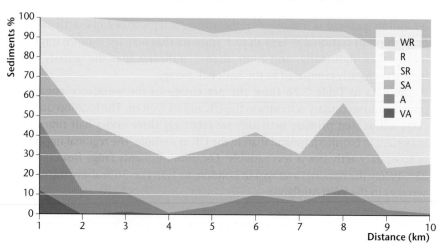

➤ Statistical correlation analysis confirms this finding at the 0.05 confidence level for well-rounded, rounded, angular and very angular sediments. However, the downstream trend in sub-angular (SA) and sub-rounded (SR) particles is not significant.

➤ The hypothesis that 'sediments become rounder with distance downstream' is therefore accepted.

➤ The relationship between roundness and distance downstream is strong but far from perfect. There is, for example, a significant increase in angularity 8 km downstream.

➤ Inputs of angular sediments from shorter tributary streams distort the overall downstream trend of rounding.

Having summarised our findings we need to evaluate the effectiveness of the investigation. Could the methodology have been improved to yield results of greater significance? Was our initial hypothesis valid or should it be modified?

The sampling methodology used was a systematic survey at 1 km intervals along the river's course. At each survey site, 50 sediments were sampled using a quadrat. This immediately raises two questions: was the sample large enough to provide enough data to test the hypothesis accurately and were sufficient sites selected along this stretch of river?

Another critical question relating to sampling method and the scale of the study is whether the length of river used was appropriate. Ten kilometres is a relatively short distance to show changes in sediment roundness, especially when sediment inputs from tributary streams can have a considerable effect on sediment characteristics in the main channel. The results may have been more significant if the study river length had been doubled.

There are also doubts concerning the representativeness of the sample data. Bedload sediment in the river comprised two rock types: limestone and sandstone. Although these rocks may erode at different rates, the sediment samples included both rock types, though not in the same proportion at each site. A further problem relates to the sorting of sediment in the river channel. Quadrats were laid at random at each site, but with a small sample of just 50 particles it is possible that some samples were unrepresentative due to fluvial sorting by size and shape.

Critical evaluation of methodology has revealed a number of problems. Some comment is needed to suggest how these problems, with hindsight, could be overcome. These might include:

➤ taking a larger sample
➤ sampling only either limestone or sandstone particles
➤ conducting the investigation over a longer stretch of river
➤ using a line transect across the channel to sample sediment, rather than a quadrat

Finally, and in conclusion, we need to state to what extent the original aims and objectives of the investigation have been achieved. In this example, with one or two caveats, we can say that the investigation has been broadly successful.

Examination-style questions

Section A: Geographical research

Table 1 *Species diversity: number of quadrats with 0 to >3 plant species*

	0	1	2	3	>3
Scar and debris slope	174	259	87	0	1
Crest	192	197	72	27	2
Dip slope	19	219	199	90	33

Figure 1 *Relief units on Whitbarrow*

Crest   Scar and debris slope   Dip slope

Michael Raw

1 Table 1 presents the results of a geographical investigation of vegetation on a slope on Whitbarrow in south Lakeland and Figure 1 shows the area of investigation. The investigation was designed to answer the following question:
   'How and why does plant species diversity vary with micro-habitat (i.e. crest, scar and debris slope, dip slope)?'
   (a) Select and justify one type of chart that could be used to represent the data in Table 1. Include in your answer a sketch of the chart you have chosen. (5 marks)
   (b) Describe and explain one relevant statistical technique that could be used to analyse the influence of the three micro-habitats on species diversity. (10 marks)
   (c) Suggest possible reasons why the results from an investigation into species diversity and micro-habitat of this type might be inconclusive. (5 marks)

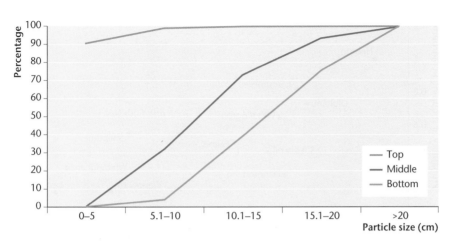

Figure 2
Cumulative frequency: particle sizes at bottom, middle and top stations on a scree slope at Austwick

Figure 3 *Scree slope at Austwick Scar*

Michael Raw

2 Figure 2 shows the results of an investigation of sorting on a scree slope at Austwick in North Yorkshire. Figure 3 shows the scree slope used for the investigation. The investigation aimed to answer the following question:
'To what extent is there evidence of sorting of scree particles by size on the slope?'

(a) Using the evidence of Figure 2 describe how the size of scree particles varies with distance down the slope. (5 marks)

(b) Describe and explain the methods you could use to obtain representative samples in either a fieldwork or research-based investigation. (10 marks)

(c) What factors would you take account of in a risk assessment of the environment in Figure 3 and what safety precautions would you take to minimise risks? (5 marks)

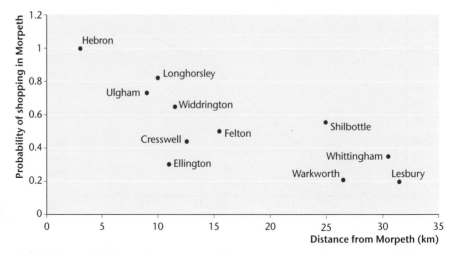

Figure 4
Relationship between distance and the probability of shopping in Morpeth from surrounding villages

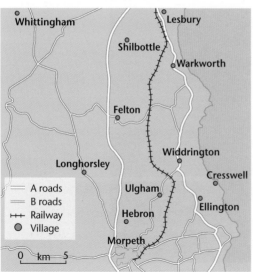

Figure 5 *The distribution of Northumberland villages in Figure 4*

3 Figure 4 shows how the probability of shopping in Morpeth by the residents in a sample of Northumberland villages varies with distance from the town. The distribution of the villages in Figure 4 is shown in the map of Northumberland (Figure 5). The geographical investigation focused on the following question:

   'How and why does the probability of shopping in Morpeth change with distance from the town.'

(a) Describe how the probability of shopping in Morpeth (Figure 4) varies with distance from the town. (5 marks)

(b) State and explain the statistical techniques that could be used to analyse the relationship between variables such as these. (10 marks)

(c) Explain why trends in a variable such as shopping probability can rarely be explained by variations in a single causal factor like distance. (5 marks)

Section B: Geographical investigation

4 State the nature of an investigation (fieldwork/research) conducted during your A-level studies. Describe and justify the method of statistical sampling you used. Evaluate the representativeness and accuracy of your sample(s) and suggest ways in which the sample(s) could have been improved. (20 marks)

5 Using your fieldwork and research experience at A-level, describe two statistical methods of data analysis you have used, and assess their value in geographical investigation. (20 marks)

Index